HAS CHRISTIANITY A REVELATION ?

HAS CHRISTIANITY
A REVELATION?

F. GERALD DOWNING

THE WESTMINSTER PRESS
Philadelphia

Scripture quotations from the Revised Standard Version of the Bible are copyright,
1946 and 1952, by the Division of Christian
Education of the National Council of
Churches, and are used by permission.

Library of Congress Catalog Card No. 67–12282

Published by The Westminster Press®
Philadelphia, Pennsylvania

PRINTED IN THE UNITED STATES OF AMERICA

CONTENTS

6 *Contents*

PREFACE

'**H**AS Christianity a revelation?' or, 'Can Christians at all justly claim to know their God?'—to these closely related questions an affirmative answer is regularly, and vehemently, given. This study attempts to show that such a positive claim, though possible, can only be a heavily qualified one—so heavily qualified, I shall suggest, that to avoid confusion different formulations are called for.

To argue this from Christian tradition—its inheritance from the Old Testament and elsewhere, its focus in the New Testament, its very diffuse growths through history to the present day—and from the 'normal' uses of words (philosophical analysis) may seem more than a little negative. I can then only suggest to the reader who finds this oppressive, but who is willing to persevere, that he turn first to the last chapter. There I have sketched the structure which I suggest may be built when at least a large part of the ground has been methodically cleared. The reversal of the printed order will not spoil the plot.

I should like to acknowledge the help given to me by Professors John McIntyre and James Barr, who both read an early version of this work in typescript and made a number of suggestions for its improvement. I should also like to express my gratitude to Professor Ian T. Ramsey, who read the proof and helped clarify some issues; to the Rev. David L. Edwards and the SCM Press; to the Rev. John Bartlett; to my brother, the Rev. John Downing, for translations and criticisms; to my colleagues at Lincoln Theological College; and to students here, who have had to bear with the book and who (not always consciously) have helped to refine its arguments.

But especially am I in delight and duty bound to thank my wife for her encouragement, patience and perceptive criticism of the form and content of this work.

Four books relevant to the present study came into my hands too late for full consideration to be incorporated: R. Latourelle, S.J., *Théologie de la Révélation*; J. L. Austin, *How to do Things with Words* and *Philosophical Papers;* and D. Evans, *The Logic of Self-Involvement.* However, their relevance will be briefly pointed in a few appended notes.

Quotations from the Bible are basically from the Revised Version, with a few stylistic changes ('you' for 'thou', etc.; and 'Yahweh' for LORD).

F. GERALD DOWNING

Lincoln
The Epiphany, 1964

I

TWO PROBLEMS

THE majority, if not all, of contemporary theologians find it
necessary to talk of 'revelation', do so often with considerable emphasis and show every sign of confidence in its use.
Emil Brunner says that 'revelation' (and its relation to 'reason')
is the 'fundamental problem of all theology', and a question at
the base of our Western civilisation.[1] Rudolph Bultmann insists
that 'revelation' is in the most ultimate sense a matter of life or
death.[2] Without 'revelation', Austin Farrer suggests, Jesus Christ
could have had no lasting effect on human history;[3] and a
similar point is made even more forcibly by Martin D'Arcy in a
pre-war collection of essays: 'If we cannot know by now what
the revelation of Christ is, then we must dismiss Christianity
despite all its comfort and arguments as a failure, and reluc-
tantly deny the claims of Christ.'[4] And for John A. T. Robinson,
though he is far from satisfied with traditional theological
language, belief in 'revelation' must be preserved when all else
is questioned; by it, Christianity 'stands or falls'.[5]

'Revelation' is vital, because it talks of the gracious initiative
that God takes towards us, without which we could have no
positive contact with him at all.[6]

And, as the collection of essays in *Revelation* referred to above
of course shows, it is not a word that is important in only one
Christian theological tradition, as say 'assurance', 'compre-

[1] In *Revelation and Reason*, SCM Press, 1947, p. ix, Preface.
[2] In *The Concept of Revelation in the New Testament*, 1929, published in *Existence and Faith*, Hodder and Stoughton, 1961, p. 71f.
[3] Article 'Revelation' in *Faith and Logic*, ed. B. Mitchell, Allen and Unwin, 1957, p. 100.
[4] In *Revelation*, ed. J. Baillie and H. Martin, Faber and Faber, 1937, p. 185.
[5] In *Honest to God*, SCM Press, 1963, p. 128.
[6] L. S. Thornton, *Revelation and the Modern World*, Dacre Press, 1950, p. 4; R. Bultmann, *op. cit.*, p. 72; E. Brunner, *op. cit.*, pp. 3, 22, 29f.; P. Tillich, *Systematic Theology (ST)*, vol. I, Nisbet, 1953, p. 122ff.; K. Barth, *Church Dogmatics (CD)* I/1, T. and T. Clark, 1936, pp. 150, 191; I/2, p. 80; etc.

hensiveness', 'Mass', might be. It is a word that can be used positively and often in very similar contexts by Orthodox, Roman Catholic, Lutheran, Reformed, Anglican and many other Christian writers.

It is fair to say that 'revelation' is widely accepted as an important, even essential theme by Christian theologians. Many books are written explicitly about it, many more with it as a basis for discussion, or as an important element in the argument. Some of them will be quoted in the pages that follow. Yet, is there any justification for offering yet another survey of this much-mapped area? The ground is important enough, but with so much written about it, it might not seem very likely that there is any significant aspect of it as yet unnoticed. This book is written in the conviction that much has still to be said. It attempts to deal with two very large issues involved in Christian talk about 'revelation' that have either been ignored or left on one side by most theological writers. One is the difficulty of using the word logically and coherently; the other is the difficulty of finding a biblical basis for the ideas it is used to convey. The present chapter offers a preliminary account of these two problems and at the same time illustrates both their importance (always supposing that they are genuine) and (with the same supposition) their 'strange' neglect. It also serves to outline the course the discussion will take.

It has been impossible to find any awareness at all of the first difficulty (the illogic of much talk of 'revelation') in the many and varied books concerned more or less directly with the topic that have come to my notice over the past five or six years.[1] And yet just the very obvious fact of the volume and variety of the discussion could itself quite easily be for anyone a first pointer to the problem.

'Revelation' suggests the removing of some obscurity, to make clear, visible, comprehensible, what had up to that point been befogged, unseen, misunderstood, or not even guessed at. And many writers who use the word actually emphasise that it is in this (quite normal) sense that they are using it.[2]

---

[1] The book that comes closest to an awareness of this problem is H. R. Niebuhr, *The Meaning of Revelation*; Macmillan (N.Y.) (1941), 1960.

[2] E.g. R. Bultmann, *op. cit.*, p. 59; P. Tillich, *ST* I, p. 120; K. Barth, 'The Christian Understanding of Revelation', *Against the Stream*, SCM Press, 1954; p. 205. J. Baillie, *The Idea of Revelation in Recent Thought*, O.U.P., 1956, pp. 19, 27.

It could of course mean only a comparative clarification. But if 'reveal' is used without qualification, it suggests a complete lucidity, openness, comprehension: ' . . . we are transposed into the greatest clarity: such clarity, that we make ourselves very definite thoughts, clear in themselves, about what is being told us, that we can react to it with our whole inner and outer attitude in life. . . . '[1] Even more strongly, William Nicholls writes: 'Revelation means, then, that God of his own free will and because he loves us has drawn aside the veil that hides him from us, and has shown himself to us as he is. Just as we must not in the slightest degree minimize the truth that revelation is God's act and not man's achievement, so we must not in any degree minimize the completeness of the act of revelation when it comes, for both errors minimize the love of God for men. God reveals *himself*.'[2]

And yet so many words are used to talk of this clarity, manifestation, revealing! They invite at first only a slight unease. If you ask at Hyde Park Corner how you can find the Albert Memorial and it takes half an hour to tell you, you will not receive seriously a final assurance of 'You see, it's quite clear'. When you ask if you may find God, and you are told 'Yes, you can, he has revealed himself', and it takes you a year to read even one month's literature, you may well wonder really in what sense the word 'reveal' is being used.

You will, of course, be told that your reaction is too superficial. It is possible to get to know clearly enough either how to cut butter with a knife, or how to build an exact replica of the Forth Bridge; but the knowledge that is fully available about the latter would need many more words for its expression, without its being, itself, any the less clear and knowable. The 'Christian revelation' is the manifesting of a 'mystery', a manifesting of the incomprehensible and 'What is essentially mysterious cannot lose its mysteriousness even when it is revealed'.[3] As it is not the revealing of something easy to understand, it is not fair to expect it to be expressed in few words. In fact a number of writers insist

[1] K. Barth, *CD* I/1, p. 198.
[2] In *Revelation in Christ*, SCM Press, 1958, p. 44.
[3] P. Tillich, *ST* I, p. 121. See also K. Barth, *CD* I/1, p. 188; I/2, p. 106; IV/2, p. 297f.; S. Bulgakoff, in *Revelation*, ed. Baillie and Martin, p. 125ff.; L. S. Thornton, *op. cit.*, p. 5; J. I. Packer, *Fundamentalism and the Word of God*, I.V.F., 1958, p. 129.

that really it is inexpressible; though this seems to be a fairly formal insistence, as they are still willing to try to talk about it. Yet this word 'mystery' is not a complete answer.

'Revelation' as it concerns Christian theologians has to do with God. And Christians have never been willing to admit that the mystery of God is difficult to understand *in the same way* as, say, the Forth Bridge is hard to understand. There are many different facts to be known about the Forth Bridge: it is complex, has lots of parts. But God is supposed not to have 'body parts or passions'. It is not because there are lots of facts to be known about him that God is 'mysterious'; he is 'incomprehensible' in the sense that three words 'God is Love' or three million are equally inadequate to tell the truth about him.[1] And this means that the problem of the many words remains. You could justify them if you were claiming that God had revealed himself as mysterious complexity: many books for many facts. But it is hard to justify them, if the claim is that God has revealed himself as one mysterious profundity.

The first problem then arises when it becomes necessary to ask, 'In what sense is "reveal" being used, when it takes so many words to talk of the "revelation" (even the "revelation of the mystery") of God who is One?'

But the many words are merely a symptom of a much deeper trouble. Suppose you were to ask, 'What is the content of this Christian "revelation"?' You would at first receive a very remarkable impression of unity from otherwise deeply divided believers. 'It is the revelation of God himself.'[2]

But as soon as this is said, the unity is shattered. Both the Roman Catholic, Martin D'Arcy, and the Anglican Evangelical, J. I. Packer, prefer to talk of the 'truths of revelation', truths about God.[3] Yet for others this is a complete misunderstanding. 'Revelation' cannot be 'propositional'; in the most nearly literal sense, it is the 'revelation of God himself, as subject'. 'What is offered to man's apprehension in any specific revelation is not truth concerning God but the living God himself.' Anything else tends to be rejected as an 'exaggerated

[1] K. Barth, *CD* I/2, pp. 268-9; P. Tillich, *ST* I, *ibid.*
[2] M. C. D'Arcy, in *Revelation*, p. 198; J. I. Packer, *op. cit.*, p. 118; E. Brunner, *op. cit.*, p. 12; P. Tillich, *ST* I, *ibid.*; K. Barth, *CD* I/1, p. 192; I/2, p. 7, etc.
[3] D'Arcy, *loc. cit.*, p. 182; Packer, *op. cit.*, pp. 42, 67; cf. H. Küng, *The Council and Reunion*, Sheed and Ward, 1961, p. 167.

intellectualism'.[1] And this is not the end of the disagreement. For Rudolph Bultmann, 'everything has been revealed, in so far as man's eyes are opened concerning his own existence and he is once again able to understand himself'.[2] Then in Paul Tillich, 'revelation is the manifestation of what concerns us ultimately . . . it is the ground of our being'; and this seems to be the 'God beyond God', 'God beyond being'.[3]

It is a brave man who will attempt to show that really these conflicting assertions are saying much the same thing. And there are still further divisions in the ranks of those who are in formal agreement. Those who see a 'revelation' of propositions cannot agree together on what the propositions are or mean; one whom we have quoted is a Catholic, the other an Evangelical Protestant. Those who see a 'self-revealing' of God such that ' . . . we are transposed into the greatest clarity: such clarity, that we make ourselves very definite thoughts, clear in themselves, about what is being told us, that we can react to it in our whole inner and outer life . . . ',[4] cannot agree, for instance, on the relation between the 'revealing' of God they claim, and non-Christian man's response to what he may call 'God'.[5]

This, then, is the first of the major problems of 'revelation'. What is the meaning of the word, when it is used to describe the source of such volumes of disagreement? In what sense, if any, can propositions or events be said to 'reveal' anything or anyone, if the actual result is this confusion and obscurity and misunderstanding? Even allowing again that it is the mystery of God (the mystery that remains a mystery) which has been 'revealed', the different theological traditions do not seem to be talking of the same mystery.

The question of the meaningfulness of the word 'reveal' as used by theologians occupies us in chapters 5 to 7. It is necessary first to look generally at the ways theological language can properly be used, to see how it could talk of a 'revealing' of 'God'. Then 'reveal' can be analysed in the various uses to which it is put (and as an aid to that, the phrase 'to know God' is also

---

[1] W. Temple, *Nature, Man and God*, p. 322; quoted in J. Baillie, *The Idea of Revelation*, p. 33—see the whole of this chapter in Baillie; G. Aulén, in *Revelation*, p. 275f.; E. Brunner, *op. cit.*, p. 9f.
[2] *Op. cit.*, p. 85.
[3] *ST* I, p. 123; *The Courage To Be*, Nisbet, 1952: Fontana 1962, p. 187ff.
[4] K. Barth, *CD* I/1, p. 198; quoted above.
[5] See the first chapter of J. Baillie, *The Idea of Revelation*.

examined). Finally, some of the arguments in which 'reveal' is used by theologians are discussed, alternative ways of expression are proposed, and their implications briefly suggested.

But not all theologians admit the usefulness of a 'linguistic analysis' of theological statements.[1] Even though Karl Barth, Paul Tillich and John Baillie, as instances, refuse to accept at any rate some forms of verbal nonsense masquerading as theology[2] (and the last makes a notable effort to take current analytic method seriously); yet they all seem to suggest that language may still usefully be employed when it has been taken beyond breaking point, to the disintegration of meaning, and made at least to look like nonsense. The mystique of words is strong and attractive. It needs something like a conversion to persuade a theologian from the (usually white) magic of verbal spellbinding. I do not pretend to be able to effect such a turn about, *metanoia*; and have quite possibly not fully undergone it myself. This being the case, the last half of the book on its own might well have little effect. It is quite possible that some just will not see any problem in talk of 'revelation' where little or nothing is in fact clear.

The second problem will perhaps seem more urgent and relevant to Christian scholars generally; and this I may outline with less argument. There seems to be a fairly genuine agreement that this believed 'revelation of God' (not questioning now what that means) happened in, through, or by Jesus of Nazareth and that this is what the New Testament, and less directly the Old, is about; that this is the foundation of the Christian Church: the 'revelation of God' in Jesus Christ, contained in, recorded in, or witnessed to by Holy Scripture. An Orthodox theologian can write: 'Jesus by Himself and in Himself revealed God the Heavenly Father.' Of this, Scripture and Tradition are the two inseparable forms.[3] And from another Orthodox writer comes: 'Le Christ est la révélation la plus bouleversante de la sainteté de Dieu dans l'humain, il est le mystère même de la vie divine posé en archétype de l'écono-

---

[1] For example, T. Boman, in his review of J. Barr, *The Semantics of Biblical Language*, O.U.P., 1961, in *SJT* 15.3, Sept. 1962, uses the phrase 'logic and word analysis' as abuse.

[2] K. Barth, *CD* I/1, p. 189; P. Tillich, *ST* I, p. 137; J. Baillie in *The Sense of the Presence of God*, O.U.P., 1962, in many places.

[3] S. Bulgakoff, in *Revelation*, pp. 143, 146.

mie de l'être humain.'¹ The Roman Catholic Hans Küng writes
of 'revelation (*sc.* of divine truth) in its entirety, in both Old and
New Testaments'.² Henri de Lubac talks of Christ joining his
sacrifice and the founding of the Church, with 'la révélation
objective de sa Personne'.³ L. S. Thornton, an Anglican, can
take for granted 'the common Christian belief that there is a
special revelation of God enshrined in the scriptures of the Old
and New Testaments'; and add that 'for Christian faith all
revelation finds its centre of gravity in the Christ'.⁴

From a rather different Anglican standpoint, J. I. Packer can
similarly assert: 'The entire New Testament outlook is determined by the conviction that the Old and New dispensations
are originally one. The writers see the coming of Christ as the
climax of a single revelatory process. . . . '⁵ And while yet
another Anglican, C. F. Evans, suggests that 'God's way of
admitting us into his revelation, it would appear, is to allow us
to overhear snatches of his conversation with the Church'
(in the Bible), he too is sure that Christ is 'God's final revelation
to us' in a way 'the scriptures themselves suggest'.⁶ Despite our
earlier quotation from him, Rudolph Bultmann, dealing ex-
plicity with 'the conception of revelation in the New Testament', concludes the first part of his discussion of his material
with: 'Thus revelation consists in nothing other than the fact of
Jesus Christ.'⁷ Karl Barth again and again insists that Holy
Scripture 'claims to bear witness . . . to the reality of God's
revelation. . . . Jesus Christ is this reality.' 'To say revelation is to
say "The Word became flesh". Of course we may also claim
to say by the word "revelation" something different, something
purely formal. . . . But then we are not asserting what the Bible
means by this word. . . . '⁸ We meet the same sort of claim in
Emil Brunner: 'In the time of the Apostles, as in that of the Old
Testament Prophets, "divine revelation" always meant the
whole of the divine activity for the salvation of the world, the
whole story of God's saving acts, of the "acts of God" which
reveal God's nature and His will, above all Him in whom the

¹ P. Evdokimov, *La Femme et la Salut du Monde*, Casterman, 1958, p. 187.
² In *The Council and Reunion*, pp. 163, 165.
³ In *Catholicisme*, Editions du Cerf, 1947, p. 188.
⁴ *Op. cit.*, pp. 2, 29.   ⁵ *Op. cit.*, p. 52.
⁶ In *On the Authority of the Bible*, S.P.C.K., 1960, pp. 32, 28-9; the article is
reprinted from *Theology* LIX 427, p. 11ff.
⁷ *Op. cit.*, p. 75.   ⁸ *CD* I/2, p. 10; I/1, p. 134, *et passim*.

preceding revelation gains its meaning, and who therefore is its fulfilment: Jesus Christ.'[1] Paul Tillich adds further that 'the Christian church has always been conscious of its vocation to be the bearer of revelation for nations and individuals'.[2]

It would be possible to multiply instances much further. Many of these confident references to the 'revelation of God in Christ' as the core of the Bible occur quite incidentally in a variety of contexts. They come, as this selection should have shown, from the works of the most heterogeneous of Christian writers. And this confidence is not peculiar to academic or dogmatic theology. A popular study of the New Testament and its background explains: 'The work of revealing God that Jesus has begun was now carried on by the illuminating work of the Spirit'.[3] And similar conclusions are stated in more technical works. W. Manson wrote that a 'conception of the revelation of God in Jesus' lay 'at the simplest level of Christian preaching' (*sc.* in the early days of the Church).[4] J. M. Robinson talks of 'the primitive Church's conviction that their *kerygma* was not merely their Spirit-led reply to God's revelation in Jesus, but rather the heavenly Lord's revelation of himself'.[5]

The problem this time arises from a glance at the concordance. The writers in the New Testament (and the Old) do not seem to have much use for the *word* 'revelation'. And if they used it, it was in a rather different way from that assumed by the writers quoted.

This time the incongruity has been noticed by some writers. It has been observed by John McIntyre: 'It is not so obvious to us that the modern predominant employment of the concept of Revelation to describe the events and significance of the Incarnation is *not* a usage of the first-century Church.' 'Not only did the Church for many centuries find it possible to describe what happened when "the Word was made Flesh and dwelt among us", without using this term, but further, because of the history of theology in the last hundred years or so, the term "Revelation" has acquired a significance for us which it has

[1] *Op. cit.*, p. 8.
[2] *ST* I, p. 134.
[3] H. C. Kee and F. W. Young, *The Living World of the New Testament*, Darton, Longman and Todd, 1960, p. 56.
[4] In *Jesus the Messiah*, Hodder and Stoughton, 1943, p. 94.
[5] In *A New Quest of the Historical Jesus*, SCM Press, 1959, p. 106, n. 3.

never had in the whole history of the Church.'[1] John Knox notes, 'There is no evidence whatever that the Early Church entertained the view that the purpose of Christ's death was to disclose the love of God.' The 'revelation of God' is 'not a characteristic New Testament idea'.[2] And James Barr comes to the same conclusion: ' . . . it is doubtful whether the common theological use of "revelation" for the divine self-communication is appropriate in the light of the biblical usage'.[3]

The first half of the discussion that follows is concerned predominantly with the facts of the use of the word 'revelation' by past Christians and, to make the study more comprehensive, with their use of other words that could convey the same sort of meaning. Did they talk of God 'revealing himself', 'manifesting himself', 'making himself known', in Christ? Do their writings even *imply* that they believed that God had done this? Do they not rather believe that God remains quite hidden in his saving activity, until the end?

We shall be concerned mainly with the New Testament authors. But as a preparation for the discussion of their writings, it is necessary to look at the material that forms the most probable background to their thought, the Old Testament; and then at other documents that may have shaped, or at least may illustrate, their thinking. And we shall take a much less detailed look at other Christian writers from New Testament times to the Reformation, in part to see how far our conclusions from the canonical literature are borne-out, and in part to see, whatever the New Testament types of usage, whether 'revelation' is none the less a necessary Christian theological word or 'concept'.

The problem then is whether 'the revelation of God in Christ' is either a 'meaningful' or a 'biblical' idea.

These two aspects of the inquiry are important enough in themselves. It only remains to mention a few of the further implications of the questions raised.

The attitude the Christian takes to other 'religions' is largely determined by the strength of his conviction that he (or probably, 'the Christian Church') has received a definitive 'revela-

---

[1] In *SJT* 10.2, p. 133; and in *The Christian Doctrine of History*, Oliver and Boyd, 1957, p. 2.
[2] In *The Death of Christ*, Collins, 1959, p. 146f.
[3] In Hastings' *Dictionary of the Bible*, T. and T. Clark, 1963, *s.v.* 'Revelation'.

tion' of God; and he is involved in speculations about 'natural' or 'revealed' 'knowledge of God', 'general' or 'particular' 'revelation'.

An idea of 'revelation' is very congenial to theologians attempting to express Christian faith in terms of existentialist philosophy, whether they draw their insights from Kierkegaard, Buber or Heidegger; and the antithesis of propositional-personal 'revelation' presents itself again.

It is often noted that 'propositional revelation' is 'intellectualistic'.[1] Propositions demand an abstract, and not necessarily committed, conscious mental activity. But 'revelation' as 'personal encounter' is just as insistent in its demand for conscious mental activity. It does not escape intellectualism by steering clear of 'abstraction'; even if it does escape some of the aridity. Gustaf Wingren suggests this in his critique of Karl Barth's *Church Dogmatics*.[2] 'Revelation' is closely bound up with intellectualism even when it is not seen as a 'revealing' of propositions.

It is interesting that Barth at the beginning of his *Dogmatics* found it necessary to defend his revelational theology against just this charge of intellectualism (*qui s'excuse . . .*); he also, perhaps unconsciously, admits that it is in answer to *our* question that the Bible presents itself as witness to divine revelation—our problem, as to whether and how far God can be known.[3]

The questioning of 'revelation' raises then the whole problem of the place of conscious cognition in man's total life; and so the question of the limits of God's interest in man and activity towards him. At the same time, it queries the reality of a metaphysically defined, conveniently non-empirical, tightly restricted area of man's life in which God may act without being proved or disproved: the 'soul', the 'mind', the 'self'.

As most of our quotations will in fact have shown, to question 'revelation' is to demand a re-appraisal of the whole Christian understanding of the purpose of God in Christ.

It is much easier to ask questions, especially destructive ones, than to provide answers. But various alternatives to the suspect

[1] See above, p. 12.
[2] G. Wingren, *Theology in Conflict*, Oliver and Boyd, 1958.
[3] Barth, *CD* I/1, p. 150; I/2, pp. 462-3; and *Die kirchliche Dogmatik* (i.e. German ed.) II/1, 1940, p. 142, quoted in Wingren, *op. cit.*, p. 42.

ways of thinking will be suggested in the course of the discussion. For better or for worse, they will be not new alternatives, but old.

> '*If I know all mysteries and all knowledge,*
> *but have not love, I am nothing.*'

> '*Beloved, no new commandment write I unto you,*
> *but an old commandment which you had from the beginning.*'

2

THE BACKGROUND TO THE
CHRISTIAN USE

A. THE HEBREW OLD TESTAMENT

'REVELATION implies for the Old Testament *the means God uses to make possible a knowledge of God for men.*'[1] Some such claim about a 'concept of revelation' in the Old Testament is often made; we here examine the very slight evidence that might support such a conclusion.

We shall look first at three Hebrew words (*galah*, *'arah* and *ḥaśap*), that have much the same meaning as the Greek ἀποκαλύπτειν and as the Latin *revelare*, from which comes our 'reveal'. If any of the writers in the Old Testament used anything that might meaningfully be called 'a concept of revelation', it would seem fair to expect it to be expressed by one of these words. However, there are other quite similar terms. There is *ra'ah* (niphal), for 'to appear', and lastly there is *yada'* (niphal), 'to make known'. It would be possible to talk of what we might call God's 'self revelation' with these, even if words that mean literally 'uncover', 'reveal' are not used. Only if we fail on each of the three occasions may we draw the negative conclusion suggested in the previous chapter. But a failure in each of the three approaches will surely be significant. If we find a few birds' feathers, but never the feathers that clothe the bird we are hunting, we must assume that it does not live

[1] L. Koehler, *Old Testament Theology*, Lutterworth Press, 1957, p. 99; Koehler's italics. See also T. C. Vriezen, *An Outline of Old Testament Theology*, Blackwell, 1958, p. 233: this writer talks repeatedly of 'the fact that God reveals himself' in the OT. Also, G. A. F. Knight, *A Christian Theology of the Old Testament*, SCM Press, 1959; G. S. Hendry, article 'Reveal', in *A Theological Word Book of the Bible* (*ThWB*), ed. A. Richardson, SCM Press, 1950; art. 'Revelation' in von Allmen, *Vocabulary of the Bible* (*VB*), Lutterworth Press, 1958; article under καλύπτω, by A. Oepke, in Kittel's *Theologisches Wörterbuch zum Neuen Testament* (*TWNT*) III, Stuttgart 1949, p. 574ff.: 'The idea of revelation is absolutely central for OT piety' (p. 579).

here. If the language that could denote it is never in fact used
to speak of the 'revelation of God', it must be very doubtful
whether God is really believed to 'reveal himself'.

I

To start with then, we look at *galah*, *arah* and *ḥaśap*. These
are the only words at all often used in the Old Testament that
convey the same basic sense as 'reveal'. When they are used
in this way, it is usually to talk of literal uncovering, stripping.[1]
As Koehler says, 'none of the words is a specifically theological
word'.[2]

Only *galah* is used at all often. It is used in talk about God
in four main ways. It can describe a 'theophany', God letting
himself be seen, as though he were materially visible. It can be
used, more metaphorically, of God's 'open' activity. It can
describe God's providing otherwise secret information about
the future, or the structure of the physical world. And there are a
couple of idioms in which *galah* is used, for the 'opening' of a
man's eyes to see a vision, or his ears to receive information;
and God's communication with men is sometimes described
in these ways.

Theophany

A cult-centre would preserve a legend of an appearance of
the god to found it, and establish its peculiar rites. I shall

[1] For instance, Ezek. 13.14, of laying bare the foundations of a house, *galah*,
niphal. These words are used very often of the stripping naked of a human body:
'*arah*, piel, Isa. 3.17; *ḥaśap*, qal, Joel 1.7; *galah*, piel, Lev. 18.6ff., *et passim*. B. David-
son, *Hebrew Lexicon*, Bagster, 1956, says that *galah* with '*erᵉwah* means explicitly
sexual intercourse, Lev. 18 and 20, etc. This is certainly the aim in view.
Galah is by far the most frequent of these words.
There is no form demanding the translation '*revelation*', no substantive of that sort.
Galah can also mean to emigrate or force to emigrate, to go, be carried into
captivity. It does not seem to be certain whether this is by way of the meaning
'lay bare a country', or whether the earlier meaning is 'remove' from whence
might come 'reveal' by way of 'remove (the covering of)'. The dictionaries are
divided. In no instance of the use of *galah* does the meaning seem ambiguous; in
no case does the pattern of a sentence suggest that the other meaning is in mind.
For all semantic purposes, these are two different words. This essay is only concerned with those uses of *galah* where it obviously means 'uncover', and refers to
God or some 'aspect' of God. This section is meant to deal with every instance in
which it might be supposed that God was said to 'reveal' or 'be revealed'. The
investigation of the other terms claims only to summarise fairly the evidence, not
adduce all of it. But the writer *has not knowingly omitted anything* that might be
relevant.
[2] *Ibid.*; cf. Oepke, *TWNT* III, p. 579, where he too has to admit that there is
no settled term for the idea he is trying to find.

refer to these again; but there are a number of them in the Book of the Judges. Just such a story for Bethel-Luz is told in Genesis 28. Jacob sees God, receives a promise for the future, and performs the appropriate ritual at a holy stone. Later (Gen. 35.7) he builds an altar there 'because there God was revealed unto him, when he fled from the face of his brother'. God appears, physically visible, to a man waking or in a dream. And probably the same sort of situation is implied by the words of God's prophet to Eli, 'I revealed myself to the house of your father' (RSV punctuates as a statement; RV as a query, which is less likely—I Sam. 2.27). In the context of a discussion of Eli's sons' abuse of the cultus, the place of Eli's family in Israel, and God's judgment on Eli and his house, the reference again can only be to a theophany that was supposed to have instituted this priesthood. The following verses make this quite clear: 'And I chose him out of all the tribes of Israel to be my priest, to go up to my altar, to burn incense, to wear (bear) an ephod before me' (there is no account of this theophany in the Pentateuch; but cf. Ex. 4 and 28).

Of the three words, only *galah* is used in this way of God.[1]

Open Divine Activity

The word is used rather less naïvely in Isaiah, of the successful outcome of Yahweh's controlling of contemporary events: 'The glory of Yahweh shall be revealed' (Isa. 40.5). It will be 'revealed' in the success of 'Cyrus', and in the return of the exiles across the transformed desert. But this does not mean that Yahweh himself is seen: the periphrasis, 'the glory', is intentional; the glory is the invisible God visibly acting.[2] Later it is said of the same event (in the present form of the book it is the same event), 'Yahweh has made bare his holy arm in the eyes of all the nations; and all the ends of the earth shall see the salvation of our God' (Isa. 52.10, *ḥaśap*). Yahweh has rolled up his sleeves for saving action, and the result will be seen (which includes 'felt') by all. However, up to the present few or none have believed our report: 'To whom has the arm of Yahweh been revealed?' (Isa. 53.1). Till now, Yahweh has acted unobtrusively through the despised and ignored servant. But soon

---

[1] *Ḥaśap* is used once of God, indirectly, at Isa. 52.10; see next paragraph.
[2] See below.

it will not be possible to ignore Yahweh's activity. The servant
is to be vindicated and the focus of God's setting right (Isa.
52.13; 53 *passim*, esp. v. 11).

'Reveal' is used in the next section of the book, again, of the
open exercise of God's righteousness, his active saving and setting right of his nation among all the nations:

'Keep judgment and do righteousness,
For my salvation is near to come, and my righteousness to be
    revealed' (Isa. 56. 1).[1]

Yahweh's righteousness is not 'revealed' primarily so that men
may know that he is righteous; nor, immediately, so that they
may respond (though both these results should follow). His
righteousness is being 'revealed for action', as a sword might be
drawn from its sheath, or a man's sleeve be rolled up his arm
for a fight. 'Reveal' is still being used pictorially, it is only an
incidental part of the illustration, which is describing the imminence of effective action. This is shown, if further demonstration
is needed, by the fact that the same thing can be said without
'reveal' being used at all:

'My righteousness is near, my salvation is gone forth' (Isa. 51. 5).

This emphasises, too, what is only a little less explicit in the
previous quotation: the active sense of 'righteousness', which is
parallel with 'salvation'. It is not an insight into God's character
that is being 'revealed'; it is an activity of God that is coming
out into the open.[2] Once this happens, then of course it is imperative that men should 'keep judgment' and themselves
'*do*' righteousness; it is imperative that they should respond.

[1] Cf. Ps. 98.2ff.:

Yahweh has made known his salvation:
His righteousness has he openly shewn in the sight of the nations.
He has remembered his mercy and faithfulness toward the house of Israel,
And all the ends of the earth have seen the salvation of our God.

[2] There is a suggestion in Ps. 92 that God grants prosperity and a long and
fertile life to show what he is like:

'They shall bring forth fruit in old age;
they shall be full of sap and green
to show that Yahweh is upright;
he is my rock, there is no unrighteousness in him' (vv. 14-15).

'To show' translates the hiphil of *ngd*. Compare also Ps. 111.6:

'He has showed the people the power of his works.'

(The only act of power explicitly mentioned is the provision of food.)
Ngd (hiphil) is more often used in the Psalms in the context of sung or spoken

not that he is righteous so much as that he does what is right,

praise; and *spr* (piel) is similarly employed (Pss. 51.15; 79.13; 89.5). Ps. 107.22 runs:

> 'And let them offer the sacrifice with thanksgiving
> and declare (*spr*) his works with singing.'

And Ps. 30.9b,

> 'Shall the dust praise you?
> Shall it declare (*ngd*) your power?'

And again, Ps. 71.14bff.:

> 'I will praise you yet more and more,
> my mouth will tell (*spr*) of your righteousness. . . .
> Hitherto have I declared (*ngd*) your works.'

It is praise, rather than information that is being offered. And this, too, is probably what is intended in Ps. 19.1ff.:

> 'The heavens declare (*spr*) the glory of God
> and the firmament shews (*ngd*) his handiwork.
> Day utters speech to day,
> and night declares knowledge to night.
> There is no speech or language;
> their voice cannot be heard.
> Their line is gone out through all the earth
> and their words to the end of the world.'

The heavens personified (or the sons of God who inhabit them) praise God. So, too, in Pss. 50.6; and in 97.6ff.:

> 'The heavens declare his righteousness,
> and all the people have seen his glory . . .
> worship him, all you gods';

and 89.5:

> 'and the heavens shall praise your wonders, Yahweh,
> your faithfulness in the assembly of the holy ones'.

Everyone, if he is wise, will join in the praise. But there is no suggestion that men or the rest of creation in their showing or telling are offering deep insights into the character of the righteous, faithful, mighty God. Of course, if God is praised, as he should be, in the hearing of those who do not yet themselves worship him, they may take the hint:

> 'Sing praise to Yahweh who lives at Zion,
> tell among the people his doings' (Ps. 9.11).

Ps. 97.6ff., part-quoted above, runs in full:

> 'The heavens declare his righteousness
> and all the people have seen his glory.
> Ashamed be all they that serve graven images,
> that boast themselves of idols:
> worship him, all you gods.'

But praise is for the sake of praise, not edification.

It may be worth noting in passing that only 'creation' is said to 'show' God's glory. His 'acts in history' do not do this; they themselves must be 'declared' by men (Pss. 102: see v. 21; 118.17, *et passim*). But the nature-history distinction is not made in the Bible, and the attempt to use Scripture to support the antithesis of 'natural or revealed' knowledge of God is not justified. On this, see J. Barr, art. 'Revelation' in *HDB* (1963) (cited above); and see also below. Contrast many writers; e.g. Oepke, *TWNT* III, p. 574ff.

But the action of God will happen, the prophet believes, whatever the response, and will be effective.[1]

Telling Secrets

'Deutero-Isaiah' finds it very important that God has declared the future in advance to Israel; this proves that it is he who controls the world's events. *Galah* is not used for this declaring by Isaiah,[2] but it is used of 'revealing' of this kind in Amos, 'Surely the Lord will do nothing, but he reveals his secret to his servants the prophets' (Amos 3.7). It is not, of course, just the future events as such that the prophets foresaw, but their meaning for Israel, and the way Israel should respond to them: 'The secret things belong to the Lord our God, but the things that are revealed belong unto us and to our children for ever, that we may do all the things of this law' (Deut. 29.29).[3] If future events are to be known, then only Yahweh may reveal them. Such foreknowledge depends on his initiative. All other ways of finding out are wicked, even if possible.[4]

[1] Cf. Jer. 33.6: 'Behold I will bring it (the city) health and cure, and I will cure them; and I will reveal unto them abundance of peace and truth.' The active sense of 'reveal', parallel here with 'bring', is particularly clear.

[2] Isa. 41.23, 26; 44.7; 45.21; 46.10.

[3] Galah is the normal term for 'telling' secrets, Isa. 23.1; Ezek. 21.29 (?); Prov. 11.13; 18.2; 20.19; 25.9; and for 'publishing' a decree, Esth. 3.14; 8.13. (See below.) The most frequent word used of providing information about the future is one that is best translated just 'tell' (at least, it is most often rendered this way in EVV): *nagad* (hiphil). (See above.) It is used quite frequently in 'secular' contexts, e.g. I Kings 10.3, 'And Solomon told her all her questions: there was not anything hid from the king that he told her not.' He answered all her riddles; cf. Judg. 14.12ff.
 If it is the future that you wish to know about, then it is to Yahweh's seer that you must go, and he may tell you: I Sam. 9-10, etc.; cf. I Sam. 15.16. This is so normal a prophetic function that Elijah is very puzzled when an event that concerns him has not been told him, II Kings 4.27.
 As well as the prophet, of course, you may ask the priest who is guardian of the ephod, I Sam. 23.9ff.
 Despite the effort in the past to explain that Israelite prophets were 'forthtellers' rather than 'foretellers', it is providing accurate information about the future that is the most important function of the prophet. This is the communication from God that man most needs. It is the ability to provide this that is for deutero-Isaiah the most telling proof of the sole relevance of Israel's God (Isa. 41.22, 23, 26; 43.12; 44.8; 45.21; 48.3, 14, 16). For the prophet, the imperative in his message depends on the future indicative, both to make the message meaningful and to authenticate it.
 It is very rare that events substantiated the prophets' claims (Jeremiah *passim*; deutero-Isaiah; Daniel). Whatever he thought he had been 'told', the future in fact had not been 'revealed'.
 For other references to *ngd* used in this way, see any good concordance. It lies only on the periphery of the area of this investigation. God never says, 'Now, I will "tell" you of myself.'

[4] I Sam. 28.2ff.; Isa. 8.19f.

The young neophyte, Samuel, 'did not yet know Yahweh, nor was the word of Yahweh yet revealed unto him'. Eli tells him how to 'know Yahweh': ' . . . thou shalt say, "Speak, Yahweh, for your servant hears" '; the child obeys, and the word of Yahweh is 'revealed' to him. It is Yahweh's judgment on Eli's house, which he is now removing from its place in Israel. Later, it is said, 'Yahweh appeared again in Shiloh; for Yahweh revealed himself to Samuel in Shiloh, by the word of Yahweh'; that is, again, probably, by explaining his purposes for Israel: ' . . . and the word of Samuel came to all Israel' (I Sam. 3.7, 21; 4.1) Similarly to Daniel are revealed the secrets of the future and the understanding of them, by an angel, who is a distinct personality, under the distant God he serves. There is now none of the unsophisticated belief in immediate contact (Dan. 10.1). *Galah* is only rarely used of this sort of disclosure, the foretelling of future events. Other terms are more frequent.

God in Job also 'discovers deep things out of darkness' (Job 12.22).[2] Here they are not even details of God's purpose, but only facts about the structure of the physical world. Ability to 'reveal' this is linked with divine knowledge in the Wisdom literature; it is marvellous knowledge and only God can cope with it.

Two Metaphors of Communication

Galah is used in the context of Balaam's vision:

'He saith, which knoweth the words of God,
    Which seeth the vision of the Almighty,
    Falling down, but yet having his eyes uncovered (*galah*) . . .'
        (Num. 24.4; cf. v. 16).

The genitive, 'of the Almighty' is presumably subjective—it is not God who is seen in the ensuing vision, but the future of Israel; and that is seen just as clearly as Balaam saw the 'angel of Yahweh' earlier (Num. 22.31). This same figure is used metaphorically by a psalmist:

'Open my eyes that I may behold
    Wondrous things out of your law' (Ps. 119.18).

---

[1] Oepke, *TWNT* III, p. 579, suggests this means 'an intuitive relationship' (*Berührung*), but does not say why.
[2] Cf. too Dan. 2.22.

As well as this (not frequent) metaphor of 'uncovering the eye', there is one of 'uncovering the ear'. For some reason, the RV uses 'reveal' when this is done by God (I Sam. 9.15; II Sam. 7.27=I Chron. 17.25; Isa. 22.14); and 'disclose' when it is done by a man (I Sam. 20.2 and 12 and 13; 22.8 and 17). The real meaning is 'speak to someone privately' ('a word in your ear'); 'reveal' is impossible as a translation, for the phrase cannot take an object, nor introduce a quotation on its own. In both these figures of speech, 'reveal' is again a subordinate part of a metaphor. The latter figure of speech is used of God telling the future; it is used in Job of God instructing men in dreams and educating them through misfortunes (Job 33.16; 36.10, 15).

This short list exhausts the instances in the Old Testament in which God is said to 'reveal', 'be revealed', etc., with the use of any word that means literally 'uncover'; and the English translators do not even find it necessary in every case to use 'reveal' at all.

The Old Testament writers do not then find this word itself very important for describing God's activity towards his world, mankind, Israel. There are some things these writers know only God can 'reveal'; but they do not often seem to think that he has made such disclosures. They never use it of God's making possible a 'knowledge of himself', nor of God 'revealing his self'. They do not build round it any 'concept' of revelation.[1]

II

We now turn to the first set of possible synonyms for 'reveal'.

Ra'ah in the niphal seems best translated 'to appear', and it comes in similar contexts to those in which *galah* is used. The two words are sometimes near enough synonymous (cf. Gen. 35.1 and 7; I Sam. 3. 21); while on other occasions they carry rather different nuances of meaning. *Ra'ah* is used in secular contexts: 'Let the dry land appear' (Gen. 1.9); and it is used of human beings, but in a religious setting: 'Your males shall appear before Yahweh.'[2] This illustrates the difference in the words; the man who 'appears', 'puts in an appearance', as it were, has not 'revealed' himself, as though God could not have seen him unless he had come to Temple.[3] God looks down from

[1] This is admitted, but its implications ignored, by e.g. Koehler, *op. cit.*, p. 99, and Oepke, *TWNT* III, *ad loc.*
[2] Gen. 23.17; Deut. 16.16.
[3] If he were hidden from Yahweh, he would hardly be alive, Gen. 4.14; Isa. 40.27.

heaven to see all that happens on earth; and therefore men come
to worship him at Zion.[1] If, though, someone does 'appear'
from some sort of hiding rather than just from a distance, then it is
the same as 'revealing'. *Galah* always implies a previous hiddenness and emphasises the precise act of uncovering (that is, when
it is being used in the ways under discussion); *ra'ah* only refers
to the actual 'being seen', and any contrast with a previous
hiddenness must be provided by the actual context.

Ra'ah in the niphal can be used (as *glh* can) to talk about God
appearing as a human sort of figure, before men's waking eyes,
or in a dream; and it can be used of the exercise of his glory in
open acts of power. From the same root *r'h* comes one of the
words for 'seer' or prophet (I Sam. 9.9!), and there are various
descriptions of the sorts of communication with God that
prophets were supposed to have. Particularly vivid are the
descriptions of occasions on which the prophet believes he has
stood in Yahweh's council hall. And lastly, the worshipper tells
of 'seeing God's face' in the temple. These are the subdivisions
under which we examine the next section of the evidence.

Theophany

The niphal of *ra'ah* is used much more frequently of theophanies than is *galah*. These are again, largely, the central event
in each case of a cult foundation legend. Yahweh, or his 'angel'
(which is a periphrasis for him, Judg. 13.21-2), puts in an
'appearance' either by just walking up, or by coming from
'nowhere', from being invisible. He gives instructions and
promises for the future and accepts the normal cult-offering.[2]
In the Chronicler's re-presentation of the story in II Samuel of
David at the threshing-floor of Araunah, it is Yahweh rather
than an 'angel' who appears to the king at the site of the later
royal cult centre (II Chron. 3.1). In the Book of Jeremiah there
is a similar reference to an 'appearing' of Yahweh, for a like
purpose, the promise of prosperity (Jer. 31.3ff.).

Yahweh twice 'appears' to Solomon in a dream, once to offer
him a gift, and the second time to accept his cult-centre and
promise to continue his covenant with the house of David (I

---

[1] Ps. 102.19ff.; cf. Pss. 42,2ff.; 84.7ff.; 139.12; Jer. 23.23-4.
[2] Gen. 12.7ff.; 18.1ff.; 26.24ff. (cf. v. 2); 35.1ff. (cf. 35.9-15 with 35.7, 28.8ff.
(!) and 48.3); see also Gen. 17.1ff., appearance for the cult-rite of circumcision;
22.14 (? RVm); Ex. 6.3ff. Also Judg. 6.12; 13.3 and 10 and 21.

Kings 3.5 ;9.2; cf. 11.9; ‖ II Chron. 1.7; 7.12). (Appearances to people awake and to people asleep were probably not all that sharply differentiated. Both could be 'true' and 'objective.')

Open Divine Activity

There are many 'appearings' of Yahweh in the Exodus traditions, though less obviously anthropomorphic. It is the 'glory' that appears. Yahweh shows that he is there by fire, light, smoke and storm (Deut. 31.15). It is explicitly said that Yahweh himself is not seen (Ex. 33.20; Judg. 13.22): a man could not see him and live. But even the glory is dangerous (Lev. 16.2). God puts in an appearance, not (God forbid!) to 'reveal' himself but to give directions to his nation, make his covenant with them (which includes, again, provisions for his cult, but in much greater detail), and to protect Israel,[2] and really as a sign to all people of his self-committal to Israel; his reputation is now openly seen to stand or fall with Israel.[3] And there are a few further instances where the 'glory' of Yahweh appears in successful action in international affairs.[4]

So far from the four words *galah*, *'arah*, *ḥaśap* (meaning uncover) and *ra'ah* (meaning in the niphal 'appear') being used to talk of 'revelation' in anything like the modern sense (*'the means God uses to make possible a knowledge of God for men'*), they seem largely to be employed in talk of 'apparition', theophany. The language becomes less anthropomorphic as the scale of action grows (and perhaps as time passes). But neither in initiating a cult nor in establishing his people are these words used to describe Yahweh allowing a 'knowledge of *himself*'. At most, he communicates some of the terms of the obedience he demands.

See also II Sam. 22.2ff. (‖ Ps. 18), esp. v. 11; also Zech. 9.14, God 'appearing', very much concealed, in the storm.

[2] Lev. 9.4, 6, 23 (especially); Num. 14.10; 16.19; 20.6; cf. Ex. 3.2, 16; 4.1, 5; 16.10.

[3] Ex. 32.12ff.; Num. 14.13ff.; Deut. 32.27ff.; Ezek. 20.9.

[4] Isa. 35.2; compare Isa. 60.2 (see above); Ps. 90.16:

'Let your work appear to your servants,
  And your glory upon their children.'

And Ps. 102.15f.:

'The nations shall fear the name of Yahweh
  And all the kings of the earth your glory;
  When Yahweh has built up Zion
  And has appeared in his glory.'

The Seer and his Vision

Another word from the same stem as *ra'ah* is *ro'eh*, seer, prophet;[1] and also connected are a couple of words for 'vision'.[2] The most frequent word for seeing a vision is *hazah*;[3] connected is *hozeh*,[4] again, seer; and again further words for vision.[5] Some of the contexts in which these words occur have been noticed already.

Not many of the remaining occasions when these words are used are important for this study. In actual fact, these are the words that are used when the ways God communicates with men are being discussed: 'And he (Yahweh) said, "Hear now my words: if there be a prophet among you, I Yahweh will make myself known to him in a vision, I will speak to him in a dream." ' But it is said explicitly that this is to speak in 'dark speeches', *not* manifestly, not clearly (Num. 12.6ff.). Yahweh makes himself known to his prophets, speaks to them; but not closely, not intimately enough for it to be called 'revelation'. He uses the indirect method of visions, and those mostly in the unreality of dreams.[6] Most of the prophets seem to have had such visions. However, from the present form of these prophecies it seems this was not the only way God spoke. Sometimes the prophets appear just to have had to speak the word of Yahweh, as his mouthpiece: 'Thus says Yahweh' ('Yahweh speaking').[7] But neither is this so sure that it is ever called 'revelation'.

The two, word and vision, are closely connected.

The content of 'vision' is very rarely Yahweh himself. The exceptions are discussed below, but usually what is seen is a picture of the future; or some physical object; and this suggests the message. It is a difficult and obscure way that God uses to make himself known; it is easy to make mistakes. So, there are many false prophets[9] and it is hard to tell between true and false.[10]

---

[1] Isa. 30.10; I Sam. 9.9.   [2] *ro'eh*: Isa. 28.7; *mare'ah*, Num. 12. 6, etc.
[3] Num. 24.4, 16 *et passim*.   [4] II Sam. 24.11, etc.
[5] *Hezew*, Dan. 2.19, etc.; *hazōn* Dan. 8.1, etc.; *hizzayōn* Job 4.13, etc.
[6] Isa. 29.7f.; Job 20.8; 33.15.   [7] Cf. Ex. 7.1. with 4.10ff.
[8] I Sam. 3.1; cf. Jer. 23.16: 'Hearken not unto the words of the prophets that prophesy unto you: they teach you vanity; they speak a vision of their own heart, and not out of the mouth of Yahweh.'
[9] Hos. 12.10; Lam. 2.9, 14; Ezek. 13.7; Jer. 14.4.
[10] Deut. 13.1ff.; compare the reception of Jeremiah, the 'true' prophet. It seems to be implied that 'true' visions are God's gracious gift. Cf. Oepke, *TWNT* III, pp. 577-8.

The meaning of 'knowledge of God', of God 'making himself known', is examined further below. But the Old Testament writers do not pretend that such 'knowledge' happens through anything that can be called 'revelation'. Yahweh's communication with men is in obscure and perhaps ambiguous visions and pronouncements.[1]

The Council of Yahweh

In the long denunciation of false prophets in Jeremiah 23, to which reference has already been made, there are some intriguing comments that throw further light on the way prophecy was supposed by some to work. 'Who has stood in the council of Yahweh that he should hear and perceive his word? . . . But if they had stood in my council, then had they caused my people to hear my words, and had turned them from their evil way, and from the evil of their doings' (Jer. 23.18, 22). It might be that when a prophet had a 'word' rather than a dream, he knew he had been in Yahweh's council chamber, and had even perhaps seen himself there. It is difficult to generalise usefully; it is possible to argue from the small number of actual references to such experiences either that they rarely happened, or that they so frequently happened it was not necessary to describe them.

The actual descriptions that are recorded rather suggest they were rare and even terrible events. Micaiah ben Imlah listened-in, he says, on Yahweh's council, and heard the courtier offer to go and deceive the royal prophets. But this was spectacular; a more normal way for Micaiah to receive Yahweh's message would be by a direct vision of the event in question (I Kings 22.17ff.). Daniel, at a very great distance, sees the aged man, but takes no part in his council (Dan. 7). Isaiah is terrified when he finds himself in the council chamber of Yahweh's palace, 'Woe is me! For I am undone . . . for my eyes have seen the King, Yahweh of hosts' (Isa. 6.1ff.). To 'see Yahweh' (now using *ra'ah* in the qal) is not something that any man would wish on himself (Judg. 13.21 *et passim*).[3] Even Moses

---

[1] Cf. I Peter 1.10; Heb. 1.1 (!).
[2] See H. Wheeler Robinson, 'The Council of Yahweh', *JTS* 15, p. 151ff. But Yahweh did not *take counsel* of his prophets (Isa. 40.13, etc.). The only exceptions are Abraham and Moses. That the visions of the council hall are intended literally is obvious; it is only modern sensitivity that finds this embarrassing.
[3] Cf. the surprise at Gen. 32.30.

must hide his eyes and only look at the back of Yahweh when he has passed (Ex. 33.17–34.35).[1]

Yahweh seen in the Temple

The elders, who in one tradition go up the mountain with Moses and behold the God of Israel, and eat and drink, may be something of an exception. But they are probably doing no more than the ordinary worshipper who went to the Temple to 'see Yahweh's face':

> 'So have I looked upon you in your sanctuary
> to see your power and your glory' (Ps. 63.2).[2]

There is nothing in the Old Testament really to suggest that the ordinary worshipper, or even Isaiah himself, normally expected a *vision* of Yahweh when he went to the Temple to 'see Yahweh'.[3] What he was 'looking for' was 'blessing'. Some prophets may perhaps have thought themselves often in God's court; but for most this more probably happened only infrequently, or never at all.

However, one thing emerges from the most cursory glance at descriptions of vision of God. These do not imply anything that could be interpreted as 'revelation' of God himself, in any modern sense of the phrase. A man goes to 'see the king's face', to pay homage, to see if the king is well disposed towards him and, if possible, to make sure that he is.[4] He does not go for the king to 'reveal' himself to his subject in any but the most superficial, physical sense, of actually putting in an appearance. So the awed visionary 'sees' God, as the most terrible King, at a

---

[1] There is an interesting treatment of this in *SJT* XIII 2 by W. J. F. Boyd. He concludes on this passage, 'Yahweh has disclosed the future of the new Israel . . . yet this by no means implies that Moses has *pierced the veil* of Yahweh's mysterious being' (my italics).

[2] Cf. Pss. 27.4; 11.7; 17.15; Isa. 38.11, cf. v. 19; and Job 19.26, 28, which are difficult for anyone to interpret. Nothing in the rest of the book suggests that it is likely to imply an experience very different from those here considered. There is also Job 34.29. The normal contrast to Yahweh's 'hiding' his face from a man is Yahweh looking in blessing on him (see below). If Yahweh refused to let a man see his face, this presumably means he refuses his requests; as in Gen. 43.5. On this whole question, see A. R. George, *Communion with God*, Epworth Press, 1953, esp. p. 93ff.; though he suggests that 'appear before God' may have in many places been substituted for 'see' God'.

[3] George, *ibid*.

[4] Cf. Gen. 32.20. 43.5. If Yahweh hides his face from a man, he dies, Ps. 143.7. The converse is for his face to shine upon his servant, which does not imply a seeing of visions, but, bluntly, prosperity. Pss. 31.16ff.; 67.1ff.; Num. 6.25; contrast Pss. 22.24ff.; 27.9ff.

great distance; but it would never cross his mind that God might reveal his 'self' to him. Rare or frequent, this sort of experience cannot be called 'revelation', at least, not 'revelation of God'. Yahweh does not 'reveal himself'.

III

It can be said that Yahweh 'makes himself known'; and this sounds in English very like 'reveals himself'. The word is *yada'* in the niphal, and again, it is used in a variety of ways in talk about God.

It serves to tell when his immense power has been exercised and experienced. It can be used of the possession of the awesome and valuable privilege of using his name. On just two occasions he seems to be said to have offered to 'make himself known'; and these passages make it necessary to see what may be meant by an Old Testament writer when he talks of 'knowing', and 'knowing' God—in case this presupposes what might properly be called 'a self-revelation of God'. The section is concluded with a glance at the way God may be said to 'know' men; and at the rarely used substantive form, 'knowledge'. It is then possible to offer some conclusions.

Acts of Power

Mostly if *yada'* in the niphal is used of God at all, it is of his making an attribute of his known; of God acting effectively, making himself felt. 'And you shall see it, and your heart shall rejoice and your bones shall flourish like the tender grass; and the hand of Yahweh shall be made known towards his servants, and he will have great indignation towards his enemies' (Isa. 66.14). At the end of a long passage in Ezekiel, describing God's coming action in wrath, fire, sword, pestilence, he says: 'And I will magnify myself, and sanctify myself and I will make myself known in the eyes of many nations; and they shall know that I am the Lord' (Ezek. 38.23; cf. 35.11ff.). This is a threat, not a promise. God does not promise to 'reveal himself', for instance, for some positive personal relationship. He is going to make himself notable.[1] He looks very like a Goliath shouting his challenge, and men are going to know more about him to their cost. He is not making himself known as a man

---

[1] Cf. Prov. 31.23. See above, p. 23, n. 1.

might to his friend; he is making himself known as great, apart, redoubtable. Similarly, but more positively, God made himself known to the Jews by bringing them out of Egypt. It is usually 'that they may know that I am the Lord' (Exodus, *passim*); but occasionally the phraseology may be more direct (? Deut. 11.2; Judg. 2.10). And still the emphasis is on God's defence of his own reputation. By and large, God's acts in history do not let us know as it were the 'inward' things of God, nor do they initiate a relationship of friends with him. They just let us know he can get his own way, he is strong.[1] And even this is only incidental to his main purposes.

To 'know God's Name'

The 'name' of Yahweh is often a sort of 'double' of himself:

'Let them that love your name be joyful in you' (Ps. 5.11).

And so, 'soul' and 'name' are almost identical.[2] It is therefore suggested that 'to know Yahweh's name' (and its use is, of course, good enough evidence that it is known!) is 'to know Yahweh's self'. If Yahweh tells his name to a man, he 'reveals himself'.[3]

However, this suggested meaning quite obviously does not fit most of the contexts which speak of 'the name'. The 'name' of Yahweh is much more like his word, his spirit, his arm, and later, his presence. It is an extension of his active power; it is that power as localisable, committed to a sanctuary or a nation and its territory. When Yahweh gives his name to a man or nation, he provides a way for the individual or group to tap his power. It is now possible 'to call on the name of Yahweh'. To know anyone's name is not primarily to know him as a person, to know his character; it is to have in your grasp that aspect of the person that normally allows you a measure of control over him.[4] So Yahweh graciously gives his name to Moses and Israel, and commits himself to them. It is the guarantee of the covenant, a sort of ambassador of Yahweh that he leaves with his people; but an ambassador that is really an extension of Yahweh himself. Now Yahweh protects Israel, 'for his name's

[1] Ezek. 20.9ff. esp. v. 14; Ex. 7.5; also Pss. 9.16; 48.3; 76.1.
[2] J. Pedersen, *Israel* I-II (1926), O.U.P., 1946, p. 245ff.
[3] Knight, *op. cit.*, p. 44ff.; Pedersen *ibid.*; von Allmen, *VB*, art. 'Name'.
[4] Cf. the reluctance of the river-god (or Yahweh himself) at Gen. 32.24.

sake', or else it might be profaned. It is for his reputation's sake, no more; there is now a part of himself in Israel.[1]

This sense of 'name' is most obvious in places where the 'name' is spoken of as resting somewhere,[2] as protecting,[3] and it is still used in this way in two passages often quoted as instances of the 'revealing' of God.

Yahweh does give his name to Moses at the burning bush. But he is not 'emptying himself' before Moses;[4] he is guaranteeing that he will be with Moses.[5] And this is even clearer in the passage where Yahweh shows his back to Moses. What Yahweh shows is not his 'self' as he has been; it is what he will do for Israel, the kindliness of his presence and care. Moses then begs that he will be Israel's God. Yahweh gives his terms for agreeing to this (Ex. 33.17-34 end).[6] All this could, of course, give some insight into God's 'character'. But it is not for that that the giving of the name is important. It is important as the guarantee of Israel's security and prosperity.

To 'know Yahweh himself'

We have still to find a passage where Yahweh is said to 'make himself known', 'reveal himself', in any but the most superficial, partial, or incidental way. There are just a few instances where this might be intended.

Thus God says to Aaron and Miriam, 'If there be a prophet among you, I Yahweh will make myself known to him in a vision. . . . My servant Moses is not so; he is faithful in all my house: with him I will speak mouth to mouth, even manifestly . . .' (Num. 12.6ff.). And in an unusually far-sighted passage, a prophet says, 'And Yahweh shall make himself known to Egypt, and the Egyptians shall know Yahweh in that day . . . ' (Isa. 19.21).[7]

The final step in examining 'revelation' in the Old Testament is to see briefly what is meant by 'knowing God'.

---

[1] Ezek. 20.9; Josh. 7.9; see above.   [2] Deut. 12.11, *et passim*.
[3] Ps. 9.9ff.; Micah 5.4.   [4] Ex. 3; Knight, *op. cit.*, p. 40ff.
[5] Vriezen, *op. cit.*, p. 235f.; M. Noth, *Exodus*, SCM Press, 1962, pp. 44-5.
[6] Cf. above, p. 23, n. 1. So far from Yahweh's name carrying an insight into his character, Moses has specifically to be told that Yahweh's name, his presence, will be kindly: 'Yahweh, Yahweh, a God full of compassion and gracious, slow to anger.'
[7] And perhaps some of the references above; though they are less obviously relevant.

(i) *The Many Uses of 'Know' in the Old Testament*   What sort of 'knowledge of God' did Jews in the Old Testament period think they could have? Fairly obviously, the term is important for this discussion: we have found that it can be said '*Revelation* implies for the Old Testament *the means God uses to make possible a knowledge of God for man*'. When we have found what sort of 'knowledge of God' these writers thought a man might have, it will then be possible to tell whether all along some idea of 'revelation' may have been implicit. If it is, then— even though, as we have tried to show, the Old Testament does not use the word itself in its own self-understanding—'revelation' is obviously an important term for understanding the Old Testament. In fact the evidence we now examine does not suggest so much as an implicit belief in 'revelation' of God.

The question is, then, what sort of 'knowledge of God' did a Jew in the Old Testament times think he could have? 'Knowledge' is a rich experience in the Old Testament. J. Pedersen says: 'Knowledge of a thing, a man, or whatever else, is identical with intimacy, friendship, fellow feeling . . .', that is, ' . . . with the totality of the object known'.[1] And 'knowing' is an activity; it is 'preponderantly pragmatic'.[2] *Yada'* can be used for an intense 'personal relationship', in something like our sense; it is used of the very close physical (and therefore in Hebrew thought 'personal') relationship of a man and a woman, a man and his wife (Gen. 4.1, *et passim*). But the Old Testament does not anticipate the Christian mystics who use the husband-wife metaphor of God and the Soul; to Hosea, the relation of himself and his unfaithful wife is a picture of the relation of God to the nation. *Yada'* can describe the relation of a man and his friend.[3] It can even describe the relation of a man and his land in its psychic whole (Jer. 16.13). But the point is, the meaning of *yada'* is determined by its object. If the object is your wife or husband, it will normally mean coitus (it may mean more than that, but not necessarily). The meaning is quite distinct from when the object is your sheep, your friend, your king; or, if you are an ox or an ass, your master's stall. And the meaning

---

[1] J. Pedersen, *Israel* I-II, p. 109.
[2] L. Koehler, *op. cit.*, p. 146. Again, of course, the Old Testament uses mostly the verbal forms of 'to know'; the substantive 'knowledge' occurs seldom, outside the Wisdom literature. It is an active 'knowing' that this literature speaks of.
[3] Ex. 1.8; Deut. 34.10, with Ex. 33.11; see below. Not frequent.

of *yada'* in *yada' YHWH*, is closest to its meaning when the grammatical object is your king or your master's stall.

(ii) *Moses' 'knowledge of God'* However, it is said that 'Moses knew God face to face' (Deut. 34.10; cf. Num. 14.14, 'eye to eye'); and this seems to be related to the description of Moses and God in Exodus, 'Yahweh spoke to Moses face to face, as a man speaks to his friend' (Ex. 33.11). 'Face to face'—this, if anything, might describe a 'revelatory' situation, God 'revealed' to his friend in 'I-Thou' meeting. But Moses is unique, and this relationship is the conclusive sign of his uniqueness, as the passage from Numbers cited above makes explicit: 'My servant Moses is not so (a "mere prophet"!); with him will I speak mouth to mouth' (Num. 12.6ff.). This is not the normal relation of man and God in the Old Testament. Not even of prophet and God. And even in this legend, meant to underline as heavily as possible the cosmic importance of Moses, Moses' relation to the nation is not lost: it is only for the sake of his people that God calls Moses and is with him (Ex. 3.2ff.).[1] The romanticism of Vigny's Moïse is a long way from the biblical narrative. This is plainest again in the story of God showing his back to Moses (Ex. 33.12ff.). This incident comes just after Moses has been called the close friend of God. 'For wherein shall it be known that I have found favour in your sight, *I and your people*? is it not that you go with us, so that we be separated, I and your people, from all the people that be on the face of the earth?' Moses is much more than an individual great man in the tradition; he is the embodiment of the real and of the ideal nation. There is no hint in the tradition that the ancient Jews ever hoped that the individual would some day be in this position, the 'friend of God' as an individual, meeting him face to face. Even Job in his long angry monologues with God is trying to pester him into restoring his, Job's right relation in his community.[2]

(iii) *To 'know' and to 'obey'* Elsewhere it is occasionally denied

---

[1] Cf. also Num. 11.29, 'Would that all Yahweh's people were prophets and Yahweh would put his spirit upon them.' This might appear at first sight to contradict the case being made here; but this wish is followed by the passage cited above, Num. 12.6ff., which shows that in the tradition in which this hope was expressed, the prophet was not seen to be in face-to-face relation with God, in the way Moses had been.

[2] Job 29, and the narrative framework of the poem.

that someone 'knows God'; the heathen (Ps. 79.6), Pharaoh (Ex. 5.2), the sons of Eli (I Sam. 2.12); and Israel (Hos. 8.1-3), who is unlike the ox and the ass, and does not know its master (Isa. 1.3ff.). It is obvious from these people's *actions* that they do not 'know' God. They disobey him, and that is why it is said they do not 'know him'. The 'knowing' and the 'obeying' are really the same activity.[1] This is borne out by the rather fewer instances where it is said that someone, or more usually some nation, perhaps represented by a great figure, does or will 'know God'. When Moses, earlier in the passage cited above, asked to 'know' God, it was not for himself as an individual that he asked, nor was it for a knowledge, an awareness, that might have been an end in itself. He asked to be told, for Israel's sake, the terms of obedience to Yahweh, so that the nation might prosper: 'Now, therefore, I pray you, if I have found favour in your sight, show me your ways that I may "know" you, to the end I may find favour in your sight: and consider that this nation is your people' (Ex. 33.13). To 'know God' is to obey him, and so to please him.

For the Chronicler, 'to search out the commandments of Yahweh', 'to know the God of your father', and 'to serve him', are all synonymous parallel expressions (I Chron. 28.8-9). The second of the two passages above[2] that talk of God being 'made known' reads in full: 'The Lord shall be known to the Egyptians, and the Egyptians shall know the Lord in that day; *yea they shall worship with sacrifice and oblation*' (Isa. 19.21): this is cultus as the focal point of obedience.

(iv) *To 'know' and to 'obey' in Jeremiah*   Jeremiah 9 contains three denunciations of those who do not 'know' God, and then (from a separate hand?), 'But let him that glories glory in this that he understands that I am the Lord that exercise loving kindness, judgment and righteousness: for in these things do I delight . . .' (Jer. 9.24). But perhaps the classical definition of

---

[1] Cf. E. C. Blackman, art. 'Know' in *ThWB*. It was 'the recognition of, obedience to, one who acted purposefully in the world'. It does not seem here necessary to discuss 'knowing that', as that is not normally taken to describe the sort of knowing that might be called 'revelation of God'. But 'knowing that' also expects a full response; it is not 'just' an intellectual acceptance of propositions. Cf. Ex. 6.7; the Israelites will know from God's actions that he is 'Yahweh their God, who brings them out from under the burdens of the Egyptians'; and the whole book details the obedient response which is to be the form the 'knowing' takes, the knowing that Yahweh is their God.   [2] P. 35.

how God is to be 'known' comes later in the same book: 'He judged (i.e. upheld) the cause of the poor and needy. Was not this to know me? says the Lord' (Jer. 22.16). This is not the same as saying, 'If you "know" God, you will obey him' (or, even, 'you ought to obey him'); it is that the *only way* to 'know God' is to obey him in your dealings with people and things, and in the manner of your worship.

It is particularly interesting to find this understanding of *yada'* so clear in the book of Jeremiah because it is often said that in him (or in his 'school') comes the turning point where Israelite religion becomes interiorised, individualised and most fully personal. The passage most quoted in this connection is the description of the 'New Covenant'. What this passage actually says is: '*I will put my laws in their inward parts*, and in their heart will I write it; and I will be their God, and they will be my people . . . they shall all know me' (Jer. 31.31ff.). It is easy to miss the drastic threat that this passage contains, if other passages which talk of God getting his own way through men's hearts are forgotten. As J. Pedersen says, 'The strong soul may turn the direction of the weak soul. If God "touches" a heart, then it is he who determines its will.'[2] God in the Exodus epic hardens Pharaoh's heart, so that he himself may receive more glory in the end. God competely controls Pharaoh. And this is what the prophet is promising here. He is completely disillusioned with Yahweh's treatment of people as free human beings, beings whom he addresses with commands;[3] and so he looks for Yahweh to set an automatic programme device in men, an internal control which they will not be able to escape.[4] At least then Israel will obey Yahweh's Torah, when it is physically part of

[1] Cf. H. Wheeler Robinson in *A Commentary on the Bible*, ed. A. S. Peake, T. C. and E. C. Jack, 1925: 'The prophetic consciousness of a Jeremiah, with its direct relation to God, will become general . . . a direct fellowship with God.'
[2] Pedersen *Israel* I-II, p. 104. The tenor of this passage seems to have been felt in this way by J. Oman: 'Why introduce a saint, or even a Christ, saying to His brother, "Know the Lord", if *by an irresistible* might, all can be made to know Him?' *Grace and Personality*, C.U.P., 1917: Fontana, 1960, p. 137 (my italics).
[3] Jer. 5.23-4; 13.10; 18.12.
[4] '*I will put* my law in their inward parts . . .' so that 'they shall know me', does stress Yahweh's initiative, and also emphasises the completeness of the result that is expected. In this it is more like the current theological term 'reveal' than any other Old Testament expression. 'Revealing' also stresses these points (see below, ch. 3). So it is perhaps significant that the prophet does not use *galah* or any synonym; nor in fact is it possible to paraphrase the expression with 'reveal'; for there is the one point of difference, that 'to reveal' is to address the conscious mind and will, and this, the prophet has decided, is

them. Then they will 'know' the Lord. The 'knowing' will be an inescapable obedience. And the following lines show that this is concerned with the individual's relation to Yahweh only as part of the nation; it is understood in terms of the nation's life; the covenant is with the nation as nation, the form of the knowledge-obedience is practical social and cultic behaviour; and the usual promise is attached, that Yahweh for his part will ensure national prosperity. This will be the realisation of right relations of individuals, and of the community and their God. There is no hint in the passage itself, despite the customary exegesis, of any close personal relationship between Yahweh and the individual. There is certainly no 'revealing' of Yahweh to him. Jeremiah himself is, to be sure, a man on his own, but only for the sake of the nation, and he hates being alone, even if it is 'with God'; just as any other Semite from Cain onwards would. He is close to God, has God's own words (Jer. 1.9, etc.), but only for the fulfilment of Yahweh's grand purpose in all history, and in Israel's history especially. Jeremiah has a series of dramatic conversations with Yahweh, but the topic is always Israel, and it fills him with grief. 'I sat alone because of your hand. . . . I will make you unto this people as a fenced brasen wall . . . for I am with you to save you and deliver you' (Jer. 15.10-21).[1]

---

not the way for God to act. The one Old Testament prophet who might have developed a 'concept of revelation' in fact chose another metaphor. This despair and seeming pessimism of Jeremiah contrasts with most of the Old Testament, for which it is enough that God's law should be 'taught': e.g. Deut. 6.4ff. Ezekiel expects much the same control by Yahweh, though he describes it a little less bluntly: the Israelites will be given malleable hearts, with God's spirit in charge, to shape their lives the right way; Ezek. 11.19; 36.26.

[1] U. E. Simon, 'The Mysticism of Jeremiah the Prophet', *CQR* CLXI 340, describes Jeremiah's experience in terms of 'mysticism' and 'communion'. Jeremiah 'is possessed by God, and his faith remains firm in face of all evidence to the contrary and increases with the realization that the *via negativa* of not knowing God also belongs to the truth of the God who reveals himself'. Simon sees the events of Jeremiah's life as being (and this probably consciously for Jeremiah himself) just the necessary background for his relationship with Yahweh, and brought about for the sake of that relationship; for instance, failure shows that God tests his servant (*ibid.*, p. 278). But there is nothing in the text to suggest this. For sure, a messenger of Yahweh has to be close to Yahweh to receive the message that is to be passed on. And being his messenger is to some extent 'being Yahweh'; and when the message is unpopular, this means separation from the people; and their refusal to hear means suffering. But the loneliness, the existence as an individual in company with Yahweh is not an essential part of the relation of Yahweh and prophet. It is incidental, it only occurs when the people disobey. And being Yahweh's servant is in fact no compensation for this separation from the prophet's people. When the people disobey, the words the prophet has to

God's 'knowledge of man'

The Old Testament literature talks of God's knowledge of men. He knows their hearts, as he knows their ways: he knows all about them, their intentions, their needs and desires.[1] God's knowledge of a man or a nation can also mean his choice, and his acceptance of the nation or the man as servant. 'You only have I known of all the nations of the earth' (Amos 3.2). 'Before I formed you in the womb I knew you . . . I sanctified you . . . appointed you a prophet' (Jer. 1.5). But mostly God's knowing is a practical knowledge of facts, future events, and what he intends to do in them. And his knowing of men comes under this head.[2] It is not a knowing as a man knows his friend.

The substantive 'knowledge'

The same applies to the substantive, *da'at*, used almost exclusively in the Wisdom Literature, and in the somewhat similar chapters in deutero-Isaiah:

'Shall any teach God knowledge
Seeing he judges those that are high?' (Job 21.22; cf. Isa. 40.14).

The whole literature is intensely 'practical', and its understanding of 'knowledge' is no exception. Only Hosea seems to use the phrase 'knowledge of God', and it is amply explained in the expected terms: 'There is no truth nor mercy nor "knowledge" of God in the land; there is nought but swearing and breaking faith and killing and committing adultery . . .' (Hos. 4.1). The parallelism of:

---

speak become pain and grief to him (15.15ff.). As Simon himself says, 'He must be among his own people to see and to hear them.' It is the separation from his people that is 'the dark night of the soul'; not a sense of separation from God, of God withdrawing his presence, his strong hand. Rather, as in the case of Job, if God had done that, it might have brought some relief. To be conscious of being Yahweh's prophet was obviously a powerful, shattering experience. But Jeremiah is still the messenger, servant, instrument; not a friend brought into relationship, communion, for his or their own sake. Following the account of Jeremiah's life is moving and humbling. But to use words like 'mystical' and 'communion' to describe his status before God is to stretch them farther from their normal meaning than they can bear. There is a very great difference between a mediaeval's or a modern's sense of communion with God (or the withdrawal of it) and the relation with God and with the disobedient people, of the prophet; the latter has a relationship aimed entirely at the fulfilling of God's purpose in the community. Just the fact that each may have found their experience very powerful is not sufficient ground for describing the one in terms of the other. Jeremiah does not suggest that God is 'revealed' to him.

[1] I Kings 8.37ff.; Ps. 139; Job 31.6.
[2] For examples of this 'preponderantly pragmatic' knowing, see Job 27ff.

'I desire mercy and not sacrifice,
The "knowledge" of God and not burnt offering' (Hos. 6.6)

speaks for itself. To 'know God' is to obey him.

Conclusions

It is necessary to examine more closely the possible implications of the contexts in which we have met the phrase *yd' YHWH*. We must decide whether this sort of 'knowing' can be called 'revelation', whether it must necessarily presuppose a belief in 'revelation'. The law, which makes God's demands 'known', might fairly be said to have 'revealed'; but we must ask whether it can be said to 'reveal' God.

(i) *Obedience and Revelation* Evidence has been found to support the contention that *yada' YHWH* in the Old Testament *means* 'he obeyed Yahweh'. The suggestion is not just that the Jews had the odd habit of refusing to admit that a man 'knew' anything of God until he proved his knowledge by various acts of obedience. It is that *yada' YHWH is best translated* 'he obeyed Yahweh'. *Yada'* in this context no more means 'know' as that word is used in current English, than does *galah*, in the contexts we have examined, mean 'exile'. The word looks the same, has the same common history; but it means, in these contexts, something distinct from what it means elsewhere. There is no cause to become mystical about this.[1] It is no stranger than the fact that *'voler'* in French can mean 'to steal' or 'to fly' (both transitively) or 'to fly' (intransitively).

Yada' can mean to know facts,[2] to experience events,[3] to enjoy a friendship with someone,[4] to have sexual intercourse,[5] to obey God. There is no one English word that can convey these various meanings. Only a circumlocution can be sufficiently general. A periphrasis such as 'have a formative relationship with' might be wide enough, and open enough, to be given its meaning by its context. And obedience is the only 'formative

---

[1] Cf. J. Barr, *The Semantics of Biblical Language*, O.U.P., 1961, especially chapter 6. Another good example of a word that demands a variety of English translations is, of course, *ntn*, give, set, place, show, etc.
[2] Ex. 6.7 *et passim*, see above, p. 38, n. 1.
[3] Isa. 47.8; 53.3; cf. Bultmann, *Gnosis*, A. and C. Black, 1952, p. 15 (E.T. of *TWNT* article).
[4] See above, p. 36.
[5] Gen. 4.1, etc.

relationship' with himself that Yahweh allows.[1] He does not allow the other formative relationships that Hebrew denotes by *yada'*; neither does he allow the relationships that English can convey with the word 'know'. ('Acknowledge' comes closest to this use of *yada'*, but is hardly strong enough.)

It would in fact, if this case is valid, be possible for *yada' YHWH* to be said of a man who had not realised he was doing Yahweh's will. It is not a description of a man's consciousness. It does not describe a 'knowing' that is perhaps 'provable' by obedience. The obedience is the full content denoted by *yada'*, the full and only possible content of a formative relationship with Yahweh.[2] (Because *yada' YHWH* is commonly translated 'he knew Yahweh', 'know' and 'knowledge' have been allowed to remain in English quotations from the Old Testament; but in inverted commas as a hint that the convention is misleading.)

If 'knowledge' of God is really 'obedience' to God, the necessary corollary is that it is impossible to talk of such 'knowledge' being 'revealed'. It is possible to 'reveal' the terms of obedience, but not to 'reveal' obedience itself. It is possible to desire it, command it, enable it, elicit it, or even in desperation compel it. But not 'reveal' it. For an Old Testament writer, 'I "know" Yahweh' does not and could not *itself entail* 'Yahweh has revealed himself'. Even in *yd' YHWH* we fail to find so much as a hidden 'concept of revelation'; still less any implicit belief in 'the revelation of God himself'.

(ii) *The Law as 'revelation'* It might be thought that in the tradition that said Yahweh at least spoke clearly to Moses, if not to anyone else (Num. 12.6ff.), the law, the codified Torah, would be seen as a 'revelation' of God's ways for men. This was his demand made clear. Moses says: 'Yahweh, shew me your ways that I may "know" (obey) you, so that I may find favour in your sight; and consider that this nation is your people' (Ex. 33.13); Yahweh then gives his law. Apart from the codified Torah, there is only uncertainty, the confusion and obscurity

[1] Cf. E. C. Blackman, art. 'Know' in *ThWB*; von Allmen, *VB*, art. 'Know'; Pedersen, *op. cit.*, p. 109; Koehler, *op. cit.*, p. 146; Vriezen, *op. cit.*, p. 129; Oepke, *TWNT* III, p. 574, notes the peculiarly moral basis of the relationship Yahweh allows with himself. But these do not draw the further conclusion here offered.
[2] Bultmann, *op. cit.*, p. 48: 'Obedience is the very essence of *yada'*.' Cf. *ibid.*, p. 18.

of prophecy. With codified Torah, God's will is plain.[1]

Though the Old Testament writers do not talk of Torah explicitly as the 'clear expression' of Yahweh's will, it may be legitimate to assume that this is how it was understood; at least, after the exile, and the codifying and integrating of the traditions. It would then be easy to produce the sequence: God's demand is made clear, his will is made plain, and that must mean that he himself is revealed. A man cannot reveal his will without revealing at least something of himself. But the Old Testament writers, as has been seen, consistently refuse to make this deduction. Despite the fact that God's acts of righteousness, faithfulness, mercy and his correlative demand for righteousness, faithfulness, mercy, should 'reveal' that he is righteous, faithful, kind, the majority do not 'see'. And for those who do to some extent understand he still remains, in himself, a hidden God (Isa. 55.9, etc.).[2] The only way in which God comes 'out of hiding' as it were is, as has been shown above, by prospering

---

[1] This clarity of communication of the terms of the agreement is probably intended in Deut. 4.13 (cf. 5.5): 'He declared to you his covenant, which he commanded you to perform, even the ten words; and he wrote them upon two tables of stone.' These latter however may be meant to be distinguished from the (nonetheless authoritative) 'statutes and judgments' of the next verse. Still, it is clearly said in Ps. 147.19ff. that the requirements of God are imparted directly:

'He told (*ngd*) his word to Jacob,
his statutes and judgments to Israel.
He has not done so with any nations. . . ?

Compare also Jer. 38.14ff.; 42.3, 4, 21 (*ngd* again). (*Ngd* is the word we saw above that is most often used of God 'telling things'.) These statutes, ordinances, judgments, can also be spoken, commanded, given, or perhaps most often taught (*yrh*, *lmd*: (Pss. 27.11; 25.4, etc.). Moses is usually the teacher (Deut., *passim*). Vriezen, *op. cit.*, p. 237ff., is obviously right not to use the ambiguous term 'the revelation of God' for 'the telling of the commands'.

Perhaps when Israelite Torah is under discussion, it is possible to discern some sense of 'particular revelation' (to use what we have noted is a non-biblical expression) of the terms of obedience (see e.g. Ps. 147, quoted immediately above). Cf. Deut. 4.6ff.: 'Keep therefore and do them; for this is your wisdom and your understanding in the sight of the peoples which shall hear all these statutes, and say, "Surely this great nation is a wise and understanding people. For what great nation is there, that has a God so nigh to them, as Yahweh our God is whenever we call upon him?"' These laws are a special gift to Israel. But at least for the Deuteronomist, the surrounding people are supposed to know enough of righteousness, to recognise Israelite law as its best expression. There is (as J. Barr, art. 'Revelation', *HDB* 1963, mentions) little attempt by the OT writers to speculate about the possibility or impossibility of the knowledge of the terms of God's demands on men outside the Israelite Torah. Just the fact is noted that many of the nations do disobey: they do not 'know' God. The possibility of God 'revealing himself' to the nations is, of course, not considered in the OT.

[2] Less directly stated in Job 28.20ff.; 36.22ff.; 37–39; 42; Ps. 40.5, Ps. 139. And the fact that theophanies are startlingly unexpected.

the individual or Israel, or if need be, defeating her enemies.[1]
And there are even weighty objections in the Old Testament,
in some of the Psalms, in Ecclesiastes, and in Job, against making deductions about the character of God from his supposed
acts in history.[2] God does not reveal himself.

IV

To draw together the discussion so far: the mere fact that
words meaning 'reveal' are not often used in the Old Testament, and are not used of God's 'revealing his self', or even his
will, is suggestive in itself. But it is not enough on its own to
settle the question about 'revelation' in the Old Testament;
and so it has been necessary to examine some possible synonyms,
to see if the same thing is being said in a less direct way. And
plainly it is not being said at all.

Part of the modern insistence on 'revelation' is due to a sense
that 'knowledge of' or even 'about' God must (for God to be
the God of Jesus and Paul) depend on God himself providing it.
It cannot be 'discovered' by human effort. There is just such
an insistence on God's hiddenness, on the impossibility of just
looking and finding him, in the Old Testament. It is a not very
important part of a general understanding that all depends on
God's initiative for his relation with men.[3] But whereas the
Old Testament is sure God retains this initiative, and remains
hidden, the Old Testament's modern expounders insist that
God must have exercised this initiative he holds, and find him
'revealing himself' on all sides. It is quite shattering to find
writer after writer admitting that for old Israel, God is hidden[4]
—and then blithely deducing from this observation God's
'self-revelation'. If he is hidden, then obviously for 'him himself' to be 'known' he must 'reveal' himself. That is fair enough.
But it does not follow (at least not without further argument)
that he therefore does, and has 'revealed' himself. Yet a greater

[1] Above p. 33; Pss. 22.24; 44.24; Isa. 54.8.
[2] See above, p. 23, n. 2; p. 44, n. 1. G. von Rad, *Old Testament Theology* I,
Oliver and Boyd, 1962, p. 453f, discusses this scepticism, and in a footnote adds
'To an increasing degree the later period spoke of the impossibility of knowing
Yahweh' (he is using 'know' in its English sense). He cites Jer. 23.23f.; Isa. 40.18,
25; 55.8f.; Prov. 30.1ff.
[3] There are very few exceptions: Gen. 18.16ff.; Num. 14.13ff.; and parallel
accounts and incidents.
[4] Richardson, *ThWB*, arts. 'Revelation' and 'Hide'; von Allmen, *VB*, art.
'Revelation'; Knight, *op. cit.*, p. 20; Vriezen, *op. cit.*, p. 234.

or lesser number of the passages we have considered are forced, though they shout their violation to high heaven, to provide an Old Testament 'understanding' of God's supposed 'self-revelation'.[1]

God's actions are primary in the Old Testament. Only then is man's response considered. God in fact makes it possible for man (Israel, at least) to be on the right side, when he acts as he wishes. He allows to be known, with greater or lesser clarity, in more or less detail, the terms of the obedience he requires of men. This is a gracious act.[2] Otherwise there is little clear communication between God and men. It might be said that the fact that the hidden God could even be spoken of, and his commands known, implies 'revelation' in some sense. It would certainly not seem too arbitrary to say that the Old Testament implies 'revelation by himself' of enough of Yahweh's own preferences for a man to be able to 'know' ('obey') him. But this 'revelation *by* himself' (and it is all along our term, not the Old Testament's) is still not 'revelation *of* himself'.

This is all that may be said positively about 'revelation' in the Old Testament. Negatively, it has to be insisted that God does not 'reveal his self'; and that his commands, which might just possibly be said to be 'revealed', are not said to 'reveal' Yahweh.

The idea that God did in the Old Testament 'reveal' the terms of the obedience that he really demands is decisively rejected in the New Testament by Jesus and by Paul.[3] For the Christian, no formula can 'reveal' the grace and demand of God. Formulae and law depend ultimately on men, and cannot be effective (Rom. 8.3). The grace and demand of God can only *happen* and then, perhaps, be increasingly appreciated, responded to. In the end, God may be 'revealed' (I Cor. 13.12). For the Christian, the Old Testament misunderstands Torah

---

[1] This is then qualified by such comments as 'even in his self-disclosure he remains a hidden God' (Hendry), art. 'Revelation' in *ThWB*, which as it stands is pure nonsense. As Augustine insisted, 'God' does not make sense of a nonsense sentence. It is just possible to make sense of the assertion, if the writer is willing to answer the further questions, 'In what sense is he disclosed; in what sense is he still hidden?' The Old Testament might be persuaded to answer, 'He is disclosed in the sense that you may see the things he has done; he is hidden in his "inner self". There is no "*self*-disclosure".' But these are not terms natural to this collection of writings.
[2] Ex. 24.12, *et passim*.
[3] Matt. 5.21ff., 27ff., 33ff., 38ff.; Luke 16.16f. and Matt.; Gal. 2.16, 21; Rom. 3.28; Phil. 3.6, 9.

where Israel went wrong was absolutizing law —

when it seems to suggest that Torah 'reveals' God's will. *A fortiori*, the Christian cannot see Torah as 'revealing' God.

The Christian may still just insist on seeing the Old Testament as a whole as 'revealing' God; the possibilities of making sense of this sort of impression are discussed in chapter 6. But it is not legitimate exegesis to read this understanding into the Old Testament itself, which is very chary of saying this sort of thing about God. Of course, if 'revelation of himself' is to be used indiscriminately as a pantechnicon word to describe every occasion on which someone thinks God has been 'in touch' with him, no matter how superficially he has been understood, no matter how poorly he himself thinks he has understood God, it may be used to paraphrase the passages we have considered, and even to describe other incidents recorded in this literature. This would still be misleading, because it is not the Old Testament's own usage; and it would evacuate 'reveal himself' of all but the shallowest meaning, if it left any at all. It would be to take a word that means 'make clear' and use it to mean 'leave obscure'. It would be to cry 'clarity, clarity', where there is no clarity.

The Old Testament writers do not pretend that the relation of God and Man is close enough or clear enough for God to be said to have revealed himself.

B. OTHER RELEVANT LITERATURE

There is little in the actual Hebrew Old Testament to act as a background for a 'concept' of 'revelation' in the New Testament. There remain the documents of later Judaism; the Septuagint version(s) of the Old Testament as the most immediate background to the Greek of the New Testament; the literature of the Qumran sect; and the other, mainly apocalyptic, Jewish writings that may be dated shortly before or contemporary with the Christian era. And there are also the somewhat sparser examples of the non-Jewish popular thought of the East Mediterranean in this period; and especially there is the now largely increased body of evidence for broadly 'gnostic' thought. Most of the documents date from later than the New Testament, but may be evidence for contemporary religious thinking, and so must be noticed. All the material we consider now is taken to illustrate very generally trends of thought that chronologically may have preceded, been exactly contemporary with, or followed the writing of, the New Testament literature. An accurate dating is often impossible; but for our purpose, as will be seen, this is not important.

1 *The Septuagint*

To know God

The LXX uses γινώσκειν and εἰδέναι for *yada'*. There is no sign of their being used to describe any increase in intensity in the God-man relation. For the Hebrew Bible's 'Moses knew God face to face', the LXX has 'ὃν ἔγνω κύριος αὐτὸν πρόσωπον κατὰ πρόσωπον' (Deut. 34.10); if the change is at all significant, it suggests that the LXX finds the same sort of difficulty in talking of a man 'knowing' God as Paul does later; and so, God is made the subject.[1] It may also be significant that the LXX version of 'the people that know their God shall be strong' in Daniel (Dan. 11.32) is 'the people that know these things . . .'.

Wisdom, which can make men 'friends of God and prophets' (Wisdom 7.27) is still severely practical. She teaches crafts, geology, meteorology: it is this 'knowledge' that she gives. The righteous man who 'knows God' will be rewarded by being set to rule the nations (Wisdom 2.13; 3.8). The thought still remains stolidly within the range of the Old Testament, for all the gloss of Greek learning.

'*To Reveal*'

'Ἀποκαλύπτειν (occasionally ἀνα-) in the LXX again means a physical stripping naked (Lev. *passim*) and is used quite straightforwardly to translate *galah*, etc.; to describe disclosing a secret, as in Joshua of the plans of the spies (Josh. 2.20); it is

---

[1] The LXX have done the same thing as later translators of the Old Testament. They have assumed that *yada'* can be translated uniformly (in their case, by a pair of synonyms). In the context of the rest of the translated work, this is not too misleading. Γινώσκειν τὸν κύριον in the LXX thus *means* 'to obey the Lord'. Out of context, the phrase could suggest a rather different relationship, a communion, a state of consciousness. There is no sign of this change of meaning occurring, save perhaps in Philo's use of the LXX. Bultmann (*Gnosis*, p. 21) says that γινώσκειν and γινώσκεσθαι in the LXX 'often . . . denote God's self-revelation as such'. But he offers no evidence other than the LXX of Ex. 29.42, 46: 'ποιήσεις . . . εἰς γενεὰς ὑμῶν, ἐπὶ θύρας τῆς σκηνῆς τοῦ μαρτυρίου ἔναντι κυρίου, ἐν οἷς γνωσθήσομαί σοι ἐκεῖθεν ὥστε λαλῆσαί σοι . . . καὶ γνώσονται, ὅτι ἐγώ εἰμι κύριος ὁ θεὸς αὐτῶν, ὁ ἐξαγαγὼν αὐτοὺς ἐκ γῆς Αἰγύπτου, ἐπικληθῆναι αὐτοῖς, καὶ εἶναι αὐτῶν θεός' which takes the terms no farther than their equivalents in the Hebrew Old Testament.

used in the passages of I Samuel 3 quoted above;[1] of the Lord 'revealing a time' to Samuel (I Sam. 9.15); and in the Psalms and in Isaiah, in the metaphors of the Lord laying bare his arm or openly exercising his righteousness. In Daniel it is μυστήρια that are revealed: 'Then the mystery was revealed to Daniel in a vision of the night . . . the God of heaven . . . reveals deep and secret things' (Dan. 2.19 and 22)[2] And it is used in an injunction to Tobit to 'reveal gloriously the works of God' (Tobit 12.7, 11). Otherwise, in the new material the LXX contains, it is only used as in Daniel (above): either of human secrets, or once in a rhetorical question: 'To whom has the root of wisdom been revealed, and who has known her shrewd counsels?' (expecting the answer, 'No one but God himself') (Ecclus 11.27; 22.22; 41.23; 1.6). The noun ἀποκάλυψις ('revealing' or 'revelation') does not seem to be used outside of the context of literal stripping, noticed already above.

To Appear

The adjective ἐπιφανής (ἐπιφαίνειν, manifest, make plain, clear) seems to have gained a rather strange use; probably because of a mistranslation of the Hebrew original.[3] A passage in Joel which talks of the 'great and terrible day of the Lord' becomes: . . . διότι μεγάλη ἡ ἡμέρα κυρίου, ἐπιφανὴς σφόδρα, and this is the adjective used to translate 'My name is great among the Gentiles' (Joel 2.11; Mal. 1.14). But it does not seem relevant to our enquiry.

The verb is used in the theophanies in Genesis (e.g. Gen. 35.7), and is of course the technical Greek term for this kind of event. It is used of the shining of light, of the sun and the stars; and so, metaphorically, of God 'making his face to shine'; it has probably no longer any sun-cult associations, but does still take the form of quite concrete well-being. The verb is used in II Maccabees of the light of a burning camp, of an apparition of Jeremiah, and one of 'The Mighty Lord'—who 'appears' as the rider of a terrible horse, and is accompanied by two attendants who beat Heliodorus for violating the Jerusalem sanctuary, 'with many sore stripes'. The thrashing makes the

[1] P. 26.
[2] The 'mystery' seems to be God's plans for the Gentiles, and provides a possible background for Paul's talking of the 'revealing of the mystery', I Cor. 2, etc.
[3] See Moulton and Milligan, *The Vocabulary of the Greek New Testament*, *s.v.*

king's chancellor recognise the sovereignty of God. Mourning turned to joy, 'now that the mighty Lord has appeared' (II Mac. 3.22ff.). Where he actually appears is uncertain; it may be in the total action of defending his cultic centre. If he actually appears as the Rider, it is, still, to do battle. It is what happens, and not the appearing as such that matters.

The noun ἐπιφάνεια is used in Amos of the grandeur of the offerings that God refuses (Amos 5.22), otherwise only in II Maccabees (in the incident quoted), and elsewhere of other manifestations from heaven, in the form of sky-armies, God making his presence felt by acts of power. They include one victory (II Mac. 15.27) where only Jeremiah has actually 'been seen', but Judas won with the sword the latter gave him; this was a 'manifestation' of God.

Φαίνειν, the simpler form of the verb, is used in much the same way. It can be used of the sun (Gen. 15.17), of the white of Jacob's peeled sticks (Gen. 30.37ff.), of lightning (Pss. 76[7].18; 96[7].4); or of the Lord in blessing (Isa. 60.2): ἐπὶ δὲ σὲ φανήσετὲι κύριος. It is used of the Lord meeting Balaam (Num. 23.3, 4). The Lord does not meet Balaam for the latter's sake (Balaam had lost all favour in the tradition by the time the LXX was made). The Lord meets Balaam solely to instruct him so that he can play his part in the drama of cursing and blessing. This verb is also used in II Maccabees, again in the scene quoted above, of the two attendants; and also of a horseman who 'appears' late in a battle (II Mac. 11.8).

The adjective φανερός is used in Deuteronomy: 'The secret things belong unto Yahweh ... but the things that are *revealed* belong unto us' (Deut. 29.29). It is used in Isaiah, of God making his name known (Isa. 64.2). Φανέρωσις is not used.

It is worth noting another word the LXX uses to make this sort of point, as it recurs in the New Testament. Δεικνύναι, 'to show', is sometimes used to translate ra'ah (hiphil): 'Show us your mercy O Lord, And grant us your salvation' (Ps. 84[5].7; cf. Ps. 90[1].16; Isa. 48.9, LXX). It is not a request to be allowed to form an accurate conception of God's loving kindness; it is a straight request for action, as the parallel clearly shows.

Nothing startlingly new has come out of the LXX, the translated or the new material, nothing to suggest a trend towards a

use of 'reveal' as a technical term; nothing to suggest even a
hope that God may be One who 'reveals his self'. We find what
we would expect of scholars steeped in the Hebrew Old Testament; and they only feel more fully their immediate predeces-
sors' embarrassment at the anthropomorphism of the theophany
stories.

The Law has been given (Ecclus 24, etc.), the terms of
obedience. Again, it might be said to be 'revealed',[1] but as in
the Hebrew Old Testament, it is not. The difficulties remain.
There is no other significant 'revealing'. It is the 'apparitional'
language that is most used in the new literature that appears
in the Greek canon. Other ways of using words like 'reveal'
are less frequent. But the appearances are of servants of God
and only indirectly of God himself. They do not even give cultic
or moral instruction, they appear solely to act. And the
'apparitions' are tangible as well as visible.

II *Apocrypha and Pseudepigrapha*

This literature does not provide any evidence that is significantly different from what we have found to date. Oddly
enough, these works rarely if ever use ἀποκαλύπτειν.

The law plays a large part in *Jubilees*, where it is the final
expression of God's will. Early in the work God promises 'And
the Lord will appear to the eyes of all, and all shall know that
I am the God of Israel and the Father of all the children of
Jacob, and King on Mount Zion for all eternity' (1.28). This
is God's epiphany as the assertion of his kingly power;[2] except
for its finality, there is little difference from some of the promises of his 'open activity' in the biblical literature.

There is a similar expectation in *The Assumption of Moses*:
'And then His Kingdom shall appear throughout all His Crea-
tion. . . .
For the Holy One will arise from His royal throne
And He will go forth from His holy habitation
With indignation and wrath on account of His sons. . . .
And He will appear to punish the gentiles' (10. 1, 3, 7).
God 'created the world on behalf of his people'. But he was 'not
pleased to manifest this purpose of creation from the foundation

[1] Oepke, *TWNT* III, p. 580.
[2] Cf. S. Aalen, ' "Reign" and "House" in the Kingdom of God in the Gospels',
NTS 8.3, p. 251ff. Translations of texts in R. H. Charles, *Apocrypha and Pseudepigrapha*.

of the world, in order that the Gentiles might thereby be convicted' (1.12, 13). We shall note again that the making-clear of God's ultimate purpose in terms of his people, and their relations with the Gentiles, is one of the most important contexts in which 'revealing' words are used.

To Enoch, in *The Book of the Secrets of Enoch* (Slavonic), appear two vast shining men (1.3ff.) and they take him up through the graduated heavens; in the seventh, they 'showed me the Lord from afar, sitting on his very high throne' (20.3). He is then taken before the Lord's face (one version takes him to a tenth heaven, to present him before the ultimate deity); and he is allowed to stand before his face into eternity (22.4-5). But the purpose of all this is just to give him information about angels and Sheol and cosmology generally. There is no more 'personal' confrontation. In fact, Enoch has to have his face chilled, to endure the terror of the closeness of the Lord.

In *The Book of Enoch* the central character has a vision; again this concerns God's purpose for his people, not to be told till a remote time. There is a prophecy of God's appearing, similar to that in *The Assumption of Moses*:

'The Holy Great One will come forth from His dwelling . . .
And appear in the strength of His might from the heaven of heavens . . .
And light shall appear to them,
And He will make peace with them . . .
And destroy all the ungodly . . .' (1.3, 4, 8, 9).

In his vision this Enoch too sees all the secrets of the universe. He sees a vision of the Judgment:

'When the Righteous One shall appear before the eyes of the righteous . . .
When the secrets of the righteous shall be revealed and the sinners judged' (38.2, 3).

In the book as it stands he sees 'the Son of Man', who has been hidden from all ages, 'but revealed to the holy and just' (48.6, 7; cf. 62.6, 7). At some point Enoch is identified with this Son of Man (70). But at no point does the vision become more than that of the courtier in the audience chamber. Only the last words (which could well be a post-Christian interpolation —along with much of the preceding) are at all exceptional: 'I and my son will be united with them in the paths of uprightness in their lives; and you shall have peace: rejoice, you children of uprightness' (105).

In *The Testaments of the Twelve Patriarchs* Simeon foresees the appearing of God on earth to punish and rule (6.5-6). Levi has a vision of the glory of the Most High, of the sort that we have now come to expect. One of his tasks afterwards will be to declare God's mysteries to men, 'concerning the redemption of Israel' (1.10).

None of these works[1] has seemed to suggest a 'revealing' of God himself, an at all intimate 'knowledge of God'.

III *The Dead Sea Scrolls*

One of the difficulties facing the theologian who has no access to the original sources is that of finding an agreed translation of the text of the scrolls, even where that text is itself complete. For instance, Millar Burrows[2] and G. Vermès[3] talk of 'all that has been revealed' by God 'concerning appointed times'; where T. H. Gaster[4] does not use the word 'reveal' at all. However, with a certain amount of cross-referencing the position should be clear enough.

Knowledge

W. D. Davies[5] discusses the various ways in which 'know', 'knowledge' are used, and the sorts of 'knowledge' actually claimed; and there is quite a lot of material. He suggests that in some passages 'knowledge of a personal or intimate kind' is to be understood. The passages he offers do not very obviously suggest such a classification; but it is certainly true that the *Hymns* in particular convey an impression of warm, personal devotion; it is much more marked than for instance in the Old Testament Psalms:

'I said in my sinfulness
   "I am forsaken by Thy Covenant".
But calling to mind the might of Thy hand
   and the greatness of Thy compassion,

---

[1] To be found in R. H. Charles, *Apocrypha and Pseudepigrapha*, Oxford, 1913.
[2] Millar Burrows, *The Dead Sea Scrolls*, Secker and Warburg, 1956, p. 371.
[3] G. Vermès, *The Dead Sea Scrolls in English*, Penguin Books, 1962.
[4] T. H. Gaster, *The Scriptures of the Dead Sea Sect*, Secker and Warburg, 1957, p. 49.
[5] W. D. Davies, 'Knowledge in the Dead Sea Scrolls . . .' in *Christian Origins and Judaism*, Darton, Longman and Todd, 1962, p. 119f.

I rose and stood,
　　and my spirit was established in face of the scourge' (IV '7',
　　Vermès).

Vermès suggests this and other similar passages may reflect the
experience of the Teacher deserted by his friends. But these
strong individual cries of anguish and knowledge of guilt and of
God's power still remain very largely within the framework of
the corporate life, and it is this that gives them meaning:

'I am consoled for the roaring of the peoples . . .
[for] in a little while, I know,
Thou wilt raise up survivors among Thy people
and a remnant within Thine inheritance' (VI '10', Vermès).

The writers seem to have been too ascetic to ask for obvious
material blessings; the 'consolations of religion', the oppor-
tunity to keep the Law, seem to have been sufficient reward.

There is deep personal devotion. But there is still a very
distant relationship between man and God. Man is only dust
and sinful; God is great in holiness and majesty; he is God of
power in the usual Hebrew way, active, creator, controller.
Man's relation to him is very unequal; it is not that of man and
his friend.[1]

'Who among Thy great and marvellous creatures
can stand in the presence of Thy glory?
How then can he who returns to his dust?' (X 15, Vermès).

And yet there does seem to be for the first time in the literature
that we have been considering a relation with God that is
enjoyed for itself, a relationship that does not seem always to be
breaking down into other terms; one that is not expressed solely
in terms of earning and enjoying and saying 'thank you' for
prosperity and fertility. Perhaps this is already to be found in the
canonical psalms, especially 119; but in the Qumran Hymns
it is unmistakable.

It is against this background that the question of the sort or
sorts of 'knowing of God' in this varied literature must be
decided.

It has been suggested that these writings are 'gnostic', that
they are concerned with the same sorts of esoteric knowledge

---

[1] There may just possibly be a reference to 'communion' with God. Gaster,
op. cit., p. 156. Vermès, *op. cit.*, p. 170, has only 'those who share a common lot
with the Angels of thy Face'.

and absorption mysticism as were the cults the second-century Church competed with. For example:

> 'I give thanks to Thee, O Lord,
> For Thou has illumined my face . . .'

sounds like a gnostic or Hermetic description of initiation. But, in fact, it continues:

> '. . . with the light of Thy covenant' (IV 8, Gaster).

One translation of a psalm from the *Manual of Discipline* runs:

> '. . . from the secrets of his miraculous power
> my eye saw the Eternal Being';

but other translations are less impressive:

> 'Through his mysterious wonder light is come into my heart;
> mine eye has set its gaze on everlasting things';

and in yet another version the whole passage reads:

> 'From the source of His righteousness is my justification,
> and from His marvellous mysteries is the light in my heart.
> My eyes have gazed on that which is eternal,
> on wisdom concealed from men,
> on knowledge and wise design (hidden) from the sons of men;
> on a fountain of righteousness
> and on a storehouse of power. . . .'[1]

In fact, where 'knowledge' is implicitly or explicitly 'of God', it is 'knowledge' in terms of obedience to revealed Law. The following are just a few instances:

> 'Thine, O God of all knowledge,
> are all works of righteousness
> and the secret of truth;
> while man's is but thralldom to wrongdoing,
> and works of deceit' (Hymns I 1, Gaster).

The antithesis makes the point clear; 'knowledge' is ethical activity enabled by God. So, too, 'Everyone who refuses to enter God's covenant, walking in the stubbornness of his heart shall not attain to his true community. For his soul has abhorred the discipline of knowledge, the judgments of righteousness he has not confirmed because of his apostasies' (*Manual* I, Millar Burrows). The same sense is obvious in an eschato-

---

[1] From the *Manual of Discipline* XI as translated respectively by Schubert in a symposium, ed. Fitzmeyer; Gaster, *op. cit.*, p. 128; Vermès, *op. cit.* p. 71ff.

logical passage from *The Triumph of Righteousness*: 'As smoke
clears and is no more, so shall wickedness perish for ever and
righteousness be revealed like a sun governing the world. All
who cleave to the mysteries of sin shall be no more; knowledge
shall fill the world and folly shall exist no longer' (Vermès).[1]

Revelation and Obedience and the Function of the Teacher

To enable this obedience God reveals his demands. 'This
(the path of which Isa. 40.3 speaks) is the study of the Law
which He commanded by the hand of Moses, that they may do
according to all that has been revealed from age to age, and
as the Prophets have revealed by His Holy Spirit' (*Manual*
VIII, Vermès). The Manual describes the function of the
Teacher 'in those times' in similar terms: 'He shall conceal the
teaching of the Law from men of falsehood, but shall impart
true knowledge and righteous judgment to those who have
chosen the Way. He shall guide them in all knowledge according to the spirit of each and according to the rule of the age,
and shall thus instruct them in the mysteries of marvellous
truth that in the midst of the men of the Community they may
walk perfectly together in all that has been revealed to them'
(*Manual* IX, Vermès). In fact, it is not just the revealing of the
terms of obedience that depends on God, but also the granting
of the actual power to obey:

'Verily I know that righteousness lies not with men
nor perfection of conduct with mortals.
Only with God on High
are all works of righteousness' (*Hymns* IV 8, Gaster).

And so Davies[2] writes: 'Furthermore not only does the eschatological character of *da'ath* in the DSS set it apart from Hellenistic *gnosis*, but its connection with the Law is significant of
another fact. As Bo Reicke[2] has remarked, the knowledge of
the DSS is often not so much intellectual as practical; it is not
so much understanding as obedience (it can also mean faith,
the fear of God). This accounts for the frequency of its occurrence in covenantal contexts, and its close connection with that
perfection of way with which we have previously dealt. In

---

[1] *Op. cit.*, p. 210. There are obviously other ways in which 'know' may be used
in the Scrolls; here we are concerned only with 'knowing God'. See Bo Reicke,
'Traces of Gnosticism in the Dead Sea Scrolls?', *NTS* 1.2; Davies, *op. cit.*
[2] *Op. cit.*, p. 140; the reference in the citation is to Bo Reicke, *art. cit.*

short, there is an unmistakable *ethical* nuance to *da'ath* in the DSS which is not always a mark of Hellenistic *gnosis*, but links the *da'ath* of which the DSS speak with that of the New Testament—where knowledge is never far removed from obedience and is a mark of the ideal future.' The enabling of this obedience that is 'knowledge of God' is the purpose of much of the 'revealing' activity of God in the Scrolls.

Revelation of the Mysteries of God

The 'perfection' of which Davies speaks is discussed in an article by B. Rigaux.[1] It is primarily the same 'obedience, fulfilment of divine orders' enabled by 'revelation of the Law'. And yet the writer feels it is necessary to go further. There is more revealed to 'the perfect' than the demands of God, the perfect way of life. Although the Law may be included in the mysteries revealed to them, there are other mysteries of God than that; compare the quotation above,

> '. . . and from his marvellous mysteries
> is the light of my heart.
> My eyes have gazed on that which is eternal.'

In Vermès' version, one of the psalms runs:

> 'Thou hast revealed Thyself to me in Thy power
> as perfect Light' (IV 7).

And this might seem at first sight to be 'God revealing himself'.

The word most often used is *raz*, the word we noted in Daniel. One of the fullest accounts of these 'mysteries of God' is given in the *Habakkuk Commentary*. God let something of them be known to his prophets, but they did not fully understand, and the full revealing was left to the Teacher, who could interpret their words:

> '. . . and God told Habakkuk to write down that which would happen to the final generation, but He did not make known to him when time would come to an end. And as for that which He said, *That he who reads may read it speedily*, interpreted this concerns the Teacher of Righteousness, to whom God made known all the mysteries of the words of His servants the Prophets.

---

[1] Fr B. Rigaux, O.F.M., 'Révélation des Mystères et Perfection à Qumran et dans le Nouveau Testament', *NTS* 4.4.

'*For there shall be yet another vision concerning the appointed time. It shall tell of the end and shall not lie.* Interpreted, this means that the final age shall be prolonged, and shall exceed all that the Prophets have said; for the mysteries of God are astounding.

'*If it tarries, wait for it, for it shall surely come and shall not be late.* Interpreted, this concerns the men of truth who keep the Law, whose hands shall not slacken in the service of truth when the final age is prolonged. For all the ages of God reach their appointed end as He determines for them in the mysteries of His wisdom' (*Habakkuk Commentary* VII, Vermès).

And much the same is said elsewhere; see, for instance, *The War*, chapter XI, and *Hymn* I. There are also parallel 'mysteries' of evil (*War* XIV); and the mysteries of God also include his past acts, his creation of the world (*Hymn* I), and the first showing of his power for the sake of his people, the delivery from Egypt (*Rule* XI; *Hymns* IV 7; '*The Words of the Heavenly Lights*' II). But the 'mysteries of God' that most concern this community are his plan for his people—their place in the scheme of things—at the end of time.

Except for the instance quoted above, there is nothing in the Scrolls to suggest that God has, does, will, 'reveal himself'. Even that passage reads in Gaster:

'. . . Thou in Thy might
hast shed upon me the Perfect Light.'

And the context would suggest that no more is meant than the sort of open acts of God's power which we noted in the Old Testament; earlier, in the same hymn, the writer hopes that God may 'manifest his might through him'; and later he explains,

'(Thou) hast shown Thyself mighty within me
in the midst of Thy marvellous Council.
Thou hast done wonders before the Congregation
for the sake of Thy glory,
that they might make known Thy mighty deeds
to all the living' (Vermès, IV 7.)

God shows his might, his mercy, his glory, in action; but he does not himself appear, as he does in some of the other apocalypses. In the *War* God is proclaimed as 'in the midst'; he will fight with the community's enemies from heaven (XI), with his troops of angels (XII), but I can find no passage where it is suggested that even his 'glory' will be visible for the fight.

There is, then, in the Scrolls, a greater stress on 'revelation'[1] than we have found so far; 'revelation', that is, of God's demand and his purpose. It is, as Rigaux says,[2] the basis of the community's life. But it is not 'revelation of God himself'; 'knowledge of God', the relationship he allows, or rather demands with himself, is as in the Old Testament, obedience to one who himself remains hidden.

iv *The Koine*

The koine Greek background was not readily accessible to the writer for first-hand investigation, but the information in Moulton and Milligan, and Liddell and Scott,[3] was not very encouraging.

To know

The former mention that γινώσκειν can be used of sexual intercourse in non-Jewish Greek. But the word is mostly concerned with 'knowing that', 'knowing about'. They note that Dibelius and Deissmann argue whether the word γνῶσις may be used of 'personal acquaintance' in the New Testament; and that to support this view, Deissmann quotes μέχρι τᾶς τῶν Σεβαστῶν γνώσεως προσκό[ψ]αντος, 'he had advanced to personal acquaintance with the Augusti'; but this use is not frequent. Γνῶσις is more likely to be 'knowledge about'; and in religious contexts, arcane speculation. But this we deal with in the next section. In the 'classical' usage it means 'to perceive, recognise, by observation'.

To reveal

Ἀποκαλύπτειν does not seem to be particularly a technical 'religious' word, and is not at all frequent in any context. It is used to describe land being left cultivable by the receding Nile waters; by Plutarch, of uncovering your head, of 'revealing the power of rhetoric' and of 'revealing your whole mind'.

---

[1] An aside in Rigaux, *art. cit.*, p. 246, would suggest that *glh* was not all that often used; but mainly the hiphil of *yd'*; however, as we have seen, the meaning is often similar enough.

[2] *Ibid.*, p. 247.

[3] Moulton and Milligan, *Vocabulary of the Greek New Testament*, Hodder and Stoughton, 1930; Liddell and Scott, *A Greek-English Lexicon*, Oxford, 1940. See also Oepke, *TWNT* III, p. 567ff.

To appear

Ἐπιφαίνειν and ἐπιφάνεια are much more often used in religious writing. They are used by Herodotus of visions; there is an inscription of (?) 300 B.C. that runs, 'ἐπιφαινομένης αὐτοῖς Ἀρτέμιδος'. Moulton and Milligan say the word ἐπιφάνεια occurs in late Greek, to denote 'any conspicuous intervention on the part of higher powers'. The adjective ἐπιφανής seems to have been used, for instance, by Antiochus IV to claim the status of Zeus incarnate. It is used later of the accession of Caligula in an inscription. Φαίνειν is used in a more metaphorical sense of appearing on the (political) scene (φαίνεις δὲ ὁ καῖσαρ . . . political hopes were fulfilled).

There is, then, nothing to suggest a hope that a deity might 'reveal himself' to his worshippers in anything but a literal, visual sense; although the vocabulary to express ideas like this was to hand.[1]

v *Philo Judaeus*

In the period we are considering, the time before and contemporary with the New Testament, the only Jewish writer of note who uses 'knowing' language at all extensively seems to be Philo of Alexandria. He is evidence of a 'cross-fertilization of Hebrew and Greek thought'.[2] It is the will of God 'to lead the race of men, wandering in trackless wastes, into a way free from error, in order that following nature they may obtain the supreme end, which is knowledge of him who truly is . . . '.[3] Moses is the recipient and transmitter of divine revelation: 'Even if we have closed the eye of the soul, and do not care or are not able to look up, do thou, O Hierophant, lift up thy voice and take command of us, and never cease to anoint our eyes until thou lead us as initiates to the hidden light of sacred words, and show us the beauties that are fenced off and invisible

[1] Oepke, *TWNT* III, p. 567, says that the oracles were not about the god himself, but were his (still obscure) pointing to the enquirer's 'Fate'. He also notes that with the 'transition to history' and the θεὸς ἄνθρωπος, e.g. Apollonius of Tyana, the purpose of a manifestation is to heal, etc., rather than reveal; which is not very different from the OT position. With an increasing confidence in the powers of λόγος, νοῦς, ἰδέα, ability of man to understand, there is, of course, less and less need for anything that might be called 'revelation' (pp. 568-9).
[2] C. H. Dodd, *The Interpretation of the Fourth Gospel*, Cambridge, 1953, introductory article on Philo.
[3] *De Decal.* 81: quoted, Dodd, *op. cit.*, p. 58.

to the uninitiate.'[1] 'To know God is to be a son of God.' The way to such knowledge is by *ascesis*. But Dodd insists that Philo does not talk of deification, mystical absorption into the One. 'Knowledge of God' is an intense mystical consciousness of absolute being; but Philo can also talk of love of God, and faith and worship. Dodd suggests that Philo's more biblical ways of thought about God often 'sort ill' with these more abstract concepts. 'Knowledge of God', then, seems to be a pure awareness of absolute being; when Philo is talking of a more 'personal' relationship, he uses words like φιλεῖν and ἀγαπᾶν.

Philo's work may, as Dodd suggests, illuminate the categories used by the Fourth Evangelist (but Dodd points out many differences); it cannot be shown to have had much influence on, or to be significantly like, any of the other New Testament writers. Even in Hebrews, the real points of contact are few.

vi *Gnosticism*

In the Hermetic literature, which cannot be dated with certainty any earlier than the beginning of the second century A.D., the phrase 'knowledge of God' does again seem to occur as a theological term in its own right, a term for an experience that is an end in itself, as in Philo.

' "I wish", I said, "to learn the things that are, and to understand their nature, and to know God; how I wish to hear this!" ' 'This alone brings salvation to man, the knowledge of God.' 'This is the happy end of those who have acquired knowledge, namely, to *become* God.' 'Deity desires to be known, and is made known to his own.' (My italics.)

It is interesting that we first find 'knowledge of God' used this way in a literature that has many features in common, including of course this stress on 'knowing', with the gnostic cults that competed with the Christian Church. 'Knowing God' is, here again, a sort of mystic absorption. Valentinus' *Gospel of Truth* provides an instance:

[1] *De Somn.* 1.164: Dodd, p. 59.
[2] The Hermetic literature is accessible in small doses in C. K. Barrett, *The New Testament Background, Selected Documents*, S.P.C.K., 1956, the first three quotations are from there, p. 8off. The fourth quotation is *Poimandres* 1.30, quoted in the Moffatt commentary on I Cor. There is further information in C. H. Dodd, *op. cit.* It is interesting to compare the long prayer, Barrett, *op. cit.*, para. 90, with the Qumran psalms. They use similar words: vision, spirit, truth, light, life. But in *Poimandres* the prayer is almost entirely abstract. The centre of life is intellectual contemplation, rather than 'right conduct'.

'Since the perfection of the all is in the Father, it is necessary for the all to ascend to him. Therefore, if one has knowledge, he gets what belongs to him and draws it to himself. For he who is ignorant, is deficient, and it is a great deficiency, since he lacks that which will make him perfect. Since the perfection of the all is in the Father, it is necessary for the all to ascend to him and for each one to get the things which are his.'[1]

The whole stress is on 'revealing'. Jesus dies so the Father of the all be no longer hidden. He proclaims what is in the heart of the Father. He is knowledge and perfection. He is the uttered 'name' of the Father. The end is unity and completeness: 'Since this incompleteness came about because they did not know the Father, so, when they know the Father, incompleteness from that moment on will cease to exist.'[2] From Ptolemaeus, 'The end will come, when all that is spiritual is shaped and perfected in knowledge.'[3] There seems to be no middle way in the thought of the early Church's nearest contemporaries between 'knowledge of God' in terms of obedience in the practical affairs of daily life, on the one hand, and this 'knowledge' that is absorption in abstract 'deity' on the other.

If the New Testament is to strike out on a new line, telling us that God has 'revealed himself', has given to men 'full knowledge of *himself*', has 'revealed himself to men' as fully as a man may 'reveal himself' to a friend, then it will have to do so definitely and unmistakably. But we must admit that the likelihood is that it will still understand God's action in Christ in the terms of the Hebrew and even more, the Greek, 'Old Testament'.

---

[1] Quoted, R. M. Grant, *Gnosticism, An Anthology*, Collins, 1961, p. 149.
[2] *Op. cit.*, p. 151.
[3] *Ibid.*, p. 175. Cf. the hymn quoted in Bultmann. *Gnosis*, p. vif.

3

THE CHRISTIAN USE: THE NEW TESTAMENT

THE clarity that 'revelation' suggests seems, as we have noted, paradoxical alongside Christian misunderstanding. Does the New Testament give any support to this paradox, either by asserting 'revelation' or by denying Christian limitations, or even by 'holding them in tension' with the help of words like 'mystery'?

The discussion of 'revelation of God' in the Old Testament included an examination of references to 'knowing God'; the same method will be followed here. Words for 'to know' will in fact introduce the discussion.

I. PAUL

To Know

General

Paul[1] uses εἰδέναι and γινώσκειν interchangeably: ἀλλὰ τότε μὲν οὐκ εἰδότες Θεὸν . . . νῦν δὲ γνόντες Θεόν (Gal. 4.8-9; cf. II Cor. 5.16).

A passage which I think throws interesting light on Paul's use of cognitive language is I Corinthians, chapter two; and it is in fact used here alongside 'revealing' language. Paul says: 'For who among men knows the things of a man, save the spirit of the man which is in him? Even so the things of God none knows save the Spirit of God. But we have received, not the spirit of the world, but the Spirit which is of God; *that we might know the things*

---

[1] Ephesians and Colossians, I and II Thessalonians are taken as sufficiently in line with 'Pauline' thought to be included in this grouping, for the sake of the present study. It does not seem that the idiosyncrasies of these various works have really affected these not very important words, though on matters that were more central to the New Testament, a separate discussion of at least Ephesians would be needed. The 'Pastorals' *are* dealt with independently.

that are freely given us of God. . . . For who has known the mind of
the Lord that he should instruct him? But we have the mind
of Christ.' This most thrilling close relationship claimed between
a man and the Lord, that we should have 'the mind' of the
Lord, the inmost Spirit of the Lord, exists in effect so that we
can 'know the things freely given us of God' (the death of Christ,
who unknown to the ἄρχοντες is the Lord of Glory; and the
results of this in terms of righteousness and sanctification and
redemption: I Cor. 1.18ff.). It is not God himself, Paul says,
that we know by this transference of 'Spirit'—but what God has
planned to do and has done.[1]

Paul does not often speak of a man's 'knowledge' of another
man. In one of his letters to Corinth he describes an experience
that happened to him much earlier in his life, as though it had
happened to another whom he speaks of 'knowing': 'I know a
man in Christ, fourteen years ago . . . such a one caught up to
the third heaven. And I know such a man . . . how that he was
caught up into Paradise.'[2] Here he is certainly not using 'know'
of any reciprocal personal relationship. He 'knows' 'this man'
in the sense of knowing facts about him. In another part of his
correspondence with Corinth he says: 'Wherefore we henceforth know no man after the flesh' (II Cor. 5.16). 'Κατὰ σάρκα'
probably governs 'οἴδαμεν' (and 'ἐγνώκαμεν', later in the verse).
Paul is saying that 'knowing a man', along with all other aspects
of Christian life, can no longer be done in a worldly way. The
'knowing' seems to be the estimating of a man's importance,
referring back to his 'we are not again commending ourselves to

---

[1] Compare the discussion of this passage in A. Farrer's essay, 'Revelation', in
Faith and Logic, ed. B. Mitchell. Farrer suggests that this (not very precise) metaphor
of the transference of 'mind', Christ's divine mind to us, is a term for 'personal
self-disclosure'. But the point is not that we 'know' the divine person by this transference of 'mind'. It is that we know 'the things that God prepared for them that
love him': the crucifixion of the one who is now *Christos*, as the act of God; 'the
things freely given us of God'. Paul is saying emphatically that understanding
God's action (and, of course, responding to it) can only happen by the act of God,
too. But he is not saying that what is given is an 'I-Thou' relation of mind to
Mind. The *nous* is not the person, it is the intellect, or at most the person *qua*
intellect, but not the whole (see Farrer himself, *loc. cit.*). 'Having the mind of
Christ' is not a self-authenticating state of being-in-relationship-with the person
of God; it is only useful in so far as it leads us to 'know the things that are freely
given us of God'. Cf. E. Schweizer, *Spirit of God*, A. and C. Black, p. 68.

[2] II Cor. 12.1ff. Vv. 6-7 make it plain that Paul is really talking about himself.
It could just possibly be his experience near Damascus, his conversion and
commission, but it is unlikely; that was a public event of which he had to speak
(Gal. 1.15ff.; I Cor. 9.1; 15.3ff.); this is private, and he would rather remain
silent. See below, pp. 82.

you' (v. 12). Then there is a further instance in an exhortation to the Thessalonians: 'And we beseech you, brethren, to know (εἰδέναι) them which labour among you, and are over you in the Lord, and admonish you: and to esteem them very highly in love for their work's sake' (I Thess. 5.12-13). Here the context suggests very strongly the Old Testament sense of 'obey'. In a similar context in I Cor. 16.16-18, Paul uses ἐπιγινώσκετε, which the RV translates 'acknowledge' (and so NEB for the Thessalonians' passage), which is the best English equivalent if it is thought necessary to etymologise; but is not, I have suggested, really strong enough. These are the only instances of 'knowing other men' that I could find in the collection of Paul's letters; he seems to prefer 'love' and 'serve' for the personal relationships of Christian people. However, there are not many occasions in his writing for talking of men's knowledge of other men. We look further, and see what he may mean by the 'knowledge of men' that God has.

God's 'Knowledge' of Men

Paul seems to prefer this way of speaking to talking of men 'knowing God': '. . . but now that ye have come to know God, or rather, to be known of him . . .' (Gal. 4.9). Against the Old Testament background, this most probably means choice.[1] This is likely in the immediate context in Galatians, where Paul is talking about Baptism, receiving the Spirit, being adopted and being made heirs. 'You have come to know God' could sound as though they had chosen God, so Paul hastens to qualify the phrase. It is always God's choice of men that is uppermost in Paul's mind when he is talking about sonship.[2] The 'μᾶλλον δὲ' certainly seems to preclude any idea of a reciprocal relationship of 'knowing'. In I Cor. 8.3 Paul again talks of God's 'knowing' men, in a context where he is belittling men's knowledge. 'We know that we all have knowledge. Knowledge puffeth up, but love edifieth . . . if any man loveth God the same is known of him' (οὗτος ἔγνωσται ὑπ᾽ αὐτοῦ). This seems to mean 'is acknowledged by', or even 'is (shown to be one) chosen by',[3] but nothing more.

[1] Cf. above, p. 41; and Amos 3.2.
[2] Cf. Rom. 8.29, on God's choice of men for sonship. This also illustrates I Cor. 8.3, quoted below.
[3] Cf. again Rom 8.28ff.: 'And we know that to them that love God ("if any man love God") all things work together for good, even to them that are called according to his purpose ("the same is known of him")'. Cf. also Bultmann, *Gnosis*, p. 35ff.

The only remaining instances are in I Corinthians 13, where Paul is talking both of God's 'knowing' us and our 'knowing' God. Present knowledge is only partial, 'through a glass darkly' (δι᾽ ἐσόπτρου ἐν αἰνίγματι); only 'then' will we see 'face to face'.[1] This 'seeing face-to-face' is the only biblical term for the 'I-Thou' relation of friends, and it is a *future* hope. Only 'then' will we know *as we have been known*. Again, there is Paul's insistence on the primacy for the present of God's 'knowing'; and it is certainly not at present reciprocal in any full sense; this is stated explicitly.[2]

However, there are further instances of Paul talking of 'knowing'; of a man 'knowing' God, the Father; or the Son; or the Man, Christ Jesus.

Man's 'Knowledge of God' and 'Obedience'

Paul most fully unpacks what he means by 'knowing God' in Romans, which contains a large number of elaborations on the theme. He writes: 'For the wrath of God is revealed from heaven against all ungodliness and unrighteousness of men, who hold down the truth in unrighteousness, because that which may be known of God (τὸ γνωστὸν τοῦ Θεοῦ) is manifest in them; for God manifested it to them. For the invisible things of him since the creation of the world are clearly seen, being perceived through the things that are made, even *his everlasting power and divinity*; that they may be without excuse: because that knowing God, they glorified him not as God, neither gave thanks . . .' (Rom. 1.18ff.)[3] 'Knowing God', 'having what may be known of God manifested in them', seems to mean recognising the difference between Creator and creation (Rom. 1.23).[4] At this point Paul seems to make a distinction between 'knowing' and the response that should follow. 'Knowing God they glorified him not. . . .' It is, however, in Paul's normal thought a very unreal 'knowing' of God that he is ascribing to the Gentiles; it

---

[1] Compare Moses, and him alone, in the Old Testament; esp. Num. 12.6ff., LXX.

[2] Cf. I John 3.2.

[3] On the meaning of 'wrath' here, see Hanson, *The Wrath of the Lamb*, S.P.C.K., 1957, p. 85: The phenomena described are not 'a proof of God's displeasure . . .' they *are* God's displeasure'. 'Wrath' in the New Testament is not an emotion or attribute of God, but the effects of sin.' In other words, when Paul says the wrath of God is 'revealed', he is not saying that God has 'revealed himself,' in his attitude to evil; he is saying God has acted to punish sin. See also below.

[4] Cf. also Wisdom chs 13-14.

did th Gentiles know Gd
via nature? No.

is a completely unrealised potential. If the Gentiles do not
worship God, nor obey him, in Paul's Hebraic thought, they
cannot really be said to 'know' him. And this Paul makes
explicit further down; he describes the Gentiles' idolatrous disobedience and God's punishment, and sums it up with: 'And
even as they *refused to have God in their knowledge,* God gave them
up into a reprobate mind.' Paul is more concerned than the
writer of the Wisdom of Solomon (on whom or on similar current arguments he may well be dependent) to show that Gentiles
as well as Jews are guilty, that they have not just 'sinned' but
have also 'transgressed', and so he has to allow the possibility of
a knowledge of the terms of obedience (Rom. 1.28; cf. Wisdom
13.1; and I John 2.4). But the whole of his argument goes to
demonstrate that this was a quite unfulfilled possibility; there
was in fact no obedience, no real 'knowledge of God', only the
unrealised potential 'knowledge' that makes the verdict 'guilty'
a just one. In I Corinthians Paul is less concerned with the
moral philosopher's questions of 'guilt' and just says plainly,
'. . . in the wisdom of God the world through its wisdom knew
not God' (I Cor. 1.21). This is not Paul's guess at the state of
men's minds; he is not talking about their religious consciousness! The pagan world's ignorance of God is an empirical fact.
This is the plainest way of stating what Paul observes of the
behaviour of those around him. They do not 'know God'. Paul
cannot really conceive the possibility of a 'knowledge of God'
that could exist in its own right, a state of being that could
authenticate itself. 'Knowing God' can only take the form of
observable worship and obedience. The 'knowledge' which
Paul at first seemed to be saying the Gentiles had is purely
hypothetical; and even this hypothetical 'knowledge of God' is
of course very far removed from an 'I-Thou' relationship; it is
a potential knowledge of God's 'power and divinity', not a
knowing of God as Person. It only becomes a real 'knowing'
when it takes the form of worship and obedience.

In II Thessalonians, 'not knowing God' and 'not obeying the
gospel of our Lord Jesus Christ' are parallel terms (II Thess.
1.8).[1] Similarly, in II Cor. 10.5 'casting down . . . every high

---

[1] 'Christian knowledge of God is service of God', Bultmann, *op. cit.,* p. 35. Cf.
also I Thess. 1.9, and I Cor. 15.34: 'Awake up righteously and sin not; for some
have no knowledge (ἀγνωσίαν ἔχουσιν) of God.'

thing that is exalted against the *knowledge* of God' is paralleled by 'bringing every thought into captivity to the obedience of Christ'. 'The knowledge of God' is the knowledge of, and obedient response to, his demand on you in the situation of your life.[1] The same may fairly be deduced from Colossians chapter 1, '. . . we do not cease to pray . . . that ye may be filled with all *knowledge of his will* in all spiritual wisdom and understanding, to *walk worthily* of the Lord unto all pleasing; *bearing fruit* in every good work, and increasing in *the knowledge of God*' (Col. 1.9-10). This is not a progression of thought, as though 'the knowledge of God' were the final stage. (It continues: 'strengthened with all power unto all patience and long-suffering with joy'.) It is a double parallelism, making the pattern *ab-ba*.[2] 'Knowledge of his will' and 'the knowledge of God' are parallel terms, and each is explained by 'walk worthily' and 'bearing fruit'; and the whole is part of a description of the ethical quality of Christian living, a prayer for its achievement.

This is the sense in which a man can 'know God' here and now. We have already noted[3] how unwilling Paul is to talk of men 'knowing' God, when it might seem to mean they had initiated the relationship with him; and Paul is equally un-willing to suggest the possibility here and now of anything approaching an 'I-Thou' relation with God. We have already looked at this, too, in connection with God 'knowing' men, but it is worth repeating the quotation. In I Corinthians chapter 13 Paul says: 'Now we see in a mirror darkly, but *then* face to face; now I know in part; but *then* shall I know even as also I have been known.'[4] Only 'then' does it become reciprocal, only then

---

[1] Cf. Rom. 2.18: ' . . . and gloriest in God and knowest his will, and approvest the things that be excellent'.

[2] This sort of external parallelism, *ab-ba*, instead of the more usual *ab-ab*, does occur from time to time in the psalms, and is an easily recognisable stylistic device. Cf. Ps. 72.1-2:

'Give the king your judgments, O God   (*a*)
And your righteousness to the king's son,   (*b*)
And he shall judge your people with righteousness   (*b*)
And your poor with judgments.   (*a*)

Cf. also Pss. 7.8-9; 98.5-6.

[3] Above, p. 65f.

[4] J. Héring, *La Première Épître de Saint Paul aux Corinthiens*, Delachaux et Niestlé, 1959, *ad loc.* suggests (following Achèlis) that the 'enigma' does not refer to the distorting effect of contemporary metal mirrors, but rather to the practice in current magic of using mirrors to see what lies in the future. (We now see dimly what lies ahead: an at present inconceivable and anyway quite impossible 'face to face' relationship with God.)

is it (perhaps) 'I and Thou', 'face to face'. At present God 'knows' *us* in choice and concern; we 'know' *him* in obedience (and that only imperfectly). It is an 'eschatological' hope, and not one that is 'realised' in any sense in Paul's present experience, that we shall know God as we now can know a friend (I Cor. 13.12).[1] 'Knowledge of God' is 'personal' in the sense that it means a personal response by the whole man in obedience and worship to the known will of God and his commands; but it does not mean the 'conversation' of two subjects, even allowing for their inequality. The content of 'knowledge of God', the actual things you do in obedience, has changed from the Old Testament (obedience is now in terms of love); but the manner of 'knowledge of God' for Paul is the same.

'Knowledge of Christ'

'Knowledge of Christ' seems to be used by Paul in much the same way. Some things that he writes may sound, out of context, rather similar to 'Gnosticism'. 'I count all things to be loss for the excellency of the knowledge of Christ Jesus my Lord.' But this continues '. . . that I may know him, and the power of his resurrection, and the fellowship of his sufferings, becoming conformed unto his death'; τοῦ γνῶναι covers all three objects, and the form of the sentence suggests that these clauses (with τοῦ γνῶναι understood) are meant to detail what 'the knowledge of Christ' and 'to know him' mean (Phil. 3. 8-10).[2] When Paul talks in similar terms elsewhere (II Cor. 4.7ff.) of 'bearing about in the body the νέκρωσις of Jesus, that the life also of Jesus may be manifested in our body', he is describing his daily life as a Christian, and all the wretched things that happen to him; they prove that the power to exercise the ministry Paul has is not Paul's own, but God's. It is these two things, the fact of being 'pressed on every side . . . perplexed . . . pursued . . . smitten down' on the one hand, and the fact of 'yet not being straitened . . . not unto despair, . . . not forsaken . . . not destroyed' on the other, that are the sharing in Christ's death and the sharing already in his Resurrection. And in the passage from Philippians

---

[1] Cf. Phil. 1.9, where, as here, it is love that is a present possibility. Even a knowledge of God's 'mind' is a rare and wonderful thing (I Cor. 2.11; Rom. 11.34); and, as we have already seen, this is not a knowing of God as *person*, but a knowing of his plans.

[2] Cf. on this passage R. Bultmann, *TNT* I, p. 180ff.

it is this sharing in Christ's death and Resurrection that Paul calls 'knowing' Christ. It is a matter of how we 'walk', behave (Phil. 3.16). This is faith describing the daily experience of the missionary in the Christian community and in the world as being in fact a close relationship with Christ. But the *substance* of the experience is the daily life and its events. Paul does not even suggest a particularly vivid 'awareness of the presence of Christ' in the things he does and that happen to him. He lives by faith, he lives and works, he is sure, by God's power; and the things that happen to him, and the things he finds he is able to do, *are* his relation to Christ, dead and raised.

Paul makes it clear to the Colossians that he sees Christian 'knowledge', 'understanding', as terms for the response to life of the Christian community. He prays 'that their hearts may be comforted, they being knit together in love, and unto all riches of the full assurance of understanding, that they may know the mystery of God (even Christ), in whom are all the treasures of wisdom and knowledge hidden' (Col. 2.2ff.)[1] He then repeats this more simply below: 'As you therefore received Christ Jesus the Lord, so walk in him, rooted and builded up in him (cf. "knit together"; all are terms for the growth of the community) and firmly founded in your faith, even as you were taught, abounding in thanksgiving.' This living of their lives together, in Christ, in love, will be 'to know the mystery of God'. For the community to mature in this way is to 'know', respond to, 'the

[1] For 'mystery', see below. Probably II Cor. 4.6, ' . . . it is God . . . who shined in our hearts, to give the light of the knowledge of the glory of God in the face of Jesus Christ' (who is the 'image of God', v. 4) means something similar. This is the nearest Paul comes to talking of God 'revealing himself in Christ'; but it is noteworthy that even in this intense and lyrical passage Paul does not quite say that (though the NEB gratuitously introduces the word 'revelation' here). 'The glory of God in the face of Jesus Christ' 'refers to his person and work regarded as one complete whole' (art. 'Face' in *VB*; cf. art., 'Presence' in *ThWB*). The 'face' is a synonym for 'person' or 'personal presence'; and when used of someone important, it refers to him in his concern with those on whom his face 'looks', those among whom he is. The person in this case is Jesus Christos, who is himself the image of God, as Wisdom was (Wisdom 7.25ff.). Christ is the image, reproduction of God, the extension of God's own self, through whom he acts; without revealing himself. The 'glory' is the activity of God who himself remains hidden (see above, and cf. Rom. 6.4, where Paul talks of Christ being 'raised by the glory of the Father'). The 'light of the knowledge' of this activity, that God has 'shined in our hearts', is much the same as the 'light of the gospel of the "glorious activity" of Christ', in v. 4. It is the fact that we know what God has done in Christ, and can respond (cf. I Cor. 2.1ff., discussed above). It is not 'revelation of God in Christ', but the understanding of God's (reconciling) action in Christ, that is here exciting Paul.

mystery'. And if the 'even Christ' in apposition is Paul's own, this just makes explicit that *this* is God's act, his mystery. The Christian's day-to-day living in love is responding to Christ, is 'knowing' him.

Again, the writer 'to the Ephesians' is unable to talk of 'knowing Christ', *tout court*, but has to explain what he means in other terms. 'A spirit of wisdom and revelation in the knowledge of him; having the eyes of your heart enlightened that ye may know what is the hope of his calling, what the riches of his glory . . .' (Eph. 1.17ff.). In Ephesians, 'knowledge of the Son of God' is paralleled by 'the unity of the faith', and contrasted with 'every wind of doctrine' and 'the wiles of error'; when the community has reached this 'knowledge' it will have come to be a 'fullgrown man'; and this is the purpose of the various 'ministers' within the total 'ministry' of all the saints (Eph. 4.13). 'The knowledge of the Son of God' is fairly explicitly *not* a communion of the individual with Christ; and even for the community is not a present fact. And for the community it seems to mean much the same obedience, faithfulness, worship, as we found in Paul. The following verses (4.17ff.) contrast the lives of the Gentiles who do not in their behaviour 'know' God; and the sort of behaviour to be expected of a community that is growing 'to the fulness of the measure of the stature of Christ'.

'Knowledge of God'. Conclusion

Paul (following the LXX of course) uses εἰδέναι and γινώσκειν as words to describe man's response to God. But while we translate them 'know', the nearest word in English is still 'obey'.[1] Perhaps again a periphrasis such as 'respond to the compelling force of' would come closer still. This relationship

---

[1] 'Knowledge' is being used in the same sort of way as in the LXX and the Hebrew Bible before it. Its nearest alternative is 'obedience' still; that is not to say that the quality of the obeying, the things that are done as a 'knowing' of God, are the same. This is of course a Christian type of 'knowing God', in terms of *agape*. And the possibility of this type of 'knowing' is new, too, created by God through the life, death, resurrection-and-ascension of Christ. But, formally, words we translate 'know', 'knowledge' are being used the same way. If, as is often the case, a language has one word that can be used with widely differing shades of meaning, it is very easy in talking or writing to slide from one to the other ('democracy', 'freedom', 'individual liberty' are good examples). So there is *a priori* a possibility that Paul himself might sometimes think of 'knowing God', 'having a relationship with God', in ways analogous to 'knowing (having a relationship with) facts', 'knowing a friend', 'knowing mystic absorption', 'having a relationship with the infinite'. But when Paul is explicit (with the one formal exception noted above, Rom. 1.18), he clearly does think of 'knowing God', 'having a relationship

is 'personal' in so far as it always means an existential reaction
and only happens at all as a personal response from the man in
question. Not the obedience of slaves to a 'Law', it is the 'free'
obedience in love of sons.[1] But the Christian relationship to God
is obeying him in the life of the Christian community, and in
the worship of the Christian community. God cannot for the
present be 'known' as a man 'knows' his friend; only obeyed as
a son freely obeys his father; though Paul hopes that 'then'
such a 'knowing', 'as we are known', 'face to face', may be
possible. So it seems unlikely that Paul will suggest that God
'reveals' *himself*. Paul seems to place 'knowing Christ' on the
same level as 'knowing' the Father; but it is 'knowledge' of the
same sort, in terms of obedience.

To Reveal

General: The Various Terms

Paul uses the prosaic words 'veil' and 'unveil' in II Corinthians (II Cor. 3.4ff. and esp. v. 12ff.).[2] He is quoting Exodus
ch. 34, in a rather strained way, both to suggest that the glory
reflected in Moses' face was waning (and this had to be concealed—not the reason given in Exodus!) and for a metaphor
of the Jews' dim comprehension of the Old Covenant scriptures.
Through Christ and through the Spirit for us the veil is done
away: we can understand the Scriptures. And we too are as
Moses was, unveiled in the sanctuary (vv. 14 and 16), facing the
Glory, reflecting the Glory.[3] But it is the 'Glory' that we face,
that which *conceals* God; Paul has specifically said in an earlier
letter to Corinth that we do not yet meet God himself 'face to
face', and there is no hint that he has gone beyond this here.[4]

---

with God', in terms of obedience, of obedience elicited by God's compelling force
in Christ. However, the fact that Paul uses these synonyms, εἰδέναι and γινώσκειν,
for a whole range of relationships does allow us to misinterpret him; unless we
look very carefully at those contexts where the sense in which he uses the words is
made explicit.

[1] Rom. 8.12-17 (and see the whole chapter); Rom. 6.15ff.; Gal. 3.23ff; 5.1;
cf. Gal. 5.16ff.; Phil. 2.6ff.

[2] The words used are κάλυμμα and ἀνακαλύπτειν. Κατακαλύπτειν, and
ἀκατακάλυπτος are used in the discussion of women's dress while prophesying,
I Cor. 11.1-16.

[3] We 'reflect' the glory, rather than 'contemplate' it; we are 'made to mirror'
(κατοπτριζόμενοι, passive) the Glory. Cf. J. Héring, *La Seconde Épître de Saint Paul
aux Corinthiens*, Delachaux et Niestlé, 1958, *ad loc.*

[4] Cf. II Cor. 5.6: Paul needs to be absent (from the body, whatever precisely
that means) to be 'with the Lord'. See below on παρουσία, p. 87, n. 2.

It is we who are 'revealed', not God. We are being changed, radically. We are being exposed to the 'glory', the activity of God who remains hidden, the reconciling activity of God in Christ. But we are not in a person-to-person 'encounter' with him whose glory is changing us.

Paul then continues with the theme of 'hidden-made-plain': 'We have renounced the hidden shameful things, we do not behave slyly, we do not (*sc.* as the Jews with veiled minds do) distort the word of God. We present the truth plain and open. . . . But if our Gospel is also veiled in any sense, it is so only for people on the way to destruction. They have been blinded in their unbelieving minds by the god of this age' (II Cor. 4.1ff.). They cannot see what God is doing in Christ.

This then leads into the passage discussed above (II Cor. 4.7ff.), where Paul recapitulates what he has said on the basis of the text from Exodus. Many do not understand. However, God has let *us* understand what he has done—is doing—in Christ. It is happening to us: we know about it, we can respond to, be changed by, the Glory. And then Paul outlines the sorts of events that are the life of sharing increasingly in this Glory, the life of ministering this glorious 'New Agreement'. The often very painful events of Paul's life show that it can only be the life of Jesus that is keeping Paul going. It is these events that are the focus of the reflecting of the Glory, 'for our exceeding light affliction, which is for the moment, works for us more and more exceedingly, an eternal weight of glory' (II Cor. 4.17). It is in these events that God's Glory is known, in the sheer physical endurance of which Paul finds himself capable; not in any 'revealing' of God, himself.

In II Corinthians chapter 3 Paul is using the literal picture of taking off a veil as a metaphor. Of the more technical terms available, he uses ἀποκαλύπτειν, ἀποκάλυψις, etc., words that come from the same stem, to do with 'veils' (though the literal meaning is very much more in the background). These are the only words that can really be translated 'reveal', 'revealing', 'revelation'.[1] But a similar idea can be expressed by φανεροῦν, φανέρωσις, 'manifest'; also by δηλοῦν, etc., though this latter is

---

[1] The NEB uses 'revelation', as noted, at II Cor. 4.6, to explain φωτισμός: the 'light of revelation'. I do not think this makes the passage any clearer; it does show how attached modern exegetes are to the word. Compare also John 8.31, NEB.

not very frequent. All describe, when not used literally, the act of someone making known something (or some person, though we have seen this is less likely) which up to that point was not known at all, or but poorly known. There is a strong emphasis on the initiative taken by the 'revealer' or 'manifester'. If these words are used, it is likely to imply that what is 'revealed' would not otherwise be knowable.

Paul seems to use ἀποκαλύπτειν and φανεροῦν interchangeably in Romans (Rom. 1.17; 3.21) and all three as synonyms in I Corinthians (I Cor. 3.13). (ἐν-)δεικνύναι (to show or express) and γνωρίζειν (to make known) also seem to be used in the same sort of way in similar contexts (Rom. 9.22).[1]

The φανεροῦν group can be used more generally than ἀποκαλύπτειν, which seems to be reserved for the activity of God. In I Corinthians the prophesying of the Christian congregation will 'lay bare' (φανερός) the secrets of a visitor's heart. In the same letter, Paul says divisions have the effect of making those that are approved in the Church 'obvious' (same word) (I Cor. 14.25; 11.19). There is a similar use in Romans 2.28, of the man who is a Jew 'in appearance' only; in Galatians Paul notes that the works of the flesh are 'obvious' (Gal. 5.19); and in Philippians Paul says his bonds are made 'obvious in Christ' (are shown clearly to be for his sake) throughout the Praetorium

---

[1] Rom. 1.17; 3.21: Δικαιοσύνη . . . ἀποκαλύπτεται; δικαιοσύνη πεφανέρωται. See I Cor. 3.13. See also Rom. 9.22; 3.25 compared with 3.21 and 1.17; 16.25-26. Oepke, art. καλύπτω *TWNT* III, p. 558ff., suggests that the words γνωρίζειν, δηλοῦν, φανεροῦν, ἐμφανίζειν, ἀποκαλύπτειν (and cognates) form a sort of ascending scale. But there is very little evidence of this (Eph. 3.5 is cited; cf. also I Cor. 3.13; Rom. 1.17; 3.21, cited here). Oepke produces a rather odd reading of statistics to show that ἀποκαλύπτειν is a completely Jewish and primitive Christian word; while φανεροῦν on the contrary has a gnostic tone, when it is not merely neutral. To obtain this 'unmistakable result' it is said that φανεροῦν, apart from the spurious ending in Mark, is only found in the synoptists at Mark 4.22 (where in Matt. and Luke it is replaced by ἀποκαλύπτειν) and not at all in Gal., Phil., Thess., James, II Peter. On the other hand it is common in John, II Cor., Col., and the Pastorals. Conversely, ἀποκαλύπτειν comes frequently in the synoptists, in the majority of the Pauline corpus and in I Peter, though never in John (12.38 is a quotation), I-III John or Col. This catalogue omits to mention that φανεροῦν occurs three times in Romans (twice as a synonym for ἀποκαλύπτειν), which is as 'frequent' as the occurrence of the word in the Pastorals. It is strange to find II Peter, by this criterion, among the completely Jewish and primitive Christian works! If phrases like φανερὸν ποιεῖν are taken into account, and φανερός on its own, and φανερῶς, φανέρωσις, it becomes even less possible to make Oepke's divisions, as a brief glance at a concordance will show. On this article, see further, J. Barr, *Semantics*, esp. p. 230ff. The *TWNT* article omits all reference to (ἐν-) δεικνύναι in the NT, though it has mentioned earlier (p. 567) that ἔνδειξις is an important word for Greek thought in this connection.

(Phil. 1.13). In Ephesians the writer says that a man's shameful secret acts are 'made manifest' by the light of Christ (Eph. 5.13). He may mean at the end time, and this passage may belong to our next section, but there is obviously a close link between this kind of 'showing up' and that which Paul expects to result from Christian prophecy. However, this group is certainly not solely 'theological'.

On all but one occasion, δηλοῦν in Paul can suitably be rendered 'it is clear (that)', 'I have been told', etc.[1] Ἐνδεικνύναι is used in a non-theological sense in Romans; the Gentiles 'shew (make obvious) the work of the law written in their hearts' (Rom. 2.15). Most of the occurrences of γνωρίζειν in Paul are 'secular' ('God' is neither subject nor object).[2]

'Revelation' and the Future

Where the words are used in a way that can at all properly be called 'theological', they have very often a future reference. The 'revealing', 'showing', are still to come. They are used of the future 'appearing' of Christ, or of the 'shewing up' of men's past actions, or of some other aspect of the *eschaton*.

The Future 'Revelation' of Christ in Glory The Corinthians are waiting for the 'revealing' (ἀποκάλυψις) of our Lord, Jesus Christ (I Cor. 1.7). The Thessalonians will receive rest 'at the revealing (same word) of the Lord Jesus from heaven' (II Thess. 1.7). The Colossians will be manifested in glory, when Christ is manifested (φανερωθῇ) (Col. 3.4). This is the same event as Paul earlier wrote about to Rome: 'The glory that shall be revealed', and 'the earnest expectation of the creation' that 'waits for the revealing of the sons of God (ἀποκαλυφθῆναι, ἀποκάλυψιν)' (Rom. 8.18ff.).[3] *This is 'revelation' in its technical sense in the New Testament*.[4] It is a future hope; other elements of the

---

[1] I Cor. 15.27; Gal. 3.11; I Cor. 1.11; Col. 1.8.
[2] I Cor. 12.3; 15.1; II Cor. 8.1; Gal. 1.11; Phil. 1.22; Col. 4.7, 9; Eph. 6.21 (cf. NEB). Phil. 4.6 is man telling his needs to God.
[3] Cf. also Eph. 2.7: God acted in Christ, so that 'in the ages to come' he 'might show the exceeding riches of his grace in kindness towards us in Christ Jesus'. This is 'show' used almost for 'do' as in the English 'show kindness'. See below.
[4] Cf. J. McIntyre, *Christian Doctrine of History*, p. 83: 'It is rather interesting that the New Testament used the term "reveal" for that final appearance, and that that is the normal New Testament connotation of the term.' See also R. Bultmann, *Existence and Faith*, Hodder and Stoughton, 1961, note 7, p. 301, where the same fact is noted—and summarily dismissed as irrelevant! So too J. Baillie, *The Idea of*

end-time may make their presence felt now; but 'revealing'
/refers to those aspects of the end that are still very much in the
future. It is largely pictorial (to put it bluntly, it is 'myth'); it
is in this context that Paul presumably hopes for the face-to-face
encounter with God; but he does not seem to use 'reveal' and
related words to describe that (which, anyway, he only mentions once in the writings we have of his).

The Future 'Revelation' of the Man of Sin   Also to be revealed in
the future is 'the man of sin, the lawless one' (II Thess. 2.3-8),
and he will be slain by τῇ ἐπιφανείᾳ τῆς παρουσίας of Jesus (the
only time 'Paul' uses ἐπιφάνεια).

The actual pattern of the future event is not within the scope
of this enquiry, which is concerned more with the formal use
of the words than with the substance of what they describe
(unless that be God). Very briefly: Paul's conception of the
state of the dead may have changed between his letters to the
Thessalonians and his 'second' letter to Corinth (I Corinthians)
on the one hand, and this third (or fourth) letter to Corinth
(that which includes II Corinthians, chapter 5) and that to
Philippi, on the other. At first he talks of sleep in Christ, and
of being 'with the Lord' only at the end-time. But later he
writes of dying, to be 'with the Lord' now. So, he expects the
raising, or 'revealing' as the case may be, of Christians who
have died, the assumption of the living, the change of all (in the
absorption of corruption by incorruption), the defeat or final
defeat of all the enemies and powers, including the man of sin;
and then Christ's triumphant reign, shared by the faithful, who
will be with him for ever. These are the events for which Paul
in the main uses terms like 'reveal': the events of this 'eschatological myth'.[1]

The Future 'Revelation' of Men at the Judgment   This future event
includes the 'revealing' of the secrets of men's hearts, in the
day of 'wrath and revealing of the righteous judgment of God'
(Rom. 2.5). In I Corinthians, Paul writes: 'Each man's work
shall be made manifest (φανερόν): for the day shall declare

Revelation in Recent Thought, p. 57. Noted also by Oepke, *TWNT* III, p. 586, who
sees this as the consummation of a 'present revealing'; but the latter is in fact
unknown to the NT writers.
   [1] The main descriptions of this future are in I Thess. 4.13ff.; I Cor. 15; II Cor. 5;
Rom. 8.18ff.

(δηλώσει) it, because it is revealed in fire (ἀποκαλύπτεται); and the fire itself shall prove each man's work, of what sort it is' (I Cor. 3.13). This may mean a testing by the ordinary or extraordinary events of the near but this-worldly future; or it may refer to the final Judgment and testing (cf. ἡ ἡμέρα), or perhaps more likely still to the former as an aspect of the latter. But there is at present no such 'revealing' of men's works. In II Corinthians Paul is more definite: 'For we must all be made manifest before the judgment seat of Christ; that each one may receive the things done in the body' (φανερωθῆναι) (II Cor. 5.10). There is little precise detail in the picture; to whom we shall be 'manifested' is not clearly stated. What is certain is that the main events which can be described in terms of 'revealing' lie in the future.

Past and Present 'Revelation'

But before this final event other lesser revealings have happened and may still happen. This is not in the grand pictorial-mythological sense we have just been looking at; rather, just as we saw above a man's thoughts may be 'revealed', so God may 'reveal' some of his thoughts and plans.

Past and Present: Prophecy In I Corinthians a 'revelation' (ἀποκάλυψις) is similar to a tongue, or a prophecy, and it is something that might come to anyone in corporate worship. 'What' is 'revealed' on these occasions Paul does not say, but he finds this sort of thing annoying, and sufficiently 'useless' to need strict regulating (I Cor. 14.26; cf. vv. 6 and 30). However, Paul seems to expect that anyone at Philippi who disagrees with him will be put right by God, 'even this shall God reveal unto you' (ἀποκαλύψει), presumably by just such a prophetic revelation (Phil. 3.15). It was by 'revelation' (ἀποκάλυψιν) that Paul after fourteen years made his way to Jerusalem; if we trust Acts at all, this might refer to the prophecy of Agabus at Antioch (Gal. 2.2; Acts 11.28). 'Revelation' in this sense (where it is 'true') is being told by God precisely what to do in a specific situation. 'Revelation' used of the present does not describe any experience of person-to-person relation with God. Paul finds it unimportant, even a little embarrassing. It is the closest he comes to 'propositional revelation'; but it is commands rather than 'pure' propositions that are 'revealed'.

Past and Present: 'Revelation' and God   God (the Father) is never said by Paul to have been (be, or be in the future likely to be) 'revealed'; but occasionally his 'attributes' (to use our term) are revealed in action.[1] Paul talks in this way mainly in Romans.[2] The wrath of God is 'revealed' (ἀποκαλύπτεται, present continuous) against the ungodly and unrighteous, in his delivering them up to uncleanness. This may be compared with what Paul writes later (Rom. 9.17ff.): God shewed (ἐνδείκνυναι) his power in Pharaoh; this fairly obviously means he exercised his power; and a few verses later Paul explains that this was 'showing' his wrath, making his power 'known' (γνωρίζειν). The actual events *were* his wrath; just as the actual events were the 'making known' (γνωρίζειν again) his kindness (next verse) to the Israelites. At this point our English phrase is just about adequate; 'showing kindness' is normally thought of as an activity that is an end in itself; you are not trying to show *that you are kind*, you are exercising, expressing the kindness so as to *be* kind. So the 'shewing' of God's wrath is the exercising of his wrath. The 'revealing' of his wrath at the start of Romans is the exercising of his wrath in the many events of Gentile sexual corruption.[3]

The 'knowledge' (τὸ γνωστόν) of God is also said to be 'manifest' (φανερόν); but this is knowledge of God's 'everlasting power and divinity', and not of God himself. We have in fact already seen that this is very much an unrealised 'potential' knowledge; those who could have exercised it have 'refused to know' God.[4] What Paul thinks must be clearly seen of God in

---

[1] In much the same way as God has shined in our hearts 'the light of the knowledge of the glory of God in the face of Jesus Christ', II Cor. 4.6; see p. 170, n. 1.

[2] Rom. 1.18ff., a passage we have already examined for its use of 'knowing' words.

[3] Compare A. T. Hanson, *The Wrath of the Lamb*, p. 85 (as quoted above): The phenomena described are not 'a proof of God's displeasure; wrath in the New Testament is not an attribute or emotion of God, but the effects of sin'. The effects are probably not seen to be as independent of God, as 'automatic', as Hanson (and Dodd) suggest; but formally the definition is correct: the events *are* God's wrath, they are his reaction to, dealing with, sin; not a display of his emotions or an aspect of his character, or his self. Cf. R. Bultmann, *TNT* I, p. 275: ' "Be revealed" means "appear on the scene", "take place" '; also A. Nygren, *Commentary on Romans, ad loc.* Cf. too II Thess. 1.4-5, where the patience under persecution of the faithful Christians is an ἔνδειγμα of the righteous judgment of God: not primarily so that people may see the righteous judgment of God, but 'so that they (the suffering Christians) may be made worthy of, fit for, the Kingdom'. This is the positive side of God's active judging, setting right. Similarly the Philippians' unity and firmness will be a demonstration, a practical proof, of their salvation, in which others should see the fact of their own dissolution.

[4] Above, p. 66ff.

the world is the fact that there must be a distinction between Creator and creature; the heathen have ignored this. This fact is 'visible' but not 'seen'; if it had been 'seen', fully accepted, they would not be idolatrous. The language is somewhat incon- sistent[1]—something is known but not known, visible but not seen—but Paul wants to prove that the Gentiles are guilty that 'they may be without excuse', that they, as well as the Jews who have the written law, can properly be the object of the wrath of God that balances the activity of the righteousness of God.

In Romans, Paul says that 'In it (the gospel which is the power of God for salvation) is revealed (ἀποκαλύπτεται) a righteousness of God.' He makes this a little more explicit later: 'But now apart from the law a righteousness of God has been manifested ... the righteousness of God (which is) through faith in Jesus (Rom. 1.17; 3.21ff.): νυνὶ δὲ χωρὶς νόμου δικαιοσύνη Θεοῦ πεφανέρωται .... δικαιοσύνη δὲ Θεοῦ διὰ πίστεως ᾽Ιησοῦ Χριστοῦ. 'Righteousness' fairly obviously means the activity of God in setting right.[2] Paul explains that this activity of setting right is effected 'freely, by his grace, through the redemption that is in Jesus'. He then goes on to say, 'Whom God set forth to be a place of expiation (ἱλαστήριον) through faith, by his blood, *to shew his righteousness,* because of the passing over of the sins done aforetime, in the forbearance of God; *for the shewing* (I say) *of his righteousness* at this present season; *that he might himself be just, and the justifier of him that hath faith in Jesus*' (Rom. 3.25-26): εἰς ἔνδειξιν τῆς δικαιοσύνης αὐτοῦ ... πρὸς τὴν ἔνδειξιν τῆς δικαιοσύνης αὐτοῦ ἐν τῷ νῦν καιρῷ, εἰς τὸ εἶναι αὐτὸν δίκαιον καὶ δικαιοῦντα τὸν ἐκ πίστεως ᾽Ιησοῦ. God does not 'set Jesus forth', etc., to *shew* that he is righteous; but so as actively to *be* righteous, δίκαιον, just; and 'shewing righteousness' is the activity of 'setting right'. It might be (though clumsily) paraphrased 'to exercise his righteousness at this present season, so as to be actively righteous, by setting right the man who accepts in faith his setting-right in Jesus'. The meaning of ἔνδειξις is the one we found in Rom. 9.17ff. There is another instance of it in II Cor. 8.24. That verse runs: τὴν οὖν ἔνδειξιν τῆς ἀγάπης ὑμῶν ... ἐνδεικνύμενοι, and the RV has to translate ἔνδειξις as

---

[1] Below, ch. 5.
[2] Cf. NEB for Rom. 1.17; Barrett, *Romans, ad loc.*; Bultmann, *TNT*, §§28-30.

'proof': 'shew unto them the proof of your love'.[1] Again ordinary 'untheological' English probably comes closest to the nuance of Paul's meaning. In ordinary English conversation, to ask someone to 'shew' or 'prove' their love is to cast doubts on its very being. 'Let's *see* your love' is a request for action; and in the same way Paul is asking for cash. To 'show love', to prove love, is to exercise it. It is not primarily a 'revelation of character' (a cruel man can 'show kindness'), it is only incidentally 'revealing'. What matters is what happens. So for Paul, in Romans chapter 3, what matters is that God becomes actively righteous, and sets men right (Rom. 3.21ff.).[2]

So too Paul can say in Galatians, 'Faith is now revealed' (Gal. 3.23); faith, obedient trust, the only true relationship to God (compare Romans chs 1-5) is now made possible, it is now a reality, it happens, because God is eliciting it. (Compare two verses later: ἐλθούσης δὲ τῆς πίστεως, 'Now that faith has come'.)

From this activity of God we can deduce that 'God is righteous', and the quality of his righteousness; i.e. we can respond in faith to his initiative in setting us right with himself. But this does not mean that he has 'revealed himself' to us, or that that was the aim of the exercise. The point is similar to the one we made on the Old Testament.[3]

Past and Present: 'Revelation of Christ'   In Galatians, Paul tells of God being 'pleased to reveal his Son in me' (ἀποκαλύψαι τὸν υἱὸν αὐτοῦ ἐν ἐμοί). Quite what Paul means is unsure; but presumably he means 'to me' (Gal. 1.15).[4] If this is so, it is parallel to I Cor. 15.8, where Paul talks of the Risen Christ last of all appearing to him, as to one born out of due season (ἔσχατον δὲ πάντων . . . ὤφθη κἀμοί); and this is then Paul's own account of what Luke

---

[1] Cf. also Eph. 2.7ff.: here the expression 'shew kindness' is actually used, in the RV: 'That in the ages to come he might show the exceeding riches of his grace in kindness toward us in Christ Jesus.' It is making us share in the life of the 'heavenlies' that *is* the showing of God's kindness.

[2] Cf. A. Nygren, *Romans, ad loc.* God does not, for Paul, have to prove he is righteous (cf. 3.5f.: it would be blasphemy to doubt it or try in any way to demonstrate it). The fact is that God has started, in his own way, to exercise his 'righteousness', by setting right men who respond by trusting in Jesus. That God demonstrates his righteousness over against sin by having Jesus crucified is not said; and it would be a hypocritical sham, if it were meant to excuse him for 'justifying the ungodly'.

[3] Above, p. 22ff.; Isa. 40.5, etc.

[4] He could mean 'in me to others', compare II Cor. 2.14, discussed below. It would not make any difference to the argument as a whole. v. 12, *q.v.*, suggests the sense accepted here.

records as a 'vision' on the Damascus Road. *Pace* (fairly) recent tendencies, whatever the fact of the Resurrection may have been, neither the kerygma nor Paul quoting it suggest that the disciples had just a 'ghostly' experience.[1] It was a 'spiritual' experience, in so far as it was the act of God who 'is' Spirit; but he, so the disciples believed, raised Jesus from death—from the grave, (the place of) the dead—in time for him to avoid decomposition; and there is no possibility of avoiding the 'crass physicalness' of their *belief*. (They had, though it may seem odd to us, no epistemology for distinguishing the fact, and the existential claim it made on them.)[2] *Ὤφθη* particularly emphasises the physical visibility of the raised Lord; Paul claims in both these places to have had sight of him; and also earlier in I Cor. 9.1: 'Have I not seen (*ἑώρακα*) the Lord?' Jesus is 'revealed' to Paul; Paul 'sees' Jesus. The point of the event is not a personal communion of Paul and the Lord; this is the commissioning of the prophet by theophany. In each case the purpose of the 'revealing' is made obvious by Paul, it is his sending as apostle to the Gentiles. It establishes the relation of

---

[1] The attempt (still made) to 'spiritualise' the Resurrection of Jesus is an attempt to by-pass the scandal of miracle (if scandal it be) In modern jargon (if it is to meet modern opinion that the attempt is being made), it would have to have been a 'physical' event of some order to have been an *event* at all. A human 'mental' change is as physical as resurrection; and if it is produced by 'God', is just as miraculous a divine 'intervention'. This is so even if you multiply your entities and invent a concept of 'mind' as distinct from 'brain'. If the resurrection, bodily or mental, is in any sense an act of God, it is a miracle. But the point at issue is that Paul was sure resurrection concerned the Lord's body, and not primarily men's hearts-minds-brains. 'See' and 'reveal' are being used physically, of actual sight; not of 'person to person meeting', or in any other metaphorical sense. To be sure, the Lord has now a 'spiritual' body, I Cor. 15.44ff.; he has been 'clothed upon' with glory and incorruption, 50-3, cf. II Cor. 5.4; he has (or 'is') the sort of body which we shall then have (or 'be') and is the possibility of our having it. But it is the sort that can be 'seen', 'revealed', II Thess. 2.8, etc.; see above. The first Christians may have been wrong. It may have been community imagination. But it is a further act of imagination to find any trace of a non-physical resurrection tradition in the stories they have handed down. Oepke, *TWNT* III, p. 587, suggests that by 'revelation' Paul implies that prior knowledge of Christian teaching became real ('revelatory'). But Paul does not say this.

[2] There is an interesting contrast in Acts between the value placed by early Christians on 'vision' as contrasted with 'reality' (this is irrespective of the historical value of the stories in question). In Acts 12.9, when the angel appears to him in prison, Peter thinks he is merely seeing a vision, and that what he is seeing isn't true. Only when he is outside the prison and in the town is he sure that a 'real' angel has been 'really' rescuing him (v. 11). This is so, even though Luke elsewhere (10.10ff.; 11.5ff., etc.) values highly the *messages* that come in visions. Luke at any rate distinguished what we might call 'spiritual vision' (which might be said to be 'very revealing') and 'real vision'. The disciples had 'real vision' of the Lord (and of angels!). See further below, p. 95, n. 1.

κύριος-δοῦλος. And the fact that Christ, the crucified and accursed one (Gal. 3.13), is raised shows that righteousness is no longer by Law, but through this act of God in Christ, through a faith-acceptance of what God has done in Christ. The curse of the Law and the power of the Law is abrogated; and so the Gentiles are accepted by God, as Gentiles, and do not have to become Jews. This is both Paul's commissioning and the charter of his mission. Paul is not claiming to have entered into a close communion with the Lord; he is claiming that he has 'seen' the Lord and been 'apostled'.

Paul uses two words related to the ones discussed above, in II Corinthians, chapter 12: 'I will come εἰς ὀπτασίας καὶ ἀποκαλύψεις κυρίου' ('to visions and revelations of the Lord'). The man—who is Paul, fourteen years back—in the body or out, he is not sure, had heard unspeakable words, had been carried right through to the third heaven. This is probably not the Damascus Road vision (II Cor. 12.1ff.).[1] It is the nearest Paul comes to describing a 'spiritual experience'. He does not think it doctrinally very important, in fact he shows some embarrassment with it, though it is very precious to him personally; perhaps it is because it is so personal, and cannot be shared (unlike the 'seeing of the Lord' that was his commission), cannot 'edify', that it embarrasses him. But this rapt state was one he entered for a short while in the distant past, and only on that one occasion. For the community as a whole, this sort of thing is unimportant (cf. I Cor. 12 and 14).

There are only a few more instances of Paul writing of 're-vealing' that has happened or does happen. In II Corinthians, Paul says 'God makes manifest the savour of Christ's knowledge through us' (II Cor. 2.14) (φανεροῦντι).[2] The main point of what Paul is saying is that he and his companions in their work are a judgment on those they meet, a savour of life to life, a savour from death to death. It is a somewhat mixed metaphor, but Paul seems to be saying that men can see in him and his companions what 'knowledge of Christ' means, and can respond positively or negatively; just as you cannot escape reacting one way or another to a strong incense. But φανεροῦν is part of the metaphor, rather than a theological term.

---

[1] Above, p. 64 and n. 2, below, p. 95.
[2] For 'knowledge', see above, p. 71.

Later in the letter, Paul says they are 'always bearing about in the body the dying of Jesus that the life also of Jesus may be manifested (φανερωθῇ) in our body (II Cor. 4.10).[1] The 'life' is the living power; it is 'obviously' the only power that could keep them going when they are so battered by events; 'that the exceeding greatness of the power may be of God and not of ourselves'. Paul is not saying more than that this is 'evident'; he is not talking of any 'revealing' of Jesus' 'self'.

Past and Present: 'Revelation' and the Spirit   In I Corinthians Paul states 'to each one is given ἡ φανέρωσις τοῦ πνεύματος *to profit withal*' (I Cor. 12.7). The Corinthians are not given the Spirit for their own spiritual enjoyment, and they have to be told that possession by the Spirit is not self-authenticating. Paul adds a comprehensive list of ways the Spirit manifests himself. The Spirit manifests himself in action, in the community, for the sake of the community; not just to show that he is there, or what he is like. He acts openly, plainly for the sake of acting; again, not for the sake of 'encounter' with himself (cf. Gal. 5.22-3).

We are nearly at the end of the evidence for Paul's use of this type of concept, of 'revealing'; we have been looking in the last few paragraphs at events in the past in which 'revealing' of some sort is said to have happened. And it is worth noticing that Paul does not seem to see the great 'saving acts' of God in the recent past in terms of 'revelation', 'revelation of God'. There will be 'revealings' in the future as the great act of God; but this is in a mythical, pictorial sense. In the present prophecy, too, effects a sort of 'revealing'. These two classes of events are events aimed at men's consciousness, meant to result in 'sight' or 'understanding'. But the 'revealing' of the righteousness of God, or his wrath, or his kindness, is not 'revealing' in the same sense; they have been 'revealed', 'shown', whether or not sight or understanding happen. You can 'show kindness' to someone without their knowing it, without being 'revealed' to them at all. It is in this sense alone that Paul talks of the act of God in Christ as the 'revealing' of his righteousness.

Past and Present: 'Revelation' of the 'Mystery'   The only places where Paul (or 'Paul and followers') employs the term 'reveal' and with it 'make known' at all consistently to describe a past

---

[1] See above, p. 69.

activity of God is in connection with the term 'mystery'
(μυστήριον): 'the revelation (ἀποκάλυψιν) of the mystery, which
hath been kept silent through times eternal, but now is manifested (φανερωθέντος) and . . . made known (γνωρισθέντος) unto
all the nations' (Rom. 16.25).[1] But the 'mystery' is certainly
not God himself, and does not seem to be Christ either. It seems
on examination to be the inclusion of the Gentiles in Israel.[2]
'For I would not, brethren, have you ignorant of this mystery
. . . that a hardening in part has befallen Israel, until the fulness
of the Gentiles be come in' (Rom. 11.25ff.). In Colossians,
Paul talks of τὸ μυστήριον τὸ ἀποκεκρυμμένον ἀπὸ τῶν αἰώνων
καὶ ἀπὸ τῶν γενεῶν—νῦν δὲ ἐφανερώθη τοῖς ἁγίοις αὐτοῦ, οἷς
ἠθέλησεν ὁ Θεὸς γνωρίσαι τί τὸ πλοῦτος τῆς δόξης τοῦ μυστηρίου
τούτου ἐν τοῖς ἔθνεσιν, ὅς ἐστιν Χριστὸς ἐν ὑμῖν, ἡ ἐλπὶς τῆς
δόξης. The 'mystery' is Christ being among, identified with
'you' Gentiles. And this is probably what Paul means a few
verses further down by 'the mystery of God' (Col. 1. 26ff. [text
unsure]; 2.2). The 'mystery' is thus another term for Paul's 'my
gospel', which came to him 'δι' ἀποκαλύψεως Ἰησοῦ Χριστοῦ'
(Gal. 1.12ff.), when God was pleased 'to reveal his Son in me
that I might preach him *among the Gentiles*'. When Peter, and even
Barnabas, refused to eat with Gentile converts, they were not
walking 'according to the truth of the gospel' (Gal. 2.14). Really
Paul's gospel was the one he had 'received' by the normal
tradition (I Cor. 15.3-8). But he had, as is obvious from early
church history, a special understanding of it, in its relation to
Law and Gentiles, Gentiles and Law.[3] The gospel of Christ, the
good news of the Resurrection of the One the Law had cursed,
implies the end of the Law, and the inclusion of the Gentiles as
Gentiles; and all this by the pure act of God in Christ, setting
them right with himself, accepting them as sons, reconciling
them, giving them peace. What Paul means when he says he
came to know this 'by revelation of Jesus Christ', is impossible
to guess at all certainly. Either in his conversion experience he

[1] The so-called 'Marcionite ending'. But most of the language can be paralleled
elsewhere in Paul, save for σιγᾶν used in this way. It is interesting to note that
μυστήριον is only used in the LXX of the secrets of God, and then only in Daniel:
2.18, cf. v. 22. And there it is the *mysteries of God's plans for the Gentiles* that are
'revealed'.
[2] See also the 'revealing of the mysteries' in the DSS (above, p. 57) and Rigaux,
art. cit., *NTS* 4.4.
[3] See above, p. 82 and next note.

believed Christ had told him (this is the view Luke seems to take),[1] or perhaps more likely, the actual experience of seeing the risen Christ convinced him. Strict Pharisee that he was, the Law was God's last word, and the Crucified One was accursed. The Crucified One vindicated by God meant a complete *bouleverse-ment.* The Law, the distinctive feature of God's people, could no longer be God's last word; he must be achieving his purpose through the Crucified One, quite apart from Law and the Law community. But whichever way Paul came to this conclusion, this was his special understanding of 'the Gospel'; it is this that was especially 'revealed' to him. This is the 'mystery'. In I Corinthians Paul speaks of 'God's wisdom in a mystery' which 'the rulers of this world' did not know; the 'things God prepared for them that love him. But unto us God revealed them by the Spirit' (I Cor. 2.10).[2] We have considered the metaphor of the transference of spirit-mind already. The 'mystery' that is 're-vealed' seems to be the same as in Colossians; like the 'mystery' there, it is 'unto our glory': it is the death (and exaltation) of Christ, in its implications for the (obviously) Gentile Corin-thians.

The author to the Ephesians certainly seems to understand 'the mystery' in the sense we have given it in Paul: 'by revela-tion (κατὰ ἀποκάλυψιν) was made known unto me the mystery . . . as it has now been revealed to his holy apostles and prophets in the Spirit; (*viz.*) that the Gentiles are fellow-heirs and fellow-members of the body' and he sees this fact as the focus of Paul's ministry. Again, it is hard to tell what the ἀποκάλυψις consisted of; it may still mean the 'seeing' of the Risen Lord that was Paul's commissioning, or it may mean an instructing, the same type of 'revealing' that the 'holy apostles and prophets' received (Eph. 3.3,5).[3]

The 'mystery' is not some esoteric doctrine that ceases to be a mystery when it is disclosed; Paul's 'mystery' is a wonder that becomes all the more wonderful for being made public.[4] It is

---

[1] Acts 26.17ff.; cf. 22.17ff.

[2] On this, see above, p. 63, p. 64, n. 1.

[3] Cf. 1.9 (γνωρίσας ἡμῖν τὸ μυστήριον). Most of the instances of γνωρίζειν used 'theologically' are when a 'mystery' is being discussed. This 'making known' is now the task of the Church, Eph. 3.10; it is by no means yet complete, 6.19.

[4] Μυστήριον elsewhere in the Pauline literature twice seems to mean what we have suggested here: I Cor. 4.1 presumably refers back to 2.1-16; at Col. 4.3 the listeners are to pray that Paul may speak the mystery of Christ, and make it

not a facet of God's character that has hitherto been unnoticed; it is a marvel planned from all ages, that has now happened. And its implications were 'revealed' to Paul. God has made possible the inclusion of the Gentiles in his purpose; and Paul is shown that this has happened. It is not that God's great act is a 'revealing'. But to Paul some time later (and for the author to the Ephesians, to others too) was 'revealed' an important aspect of what the act of God in Christ effects.

'Revelation': Conclusion

'Revelation' is a subordinate motif in Paul. 'Revelation' (and similar words) can be used in an apparitional sense of the future, of Christ and of the sons of God at the End Time; it can be used of the making visible then, or now, of the secrets of men's hearts; it can be used of the 'appearances' of the risen Christ, in the sense of a physical making-visible. It can be used of God imparting information to 'prophets' and the like. And Paul does not think all this very important; except for the one occasion when he, Paul, saw the Lord, and realised, or was told, the mystery of God, the meaning of the Cross, for the whole world. Also, the words can be used in a more dynamic sense, akin to that of the English 'shewing', as Paul himself suggests by using ἐνδεικνύναι, God 'showing' kindness, righteousness, and wrath.[1]

'Revelation' is a term which emphasises the initiative of the 'revealer'; it might have been expected that Paul, with his strong sense of God's initiative in human affairs, his conviction of God's sovereign power, would have found this term more useful. He does see the 'revealing' to himself of the mystery of the Gentiles' inclusion in God's people as an act of God's power, appointing Paul *the* apostle to the Gentiles. But this is totally subordinate to the Cross and the exaltation, where the mystery *happened*. For Paul, God has acted decisively to reconcile the world to

---

manifest, referring to 1.26ff. Twice it just means 'hidden things', somewhat disparagingly, I Cor. 13.2; 14.2; and twice it is used of other 'mysteries', I Cor. 15.51, of the end-time events; Eph. 5.32, the unity of Christ and his Church: but this is the same as the mystery of Christ and the Gentiles. Cf. J. A. Robinson, *Ephesians*, Macmillan, 1904².

[1] Compare the entries ἀποκαλύπτω, ἀποκάλυψις in Arndt and Gingrich, *A Greek-English Lexicon of the New Testament*, C.U.P., 1957. This offers four divisions: general; of supernatural events; of the interpretation of visions; of the eschatological revealing of persons and events. But it nowhere suggests that there is a 'revealing of God'.

himself.[1] But Paul nowhere says that this means that God has
'revealed himself' to the world.[2] And this was only to be expected, once it was realised that for Paul, the only 'knowledge of
God' yet possible is our obedience as sons to what are believed to
be his demands.

II. THE SYNOPTICS

'Knowledge' and 'Revelation' in the Great Thanksgiving

The obvious place to begin discussion of the use of the idea
of 'revealing', and the related concept of the imparting of
'knowledge' in the Synoptic Gospels, is the 'Johannine bolt in
the Synoptic blue', the Great Thanksgiving (Luke 10.21ff.;
Matt. 11.25ff.). To attempt to find a 'new' solution to this
formidable crux is certainly beyond the scope of this essay. All
that can be done is to summarise the conclusions of the standard
works.[3] The first two verses are almost identical in Luke and in
Matthew. The latter has:

> 'At that season, Jesus answered and said, I thank you, O Father,
> Lord of heaven and earth, that you did hide these things from the
> wise and understanding and did reveal them to babes; yes,
> Father, for so it was pleasing in your sight. All things have been
> delivered to me by my Father: and no one knows the Son save
> the Father; neither does any know the Father, save the Son, and
> he to whomsoever the Son wills to reveal him.'

Matthew continues with the 'invitation': 'Come unto me, all
you who labour and are heavy laden, and I will give you rest.

[1] Rom. 5.10; II Cor. 5.18, 19, 20.
[2] It is probably significant that Paul sees the παρουσία of Christ always as future
(I Thess. 2.19; 3.13; 4.15; 5.23; II Thess. 2.1, 8; so elsewhere in the NT: I John
2.28; Matt. 24.3, 27, 37, 39; II Peter 3.4, 12; and perhaps 1.16; James 5.7 (?)).
It is a term Paul uses for his own presence, or coming to be present as a friend (Phil.
1.26; 2.12; cf. II Cor. 7.6; 10.10). But he cannot use this of Christ now. In fact,
he wishes to 'depart and be with Christ' (Phil. 1.23), 'to be absent from the body
and be at home with the Lord' (II Cor. 5.8). Paul certainly sees the Christ active
now in the community and the individual (Gal. 2.20, etc.); and perhaps it is fair
to guess, 'present in (the) spirit' (cf. I Cor. 5.3 of Paul himself). But this in a hidden
way, not in the way of a friend who is presenting himself for 'encounter', 'revealing'
himself. It is very real, but it is not aimed at confrontation; it can fully achieve
present (limited) aims with little 'revelation' as such. Certainly there is now no
'revelation' of God.
[3] Such as A. H. M°Neile, *The Gospel according to St Matthew*; J. M. Creed, *The
Gospel according to St Luke*, both Macmillan. Also R. H. Fuller, *The Mission and
Achievement of Jesus*, SCM Press, 1954, p. 89ff.; W. Manson, *Jesus the Messiah*,
p. 71ff.; R Bultmann, *Gnosis*, p. 50ff.; A. M. Hunter, *NTS* 8.3 [*Teaching and Preaching
the N.T.*, SCM Press, 1963, p. 41ff.]; F. W. Beare, *The Earliest Records of Jesus*,
Blackwell, 1962, *ad loc.*

Take my yoke upon you, and learn of me; for I am meek and lowly in heart; and you shall find rest for your soul. For my yoke is easy and my burden is light.' Luke has τίς ἐστιν ὁ υἱὸς . . . τίς ἐστιν ὁ πατήρ, which is a little strange, but Creed suggests it is only a stylistic change. Luke's form makes it clear that he did not understand this as a 'personal knowing'. It is best to work on the assumption that Matthew's form is 'original' (which cannot of course, mean anything more than 'closer to "Q" '), as that is the slightly more difficult assumption for the case this essay is making.

The passage is then to be explained, either against the background of the Old Testament and Judaism in general, or against the gnostic background proposed by Norden and Bultmann, among others.[1] There are no further synoptic parallels to work from. And we have seen that there is nothing in the Dead Sea Scrolls as so far published which provides an alternative background for this sort of language to that provided by the 'canonical' Jewish scriptures. Nor is there anything like this in Paul. If the gnostic background is chosen, or if the parallels with John are pressed,[2] then the passage ceases to be immediately relevant, and it should be studied along with the Pastoral Epistles, and the Johannine literature, as evidence for second or third generation Christian belief.[3] In this case, Luke's τίς ἐστιν is probably best taken as a fair interpretation, the hidden gnostic saviour is talking of the unknown God of an abstract mythology. This would then be a different type of 'knowing' from the one we have found so far, probably more like that of the Hermetic literature.[4]

I believe that this is how the passage should be read. As Bultmann says, the 'he to whomsoever the Son wills to reveal him' rules out its association with the 'knowledge of Yahweh'

---

[1] Norden, *Agnostos Theos*, p. 277ff.; quoted, J. M. Creed, *op. cit.*, *ad loc.*; cf. Bultmann, *op. cit.* See also K. Stendahl, 'Commentary on Matthew' in *Peake*, Nelson, 1962; S. M. Gilmour, 'Commentary on Luke', *Interpreter's Bible*, Abingdon Press, 1952: 'a Christian version of an idea that had been popularised in the Hellenistic world by various gnostic cults'; F. W. Beare, *op. cit.*, p. 89f.: 'evidence for the early emergence of Hellenistic influences in the thought of the Church'.

[2] John 10.14ff.; 'I am the good shepherd; and I know mine own, and mine own know me, even as the Father knows me and I know the Father'; 17.25f.: 'O righteous Father, the world knew you not, but I knew you; and these know you did send me; and I made known to them your name, and will make it known. . . .' But see below *ad loc.*

[3] See below, on the Pastorals.   [4] Above, pp. 61ff.

in the Old Testament. 'No one knows the Father save the Son' cannot, without leaving a great logical gap, be followed by 'and he to whomsoever the Son wills to reveal him' if 'know' in the first part of the sentence means 'obey'.[1]

However, as we have noted, other scholars have found it possible to interpret this against an Old Testament background and, again, it is necessary to consider the understanding of the passage that is less congenial to the present thesis. The saying is then to be taken as coming from the very early Church, or from the Lord himself, and is to be explained against the background of contemporary Jewish thought. It is to be taken as it stands in Matthew, not excluding the invitation.[2] If this is done, then the πάντα that are delivered become the 'reign of God'; the Father's 'knowledge of the Son' becomes his 'choice of him to fulfil the role of the Servant'; the Son's 'knowledge of the Father' is his response to that choice 'in faith and obedience'. The 'revealing' of the Father by the Son becomes 'the proclamation of the impending advent of the eschatological Reign of God'. This is the 'revealing' spoken of in the first part of the saying. The 'Invitation' shows a blending of a rudimentary 'Wisdom Christology' with the 'Sonship of Jesus conceived in terms of the obedient Servant'. This is, however, as it stands, in all probability a writing-up by the first Christians of the tradition of Jesus' self-understanding; rather than *ipsissima verba* of Jesus himself.

And it at once becomes obvious that when this saying is made to fit the life of Jesus, or the earliest Church, there is no room in it for any 'revealing' of *God himself*. That aspect of the saying is ignored or re-interpreted. If Jesus 'reveals' anything, it is the demand of God, the demand inherent in this being the end-time. He does not 'reveal' God.[3]

[1] Bultmann, *ibid*. See above, p. 37ff.

[2] There is a Thanksgiving in Ecclus 51.1ff., followed a little later by an invitation from Wisdom, v. 23ff.: 'Draw near to me . . . put your neck under the yoke. . . .' Cf. also 24.19.

[3] The citations are from Fuller, *op. cit.*, p. 90ff. Hunter (*art. cit.*), however, accepts them as *ipsissima verba*. He interprets them in much the same way as Fuller, not quite ignoring the final 'revealing' of the Father by the Son, but offering this rather odd comment: 'If the Son knows the Father with the same knowledge as the Father has of (? the Son) himself, it is not a knowledge which is transferable. The power Christ claims to give is not the power to know the Father *as he did*, but rather the power to know the Father *in him*.' No Old Testament references are offered as background for this 'interpretation'. (Hunter also adds that the Old Testament thinks of a man's knowledge of God as an I-Thou relationship, for which we have been able to find no evidence.)

If Jesus 'reveals' the Father's identity, or, even, 'self', the passage is late and gnostic. Only if it talks in terms of God bringing his kingdom, God acting, is it possible to set it in the context of Jesus' understanding of himself, or his first followers' belief in him.

This is the only saying in the Synoptic Gospels that sees Jesus' mission in terms of 'revealing'. As an understanding of his work, it may be particularly appropriate to a collection of his teachings (Q?). But it occurs nowhere else.

'Knowledge' in General

For the rest, γινώσκειν, ἐπιγινώσκειν (of a *person*), are used in straightforward narrative. The walkers to Emmaus (Luke 24.16 and v. 35) 'know' the Lord—they were made to 'recognise' him —in the breaking of the bread (ἐγνώσθη αὐτοῖς), having failed to recognise him earlier (ἐπιγνῶναι). The two words seem to be used synonymously; Luke appears to imply just physical recognition and no more. *That* Jesus is raised is quite momentous; but the author does not emphasise any existential demand that we might think implicit in the encounter. It is a recognition of the fact of his identity. One or other of these verbs are used of the 'recognition' of men by their fruits (Matt. 7.15); of the men of Gennesaret who 'recognise' Jesus and bring out their sick (Matt. 14.35); of the Lord's refusal to 'acknowledge' those who have done nothing more than invoke him (Matt. 7.23); of the men the Lord says have not 'recognised' 'Elijah' even though he has come, in Matthew only (17.12); of the Lord by the Pharisees, who think he might have 'recognised' the sort of woman who was anointing him (Luke 7.39); of the crowd which 'recognised' the lame man (this is in Acts—3.10—but it is evidence for synoptic-type usage); of another crowd that 'recognises' that Paul is a Jew (Acts 19.34); and of the sailors who recognise the island as Malta (Acts 28.1). In all these cases, γινώσκειν, ἐπιγινώσκειν, mean just 'recognise'. They do not mean 'know' in the sense 'establish, enjoy, a personal relationship with'. In Luke, the Lord quotes the prophetic belief that God 'knows' men's hearts (Luke 16.15); and in Mark, the Lord 'perceives' 'in the spirit' the thoughts of his Pharisaic opponents (Mark 2.8 and ‖s). In all these instances it is a 'knowing of facts about' a person that is at issue. It is of course assumed that this is more than a 'bare' knowing; in the normal way, people are said to know a fact, when they act appropriately.[1] There is no hint of the (probably necessary) sophistication that allows for a 'knowledge' that has no observable form. But this is ordinary usage, and there is no sign of any specialised use of the terms, for a man's 'knowing his friend', for instance.

There is a rather more technical use of γινώσκειν in Matthew, 'paralleled' in a slightly different form in Luke: the Lord's assurance that 'there is nothing veiled that will not be revealed, nothing hidden that will not be *known*'; in the Markan form of the saying it is combined with 'the lamp on the stand', and only φανερός, φανεροῦν are used (Matt. 10.26; Luke 12.2; Mark 4.22).

The actual content of what is to be 'known' is not clear. Matthew, and Luke, in the discussion of parables in their version of Mark 4, say, 'to you is given to *know* the mystery of the kingdom'. This is presumably its relation to Jesus and his death and Resurrection, how a man can 'enter' it, and its imminence and futurity (Matt. 13.11; Luke 8.10; Mark 4.11).[2] So perhaps the Kingdom is the subject of these 'hidden-known' sayings also. Unless they are just general assurances of 'the truth will out' sort,[3] they are part of the 'Great Assurance', that what is being done in an out-of-the-way sort of place will be 'known' (and included in that is, of course, 'responded to') more widely.

This seems to have been quite genuinely part of the Lord's teaching,[4] and these sayings can fairly be taken as his, with this meaning: What he is doing *will be known*. It is not his own task to spread this knowledge; and it is knowledge of what he is doing and teaching, not 'knowledge' of God as such, nor 'knowledge of himself'.

---

[1] See above, p. 47, n.1.

[2] So M'Neile, *op. cit.*, *ad loc.* Mark just has 'to you is *given* (δέδοται) the mystery of the kingdom of God; but to them that are without, all things are done in parables'. Cf. J. Jeremias, *The Parables of Jesus*, SCM Press, rev. ed. 1963, p. 13ff. The disciples are inside, they have accepted the rule of God; for those outside, everything is *done* secretly. There is not the stress on 'knowing' in Mark.

[3] See below. Luke 12.2 seems to use the saying this way—the hypocrisy of the Pharisees will become evident. But the sayings that follow in Luke are the same as the 'fear not' exhortations in Matthew, which seem to be addressed to the disciples in their mission (or the early Church in its).

[4] Cf. Jeremias, *op. cit.*, p. 146ff. I think the phrase 'The great Assurance' is his. Though of course these sayings have been used by the Church of its post-Resurrection mission.

*so devrous "know" = recognize the_*
but not = to a saving knowledge

Γινώσκειν is used in the Infancy Narratives of the union of husband and wife (Matt. 1.25; Luke 1.34).

'Εἰδέναι is used a few times (with a person as object); the demons 'know' the Lord, 'who' he is (Mark 1.24 and v. 34; ‖ in Luke). This may be 'supernatural' knowledge similar to that claimed by the Lord in the Lukan form of the 'Thanksgiving'. The demons know that Jesus is the 'Holy One of God'. It is used of 'recognition' (but as with γινώσκειν, recognition includes recognition of status, and implies response of some sort), of the wise and the foolish virgins (Matt. 25.12) and in Peter's denial of any 'knowledge' of the Lord (Mark 14.66ff.). This is terrible apostasy by Peter; but it is no deep 'knowledge', as, for instance, of a friend, that is in question (even if it might have been at the back of the evangelist's mind). Peter is just saying, 'He's not even an acquaintance of mine.' And lastly, the Lord uses it to deny that his opponents 'know the scriptures, or the power of God' (Matt. 22.29).

Γνωρίζειν, 'to make known', is used by Luke, of the angels telling the shepherds and others of the birth of Jesus (Luke 2.15, 17); in Acts, in a quotation from Psalm 16, where 'David' talks of being made to experience life (ἐγνώρισάς μοι ὁδοὺς ζωῆς); and later, in the speech of Stephen, of Joseph letting his brothers know his identity (Acts 2.28; 7.13).

'Knowing' is not an important term in the Synoptic Gospels; they do not speak even as frequently as Old Testament writings do, of 'knowing God'; they do not talk about 'knowing' a friend; they do not at all suggest that God is to be 'known' as a friend.[1] The instances we have examined have largely been ones where 'knowing a friend' or 'knowing God' might possibly have been intended; but on examination, they seem to resolve easily into 'knowing that'-type language. And we found this to be the most probable sense of the 'knowing' in the Thanksgiving, if that be 'authentic'. It is a 'knowing that' which includes a response (or else the knowledge is denied). But that is as far as it goes.[2]

[1] To address God as Father, even as 'Abba', implies a different type of 'knowing' from the 'knowing' of a friend; obedience is still the uppermost idea: 'Your will be done'; 'However, not my will, but yours be done' (Matt. 6.9; Luke 11.2; Mark 14.36 and ‖).

[2] Again, explicit instances of 'knowing that' have received attention only in passing in this essay, which is concerned with the use of 'know' in phrases like 'to know God', 'to know a person'.

'*Revealing*'

As in Paul, words from this vocabulary are used in recounting the myths of the end time; of the physical visibility of Christ after the Resurrection; of the making known of secret information by God (directly or indirectly); and in general narrative and discussion. 'Revealing' language is used, of course, in the Thanksgiving; and this we have already discussed. Again as parallel terms, ἀποκαλύπτειν and γινώσκειν are used in another passage already noted, 'There is nothing that is covered that shall not be known.' The Markan parallel, as already noted, uses φανεροῦν, etc. In Matthew the saying is set in a missionary context. This is the activity of the disciples (Matt. 10.26 and Luke; Mark 4.22 and ‖s). They are going to 'reveal' what Jesus has done and told them secretly and privately. There are no gnostic, cosmological secrets recorded; the nearest the Synoptic Gospels come to such secrets is the teaching about Jesus' Passion and Resurrection; and the teachings about the end time, 'the mystery of the kingdom' (Mark chs 8-10 *passim*; and ch. 13 and ‖s). It seems probable that it is Jesus' teaching about the rule of God, its nearness and distance, and the attitudes and behaviour that are appropriate to it, that is in question. Jesus has been among and taught his closer circle of followers (literal followers), who have ears to hear, and do hear; and in these sayings, as part of his 'great assurance', he (and the early Church) is telling of the future spreading of his work. It is this spreading that is the 'revealing'. By inference, perhaps his own teaching is in a sense a 'revealing' too; but this is not explicitly said. It is the 'making known' to a wide, as opposed to a small, circle that can be called a 'revealing'; this is the taking of the light from under the measure, where it was already burning, for it to give light to the whole house.

In Matthew (only) the Lord replies to Peter's confession of him as 'the Messiah, the Son of the Living God', with, 'Flesh and blood have not revealed it to you, but my Father which is in heaven' (Matt. 16.13ff., esp. v. 23). This is a 'revelation' of facts about Jesus, of 'propositions'. Peter does not understand, does not 'know' more than the mere words: he minds not the things of God, but the things of men.

These sayings are to be taken, then, in much the same way as the ones in which, we decided above, the Thanksgiving must be understood, if it is to be taken as a logion of the Lord or the earliest Church. The 'revealing' here is 'propositional'. The propositions should of course be seen as significant for us as people, but they may not.

In the synoptics ἀποκαλύπτειν is used elsewhere only in Luke. It is used of the future 'revealing' of the Son of Man (Luke 17.30); this is in the literal sense of 'making visible' in the drama of the end time. We found the same use in Paul. And, it is said, the coming of Mary's Son will lead to the 'revealing' of the thoughts of many hearts (Luke 2.35); again, a use of 'reveal' that can be paralleled in Paul. (Luke, of course, seems to have understood the 'covered-revealed' saying in this way: Luke 12.2.)

In Mark, δεικνύναι ('to show') is used in a normal physical sense, 'Shew yourself to the priests' (Mark 1.44); and so later: 'He will shew you an upper room . . .' (Mark 14.15). It is used in the 'Q' Temptation story: the devil 'shows' the Lord all the kingdoms of the earth (Matt. 4.8; Luke 4.5). In Acts, God 'shows' Peter that nothing is common or unclean (Acts 10.28). This is 'revelation' of a command of God, in the normal prophetic way, through a vision.

Ἐπιφαίνειν is used in Acts of 'shining', literally and metaphorically, as in the Psalms; and ἐπιφανής for 'terrible' (or 'wonderful') in quoting Joel (Acts 2.17ff.). Matthew 1.20 uses φαίνειν of the apparition of an angel in a dream (which just means, of course, that in the dream the angel was 'visible'). It is used by Matthew of the future apparition of the sign of the Son of Man (24.30), and again by him in a quite ordinary way, when the Lord attacks religious ostentation, 'being seen by men' (Matt. 6.5ff.).

Φανεροῦν, etc., are used by Mark in his version of the 'Q' hidden-revealed saying (4.22; see above). Mark has the Lord tell the people he has healed not to make him 'known' (φανερός) (Mark 3.12 and ǁs); and Herod becomes interested because his 'name' has become 'known' (Mark 6.14). Φανεροῦν is used in the longer ending of Mark, of the 'visibility' of the Risen Lord (Mark 16.9ff.).

Ὁρᾶν is used in a similar way, mostly of the appearances of the Risen Lord (Luke 24.34; Matt. 28.7, 10) or of an angel (Luke 1.11; 22.43—some texts). It is used of the apparition, on the Mount, of Moses and Elijah (who are however physical enough for the moment for Peter to offer to build tents for them) (Mark 9.4 and ‖s). It occurs in a quotation in Luke, 'All *flesh* shall see the salvation of God' (Luke 3.6). Similarly, the Lord prophesies that the days will come when his hearers will long to 'see' 'a day of the Son of Man, but they will not see it' (Luke 17.22). In the last two instances 'see' means experience, live through, as in the Old Testament phrase, 'see good days'. It is used in prophecies of the future seeing of the Son of Man, twice in Mark (13.26 and ‖s; 14.62 and ‖s).

In Acts, Stephen says that God 'appeared' (ὤφθη) to our father Abraham; this is just a quotation of the Genesis theophany story (Acts 7.2, citing Gen. 15.7). Ananias, going to heal the blinded Saul, says he has been sent to him by the same Jesus who 'appeared' to him on the way to Damascus (Acts 9.17). The Lord himself, according to 'Paul's' later account in Acts (26.16), says he 'appeared' to make Paul a minister and a witness. These passages are best taken as referring to the Lord being actually 'seen'.[1] The same word is used of the Resurrection appearances in one of the 'kerygmatic passages' (Acts 13.31); and of the 'vision' of the Man from Macedonia. Luke has to note explicitly that it was a 'vision' (ὅραμα). Ὤφθη on its own would not necessarily mean that (Acts 16.9).

Finally, and this is quite unique, the verb is used in the Matthaean Beatitudes, 'Blessed are the pure in heart, for they shall see God' (Matt. 5.8). This, as M'Neile hints (*ad loc.*), is blessedness in terms of worship, seeing God as he was 'seen' by the worshipper in the Old Testament; like the other descriptions of bliss, this is a promise for the *eschaton*. It is not the immediate or inherent result of purity of heart: 'Great is your reward in heaven.' It is impossible to tell if this is Paul's 'face to face' (I Cor. 13.12), or the rather more distant joy of being in

---

[1] See above. Luke in Acts makes Paul talk of 'seeing' *a light*, and may be suggesting a difference between Paul's 'seeing' of the Lord, and that of the earlier apostles. For Luke, the Lord has ascended for the duration, and ordinary appearances have stopped. However, Paul, at I Cor. 9.1; 15.8, is quite sure he has 'seen' the Lord in precisely the same way as the others, even though it was last of all (contrast Acts 13.30-31, where 'Paul' relies on others' witness!). Luke may have thought that Paul saw the light as a sign of Jesus' presence; or that Jesus was there in more than Resurrection glory, more as at the Transfiguration. But it was a physical light, which Paul's companions, too, saw (22.9)—not an inner personal experience that has to be described in picture language—just as the voice was audible, but only Paul understood (Acts 9.7; 22.9). For this distinction, though with a somewhat different final conclusion, see also J. Knox, *Chapters in a Life of Paul*, A. and C. Black, 1954, pp. 113, 123.

God's court that the Apocalypse of John describes. The other terms, 'Sons of God', 'inherit the earth', suggest the less personal sense is more likely.

Θεωρεῖν is used once, in Acts (7.56),[1] when Stephen announces his vision: 'Behold, I see the heavens opened, and the Son of Man standing on the right hand of God.'

Conclusion

There is only the one suggestion, in the Thanksgiving, that it was in the work of Christ to 'reveal' in any sense at all. It could mean he was to 'reveal' the person of the Father; but defenders of the 'authenticity' of the saying seem mostly to reject this interpretation. Even if the saying is allowed to stand as a logion of the Lord or the earliest Church, it is an exception that emphasises the general conclusion, that neither Jesus nor the synoptists themselves seem from the records to have thought 'revealing' of any kind to have been his real task or achievement. Neither he nor they say that he is imparting 'knowledge of God' (or of himself for that matter), or suggest that this is what in fact came out of his life and work. He taught, and obviously what is taught and learnt can be called 'knowledge'; but it was 'knowledge-how' that he taught—how to respond in a world into which God's rule was breaking in the Person and work of the Teacher. Neither he nor his disciples talk much about him as 'Teacher' (contrast the leading figure in the Qumran sect). It is not even implied 'between the lines' that it is as Teacher, and so imparter of 'knowledge' and so (perhaps) 'revealer', that he is important. He came to live, work miracles, proclaim the rule of God and the way to respond—privately, among a small circle—and then, a little more publicly, to die. The small circle would then 'reveal' (perhaps he said this) what he had done and said. But this is only an incidental use of the term. His own mission was not concerned with anything that needed to be called a 'revealing'. This at any rate is the understanding of the churches and writers that produced the Gospels. We might use 'reveal' more freely than they.[2] But it is not our use that is, at present, in question.

---

[1] The 'seeing' in dreams is analogous, but less immediately trustworthy: Acts 10.17; 12.9.
[2] E.g. Oepke, *TWNT* III, p. 583f., talks of the 'revelatory acts' of Jesus 'to reveal (God) in his seriousness and his love'.

The most frequent way 'reveal' and similar words are used, with Jesus himself as the object, the 'person revealed', is of the Resurrection appearances, and of the coming of the Son of Man (= Jesus?). Whatever we may think about the appearances or about the eschatological myth, the words are intended to describe physical visibility.[1]

III. THE JOHANNINE LITERATURE

'John'[2] brings us closest yet to a theology where 'revealing' might seem likely to be an important 'concept'. But first, following our usual pattern we consider his use of 'knowing' words.

To Know

He does not use the noun γνῶσις at all; perhaps, as is often suggested, because it was a technical term of contemporary 'gnosticism'. He seems to use εἰδέναι and γινώσκειν as synonyms (John 8.55, etc.).[3]

General

The normative, everyday use can be seen in John ('the Baptist')'s witness to Jesus: 'In the midst of you stands one you do not know'. 'I knew him not, but that he should be manifested to Israel' (John 1.26, 31), and in the question later of the crowd, 'Is this not Jesus, the son of Joseph, whose father and mother we know?' (John 6.42). It here means knowing and recognising people in a non-relational sense. John's first statement may bear the overtones of later Christian recriminations against the Jews who do not 'obey'; but in the actual context in John it means no more than the Baptist's admission, immediately afterwards, that when he started preaching he did not know the identity of

[1] And the language seems nowhere to imply an at all deep level of 'personal encounter'.

[2] This is not the place to discuss questions of authorship in detail. The Gospel and Epistles could have come from the same pen; they are certainly from the same 'school'. The decision would not greatly affect the ensuing discussion. There is sufficient general similarity between them for each to be the best interpreter of the other; while even if they are by the same writer, they differ enough for supposed parallels to need to be checked carefully. Compare C. H. Dodd, *BJRL*, and W. F. Howard in *JTS*: 1946-8. We also examine the Apocalypse in this section; there is little enough relevant material in it, and it fits this group better than any other.

[3] W. F. Howard, *op. cit.*, notes that this use of synonyms in close conjunction with each other is a distinctive feature of Johannine style. Attempts to produce a progression where the words seem synonymous are usually based on a selection of evidence and are not very successful.

the man he was proclaiming. (The verb in these cases is εἰδέναι.)
Γινώσκειν is used in much the same way when Nathaniel says,
'Whence do you know me?' (John 1.48). It is more than a superficial recognition. Jesus knows quite a lot *about* Nathaniel. As the
evangelist later says, 'he knew all men . . . he needed not that
anyone should bear witness concerning man; for he himself
knew what was in man (John 2.24-5). This is knowledge of men's
minds and ways, like the knowledge of men that God has in the
Old Testament. So again, Jesus says to the Jews, 'I know you,
that you have not the love of God in you' (John 5.42). This is
knowledge *about* a person. To be sure, it is a practical knowledge, of how to behave toward them; but it is not, at any rate
so far, the knowledge of the other's 'self'; it is not used to describe
an 'I-Thou' relation.

God's 'Knowledge'

It is never said that the Father 'knows' or 'will know' the
disciples; only that the Father 'knows' the Son (John 10.14, 15,
etc.). The disciples are 'known' by the Son, and they will 'know'
the Son as the Son is 'known' by the Father, and 'knows' him.

Men's 'Knowledge' of God

The Lord frequently denies that the Jews, crowds, etc., 'know'
the Father (John 7.29, etc.). The disciples should be able to
'know' the Father, 'in' Jesus (John 14.7). The crowds ought to
have been able to 'know' the Father in the same way (John
8.19). Something more than recognition and knowledge of
identity is implied in these passages; for it is admitted that the
crowd does 'recognise Jesus', as the man from Nazareth, whose
parents they 'know' and yet they do not 'know him' (*ibid.*). This
is a deeper sense of 'know'; and in this sense even the disciples,
who have been a long time with Jesus, have only a very hazy
'knowledge' of him; 'Have I been so long time with you, and
do you not know me, Philip?' (John 14.9). What this deeper
sense of 'know' is, nowhere clearly appears. This is largely the
fault of the writer's style. He is deceptively translucent in his
constant repetitions of a few simple bold words, in short phrases
and sentences; he sets alongside each other his major concepts,
and says, 'Can you not see?' and for the life of you you cannot,
until you have fought your way inside the charmed circle of his

ideas. (And even when you think, after a struggle, that you are inside, you are constantly worried—if still awake—by the irritating doubt, 'Have I really understood?') The writer only very rarely gives you a key to the sense of even one of his linked concepts, from which you can deduce the real meaning of the rest.[1] An example of this is the ἐντολαί. He frequently makes the Lord talk about his 'commandments', but unlike the synoptists, he never seems to tell you what they are; there is nothing about divorce, or wealth, or fasting, or how to pray, or forgive. Only in chapter 13 does the Lord say, 'A new commandment I give you, that you love one another' (John 13.34). But that has not taken us much further; we are not told the form love takes; we are still not told how '*the* commandment' can be expanded into 'commandments'.[2] Either the writer expects his reader already to be able to give content to his major words, or he expects the Spirit to provide content; or both.

'*Knowledge*' *of God and Love for God and Men in the First Epistle*

The key that seems to explain how this writer is using 'know' is provided by the First Epistle: 'Beloved, let us love one another: for love is of God, and everyone that loves is begotten of God, *and knows God*' (I John 4.7ff.).[3] That this means what it appears to mean is shown by what follows: 'No man has seen God at any time; *if we love one another*, God abides in us, and his love is perfected in us.' And he goes on to say that this 'knowing God' by 'loving man' links with the whole Christian tradition of faith in the saving activity of God. We can know that what he has just said is a correct statement of the Christian experience, because we have the Spirit. We know we have the Spirit, because we confess Christ came in the flesh. Then he makes it quite clear that he is not talking what we (today) would call sentimental humanism. He is not suggesting that 'the love of man is every-

[1] For this reason, Bultmann (*TNT* II, SCM Press, 1955) supposes that John only provides a purely 'formal' analysis of the Christian life. Bultmann's exegesis of this analysis is helpful and persuasive. But to make his case, that this is all that is offered, he has to expunge all reference to the sacraments, and ignore the few other anchors the Evangelist provides to link his scheme with actual Christian life. It is probably this all but formal approach that has earned John the reputation of being a mystic. It is a style that fascinates, but is in danger of saying nothing, excitingly.

[2] Though there is a hint in 'Greater love has no man than this, that a man lay down his life for his friend', John 15.13.

[3] Cf. 2.4: 'He that says, I know him, and does not keep his commandments, is a liar.'

one's inherent divine possibility'. He asserts: 'Herein is love, not that we loved God, but that he loved us, and sent his Son to be the propitiation (expiation) for our sins.' It is the love God himself exercises, it is this love 'abiding in us' that makes possible our love of our brothers, and it is our exercising of this love that is the 'knowing of God'.[1] And at one point in the epistle he comes to a concrete definition of what this love is: 'Whoso has the world's goods, and beholds his brother in need, and shuts up his compassion from him, how does the love of God abide in him?' (I John 3.17). We love, because he first loved us; God abides in us, and his love is perfected in us. But the love of God in us, and our love for him, *only* becomes real, and more than talk, in our love of the brethren; and a very practical love and concern that is. And this is 'to know God'.

To make this even clearer, he says: 'And hereby we know that we know him, if we keep his commandments' (I John 2.3-5). For 'John' 'knowledge' of the 'eternal Thou' is not a self-authenticating experience. It is only authentic when it takes the form of obedience. 'He that says, I know him, and does not keep his commandments, is a liar' (*ibid.*).[2] Unless John is using 'know God' in something very like its LXX sense, this is an untrue generalisation. John is in fact insisting that there is no relationship with God which does not consist in obedience. There is no possible relationship for 'know' to denote, apart from that of keeping the commandments. 'Knowing God' is still understood, formally, in the same way as in the Old Testament. It is obedience; it is, of course, an entirely new quality of obedience, it is obedient love of the children of God for each other; it is the obedience of those who are free, not slaves (John 8.31ff.); just

---

[1] Cf. I John 3.16; 4.7, 8.

[2] Bultmann, in *Gnosis*, is obviously right when he says there is a 'paradoxicality' between this contention of John that 'knowing' is only real in 'obeying' and the gnostic sense of 'know' which the writer seems to use. *But the writer uses the gnostic sense only to contradict it.* It is doubtful, however, whether this is a good pastoral or apologetic method; it is so very easily misunderstood. It is unnecessarily quixotic to fight for the integrity of words that are losing their virtue among your fellow-men. It is better to find some that are not yet ambiguous. Still John is certainly contradicting the gnostic use, and insisting that the OT one is the only proper one; he is not juggling with the two in his own thought. For 'He that says, I know him, and does not keep his commandments, is a liar' to be true, 'know' must *mean* 'obey'. If it means *anything else at all* (within the range of meanings γινώσκειν—*yada*'—know cover in the literature under discussion) then John's assertion cannot be true. Every other at all appropriate meaning that 'know', etc., can convey would allow 'I know even if I disobey' to be true.

as God in Christ has created an entirely new possibility of
obedience. It may seem rather strange that this writer, to all
appearance very 'religious', should 'reduce' Christian faith to
so mundane a level. But he does. And it will be my contention
later on that this is the only way that these terms can be made
'meaningful'. To repeat, I am not saying—the First Epistle is
not saying—that human love is self-sufficient and all that God
demands. It is God loving first, and sending his Son, that makes
real human love possible; God loving both elicits our love and
makes it real. But it is our love of the brethren that he empowers,
and this is the return of our love to him. This is to love and to
'know' God.

'Knowledge of the Father' (in the Gospel)

In the Gospel, this still seems to be the underlying meaning
of 'knowing' God, though admittedly the writer is here less
concerned to explain his terms, and just uses them and expects
to be understood. Jesus says to the Jews: 'It is my Father who
glorifies me, of whom you say that he is your God; and you have
not known him: but I know him . . . I know him and keep his
word' (John 8.54ff.). And the Jews, though they claim he is their
God, obviously do not 'know' him: they disobey. They do the
works of their real father; they do not 'know', obey, God as
Father (John 8.41). John is again allowing claims to a relationship with God to be made, and then insisting that obedience to
God is the only possible genuine and positive relationship with
him that can happen.

This appears again in the sequence considered above: 'I
know the Father; and *I lay down my life* for the sheep'; and later,
even more explicitly, 'Therefore does the Father love me,
because I lay down my life. . . . This commandment received I
from the Father.' There is the same close link of 'knowing God',
'love' and 'obedience' (here in the very concrete form of dying
for men) that we found in the First Epistle. And again, 'It is the
Father abiding in me who does his works' (John 14.10ff.).

When the Evangelist becomes that little more specific, and
tells what his words and ideas mean, he shows that in his view,
even for Jesus, 'knowing God' is real only in love and obedience.[1]
And love is love for 'the sheep'.

[1] Cf. John 5.30; 6.38; 7.18.

This obedient loving service of men, which God himself empowers, is then, *a fortiori*, for the 'ordinary disciple' the only possible, the highest possible, relationship with God. It is certainly a 'personal' relationship, in so far as God abiding in a man has a quite catastrophic 'personal' effect. But it is not a person-to-person relation with God. Nor is it a sequence, 'know God, and then love men', 'love men and so grow to love God'. In letting God abide in you, in letting his love empower yours for men, you are 'knowing' God; just as in keeping Jesus' commandments the disciples will be 'abiding in' Christ, 'knowing him', and so 'knowing the Father', and having the Father come and make his abode with them (John 14.17, 23ff., etc.). The Evangelist does not resolve the 'paradox of grace', he maintains both sides in tension: the obedient keeping of the commandments on the one hand, and the gracious abiding of Father and Son, and coming of the 'other Paraklete', on the other.

It remains to be seen if other instances of the use of 'knowing' words by the evangelist bear out this conclusion; and to see what part the Son, Jesus, plays in the producing of this 'knowing'; whether he is thought of as a 'revealer'.

'You worship that which you know not, we worship that which we know' (John 4.22): the impersonal neuter (ὃ οὐκ οἴδατε) may imply that it is 'factual' ignorance; but in the context of the discourse with the Samaritan woman as a whole, the strong overtone of 'obedience' that the word 'know' carries in the Old Testament may also be intended.

Because the world does not 'know' the Father, it will persecute the disciples (John 15.21; cf. 16.3; 17.25). 'Not knowing the Father' can, it seems, take no other form than hatred of the disciples. This is just the obverse of what is stated in the First Epistle (I John 3.16). 'You know God' is said three times in the First Epistle, to various groups of people (I John 2.12ff.); but it is explained by such phrases as 'You have overcome the evil one', 'You are strong, and the word of God abides in you'; and the abiding of the word of God, of course, means observable obedience (I John 2.3-6).

John twice uses the word γνωρίζειν (rare in the New Testament); once when Jesus says, 'I have made known to them your name, and will make it known, that the love wherewith you love me may be in them and I in them' (John 17.26). The abiding of the love in the later part of the sentence at once links it with the keeping of the commandments and love of the brethren that we have seen above to be the content, the entirely *observable* content, of 'abiding' and 'knowing'.

'Name' (ὄνομα) can be used just of the syllables, with which you address someone;[1] but even then it usually means that the user of the name has a certain personal relationship with the one addressed; a relationship of obedience, of friendship, or of authority. So, properly to use 'the name' of Christ or of the Father is to accept the relationship that they each both offer and demand. To make known the Father's name is thus to make possible that relationship—'that the love wherewith thou lovest me may be in them . . .'. But this means in fact that the 'name' of Christ or of the Father is very much more than the syllables used to address them; it means something more like the *power* of each.[2] So, Jesus prays 'Father, keep them in your name' (John 17.11), where 'powerful protection' or something of the sort seems to be the meaning. The 'name' of the Father is his active personal power. In the same way, when (in the same verse) Jesus says the Father has given the Son his own 'name', it seems to be another way of saying 'all things that are mine are yours, and yours are mine'. Again, the 'name' seems to have something of the sense of the 'glory' (John 17.10 and v. 5).

This does imply that Jesus in 'making known' the Father's 'name' has made possible a very close relationship with the Father, closer than is implied by the 'making known' of God's name in the Old Testament. But the terms of the relationship, the effect of the closeness implied in 'knowing his name' (and elsewhere, in 'abiding in' him, and he 'in' the disciples), do not seem to consist in a vivid awareness of the Father, person to person. It is not a 'making known' in that sense. It is a making felt his power, formally analogous with the way Yahweh's name is 'made known' in the Old Testament. John tells us what the effects of the closeness in the various ways in which he describes it are to be. 'Holy Father, keep them in your name, which you have given me, *that they may be one* even as we are . . . even as

[1] John 10.3, 'I call my sheep by name'; see above, p. 34ff.
[2] Cf. 5.43. This understanding of 'name' also makes more sense of 'asking in my name', 14.13, etc. Of course, primitive magical ideas lie behind all this. But the point is that for John just the incantation of the 'name' is not its powerful use.

you, Father, are in me and I in you, that they may also be in us . . . and the glory you have given me, I have given them; that they may be one, even as we are' (John 17.11, 21, 23). If John makes the aim of this closeness to God the unity of Christians, it seems unlikely that he means by 'abiding', etc., an awareness of God as a close friend; he could hardly ask for that as a means to human unity. It is more likely that he sees the abiding, etc., in a less sophisticated, more 'mythical' sense: God is present as an invisible person of whom you are aware only as he affects your relationships with the people visibly present with you. 'Making the name of the Father known' is making the disciples respond to the powerful love of the Father by becoming a unity together.

The Evangelist uses γνωρίζειν earlier, in chapter 15: the disciples are Jesus' friends, because he has 'made known to them all the things he heard from the Father' (John 15.15-16). These 'things' are then said to be 'the things commanded' (John 15.17); and the 'commandments', we have seen, are the (unspecified) working-out of the one 'commandment', to love. This is the same as the commandment Jesus himself received, to lay down his life, in love for the 'sheep' (John 10.18; cp. 15.13). John is never more precise than this; but he does specify this one particular act of obedience, presumably to show the very definite and practical quality of the obedience and response he expects (compare the demand in the First Epistle, to share the world's goods). To 'make known' the things of God, what God commands, is not by John's day primarily to make the terms of obedience known (this has already been done in Christian catechesis). It is to demand and make possible by the Son's and the Father's, or the Spirit's abiding, the love of men (John 14.23, 26).

There is no significant use of 'knowing' words in the Apocalypse.

Revealing

Having examined the use of 'knowing' words, we have again a background against which to understand any use of 'revealing' words. If it is 'knowledge of God' that is 'revealed', it will be in the sense outlined above.

General

Almost the first thing that meets you in the Gospel, at the end of the prologue, is the blunt statement, 'No man has seen God at any time' (John 1.18; and this is repeated in the First Epistle —I John 4.12), 'but the only begotten Son, which is in the bosom of the Father, he has declared him (ἐξηγήσατο).' And this seems at the outset to be a declaration that 'seeing' type language (of which 'reveal' is a part) is inappropriate; and that only 'making known' should be used; and this would of course be in the sense we have just determined. Ἐξηγοῦμαι is a technical term for declaring divine secrets; these in John can only be 'the commandments'; to 'declare the Father' means much the same as to 'make his name known', or to make 'these things known'.

The Evangelist does not in fact use 'reveal' of this declaring. He only once uses the word (ἀποκαλύπτειν) that can be strictly translated this way, and that is in a quotation from Isaiah (John 12.38): 'To whom has the arm of the Lord been revealed?' And he seems to understand this in the normal Old Testament sense. Who has seen God's work? The work of God is not specifically intended to 'reveal' his arm; his work is effective anyway. The prophet, and the Evangelist, are just both sorry, in their own ways, that God's powerful action has gone without notice and response. The only other instance, in the writings we are examining, of the use of a word of this sort is in the first words of the Apocalypse, Ἀποκάλυψις Ἰησοῦ Χριστοῦ (1.1); the book describes events that will happen, and the reality of heaven now. But it is not a 'revelation' of the Father or Jesus; the seer never 'meets' either. The setting is the heavenly court. The book does not use the word more than this once. 'Revelation' as such is not a Johannine word.

The other noun with a similar though not identical sense, ἐπιφάνεια, is absent too. Only verbal forms of it and other similar words are used. This is perhaps further evidence of the author's dislike of substantives.

In its normal sense of displaying for view something physical, δεικνύναι is used when the Lord displays his hands and his feet (John 20.20; cf. Luke 24.40, some texts). Compare also 'What sign do you shew?', the question asked by the Jerusalem authorities when Jesus has cleared the Temple (John 2.18).

Jesus says: 'The Father loves the Son, and shews him all the

things that he himself does; and greater works than these will
he shew him, that you may marvel' (John 5.20); and he goes
on to talk about Resurrection. This is (if the term must be used)
'revelation' of the mighty acts of God (not of God himself), in
this case to *the Son*. But it is like the shewing of a sign, demanded
above. So too Jesus says to those who want to stone him, 'Many
good works have I showed you from the Father' (John 10.32).

Past 'Seeing' of the Father and of Jesus

Philip says, 'κύριε, δεῖξον ἡμῖν τὸν πατέρα', 'Lord, show us
the Father' (John 14.8). Δεικνύναι has been used so far of
making physically visible, and it does not have quite the same
overtones as ἀποκαλύπτειν. None the less, this looks to be a
request to Jesus to 'reveal' God. The ensuing monologue is then
important for an understanding of the Johannine use of this sort
of word. Jesus says, 'Have I been so long with you, and do you
not know me, Philip? He who has seen me has seen the Father'
(ὁ ἑωρακὼς ἐμὲ ἑώρακεν τὸν πατέρα) (John 14.9).[1] That Jesus is
talking straightforwardly of physical seeing, at least of himself,
seems obvious; compare what he later says to Thomas, 'Because
you have seen me' (ἑώρακας again), 'you have believed; blessed
are those that have not seen (οἱ μὴ ἰδόντες), and yet have
believed' (John 20.29). The Son and the Father are so close a
unity (ἐγὼ καὶ ὁ πατὴρ ἕν ἐσμεν) (John 10.30) that when the
Son was physically visible, so was the Father. Anyone, then,
who had seen and 'known' Jesus would have realised that he
was seeing the Father as fully as that would ever be possible.
But Philip and the rest of the disciples did not 'know' Jesus,
and so had not 'in' him been able to see the Father: 'Have I
been so long with you, and you do not know me, Philip?' (John
14.9).[2] And now that Jesus has 'gone to the Father', 'seeing'
and 'revealing' words, with the possibility of person to person
awareness that they suggest are no longer appropriate: 'A little
while and you see me no more . . . (οὐκέτι θεωρεῖτέ με) because
I go to the Father' (John 16.16ff.; cf. vv. 28ff.). Then, except

---

[1] Cf. 12.45: ὁ θεωρῶν ἐμὲ θεωρεῖ τὸν πέμψαντά με (again, there is no important
graduation of meaning between θεωρεῖν and ὁρᾶν, either way).

[2] Even when Jesus has explained to his disciples at length his relation to the
Father and the Spirit, they still do not really believe; so he asks the rhetorical
question, 16.32: 'Do you now believe? Behold the hour comes, yes, is come, that
you shall be scattered.' This will show that in fact they have not believed or known
him.

for the further 'little while' of the appearances ('again a little while and you shall see me', ὄψεσθε), 'seeing' language becomes inapposite for an indefinite period; during the latter, faith-without-sight is the only way of 'knowing': 'Blessed are those who have not seen and yet have believed' (John 20.29).

The First Epistle certainly understands the seeing of Jesus in this way: 'That which was from the beginning, that which we have heard, that which we *have seen with our eyes* (ἑωράκαμεν, perfect tense) that which we beheld (ἐθεασάμεθα), and our hands have handled, concerning the Word of life (and the life was manifested and we have seen [ἐφανερώθη and ἑωράκαμεν] and bear witness . . .), that which we have seen and heard we declare unto you' (I John 1.1ff.). At one time the life was 'manifested', and 'we', in the person of the first followers,[1] 'saw', but now there is no more 'seeing'; God, Christ, God in Christ, do not 'stand revealed'. God was physically visible for a while (but that still does not mean that his 'self' was 'revealed') when Jesus was; but he is not now visible for us. Fairly obviously, in the sense of *physical visibility*, he is not 'revealed' for us. We look forward to 'seeing him', in the future: 'We know that *if he shall be manifested* (ἐὰν φανερωθῇ) we shall be like him; for we shall see him even as he is (ὀψόμεθα)' (I John 3.2). We shall look below at some possible instances of the author using 'seeing' words metaphorically of the present relation of the follower and Jesus or the Father. Up to now, 'seeing' language has been used quite literally, without suggesting any deeper 'revealing'.

The writer uses ὁρᾶν (and the other 'parts' that provide its future, aorist, etc.: ὄψομαι, εἶδον ὤφθην) quite frequently, and θεωρεῖν in much the same way,[2] and also θεᾶσθαι and βλέπειν. The words are used of ordinary physical seeing, and this hardly needs illustrating; but of course as we have already noticed it is often a physical seeing which has great 'theological' significance. The Baptist 'saw' (ἑώρακα) the dove (John 1.34; cf. 1.32, τεθέαμαι). The Galileans have 'seen' (ἑωρακότες) Jesus' signs (John 4.45); here there may be some contrast between the seeing and the refusal to believe; compare the blind man who is

[1] That the 'we' is the later Church, implying its solidarity with the first apostles, seems to be accepted by many commentators; see the article 'The Authority of the Fourth Gospel' in Hoskyns and Davey, *The Fourth Gospel*, p. 86ff.

[2] Cf. John 4.45; 6.2; 4.48; 11.42; where the verbs are both used of 'seeing' signs, without there being any difference in the depth of perception described.

healed at the pool Siloam (John 9.1ff.),[1] who sees and believes. When onlookers 'see' Jesus' signs being done, they should 'see' that God is doing his works. John does not suggest that they should 'see God'.

It is probably not significant that βλέπειν is not used with Jesus as object; it *is* used of the Son seeing what the Father does (John 5.19).

'Seeing' God as a Present Experience

The problem is, does John also use these 'seeing' words, at any rate on some occasions, of the relation of disciple and Jesus, or disciple and the Father, quite apart from physical seeing? Does he use 'seeing' words of the relationship of Jesus and the disciples after the Resurrection, and after the last Resurrection appearances? This would then be metaphorical, and might be a metaphor of 'revelation', in its modern sense, the 'making seen' of the Son or the Father to the 'minds' or 'souls' of Christians.

The 'glory' of God is to be 'seen' in the raising of Lazarus, and in the healing of the man born blind (John 11.40; 9.3; cf. 1.14; 2.11); in the latter narrative Jesus says: 'Neither did this man sin, nor his parents: but that the works of God should be manifest in him'; and this shows that the making visible of the 'glory' of 'works' of God is to be understood in the same way as the 'revealing of the arm of the Lord', John's quotation from Isaiah, mentioned above (John 12.38). God is most fully glorified in the death of Jesus on the Cross (John 12.23; 13.31, etc.). Jesus does not glorify the Father so that men can see the Father's glory, but just because the Father must be glorified. If men see the glory—and respond—then so much the better. And 'the glory' is still that which conceals God himself. God 'revealing' his glory is not God 'revealing his self'. John refers to Isaiah's vision. The Hebrew version has 'I saw *the Lord*'; the LXX, '*the glory* of the Lord'. And John quotes the LXX: 'Isaiah

---

[1] Most of the occasions on which βλέπειν is used in this Gospel are in this chapter; but it is used in a way very similar to ὁρᾶν, etc., above. Cf. 1.29, 38; 5.19, and the examples quoted p. 107, n. 2.

[2] In the 'biblical' use, the important point is the happening, the event; it 'happens' in the observable sphere of human history; this sort of event could not happen other than visibly, and its visibility is the guarantee of its reality. But it is only incidentally visible, for the sake of really happening; it does not happen for the sake of being made visible.

said this, because he saw his (Jesus!) *glory*' (John 12.41). If you
see 'the glory', you see that God is there (and active); but you
do not see God. You can infer the character and purpose, as
well as the presence of God, from the action; but the action is
not, at any rate primarily, performed for the sake even of the
inference.

The remaining instances demand a rather fuller treatment; at
least on first sight they fit less readily into the case being made here.

In the Feeding Discourse, Jesus says: 'It is the will of my
Father that everyone who beholds the Son of Man, and believes
in him, should have eternal life.' Then he asks, 'What then if
you should behold the Son of Man ascending where he was
before?' (θεωρῆτε) (ch. 6; esp. vv. 41ff.). Just prior to the
saying of Philip, 'Show us the Father', discussed above, the
Lord has said, 'If you had known me, you would have known
my Father also; from henceforth, you know him and have seen
him' (ἑωράκατε) (John 14.7). In the same chapter he says: 'The
world . . . beholds him (the Spirit) not, neither does it know
him; you know him, for he abides with you, and shall be in you'
(John 14.17). All these, and especially the last, may be intended
to suggest a metaphorical sense of 'beholding' (θεωρεῖν) or
'seeing'. Two verses on, Jesus says: 'Yet a little while, and the
world beholds me no more; but you behold me (present, continuous action); because I live, and you shall live also.'

Whether or not in the first part of each sentence, θεωρεῖν is
intended literally, John does seem to mean that the disciples (in
contrast with 'the world') *are* to have some continuing relationship (presumably non-visual, see above) with the Spirit and
with Jesus, a relationship that can nonetheless, implicitly, or
in the latter case explicitly, best be expressed in a visual metaphor. How then does he use this metaphor? Would, for instance,
'I shall be revealed to you' be a proper paraphrase? The way
John is using the metaphor is probably explained a few verses
later on still. Jesus says: 'He that has my commandments, and
keeps them, he it is that loves me: and he that loves me shall
be loved by my Father, and I will love him, and will manifest
myself to him. Judas (not Iscariot) says to him, "Lord, what is
come to pass that you will manifest (ἐμφανίζειν both times; not
elsewhere in John) yourself to us and not to the world?"' Jesus'
answer to this is: 'If a man love me, he will keep my word; and

my Father will love him, and we will come to him and make
our abode with him. He that loves me not, does not keep my
words. . . .' This is how Jesus is 'manifested'; so, presumably,
this is how the disciples 'behold' him (and the Spirit?—it is
difficult to talk of 'beholding' the Spirit, having the Spirit
('revealed', anyway). We 'behold' Jesus, he is 'manifested', in his
and the Father's abiding in us.[1] In the First Epistle, at any rate,
we found that the form and manner of the abiding was the new
possibility of love of the brethren. Again, John is not suggesting
we love first, and then God loves us and so abides in us (this is
explicitly denied at I John 4.10[2]): compare 'Even as the Father
has loved me, I also have loved you; abide in my love. If you
keep my commandments, you shall abide in my love' (John
15.9f.). If John can alternate between the priority of our love
and the priority of the love of the Father and the Son, it seems
that he is saying here (what is said more clearly in the First
Epistle) that the keeping of the commandments *is* the abiding of
the Father and the Son.[3] The Son is manifested to us in the
abiding, in our keeping of the commandments. When he abides
in us, we can keep the commandments, we can love the brethren.
In our love of the brethren he is manifested to us; his abiding
becomes real, appreciable. And this is why John can make the
abiding both the pre-condition and the result of keeping the
commands. This being so, 'beholding' and 'manifesting himself'
are both radically re-interpreted (and, of course, have little of
their original meaning left: this is not necessarily the best way
to treat words). When John explains his words in these ways, he
is leaving no room for any 'awareness of God', any 'revealing of
God', other than in men's love for each other.

The next instances are in chapter 16. There is a constant
repetition of 'A little while and you behold me no more ($\theta\varepsilon\omega$-
$\varrho\varepsilon\tilde{\iota}\tau\varepsilon$); and again a little while, and you shall see me ($\check{o}\psi\varepsilon\sigma\theta\varepsilon$)'
(John 16.16ff.).[4] The question is, does John intend an (un-
balanced) contrast between temporary physical invisibility and
a subsequent non-physical 'seeing'? Or does this refer solely to

---

[1] However, see further, below.
[2] Cf. especially John 15.16.
[3] Above, p. 102ff.
[4] See above, p. 106. (At John 15.24, ' . . . but now have they both seen and
hated both me and my Father', 'seen' probably governs the antecedent 'the works';
cf. Barrett, *The Gospel according to St John*, S.P.C.K., 1958, *ad loc.*)

the physical seeing in the post-Resurrection appearances? C. K.
Barrett (*ad loc.*) suggests that the future ὄψεσθε (used in Mark
only of the seeing of the Son of Man on the clouds) is used here
to suggest that the Parousia will have happened for the disciples.
(This would then also explain how they could 'behold him'
while the world could not.[1]) However, John himself does not
reserve this verb for eschatology: he uses θεωρεῖν in an eschatological saying: 'What if you should behold the Son of Man
ascending where he was before?' (John 6.62). He uses the
present tense of the same verb ὁρᾶν of Thomas seeing the Risen
Lord (John 20.29; cf. vv. 18 and 25), where quite ordinary
seeing is intended. And it is used twice more in the same chapter,
in this way. Θεωρεῖν is used in the same chapter of seeing the
linen cloths, the angels, and the Lord (John 20.6, 12, 14).
'Ορᾶν (εἶδον) is used again, of seeing the contents of the tomb,
the Lord, the Lord's hands and the place where his side was
wounded (John 20.8, 25, 27, 29). This being so, it is probable
that for John these promises that the disciples will 'see' the Lord
were fulfilled quite literally in the Resurrection appearances.
The saying to Thomas, 'Blessed are they who have not seen,
and yet have believed', does not suggest that for John 'seeing'
was a metaphor, normally to be used of the later relationship of
the disciples and their Lord who was no longer physically
with them.

After the 'a little while and you shall see me no more; and
again a little while, and you shall see me', Jesus goes on to say:
'You shall be sorrowful, but your sorrow shall be turned to
joy. . . . And you therefore now have sorrow; but I will see you
again and your heart will rejoice (πάλιν δὲ ὄψομαι ὑμᾶς καὶ
χαρήσετα ὑμῶν ἡ καρδία), and your joy no one takes away from
you' (John 16.20ff.). This is echoed in: 'The disciples therefore
were glad, when they saw the Lord' (ἐχάρησαν οὖν οἱ μαθηταὶ
ἰδόντες τὸν κύριον) (John 20.20). Again, the Resurrection
appearances fulfil the promise. And in chapter 16, Jesus says
that the Paraklete will convict the world 'of righteousness,
because I go to the Father, and you behold me no more'
(οὐκέτι θεωρεῖτέ με) (John 16.10). This may of course mean
that the exegesis offered for 14.17ff. ('seeing' and 'beholding' =
'abiding', 'obeying') was too complex. John may have meant

[1] Mark 14.62, etc.; John 14.21-3.

no more than in these other passages. The fact is that he there
does talk of a continuous 'beholding' and does describe the
constant abiding as a 'manifesting'. '*In a sense*', he is saying,
'Jesus will be obviously around, you will be able to "behold"
him.' But he makes clear what this sense is—it is the abiding.
It is further possible, though somewhat less likely, that John is
then using 'behold', 'see', in a double sense in chapter 16 also.
He does use other words to mean two things at once (e.g.
ὑψοῦν, 3.14; 8.28; 12.32 and 34). He may be referring both to
the appearance-manifesting and to the abiding-manifesting.
But he never gives any explicit hint in these later passages that
this is his intention, no hint, that is, comparable to that offered
in chapter 14. In neither case, of course, is he talking of a
'revealing' of God.

We have to conclude that in the majority of cases John means
most of these promises of 'seeing' in the future quite literally of
the short period when, he believed, the risen Lord was from
time to time physically visible to the disciples. The Greek desire
to 'see God' (which Barrett refers to) was fulfilled for the first
disciples only. Thomas could 'see' his 'Lord and God' (John
20.24ff.). For those who come after, the closest possible relationship is by believing. In the lifetime of the Lord, the disciples
could have physically seen and believed and known God, but
did not.[1] In the period of the Resurrection appearances (according to John) the disciples *did* see and believe God; but now,
until 'he shall be manifested' (I John 3.2), there is no 'revelation' for us, even in this sense. What we have is the abiding of
the Father and the Son, the abiding of the Spirit: and this is in
fact better! (John 16.7). It is the only sort of 'manifesting' of
the Father, Jesus, or the Spirit that happens at the time the
Evangelist writes.[2] It is not 'revelation'.

There is nothing of theological importance in the Fourth
Gospel that explicitly demands a term like 'revelation', at least
in any of the modern senses that we examined in the first
chapter. The words that could be used in the latter sorts of way
are here used still quite literally, of straightforward 'seeing'.

---

[1] Above, p. 106ff.
[2] I have to admit that while this seems to offer the best account of by far the
greater part of the material we have considered here, I am still not really sure of
the sequence 14.6ff. But that is the only one that really seems to object at all to my
treatment, and it is very obscure.

There might be an exception to this in the First and Third Epistles: 'Whosoever abides in him (God) does not sin; whosoever sins has not seen him, neither knows him'; and, 'He that does evil has not seen God' (I John 3.6; III John 11). This could imply that the obverse was possible and John's normal use of parallelism would suggest it; those who do not sin, and do abide, *have* seen and *have* known God. However, even understood this way, these two pronouncements seem only to reinforce what we have seen already of John's understanding of the relation of the disciple and God. 'Seeing God' is no independent self-authenticating vision (or 'meeting'). It consists of 'not sinning', or of 'abiding', which, as we have seen, also means keeping the 'commandments', loving. This is said even more clearly in the second part of the saying in I John, and in the one in III John. Yet, if you have 'seen' or 'encountered' someone, you *have*, and nothing else you do can alter the fact. Only if the 'not sinning' is the *same event* as the 'seeing', is it possible to say 'whoever sins has not seen him'. John is saying again, 'There can be no relationship with God (seeing, knowing, or any other), save one that takes the form of obedience.' However, it is doubtful whether in this case a strict antithetical parallelism is intended; John is probably denying the mystic claim of some opponents, without implying that the sinless man could be said to have 'seen God'. He has just said, '*If* he shall be manifested, . . . we *shall* see him even as he is'; and he says, twice, explicitly, 'No man has beheld God at any time' (οὐδεὶς ἑώρακεν) (John 1.18; I John 4.12), and 'he who does not love his brother, whom he has seen, how can he love God, whom he has not seen' (ἑώρακεν, the verb used above) (I John 4.20).

Appended Notes There are a few more passages where 'manifest'-type words are used, and two related 'themes', that need to be noticed. They do not materially affect the foregoing conclusions, and would only have further complicated the train of the argument; but they need to be included for completeness' sake.

There are some uses of φανεροῦσθαι that we have not yet noted; they seem quite unmistakably to be referring to the past or future actual physical visibility of Jesus. John the Baptist says, 'I knew him not, but that he should be manifested to Israel' (John 1.31). Jesus' brothers complain of his staying hidden: 'Manifest yourself to the world' (John 7.4). Jesus 'manifests' himself to the disciples at the sea of Tiberias (John 21.1); this was the third time he 'was manifested to them'. We have already noted the beginning of the First Epistle '. . . we beheld, and our hands handled . . . (and the life was manifested, and we have seen . . .)'. So the writer says later on, 'He was manifested to take away sins. . . . To this end was the Son of God manifested, that he might destroy the works of the devil.' He lived, physically visible, to effect God's purpose. He is not 'manifest' in any other sense than that (I John 1.1ff.; 3.8).

We have already noted the use of the verb of God at the end time (I John 3.2); it is used a little earlier, presumably also of God, 'Abide in him, that if he shall be manifested, we may have boldness . . .' (I John 2.28).

Revelation 22.4 (καὶ ὄψονται τὸ πρόσωπον αὐτοῦ) promises for the future perhaps a more intimate relationship with God than the seer has himself had in his visions of the abyss and heaven and heaven's court (cf. 21.3, 7).

Φανεροῦν is used once, in the dynamic sense of 'show', rather than 'put on view'—'Herein was the love of God shown us: God sent his only begotten Son into the world, that we might live through him' (I John 4.9).

The Apocalypse prefers δεικνύναι to describe what happens to the seer, 'I heard a voice as of a trumpet speaking with me, one saying: 'Come up hither, and I will show you the things which must come to pass hereafter' (Rev. 4.1, *et passim*—eight times). Φανεροῦν is used twice, of disclosing nakedness (Rev. 3.18); and after most of the plagues of judgment have been poured out, the victors over the beast praise God, because his righteous acts are now 'manifest' (Rev. 15.4).

'Enlightenment' and 'the Word'

There are two more terms that we need to examine in this literature. These are 'illumination' (the 'shedding of light') and 'the Logos'.[1]

'The light shines in the darkness, and the darkness does not overcome it (οὐ κατέλαβεν)', did not comprehend it (John 1.5). This is taken up a few lines later in the prologue with 'That was

---

[1] Cf. NEB for II Cor. 4.6, 'the light of revelation', and Oepke, *TWNT* III, pp. 591-2, quoted below.

the true light, which shines on every man, coming into the world' (John 1.9).[1] But the light is not one which, as it were, shines on the mystery of the Godhead; it is never at any rate said in John that the coming of the light 'reveals' God in any way. The light that shines, shines on *men* to 'reveal' them, to show up their works for what they are. 'And this is the judgment, that the light is come into the world, and men loved the darkness rather than the light, for their works were evil. For every one that does ill hates the light, and does not come to the light, lest his works should be reproved. But he that does the truth cometh to the light, *that his works may be manifest* (φανερωθῇ) that they have been wrought in God' (John 3. 19-21).[2]

Christ has come so that men may not walk in darkness—do the works of darkness (I John 1.6; 2.9; John 12.46; 8.12 again). In our own rather dull language of morality we might say that Christ and his teaching are a standard by which our actions are judged. John means more than that. The light is to do with men's conduct rather than with 'revelation of God'. But God is light (I John 1.5), and when the doer of truth comes to the light for his works to be manifest, it will be seen that 'they are wrought in God' (τὰ ἔργα . . . ἐν Θεῷ ἐστιν εἰργασμένα) (John 3.21). If a man walks in light, it does not just mean that he has accepted Jesus' teaching (it includes that, but John does not give us much of Jesus' ethical teaching) nor does it mean that he has 'accepted revelation'. It means that God has entered his life, is loving through him by abiding in him; and so, the man is walking in light; his works (whether he knows it or not?) are being done 'in God'. 'God is light . . . the darkness is passing away and the true light is already shining. He who says he is in the light and hates his brother, is in the darkness right up to this moment. A man loving his brother is abiding in the light (ὁ ἀγαπῶν τὸν ἀδελφὸν αὐτοῦ ἐν τῷ φωτὶ μένει)' (I John 1.5; 2.8ff.).

---

[1] NEB adopts this punctuation; cf. 8.12; 12.46.

[2] Cf. 12.46: 'I am come a light into the world, that whosoever believes in me may not abide in darkness. . . . I came not to judge the world, but to save the world. He that rejects me has one that judges him; the word that I spoke, that shall judge him on the last day.' Cf. also, again 8.12; and 9.39: 'For judgment I came into the world.' These are not contradictory (see Barrett, *op. cit.*, *ad loc.*); the 'light' is discriminatory: some accept salvation, some refuse. The latter is judgment. (In much the same way, 'light' in the Old Testament, light from God, illuminates men's 'paths', or is God's blessing to them, or both; but does not shine on God. It shines 'from', not 'to'—Psalms, *passim.*)

John does not say how the 'abiding' works, how a man is 'of the light', how he does his deeds 'in God'. He just believes that this does happen, in connection with the coming of the light, and the confession of Jesus come in the flesh.

The 'shining' of the light is Jesus' coming into the world, his being made 'manifest': 'I am come a light into the world, that whosoever believes on me may not abide in darkness' (John 12.46). The coming of the light, its abiding in men, makes love possible. It also lets men see themselves much more clearly. Am I for God or against him? This is judgment. Either when Jesus is physically there, or when the Spirit is there in the disciples (John 16.7ff.), men are driven to decide whether to be in the light, and so to love; or to be in the darkness, the negation of love and life. But it is a light which shines on men, rather than one which lights up—'reveals'—God.

Much the same must be said of 'the Word'. Its use as a title for Jesus in the Fourth Gospel (1.1, 14; cf. Rev. 19.13) may seem to imply 'revelation'; but a closer examination would suggest that this is not so. To be sure, Oepke explains that 'in so far as it (Johannine theology) transfers the Logos concept to Jesus it brings Christianity's absolute claim to revelation to its most comprehensive expression'.[1] Barrett notes[2] that in ordinary Greek λόγος could mean both inward thought and its outward (communicated, comprehensible) expression. It could (but did not have to) convey an idea of actual 'revealing'.

The commentaries debate at length the question of the proportions of Greek and Old Testament thought that lie behind the Johannine use of the term, and this is no place even to summarise the arguments. But however much Stoic (or Platonic-Stoic) thought may have influenced the Evangelist in particular, one thing is clear, and we have already noted it in looking at 'enlightenment'. 'The Word' that is 'the light' is not the universal 'light of reason', enabling men to understand truth. It is the light that Jesus came as, the light that judges those who refuse to 'do' the truth (1.9; 12.46; 3.16-21). The Word is not the light of a 'general revelation'.

However, 'the Word' has come to some who believed, and

---

[1] *Op. cit.*, pp. 591-2, noticed above, p. 114; see also Barth, *Against the Stream*, p. 214; Barrett, *op. cit.*, p. 61.
[2] *Op. cit.*, p. 127.

received him (1.11-12). It still might be that he had come to
be the expressed mind of God for them to apprehend. There is
no explicit explanation of the term in the body of the Gospel; in
fact 'the Word' is not of course used. But Jesus is 'the Truth'
(14.6), and the Truth is the Word of God' (17.17), and the
word of God is spoken in the words of Jesus, or acted in his
deeds (14.24, see 14.10). Jesus by his teaching and his total
activity makes known the words of God. The words of Jesus
that are the words of the Father are, as we have already seen,
commands, summed up in the command to love. John does not
use the word 'reveal' (save once in a quotation, as noted). But if
the term is very precious, it would be pedantry to refuse to allow
it to be said that Jesus, for John, 'reveals' the demand of God.
We have already discussed this. It is not the same as 'revealing
God'.

In the prologue itself it is the creative function of the Word
that is to the fore, as in the few Old Testament instances where
'the word of God' is mentioned (Gen. 1.3; Ps. 33.6, 9; Isa.
55.10-11) and in the rather more prominent descriptions of the
similar extension of Yahweh, his Wisdom (Prov. 8, Ecclus 24,
Wisdom 7). It is more nearly analogous to the human word that
magically achieves its purpose quite apart from any understanding ('Open, Sesame'), than to the human word that con-
veys information, or enables 'revealing encounter' between
persons.

Jesus is 'the Word of God' as the creative act of divine love,
making obedient love of men and God possible for us. But he
does not, at least not yet, 'reveal God'.

What the writer seems to be doing with both λόγος and φῶς
is taking terms from conventional religious language (gnostic,
philosophic, biblical), and insisting that they are only meaningful in terms of the ethical behaviour that is demanded of (and)
in his view, only possible for) a Christian.

This is, of course, part of his over-all programme, which is to
show that the events of the life, death and resurrection of Jesus
are not just odd, past, ambiguous happenings, no longer of any
importance. They created the possibility of Christian life; and
thinking about them in the correct way is part of the coming to
a fuller understanding of that life, and so to a fuller response in
love to man and God.

Conclusion

The Evangelist quite frequently uses 'seeing' and 'revealing' words, but he uses them mostly literally of the physical visibility of the man Jesus, who was the Word become flesh. His obedient love in life and death makes our obedient love of the brethren possible. This is 'knowledge of God'. There is no other 'knowledge' or 'revelation' for us.

IV. THE DEUTERO-PAULINES, ETC.

Knowing

In Hebrews γινώσκειν occurs only once in a relevant context (Heb. 8.11), in quoting Jeremiah on the 'New Covenant', and the passage is quoted more for its reference to forgiveness than for anything else. The Pastoral Epistles are rather chary about γνῶσις, perhaps for the same sort of reason as John is; there is talk of τῆς ψευδωνύμου γνώσεως (I Tim. 6.20). They use ἐπίγνωσις more readily, the knowing of something more specifically. God wills 'that all men should be saved, and come to the knowledge of the truth'. This makes the 'facts' of the faith ('there is one God, one mediator between God and men, the man, Christ Jesus . . .', etc.—I Tim. 2.4ff.) sound rather like the content of a Christian 'gnosis'. But in II Timothy, 'coming to the knowledge of the truth' is paralleled by being taken 'captive to the will of God' (II Tim. 2.25f.). The 'silly women' are ever learning, never able to come to the 'knowledge of the truth'; 'Timothy', on the other hand, did follow my 'teaching, conduct, purpose, faith, longsuffering . . .' (II Tim. 3.7, 10). In Titus the writer dismisses the 'gnostic' claim, 'I know God', with the Hebraic refutation: 'They profess that they know God; but by their works they deny him, being abominable, and disobedient, and unto every good work reprobate' (Titus 1.16). It is a very sober 'gnosis' (cf. Titus 2.11ff.).

II Peter uses γνῶσις in a conventional rounding off to the work (II Peter 3.18), but there is little in the context to show what it means. But earlier the writer uses it in an ethical sorites 'faith . . . virtue . . . knowledge . . . self-control . . . brotherly affection . . . love' (II Peter 1.5-6). In this stylistic play the words are not necessarily in a logically ascending scale; but neither are they part of an intelligence test for spotting 'the stranger'. 'Knowledge' is, then, presumably again, 'knowing-obeying' ('the will of God'). The writer then goes on to use ἐπίγνωσις: these ethical attainments will make their possessor 'not idle nor unfruitful unto the knowledge of our Lord Jesus Christ' (II Peter 1.8). Admittedly, 'knowing' words are used in some profusion, in the opening of the 'letter' (II Peter 1.2-3, etc.) and this may be due to 'gnostic' influence; compare the θείας κοινωνοὶ φύσεως and τῆς ἐν τω κόσμῳ . . . φθορᾶς (II Peter 1.4), and the world-renouncing section 'escaping the defilements of the world through the knowledge of the Lord and Saviour, Jesus Christ' (II Peter 2.18ff.). But the writer parallels this 'knowing' with the 'knowing' (ἐπίγνωσις) of the way of righteousness' and of 'the holy commandments'. Salvation may be in terms of 'knowledge'; but it is still the severely ethical and practical 'knowing' of the earlier Christian and Old Testament teaching. 'The way to perfection' would be expected from a Christian gnostic, rather than 'the way of righteousness'. The writer accepts some beliefs that are fundamentally opposed to the main stream of Christian faith, but at this point he seems to be defending a traditional understanding with the use of his opponents' terminology.

Revealing

Again, broadly speaking, the usage we found in Paul prevails. 'Revelation of Christ' is part of the myth of the end time; he will 'appear', as visible as he was before in Palestine. Also God has made various important pieces of information 'known'. And the words can be used quite generally in ordinary narrative.[1]

Hebrews uses δεικνύναι (Heb. 6.10) in the way we have frequently met: 'God is not unrighteous to forget your work and the love which you showed toward his name in that you ministered to the saints, and still do minister.'

The same use is met in the Pastorals: 'Alexander the copper-smith showed (RV, "did"!) me much evil.' So 'showing fidelity' means 'acting faithfully', 'shewing meekness' means 'acting' meekly' (II Tim. 4.14; Titus 2.10; 3.2). And when the author

---

[1] I suggested above, p. 88, that 'The Great Thanksgiving'—Matt. 11.25ff. ‖ Luke 10.21ff.—might better be placed in this section than with the rest of the synoptic material.

makes Paul say: '. . . for this cause I obtained mercy, that in me as chief might Christ Jesus show forth all his longsuffering, for an example for them which should hereafter believe on him to eternal life', presumably what he means is 'that Christ might be openly merciful to me'. If the idea of Christ seeking to 'disclose' himself comes into the passage at all, it is at several removes; 'Paul' is the example who is seen (I Tim. 1.16).

As in the Johannine writings, there is a warning against thinking of God 'revealing' himself, quite explicitly: 'whom no man has seen nor can see' (I Tim. 6.16).

The 'man of God' is charged to hold the commandment without spot, etc., *'until* the appearing (ἐπιφάνεια) of our Lord Jesus Christ' (I Tim. 6.14). This God will 'show' (δείξει). Ἐπιφάνεια is used the same way elsewhere; for instance in Titus: 'Looking for the blessed hope and appearing of the glory of our great God and Saviour, Jesus Christ' (Titus 2.13; cf. II Tim. 4.1).

However, these terms are also used of the past. God 'manifested his word in the message wherewith I was entrusted' (Titus 1.3). This is God letting his purpose be known. This 'manifesting' (ἐφανέρωσεν) is not the work of Christ (though of course, the 'word' is about Christ). It is similar to the Pauline 'revealing of the mystery'.

'The grace of God has appeared, bringing salvation to all men, instructing us . . . that we should live soberly and righteously and godly in this present world' (Titus 2.11f.). The 'appearing of the grace' happens in the events of the 'appearing of our saviour, Jesus Christ' (II Tim. 1.9-10). It is possible that 'grace', personified in Titus ch. 2 as a teacher (ἡ χάρις . . . παιδεύουσα ἡμᾶς), actually is Christ; but the rather odd personification may only be incidental. A passage later in the letter suggests that only a literary personification of an attribute of God is intended: 'When the kindness (χρηστότης) of God our Saviour and his love appeared . . . he saved us . . .' (Titus 3.4).

However, 'epiphany' is used frequently by this writer to describe aspects of the central Christian events. He *may* be implying that God's gracious and kindly character is 'revealed' in Christ. But it seems more likely that he is saying that God's grace and kindness become 'available', rather than that God himself is 'revealed'. The writer also says: 'God . . . saved us . . . according to his own purpose and grace, which was given (δοθεῖσαν) us in Christ Jesus before times eternal, but now has been manifested (φανερωθεῖσαν) by the appearing (διὰ τῆς ἐπιφανείας) of our Saviour, Jesus Christ.' The grace was given from all eternity, but has now become available, accessible, through the epiphany of Jesus Christ. He 'abolished death, and brought life and incorruption to light, through the gospel whereunto I was appointed preacher' (II Tim. 1.9ff.). This 'grace' that already belongs to us is the possibility of 'life and incorruption', and Christ makes them available by 'revealing them', bringing them to light (φωτίσαντος). In his theophany, Christ 'reveals' the secrets that the gnostic-minded man was hoping to discover, or falsely thought he knew. That the central Christian events are seen in terms that are at least formally gnostic is further suggested by the hymn in I Timothy (τὸ τῆς εὐσεβείας μυστήριον): ⟞

> He who was manifested (ἐφανερώθη) in the flesh,
> was justified in the spirit,
> seen of angels,
> preached among the gentiles,
> believed on in the world,
> received up in glory (I Tim. 3.16).

The writer worships in a gnostic atmosphere (though strongly opposed to 'heretical' gnostics) and the hymn to the Spirit-Christ hero-god who made a theophany in flesh comes immediately to his mind. It is the 'appearing' that is being wondered at; there is no notion of conquest, or of redemption. But it must still be remembered that this writer's was a very sober 'gnosis' of obedience (if uninspired obedience) to God. 'For the grace of God has appeared, bringing salvation to all men, instructing us to the intent that, denying ungodliness and worldly lusts, we should live soberly and righteously and godly in this present world.' This is the gnosis, and the way of salvation! (Titus 2.11ff.).[1]

The writer to the Hebrews uses ἐμφανίζειν once in a 'normal' context, 'they that say such things make it plain that . . .' (Heb. 11.14). Earlier he uses it to speak of Christ coming before God in the 'once-for-good' atonement ritual, and in the same context

---

[1] It is interesting that if Christ's work is not seen as 'revealing', early Christianity look much less gnostic than is suggested by e.g. A. E. J. Rawlinson, quoted in W. D. Davies, *Paul and Rabbinic Judaism*, SPCK, 1955, p. 199; J. N. D. Kelly, *Early Christian Doctrines*, A. and C. Black, 1958, p. 27; R. Bultmann, *Primitive Christianity* . . . , Fontana, 1960, p. 235.

uses φανεροῦσθαι and then ὄψεσθαι in the same way: 'Christ entered . . . into heaven itself, now to appear before the face of God for us . . . now at the end of the ages has he been manifested to put away sin by the sacrifice of himself.' This manifesting took place in heaven; and here too, probably, 'Christ also . . . shall appear (ὀφθήσεται) a second time, apart from sin, to them that wait for him for salvation' (Heb. 9. 24, 26, 28). The picture is a little confusing, but he seems to be going to appear to those waiting 'outside' the heavenly sanctuary, as the Jerusalem High Priest did, for a second time, to show them that the atonement has been effected (Lev. ch. 16, esp. v. 17). This is still a literal use of the terms in a myth-picture of the world's atonement. He also looks forward to a future 'seeing' of God, probably in a court setting (12.14; cf. vv. 22ff.).

There is no 'revealing' of God now; Christ is only 'revealed' in terms of the myth.

I Peter uses φανεροῦσθαι of the lamb, foreknown before the founding of the world, but 'manifested at the end of time for your sakes' (I Peter 1.20). But the manifesting is here subordinate to the redeeming through his precious blood. It means the coming as a person, physically visible. The same verb is used again of the future 'appearing' for judgment of the Chief Shepherd (I Peter 5.4).

V. CONCLUSIONS

G. S. Hendry says that for the Bible 'God reveals himself, and we are dependent on his revelation of himself for all our knowledge of God'.[1] According to W. Manson, a 'conception of the revelation of God in Jesus "lay" at the simplest level of Christian preaching'.[2] J. M. Robinson writes of 'the primitive Church's conviction that their *kerygma* was not merely their Spirit-led reply to God's revelation in Jesus, but rather the heavenly Lord's revelation of himself'.[3] We quoted these and many more instances in the first chapter.

In contrast, our survey of the background in the Old Testament and further afield made such claims as these seem unlikely, and our examination of the New Testament literature itself has

[1] Article 'Revelation' in *ThWB*.
[2] W. Manson, *Jesus the Messiah*, Hodder and Stoughton, 1943, p. 56.
[3] J. M. Robinson, *A New Quest of the Historical Jesus*, SCM Press, 1959, p. 106, n. (3).

shown that its writers never clearly and explicitly say that 'God reveals himself (in Christ)', or that 'God has revealed himself'.[1] There are quite a few suggestions that we depend on God for our obedience to God (our 'knowledge of him'), our 'free obedience' as sons, not slaves (Luke 11.2; Gal. 3-4; Rom. 8; Heb. 2-3; John 8; Matt. 21.28ff.). But this is not 'knowledge of God himself'; nor do we depend for this knowledge-obedience on any 'self-revealing' by God.[2]

It is more or less assumed that we know the broad outline terms of this obedience. (The Pastorals seem to suggest that the 'revealing' of the terms of obedience *are* the central gracious act of God.) It is supposed, more obviously in Paul and John than in the other writers, that the death and resurrection of Christ and the coming of the Spirit make this obedience possible, one way or another. It is possible now to obey God (in gratitude and in his strength) in the actual situations in which we find ourselves. In this sense only is it possible to 'know' him, now.

Christ is expected to be 'revealed' in the future, as he was for a time in the past. This means, as it did then, becoming physically visible; as visible as he was in Palestine.

There are a few signs, again mainly in John and Paul, of a hope that ultimately 'God' or 'the Son of God' may be 'seen as he is', met 'face to face'.[3]

'Revelation', in any of its modern theological uses, as a major term (or even the sole adequate term) with which to convey the purpose of the life, death, resurrection of Jesus, does not occur in the New Testament.

But it is unsatisfactory to leave the New Testament evidence with just these negative conclusions. If the earliest Christians did not see God's purpose in Christ as the 'revealing of himself', how did they see it? A full answer would need a 'New Testament Theology'; and as that is provided by a number of writers already, there is fortunately no need to attempt it here. The evidence is offered in a variety of schemes that makes it easy to

[1] Only the 'Thanksgiving' in the Matthean form may be an exception; only there and in the Pastorals have we found Jesus presented at all as a 'revealer', and in the latter it is of the demands of God rather than God himself.

[2] It is interesting to compare these conclusions with the not dissimilar ones of A. R. George, *Communion with God in the New Testament*, Epworth Press, 1953; especially his treatment of 'vision' and 'knowledge'. His term κοινωνία is much more useful in quotation or as exegesis.

[3] I John 3.2; I Cor. 13.12; cf. Matt. 5.8; Heb. 12.14; Rev. 4.1ff.; but these latter are probably to be understood in a less intimate sense, more in terms of the courtier and the sovereign. Rev. 22.4 may be more 'personal'.

survey, even when the reader might find it necessary to disagree with details (or more) of interpretation.

It is perhaps enough to mention a few of the words which the present writer sees as proper keys to New Testament interpretation: not so much the words themselves as the contexts in which they are used. 'The (Holy) Spirit', 'Spirit of God', 'Spirit of Christ'; 'sanctification' and 'the saints'; 'the body of Christ', 'the Church', 'the people (of God)'; 'sons (or children) of God' and 'adoption'; 'peace', 'grace', 'reconciliation', 'forgiveness', 'rightwising' ('justification'); 'call' and 'calling'; 'save' and 'salvation'; 'redeem' and 'redemption'; 'lord' (Christ); and pre-eminently 'love'. It is in terms like these that the earliest Christians tried to understand the activity of God in Christ.[1]

As we have clearly seen, none of the canonical writers who use these terms *explicitly* presupposes God's 'revelation of himself'. Nor is such a 'revelation' even necessarily *implicit* in any of these descriptions of what God *is* believed to have done. It is quite possible to be an enigmatic de Gaulle, and still make for yourself a people; it is only normal to be father to a child long before the child knows you well, if he ever does; you rarely find you 'know' a friend's character until you have accepted his friendship, and enjoyed it for a good many years. These (and other) paradigms from ordinary human life are used to describe what God has already done and still does. But he has not yet 'revealed himself' and this was not his intention.

'Revelation' is used by contemporary theologians to talk of God's completed 'act' in Christ.[2] The New Testament talks rather in the terms we have listed above (and more) of what God has done and is doing. What he has done and is doing is to prepare a people who may learn to love, be brought to conform to the image of his Son; and only then may God (Father or Son)—some say—be 'revealed'. Only 'then' will perception of God be made so clear that we would be justified in calling it 'revelation of God himself'. Already we are 'redeemed', 'accepted', 'made holy'. This is as sure and complete as the Cross and Resurrection and presence of the Spirit. It is final. But 'revelation' cannot yet be said to be complete; it is barely

[1] See the table at the back of the book.
[2] See chapter 7.

begun; it is, we may believe, the ultimate but still very incomplete aim of what God has already done, and still does.

The words in which the New Testament writers choose to talk of what God has done in Christ have the disadvantage from many points of view of being undisguisably 'mythological'. A related but not quite identical criticism might be that they do not answer many of the questions that modern theologians would like them to. They do not talk about how to 'know God'; or how to 'meet him' in 'existential encounter'. This is perhaps why the very tiniest (and in fact irrelevant) seeming hints of a different vocabulary are so eagerly seized on. It seems much easier, superficially, to make good in some way a claim that Christians have a special 'knowledge', than a claim that they have been 'redeemed', 'saved'. Saved? What from, what for? Where's the difference? It seems easy to destroy a claim to 'salvation'. It seems much harder to show that a man has not the 'knowledge' he claims, and it is tempting to grasp what seems to be the more readily defensible position.

But I still think that much of the language the New Testament writers in fact use does make sense. It can only make sense (but it *does* make sense) where people find themselves in a community of those who do love; love and serve each other, and the world. Then it, too, is fully defensible.

'Revelation of God' and 'salvation by God' are both 'myth' (the first only a little less obviously so)—but the myth of 'salvation' makes sense where the myth of 'revelation' does not: because people *are* 'saved' from hate and apathy to love in) community—sometimes. But people do not have a clear 'knowledge of God'.

However, that is to anticipate the discussion in the second part of the book.

4

THE CHRISTIAN USE FROM THE
NEW TESTAMENT ONWARDS

THE documents of the 'New Testament' do not, by and large, give a very large place to 'revelation' in any sense as a metaphor, concept or category to express their understanding of the purpose of Jesus or of God 'in' Jesus. For some this might conclusively rule the term out of court, theologically: it is not 'biblical'. For those who really claim to produce a 'biblical' theology this should be a serious argument.

Still, many others might argue that to keep to purely biblical terminology or 'concepts' is an artificial and even destructive limitation. Later Christian understandings of Christ have a right to be taken seriously; later terms and ways of thinking may enrich our own theology and response. If more recent Christians have believed that 'God was in Christ, "revealing himself" to the world', we might do well to follow them.[1] This could be a true compulsion of the Spirit, guiding us to a fuller insight into the purpose of the events (including the thoughts) recorded in the New Testament. Chapters 5-7 deal with this question of the value of 'revelation' as a Christian theological word, the problem of 'meaning' which we posed in the first chapter. In the present chapter, we look very briefly at a few 'fathers' of the Church, at their understanding of 'revelation of God himself', of the granting of 'knowledge of God', in relation to the past 'Christ event'. The field is too vast for a comprehensive survey even of the whole of the work of the few fathers chosen; so attention is focused on their understanding (where it is known) of the 'Great Thanksgiving' (Matt. 11.25ff.; Luke 10.21ff.) and its relation to Paul's disparagement of his present

[1] Both J. Knox and J. MacIntyre, whom we quoted (above, p. 16ff.) as noting the absence of this term from the NT, themselves use it positively in the books from which the citations were taken.

'knowledge' by comparison with the 'knowledge' and 'encounter' he awaits (I Cor. 13.9-13). It is interesting to find how often this latter is allowed explicitly to qualify the understanding of the former.

In this way we try to answer the question, 'Do these theologians believe that God did or does "reveal himself" in Christ?'

We also note one or two factors that may contribute to, or at least be corollaries of, a belief in 'revelation': a growing intellectualism, and spasmodic tendencies to doctrinaire exclusiveness.

Clement of Rome[1]

In his letter to the Corinthians, Clement uses ἀποκαλύπτειν itself only in his quotation from Isa. 53.1ff., 'To whom hath the arm of the Lord been revealed?'; and he is using it only to talk of Jesus' humility and self-effacement (16.3).

He does not use our 'test quotations' from the New Testament.

However, he does seem to suggest that God may be 'seen' with 'the eyes of the soul', in natural events (!): 'Let us look steadfastly at the Father and Creator of the whole universe, and let us hold fast to his excellent and pre-eminent gifts of peace and his beneficent actions. Let us see him with our mind and look with the eyes of the soul at his long-suffering will. Let us consider how imperturbable he is towards his whole creation' (19.2-3). We look, not to see God himself, to contemplate him or 'encounter him as person'; but in fact, to encourage ourselves to patience, peace and concord, by the example of certain regularities in the world at large (20). Any Stoic might have said as much. In fact, the 'let us look . . .' is no more than a literary device.

Parallel with this finding of the will of God through meditating on nature, however, is a more specifically Christian contemplation:

'Through him (Jesus Christ, the High Priest of our offerings) let us gaze into the heights of heaven. Through him we see as in a mirror God's spotless and glorious countenance; through him the eyes of our heart were opened; through him our senseless and

[1] *I Clement*, written *c.* AD 95. The quotations are from the translation by W. K. Lowther Clarke, SPCK, 1937; with the Greek text of J. B. Lightfoot, *Apostolic Fathers*, Macmillan, 1898.

darkened mind rises up towards his marvellous light; through him the Lord desired us to taste the immortal knowledge; "who, being the effulgence of his majesty, is by so much greater than the angels, as he hath inherited a more excellent name" ' (36.2-3).

He is quoting Heb. ch. 2, and perhaps II Cor. ch. 3, for the 'mirror'. The former has, as we have seen, no suggestion that Jesus is the 'revelation' of the Father, and in the latter we are made to reflect the glory (κατοπτριζόμενοι, passive) rather than 'see in a mirror' (ἐνοπτριζόμεθα, middle) as here. Still, Clement himself does have this penchant for visual metaphors, and this may well be an intentional re-interpretation of his Pauline passage. He quite explicitly offers this as 'the way in which we found our salvation' (35.1): 'revelation of God' (in this 'contemplative' manner) is here for the first time, apparently proposed as the key-term for expressing the purpose of Christ.

Unfortunately, he nowhere else expands what he writes here. A correct understanding of his intention depends rather on whether the five phrases are all in parallel, or supplementary, or quite distinct. He does often use parallelism:

'For by his supreme power he established the heavens and by his incomprehensible wisdom he ordered them' (33.3),

soaked as he is in the LXX. And the first four phrases of 36.2-3 certainly appear to be saying much the same thing. If it be accepted that this is so with the fifth, then there is a fairly good clue to the whole passage, because he discusses elsewhere the 'knowledge' that Christians possess. In summing up all the surrounding material he says: 'Now that all these things are clear to us, and we have studied the depths of *divine knowledge*, we ought to do in due order *all things which the Lord hath commanded us to perform* at appointed times' (40.1). 'Divine knowledge' is knowledge of how to obey. And earlier still, when he had just finished describing our salvation in terms of 'gazing into the heights of heaven', he explained the point of it with these words: 'Let us therefore, brethren, with all earnestness serve in his army, under his faultless orders' (37.1).

From chapter 31 onwards he has been exhorting his readers to 'good works' (which is what he means by 'faith') as gifts of God, not their own acts. In 35 he describes the gifts of God in more detail: 'How blessed and wonderful are the gifts of God beloved! Life in immortality, joyousness in righteousness, truth in boldness, faith in confidence, self-control in sanctification: all these things are within our understanding.' In 36, then, he describes how it is that these gifts, including the 'faultless orders' are 'within our understanding'; all the while maintaining his encouragement to obedience, so that finally we may gain the greater gifts that still as yet 'eye has not seen nor ear heard' (34.8); 'if our mind by faith is firmly set towards God; if we seek out what is pleasing and acceptable to him; if we perform what benefits his spotless will and follow the truth . . .' (35.5).

The whole section (in fact the whole letter) is concerned with obedience to God's known will; and it is most likely that this is the 'knowledge' to which he refers at 36 in the somewhat flowery language of 'seeing in a mirror God's spotless and divine countenance'. If this still seems a forced exegesis, it is only possible to point out that it would be a little odd to suggest that all Christians have an intense mystical awareness of God mediated through Christ, and yet are sufficiently unaware of him for his demands to need to be made clear with a variety of rather weak arguments from the Old Testament and 'nature'.

However, further contexts in which Clement talks of 'knowledge' make the interpretation offered almost certain. 'Those who do anything contrary to *what befits his will* incur death as the penalty. You see, brethren, the greater *the knowledge of which we have been counted worthy*, the greater the danger to which we are exposed' (41. 3-4). 'But if any *disobey the words spoken by him* (Jesus Christ) *through us*, let them know that they will involve themselves in transgression and no small danger. But we shall be innocent of this sin; and we shall ask with earnest prayer and supplication, that the Creator of all may keep unbroken the fixed number of his elect in all the world through his beloved Servant Jesus Christ, through whom he called us from darkness, to light, *from ignorance to knowledge of the glory of his name*' (59.1-2).

That *I Clement* contains an outlook very similar to that of the Pastorals is almost a truism for New Testament scholarship.[1] Clement's understanding of the purpose of Christ is just one instance of this. Jesus came to make God's demands known, the real point at issue, as in the quotation from 41 above, being

---

[1] E.g. Bultmann, *TNT* II, p. 187: 'closely related to the Pastorals'.

God's will for the ordering of his community. Obedience to his will (an obedience that is 'not through ourselves or through our own wisdom or understanding of piety or works', 32.4) is the way of life and salvation. It is 'knowledge of God's wishes' that Christ came to impart. He did not, does not 'reveal God', or 'knowledge of God himself'.

'In regard to faith and repentance and genuine love and self-control and discretion and patience, we have exhausted every topic' (62.2), is Clement's own concluding catalogue of the contents of his letter.

Ignatius[1]

Ignatius, 'bishop' of Antioch, wrote his letters to the various churches, on his way to the arena in Rome (or so he hoped), in the first or second decade of the second century.

To the Magnesians he wrote: 'There is one God who manifested Himself through Jesus Christ His Son, who is His Word, proceeding from silence, who was in all things well-pleasing unto Him that sent Him' (8). Ignatius can also call Jesus 'the unerring mouth in whom the Father hath spoken truly' (*Romans* 8); and describe him as 'the mind of the Father' (*Ephesians* 3). Again, at first sight it looks as though Christ is being seen as 'revealer of God'. But a closer examination shows that here too this sort of language is used subject to a number of qualifications, some of which we have met already.

Not only is Jesus Christ 'the mind of the Father', but the bishops (in whom Ignatius has immense confidence) 'are in the mind of Jesus Christ'; and this is how the mind of God is known. So now, men can 'run in harmony with the mind of the bishop' (*Ephesians* 4), 'in harmony with the mind of God' (*Ephesians* 3). Then God will 'acknowledge them by their good deeds to be members of His Son'.

And just as Jesus is the Word of God from silence, so Ignatius himself may be a word of God, if men keep silence and do not prevent him (*Romans* 2).

Jesus Christ is our Teacher, and he may raise us from the dead: 'for this cause, seeing that we are become His disciples, let us learn to live as beseemeth Christians' (*Magnesians* 9-10). We should be 'arrayed from head to foot in the command-

[1] Text and translation in J. B. Lightfoot, *op. cit.*

ments of Christ'. There is an enigmatic passage in *Ephesians*
where, again, Jesus is styled Teacher: 'Now there is one teacher
who spake and it came to pass: yea, and even the things He
hath done in silence are worthy of the Father. He that truly
possesseth the word of Jesus is able also to hearken unto His
silence, that he may be perfect; that through his speech he may
act and through his silence he may be known' (15). The writer
seems to mean that a man can learn both from Jesus' teaching
and his actions, and can obey whether or not he explains his
obedience in words; and so, as Ignatius has just quoted, 'The
tree is manifest from its fruit; so they that profess to be Christ's
shall be seen through their actions' (14). It is reasonable to
suppose that this implicit and explicit teaching on Christian
behaviour forms much of the content of 'the knowledge of
God, which is Jesus Christ', which can prevent us from 'perish-
ing in our folly' (17). So, too, to 'receive the pure light', Ignatius must become 'an imitator of the passion of my God. If any
man hath Him within himself let him understand what I desire,
and let him have fellow-feeling with me, for he knoweth the
things which straiten me' (*Romans* 6). Ignatius' 'Christ mysticism', his awareness of 'Christ in him', is no self-sufficient
'knowledge of God'; it is a deep and urgent desire to die and so
'come to the Father' (*ibid.* 7).

When Ignatius talks of 'the hidden things' or 'the mysteries'
they also seem either to be the actions of Jesus or details of
church life and Christian conduct. Shortly after he has spoken
of the 'word' and 'silence' of Jesus, in the passage we have just
noted, he adds: 'And hidden from the prince of this world were
the virginity of Mary and her child-bearing and likewise also
the death of the Lord—three mysteries to be cried aloud—the
which were wrought in the silence of God' (*Ephesians* 19).
Another 'mystery' is the resurrection of Jesus (*Magnesians* 9).

In his letter to Polycarp, bishop of Smyrna, he writes, 'as for
invisible things, pray thou that they may be revealed unto
thee' (2); to the Ephesians he mentions the possibility that God
might 'reveal' something to him, so he could tell them more of
the implications of the 'dispensation relating to the new man
Jesus Christ, which consisteth in faith towards Him and in love
towards Him, in His passion and resurrection' (20). (These are
the only occasions on which he uses the word ἀποκαλύπτειν.)

And fortunately, in *Philadelphians*, he cites an occasion when he himself 'spoke . . . with God's own voice' a 'hidden thing': 'Give ye heed to the bishop and the presbytery and deacons. . . . He in whom I am bound is my witness that I learned it not from flesh of man; it was the preaching of the Spirit who spake on this wise; do nothing without the bishop; keep your flesh as a temple of God; cherish union; shun divisions; be imitators of Jesus Christ, as He Himself also was of His Father' (7).

The only other contexts in which he uses 'revealing' language is to talk of the time when 'God appeared in the likeness of man'. He appeared, 'put in an appearance', not to be seen, known, comprehended; but to make 'newness of everlasting life' possible; 'the abolishing of death was taken in hand' (*Ephesians* 19). What matters to Ignatius was not that in Jesus God could be 'known' (except in the sense we suggested above), but that Jesus was God made really 'like' man (*Smyrneans* 1-6). Then his resurrection makes our 'immortality' possible (*Magnesians* 9, etc.); the bread of the Eucharist becomes a φάρμακον ἀθανασίας (*Ephesians* 20).

For Ignatius, God through Christ, and Christ through the leaders of the community, has made his 'mind' known, for the ordering of the life of church and individual; and God also empowers the obedience he demands (*Smyrneans* 11), which is conformity to the life of Jesus. At best this takes the form of a 'martyr's' death. And so the Christian may 'attain God' (*Romans* 8, *Trallians* 13, *Magnesians* 14). Not even this does Ignatius explicitly call 'revelation of God'.

'*Barnabas*', '*Hermas*', '*The Didache*'[1]

The pseudonymous *Epistle of Barnabas*, written probably by the end of the third decade of the second century, is very largely concerned with 'revelation'—of a sort: 'We ought therefore to be very thankful unto the Lord, for that He both revealed unto us the past, and made us wise in the present, and as regards the future we are not without understanding' (5). God has done this through the prophets (1); even though things are not so clear that there is no need for us to search: 'It behoves us therefore to investigate deeply concerning the present, and to search

---

[1] Text and translation in J. B. Lightfoot, *op. cit.*

out the things that have power to save us' (4). What interests the writer as a Christian (in the past, present and future) is of course Jesus: 'the Father revealeth all things concerning His Son Jesus' (12). The Old Testament tells of his life in the flesh, his cross and ascension, the atonement he effected and the covenant we received, in a variety of often enigmatic ways.

Finally the Son of God was himself 'manifested in order that at the same time they (Israel) might be perfected in their sins, and we might receive the covenant through Him who inherited it, even the Lord Jesus, who was prepared beforehand hereunto, that appearing in person He might redeem out of darkness our hearts which had already been paid over unto death ... ' (14). Also foreshown in the Old Testament is the six thousand years from creation till the end, and the judgment, when God will 'set all things at rest' (15). Then we shall be the perfect 'incorruptible temple' for God to dwell in (16).

Jesus 'in the flesh' manifested the resurrection, and that he will be judge. By choosing great sinners as apostles, 'He manifested Himself to be the Son of God.' He came 'in the flesh' because otherwise he would have been too glorious for men to bear it (5). He was 'manifested' in the sense of 'being present, physically visible', to perform the foretold saving acts. But not to 'reveal', himself or the Father.

The writer then goes on to elaborate the 'two ways' of light and of darkness (18ff.). 'This is the way of light, if anyone desiring to travel on the way to his appointed place would be zealous in good works. The knowledge then which is given to us whereby we may walk therein is as follows. ... 'Thou shalt love him that made thee ... hate all hypocrisy. ... Thou shalt not commit fornication ... ' (19). 'He that doeth these things shall be glorified in the Kingdom of God. ... The day is at hand ... ' (21).   X 14

Again, the important 'knowledge' is of what God commands. The 'manifesting of Jesus' is not the reason for his coming, but the essential prerequisite of his effective saving activity. The only 'revealing' God does is of important events to come.   )

The *Shepherd* of 'Hermas' dates from around the middle of the second century. It describes a variety of visions and 'parables', often tortuously allegorical. Its main point is the offer of one more chance for repentance after baptism.

Cryptic writings and strange visions have their meaning 'revealed' to him (e.g. Vision 2.2, 4) in trances and dreams. But what is 'revealed' is not all that 'revealing'. Hermas has to go on and ask for a 'complete revelation concerning the three forms of the aged woman'; and even that does not add much (Vision 3.10f.).

He explains that the Son of God was 'made manifest in the last days of the consummation' (Similitude 9.13); this was so that men might be saved by entering through him as the 'gate' into the Kingdom of God.

'The name of the Son of God is incomprehensible'; but those who have borne it (by baptism) live, and have come to 'a full knowledge of it' (Similitude 9.15-16). A little later the writer argues: 'Therefore they that have not known God, and commit wickedness, are condemned to death; but they that have known God and seen His mighty works and yet commit wickedness, shall receive a double punishment, and shall die eternally' (Similitude 9.18). Since 'knowledge of God' plays so small a part in the work, and there is no 'revelation' of God, it is safest to assume that no more is meant than acquaintance with his characteristics and his moral demands. There is really not enough evidence to argue from.

There is very little in the *Didache*, either. It could be dated as early as the first century, but it is hard to tell. The 'thanksgivings' at meal times (perhaps at 'the Eucharist', but probably not) include the following: 'for the holy vine of Thy son David, which Thou hast made known to us through thy Son Jesus' (9), which could mean just about anything; in the imagery of the Fourth Gospel it might signify the Church, which comes into the grace over bread, and that is quite probably dependent on John ch. 6. However, the prayer continues: 'for the life and knowledge which Thou didst make known to us through Thy Son Jesus'; and similarly in the next prayer: 'for the knowledge and faith and immortality, which Thou hast made known unto us through Thy Son Jesus' (10). And gnostic though this may sound, it is probably explained by the first chapters, which describe the teaching of Jesus as 'the way of life' (similar to the 'Two Ways' in *Barnabas*). This is the only 'knowledge' the book contains, and it is said to 'give life'. The 'knowledge' Christ gives then is much the same as in *Barnabas* 18.

At the end, 'The Lord shall come and all His saints with Him. Then shall the world see the Lord coming upon the clouds of heaven' (16).

In the sub-apostolic age, in the Pastorals, *I Clement*, Ignatius, *Barnabas, Didache*, there is a fair amount of agreement in the use of words like 'knowledge' (as given by God), 'manifest' and (though it is rarely used) 'reveal'. The 'knowledge' God gives is how to please him and qualify for immortality. This is taught by Christ. The life of Christ and other important events may be 'manifested' beforehand, chiefly in the 'Old Testament'. Christ himself was 'manifested' to impart this 'knowledge' of how to please God, and perhaps also to enable its use. And at the end time, Christ will be 'manifest' again.

There is nothing that can clearly be called 'revelation of God himself'. If any such possibility is foreseen, it lies beyond the end, or at least beyond death.

The Letter to Diognetus[1]

The '*Letter to Diognetus*' is mentioned for its interest, although it is difficult to date. Lightfoot suggests somewhere around A.D. 150 for the first ten chapters.

This letter outlines, for the first time, something like a 'theology of revelation'. 'No man has either seen or recognised Him (God), but He revealed Himself.' 'For what man at all had any knowledge what God was, before He (Christ) came?' (8). And now, it is possible to apprehend 'full knowledge of the Father' (10). He 'revealed Himself by faith, whereby alone it is given to see God' (8). God's hiddenness beforehand; and then his act in Christ, not just to tell how to obey him, but 'to reveal himself', to give a *complete* 'knowledge of himself', so that, albeit 'by faith' he may be 'seen': all this amounts to an acceptance of 'revelation' as a major theological concept.

There are only a few qualifications to note. The 'full knowledge of God' that is now possible is propositional—it is 'knowledge about God', 'what God is'; it is the ability to make correct

[1] Text and translation in J. B. Lightfoot, *op. cit.*

statements about him, such as: 'For God loved men for whose sake he made the world . . .' (10). And the purpose of this 'revealing' is to enable our imitation of the love of God.

And the writer has more to say about God's purpose than this. God had a plan, secret till he 'revealed' it through his Son, 'the purpose which He had prepared from the beginning' (8). 'He bore with us, not because He approved of the past season of iniquity, but because He was creating the present season of righteousness, that, being convicted in the past time by our own deeds as unworthy of life, we might now be made deserving by the goodness of God . . . ' (9). God 'manifested His goodness and power' *in action*: 'in pity He took upon Himself our sins.' This section could well be based on an intelligent reading of Paul and Ephesians.

'Revelation' is still only one aspect of God's purpose in Christ; by itself it would not have been enough; men had to be fitted, made able. But this writer does see it as God's intention that men should, by faith, have a clear knowledge about himself, here and now, through the saving activity of Christ.

This is 'revelation of God's self', in one sense. But still not in a sense acceptable to many modern theologians, for whom 'revelation' must be 'personal', not 'propositional'.

A last point to note, one to which we shall have occasion to refer again, is the 'anthropology', understanding of man, of this letter. Man is a soul imprisoned in a body. This is so natural a description that it can be used to illustrate the position of Christians, who are 'the soul of the world' (6). Man as an (intellectual) 'soul' warring with his body is the view, broadly speaking, of 'Greek Philosophy', certainly of popular Platonism: 'Whence come wars and fightings and factions? Whence but from the body and the lusts of the body? . . . having got rid of the body we shall be pure and have converse with the pure, and know of ourselves the pure light everywhere, which is no other than the light of truth.'[1] I suggest, very tentatively, that there may be some connection between the acceptance of this rather 'intellectual' definition of man on the one hand, and on the other, the interpretation of God's purpose in Christ

[1] Plato himself, quoted in B. Russell, *A History of Western Philosophy*, Allen and Unwin, 1946, p. 159.

as 'revelation', as directed largely or entirely to the mind-soul of man. If you start off with a view of man in which ratiocination, or even, more widely, conscious cognition, is his *esse*, then the situation with which you believe God in Christ has dealt is defined in advance in these terms, and you are almost certain to look for *knowledge* of or about God as the saving results of Christ's coming and life.

And further, of course, man is already the 'soul' he will ever be. He is always (at least in theory) capable of comprehending ultimate truth, if only he will free his intellect from the effects of being embodied. If his soul is ever to know the truth, contemplate 'reality' (and he is confident it may), 'now' is as possible as any other time. It is the same 'soul' with the same characteristics, 'faculties', powers. There is perhaps room in this understanding for 'progress'—progress in the mind's control of its body. But there is no room for 'eschatology', no room for Paul's '*then* shall I know', 'then' at the Resurrection, at the transformation and glorifying of 'the body' (the total individual, or perhaps the total community of individuals). In the philosophical intellectual view, man has already, (or 'is' already) the only mind there will be for him. He is able *now* to receive as full a 'knowledge' of, for instance, 'God' as he may. 'Revelation', as complete a clarity as will ever be possible for him to appreciate, he may now appreciate.

This may, of course, be modified by one element in Old Testament and early Christian thought: the emphasis on the initiative and supremacy of God. So it may be said, as by this writer, that a man cannot 'reveal' God, God must disclose himself. But still man is such that his mental powers can here and now receive this 'revelation', or can here and now be fitted to receive a 'complete knowledge of God'.

This understanding of man may then, I suggest, lead to an understanding of the activity of God in Christ very different from that offered by the New Testament writers. It is not necessarily an invalid impression. I shall discuss its value later. For the present we just notice the possibility that it does affect the question we are examining: the question of the extent to which Christians have believed that (to adapt Paul) 'God was in Christ, "revealing" himself to the world.'

Though most Christian writers from the second to the

twentieth centuries have accepted the Greek philosophical picture of man, they have usually modified it with elements drawn
from early Christian eschatology, have often made it less barely
'intellectual' and more 'personal' by demanding love, 'ethical'
activity, and have not drawn all the conclusions from it that
they might. So they will often qualify what they mean by 'revelation', and insist that God is still in some sense hidden: the
eschatology may not always be fully 'realised'. But the emphasis
is still on cognition, conscious will, intellect, alone; rather than
intellect being seen as just one part of the much wider life of
man.

However, this is only really an 'aside' (to which we return in
chapter 7), and the main case of this essay stands or falls without
it.

Justin Martyr[1]

Knowledge

Justin, writing about A.D. 150 is the first to quote our 'test
passage' (Matt. 11.25ff.; Luke 10.21ff.). It means that 'He
(Jesus) revealed therefore to us all that we have understood
from the Scriptures by His grace, having come to know Him
as First-born of God and before all created things, and son of
the patriarchs, since He became incarnate by the Virgin who
was of their race, and He endured becoming a man without
form or honour, and liable to suffering' (*Dialogue with Trypho*
100.2). It is 'revelation' of 'knowledge about' his role and
status. The same appears when Justin again quotes this passage
in his *First Apology*. Jesus, according to Justin, is here promising
to deal with the situation in which the Jews did not know 'what
the Father was, and what the Son'. Jesus 'is called Angel and
Apostle; for he declares whatever we ought to know, and is sent
forth to declare whatever is revealed' (*Apology* I, 63).

Justin thinks that many 'stoics, poets, and historians', and
especially Plato, had a share in the σπερματικὸς λόγος, and
'whatever things were rightly said among all men are the
property of us Christians'; but they do not 'on the more important points appear . . . to have possessed the dimly seen wisdom,
and the knowledge that cannot be spoken against' (*Apology* II,

[1] M. Dods, etc., T. and T. Clark, 1867; A. L. Williams, *Dialogue with Trypho*,
SPCK, 1930.

13). So, too, the Jews 'know God', though they 'practise none of these things which they that fear God do' (*Trypho* 10); and there is, as in Hermas, a clear distinction between 'knowing', which can be quite abstract, and the response that ought to follow. It is interesting that there are nevertheless a few passages where Justin may be using 'know' in a more 'biblical' way. In the passage, 'you are prone and apt to depart from the knowledge of Him. As also Moses says: The people ate and drank and rose up to play' (*Trypho* 20), the abstraction of knowledge from obedience is not so apparent; nor again when Justin sums up an appeal to repent with 'Know Christ', and backs it with Old Testament quotations that demand 'obedience' (*Trypho* 28).

Mostly knowledge is explicitly 'philosophical'. But it is a very practical philosophy: it is words of the Saviour that are meant to be 'carried out in practice' (*Trypho* 8). 'And as an eternal final Law was Christ given to us' (*Trypho* 11). To know how to describe God correctly, and the obedience he demands—this is the knowledge Justin is concerned with.

Revelation

Justin uses words of this sort largely in describing the prophets' telling of the future and of the truth about God: 'They and they only saw the truth and declared it to mankind . . . it is open to anyone to consult (their writings) and to gain most valuable knowledge both about the origin of things and their end, and all else that a philosopher ought to know' (*Trypho* 7). However, 'what the prophets said and did they revealed in parables and types' and this makes it necessary for someone to 'reveal the mystery of things that cause even the precepts of the prophets to be attacked' (attacked for their inconsistency and apparent lack of sense) (*Trypho* 90ff.). Properly understood, the Old Testament will provide information that shows that the life and death and resurrection of Jesus for the world's salvation were planned in advance, by the world's Creator, and will throw some light on the relation of the Son and the Father (and the Spirit) (*passim*). In so far as the philosophers did know any truth about God, they too must have learned it from the Old Testament (*Apology* I, 44).

Justin also uses 'reveal' for more recent communications by

God; for instance, in the Nativity stories (*Trypho* 78, 103, 115).

He talks of Christ 'appearing', once in humility and again in glory (*Trypho* 14); and the Son was the divine figure who 'appeared' to the Old Testament heroes, was 'revealed' to them —in the sense, 'became physically visible' (*Trypho* 51, 62). It could not have been the 'ineffable Father and Lord of all' but Christ made visible (*Trypho* 127). God the Father cannot be 'seen'; nor Christ, unless he takes some physical form.

Right at the beginning of the *Dialogue*, Justin tells how he was convinced by a Christian stranger of the nonsense of Plato's belief that 'the eye of the mind is itself of such a kind that it can see BEING', 'see God' (*Trypho* 4). The most that can happen is that souls 'can understand that there is a God, and that righteousness and piety are good' (*ibid.*). This itself depends on God giving them understanding (*Trypho* 7). But even the Christian can have no closer perception of God than this. Justin here accepts the philosophical body-soul description of man only with heavy qualifications. When he describes man once more at the end of the work, there is again no hint that he sees him now or even ultimately, as made for 'communion' with God, or to know him 'personally': 'He (God) desired to make . . . persons possessed of Freewill to practise righteousness, and possessed of the sense of Reason, that they might know by Whom they have come into being, and because of Whom they exist, though once they were not, and of a Law, that they should be judged of Him, if they act contrary to sound reason' (*Trypho* 141).

It is significant that Justin's Christian faith made him more agnostic, less inclined to suppose a full appreciation of deity possible, than Platonic philosophy would have done. Admittedly for Justin's Platonist friends experience of God could not be put into words; but the 'ineffable' experience as such was possible. And it was this that Justin's Christian stranger firmly denied. Justin followed him and chose instead that 'philosophy' (Christianity) which offered only such 'knowledge about God' as was necessary to obey and worship him.

It is probably fair to connect this agnosticism, and this stress on ethical conduct as the mode of our relationship with God, with Justin's willingness to accept anyone who reproduced a broadly 'Christian' pattern of behaviour as a fellow Christian (*Apology*

I, 46; *Trypho* 45); and also with his willingness to allow for certain quite important differences of opinion and practice among consciously committed Christians (the voluntary keeping of the Jewish Law, *Trypho* 47). In this he contrasts with, for instance, Jerome, and probably with Irenaeus.

Such 'knowledge' as God provides is strictly subservient to the salvation he wrought in Christ. It is 'knowledge how to respond to', how to accept, fit in with, the saving events. And it is the saving events that occupy most of Justin's often tortuous exegesis. It is for creation and for salvation from evil and evil powers and for belonging to the priestly community of the Church that the president gives thanks at the Eucharist (*Trypho* 41; *Apology* I, 65); not for any 'revelation' of God. Justin's theology is very 'biblical', even absurdly so; this means that automatically 'revelation' (in any sense) becomes a very subordinate motif.

Irenaeus[2]

Irenaeus, writing twenty or thirty years later than Justin, has rather more to say about 'revelation'. This is because he is arguing against opponents for whom the term is important, gnostics who claim that Jesus came 'to reveal the *unknown* Father', who is other than the Creator God of the Old Testament. And the 'corner-stone' (*sic*) of their system is, significantly, 'The Great Thanksgiving' (*Adv. H.* I 20.3). So Irenaeus insists again and again, 'Wherefore, to teach us that the Son who is coming is the same who makes the Father known to such as believe Him, He said to His Disciples, No man knoweth the Father, but the Son, nor the Son but the Father, and those to whomsoever the Son will reveal Him: teaching of Himself and the Father, as the truth is, that we might not receive another Father, save Him who is revealed by the Son. Now He is the Framer of Heaven and Earth: as is shown by our Lord's discourse: not the pretended Father who hath been invented by Marcion, or by Valentinus . . ., etc.' (*Adv. H.* IV 6.3-4). The Lord says these words to make it plain that 'no one can know

---

[1] It is not that Justin believes that men can set themselves right with God; the obedience of these 'unconscious Christians' depends on Christ, and so, too, their ultimate salvation (*ibid.*).

[2] In *Adversus Haereses*, translation by J. Keble, Parker (Oxford), 1872.

God except on God's teaching . . . for God to be known is itself the free-will of the Father' (*ibid.*).

In the context of this sort of argument, Irenaeus can make 'revelation' the purpose of Jesus' coming: 'And to this end did the Father reveal the Son, that by Him He might be manifested to all men, and that such as believe Him, being righteous, He may receive into incorruption, and into eternal refreshment: (now to believe Him is to do His will:) but those who believe not, and therefore fly from His light, He will justly shut up in the darkness which they have chosen for themselves. To all therefore the Father hath revealed Himself, in making His Word visible at all: and the Word again in being seen by all was shewing to all the Father and the Son' (*Adv. H.* IV 6.5). Though·even here, there is the same further purpose of 'revelation' as we have noted before: obedience.

'Revelation', then, is important. It is perhaps not quite fair to argue from his silence; but Irenaeus does seem to accept the philosophical definition of man as body governed by mind-soul, with less reservations than does Justin. Using arguments similar to his, Irenaeus 'refutes' Plato's metempsychosis, but makes none of Justin's strictures on the soul's incompetence in spiritual matters. 'The apprehension of the man, his mind, and reflection, and the purpose of his heart, and whatever is of that sort . . . are the motions and operations of the soul' (*Adv. H.* II 33ff.; 29.3). The body cannot make the soul lose its 'power of knowing' (*ibid.* 33.4). The 'soul' can even now so escape the body as to be capable of 'vision' (*Adv. H.* II 30.2). (Contrast Justin, *Trypho* 5; though the examples are only of the prophets and Paul, II Cor. 12.) Of course Irenaeus modifies this with the traditional Christian belief in Resurrection. But man is predominantly intellect, and 'spiritually' a fairly highly competent intellect at that, if God grant him knowledge. So again we may suggest that a willingness to see God's purpose in Christ in cognitive terms is prepared for by an understanding of man primarily in terms of conscious mind.

A further aspect of Irenaeus' position that it may be fair to link with his stress on 'revelation' is his insistence on the uniformity of Christian belief, over against the varieties of gnosticism: 'For erroneous as their views are, yet for the present they refute themselves, by their not having the same thoughts on the

same subjects. But we, following as our Teacher One only, and
Him the only true God, and having His sayings for the rule of
truth, say all of us always the same words about the same
things' (*Adv. H.* IV 35.4). If Christ is the teacher who 'reveals',
then Christians must be those who hold one clearly defined
unvarying set of beliefs. The contrast with Justin's position is
worth noting. And it is also important to see, as I shall show in
more detail in the next chapters, that the converse to Irenaeus'
position must also hold true. If Christians, in circumstances
other than those of the small second-century Church, find
that they cannot always say 'the same things on the same subjects', doctrinal or ethical, then it must be difficult for them to
talk at all confidently of 'revelation'.

Important though 'revelation' is with Irenaeus, to describe
the purpose of God in Christ, it is still not an end in itself. It is a
means to an end; and in the last resort God's plan in Christ (for
this world at least) has to be expressed in other terms. We have
already seen Irenaeus describe the 'revealing of God' by Jesus
in the Johannine terms of the light that demands decision to
obey or disobey, to choose life or condemnation. But 'revelation'
is also used of making the Son physically visible, as the pattern,
matrix, image (εἰκών), of man for man to see what he was
meant to be like. And this itself only becomes useful when the
'resemblance' (ὁμοίωσις) is restored, when men are actually
shaped to the pattern displayed (*Adv. H.* V 16.2).

The purpose of the Incarnation is more fully expressed in
terms like these: 'And therefore in the last times the Lord restored us to friendship by His Incarnation, being made Mediator of God and men: on the one hand, appeasing the Father
on our behalf (*sic*!), against whom we had sinned, and assuag-
ing our disobedience by His own obedience (earlier, 'healing the
disobedience which was wrought at the tree by the Obedience
which was also at the Tree'); on the other hand, granting us to
be on terms of *citizenship* and *dutifulness* with our Maker' (*Adv.
H.* V 17.1, and 16.3; my italics). So too, Irenaeus explains that
the 'all things' that Jesus says in the Thanksgiving are 'delivered' to him, means all power to save (not all knowledge to
communicate) (*Adv. H.* IV 20.2).

The 'revelation' of God in Christ does not mean anything
that could be called 'vision' (*Adv. H.* IV 9.2, V 7.2); and

Irenaeus quotes I Cor. 13.9ff.: 'We shall have our growth and increase, so as to enjoy the gifts of God, now no more through a glass and darkly, but face to face' (*ibid.*). 'In respect of His Greatness, then, one cannot know God, for it is impossible to measure the Father. But in respect of His Love (for this is it which by His Word leads us to God), we, obeying Him, are ever learning, that God is so great, and that it is He who by His Own Self created, and elected, and beautified and pre-served all things' (*Adv. H.* IV 20.1).

As with Justin, and the '*Letter to Diognetus*', the 'revelation' is 'propositional'. For the present, what is 'revealed' is correct information about the Father. And the importance of this 'revelation' is its clear assurance, that the Father of Jesus, and the Creator of whom the Old Testament speaks, are the same God; just as the speakers in Creation and in the Old and New Testaments are the same Word (*Adv. H.* IV 6.1-6). The 'revela-tion' that concerns Irenaeus is the 'revelation' of this identity. He quotes with approval Justin against Marcion, 'I could not have believed the Lord Himself, if He announced another God beside the Creator' (*Adv. H.* IV 6.2). Quite incidentally, the Christian experience of forgiveness 'reveals' that it is the God who laid down the Law in the Old Testament who in Christ accepts the penitent (*Adv. H.* V 17.1). Irenaeus is being driven to talk a great deal about 'revelation' (but only in this limited sense of the 'revelation' of propositions that make clear the identity of the Creator, and the Father of Jesus) because of its denial by his opponents. But it is not a belief that God has 'revealed his self' that he is defending. It is the total Christian experience of acceptance and renewal, while comprehension of God is still dim. To this Christian experience, its continuity with pre-Christian Jewish, and total human experience is integral. Deny that, says Irenaeus, and you shatter the whole. But you cannot: the continuity is clear from statements in the earliest documents of Christian faith onwards. It is 'revelation' of Jesus' Father's *identity*, then, not of his character or person, that plays this vital but subservient part in Irenaeus' theology (see finally *Adv. H.* V 36.3, his concluding words).

Only at the end will Jesus be 'seen', 'appear' again, clearly; and he will be our slow preparation for encounter with the Father: 'The just shall reign upon earth, growing by their sight of the Lord, and by Him shall be accustomed to comprehend the glory of God the Father' and finally to abide in 'communion with God' (*Adv. H.* V 25.1, 26.1).

Irenaeus only stresses 'revelation' because he is willing to argue on the same ground as his heretical opponents; though he is perhaps prepared for this by his acceptance of the contemporary philosophical definition of man in intellectual and cognitional terms. 'Revelation' is still subordinate to more 'biblical' categories; but its frequent use may be tending to produce a Christianity concerned basically with the intellectual acceptance of certain propositions. And this understanding easily leads to a yet further narrowness, that leaves little room for differing opinions or even the reverence of agnosticism.

Origen and Chrysostom and the Incomprehensibility of God[1]

The main lines of early Christian thought on the 'revelation of God' should now be fairly clear. Man on his own cannot know very much, if anything, of the truth 'about' God; even though his intellectual curiosity demands that he should. God must take the initiative, and 'make himself known'. And to a greater or lesser extent he is seen as having started to do this in Christ. Even so, it is admitted that, this side of death, things are still not as clear as they might be. 'Then' (which in Irenaeus still means after the Final Judgment) there will be a deal more clarity, even direct contemplation.

Most of this is reproduced in Origen (A.D. 185-253/4). God, as the Old Testament says, hides himself; men have, 'according to their merits', only obscure ideas about him (VI 17, VII 44). So even Plato, who said some pretty useful things, did not know enough not to commit idolatry (VI 17, and VII 42). But a 'true man' is one who wishes 'to look up and ascend in his mind from all visible and sensible things to the Creator of all who is Light' (VI 66, cf. VII 44).

And so, to those who have a pure heart (VII 45), 'by a mira-

[1] Origen, in *Contra Celsum*, trans. H. Chadwick, Cambridge, 1953; John Chrysostom in *Jean Chrysostom sur l'incompréhensibilité de Dieu*, Intro. F. Cavallera, J. Daniélou, trans. R. Flacelière, Éditions du Cerf, 1951; and in *Homilies on the Scriptures*, translations published in Oxford by Parker, 1854-5. Obviously, if this were intended as a full account then Clement earlier, and the Cappadocians and pseudo-Dionysius and many more, would have to be included. But it is in fact only an illustrative selection, and not a history.

culous divine grace the knowledge of God is extended ... to those who by God's foreknowledge have been previously determined, because they would live lives worthy of Him, after He was made known to them' (VII 44). 'When the Logos of God says that "No man has known the Father except the Son, and the man to whom the Son may reveal Him", he indicates that God is known by a certain divine grace, which does not come about in the soul without God's action, but with a sort of inspiration' (*ibid.*). 'Knowledge of God' is made possible through the coming of the Logos; and this is salvation: 'Accordingly, if Celsus asks us *how we can come to know God, and how we imagine we shall be saved by him*, we reply that the Logos of God is sufficient; for he comes to those that seek him, or accept him when he appears to make known and reveal the Father, who before his coming was not visible (*sc.* to the eyes of the soul). And who but the divine Logos can save and lead the soul of man to the supreme God?' (VI 68). The Word became flesh, to lead men up from a comprehensible 'image of God' to higher stages of knowledge (*ibid.*).

This is still 'knowledge about God': Jesus' words in the 'Thanksgiving' mean 'He revealed to his true disciples the nature of God and told them about his characteristics' (II 71). And it is as yet not very clear; Origen quotes Paul in I Cor. 13.9ff. (VII 38, VI 20).

Only '*after the troubles and strivings here*' shall we come to 'the topmost heavens', and 'be always engaged in the contemplation of the invisible things of God', which will no longer be understood by us 'from the creation of the world by the things that are made but, as the genuine disciple of Jesus expressed it, when he said: "But then face to face"; and "When that which is perfect is come, that which is in part shall be done away" ' (*ibid.*). H. Lietzmann offers this summary: 'The way led higher up into the regions of the invisible: the soul became more and more spiritualised, and grew to perfect knowledge until at last it was no longer soul, but wholly *nous* and spirit, and was able to behold "face to face" the world of intelligible being and essence.'[1]

So far, we have met nothing very new; except that it seems

[1] H. Lietzmann, in *The Founding of the Church Universal* (1938), Lutterworth Press, 1955, p. 311; quoting Origen, *de Princ.* 2, 10, 4; 11, 3-7; 3, 6, 1. 3).

fairly clear that our final 'knowledge' is still 'propositional', it is
knowledge of 'the things of God'; the Pauline 'face to face'
has to be understood 'allegorically'. It is no longer a metaphor
for 'personal encounter', but just for clarity (VII 38; though
this is clearer in Chrysostom, below).

And this leads into the important new point. Our 'knowledge', Origen affirms, will never be complete. This is what
Jesus means in the very words of the Thanksgiving (!): 'Although a derived knowledge is possessed by those whose minds
are illuminated by the divine Logos himself, absolute understanding and knowledge of the Father is possessed by himself
alone, in accordance with his merits, when he says: "No man
has known the Son save the Father, and no man has known the
Father save the Son, and him to whom the Son will reveal him."
Neither can anyone worthily know the uncreated and firstborn
of all created nature in the way that the Father who begat
him knows him; nor can anyone know the Father in the same
way as the living Logos who is God's wisdom and truth'
(VI 17).

The provenance of this understanding of the 'incomprehensibility of God' is debated.[1] Norden apparently proposed
Greek philosophy before Christianity, but H. A. Wolfson suggests Philo of Alexandria: 'The greatest good is to understand
that God, in his essence (κατὰ τὸ εἶναι), is incomprehensible
(ἀκατάληπτος) to every being.' 'We can only know his existence
and manifestations.' 'He who would see the sovereign Being
would be blinded by the brightness of his radiance before he
saw him' (*de Fuga* 164).[2]

We have already seen that Justin Martyr said God could not
be described, he is 'ineffable' and that our minds cannot now
grasp him; and that this will always be so, may be implicit in
his silence, which we also noticed, as to any 'vision' of God as
part of the ultimate destiny of men. And Irenaeus talked of
God being at present unknowable in his greatness, though he
set no bounds to our future contemplation. With Origen this
speculative limitation on the final possibilities of 'knowledge of
God' becomes explicit.

It is developed a good deal further by John Chrysostom and

---

[1] See the introduction to *L'incompréhensibilité*.
[2] H. A. Wolfson, *Philo*, Harvard, 1947; quoted in *L'incompréhensibilité*.

the Cappadocian Fathers,[1] and, of course, by pseudo-Dionysius, and after him by the 'apophatic' mystical traditions of eastern and western Christendom.

Eunomius sparked off the process by asserting on the one hand the impossibility of knowing God by ordinary human powers; and on the other, that God had dealt with this by a complete self-revelation, that could be summed up in the word ἀγέννητος, 'unbegotten'. Now we can know God as he knows himself.

Chrysostom's answer is interesting because it is not primarily philosophical, but argued 'au plan du sens réligieux commun'.[2]

The 'Great Thanksgiving' has the usual suggestions for him; 'revelation' is a gracious act of God, who is otherwise hidden. And in its own terms it gives information about the first two persons of the Trinity. But his predominant exegesis is identical with Origen's. He finds it still necessary to make the anti-Marcionite point, that this is not the revealing of a hitherto totally unknown God; but explains that it is really making clear the limitations of possible human knowledge: 'He means not this, that all men were ignorant of him, but that with the knowledge wherewith He knows Him, no man is acquainted with Him (the Father); which may be said of (our knowledge of) the Son too.' And then he quotes in support, I Cor. 13.9: '. . . it is the perfection of knowledge that He is here intimating, since neither do we know the Son as He should be known; and this very thing, to add no more, Paul was declaring, when he said, We know in part and we prophesy in part' (*Homily on Matt.* 38.2).

On I Cor. 13.9-13, he explains that we shall have a much clearer knowledge than now (this is all that 'face to face' means); but it is not that 'we shall know Him as He us'. 'Then shall I know even as I am known', means I shall know God with as much intensity and self-giving as that with which he now knows me. For the present, we know that he is, but not 'essentially' what he is. We cannot claim a greater knowledge than the apostle Paul (*Homily on I Cor.* 34.2-4).

Nor is it just the 'essence' of God that is beyond compre-

---

[1] Chrysostom, in *L'incompréhensibilité*; Basil, *Against Eunomius* and Gregory of Nyssa, same title.
[2] *L'incompréhensibilité*, p. 18.

/H *good*

hension; the ways he achieves his purpose on earth are, as Paul says, past finding out (*On Romans* 11.33ff.). The Christian must allow God to act, without expecting to know at all clearly how (*L'incompréhensibilité*, 12off., 711 Aff.).

The reasons that Chrysostom and these other writers offer for denying that God may be comprehended, vary. Some are biblical, like the few just quoted: as we have ourselves seen, the writers in the Bible do not think of God as one who 'reveals himself'. Some are philosophical; the hiddenness of God in this sense is obviously not the same—it is the difficulty of framing adequate concepts in which to talk about him. But even if this difficulty is seen as a largely artificial one, as a difficulty caused more by the nonsense of an idealist philosophy than by any reticence of its subject-matter, the fact remains that when adequate terms with which to talk of God are not available, we can be pretty sure that there is no clear impression of him. And the remaining reasons are a proper reverence, and a perhaps improper fear of God. At least, in the later liturgies, which echo this language, there is an awe of God that seems to amount to a failure to trust that we are accepted. Whatever the reasons offered, and whether we judge them good or bad, it is important to note that even when the intellectualist definition of man has been fully accepted, Christians have refused to pretend, without heavy reservations, that God is 'revealed' to them.

Augustine of Hippo[1]

Augustine offers yet another variation on the theme: 'Man . . . on account of the uncleanness of sins and the punishment of mortality cannot see God' (*de Trin*. VII 3). ' "The light shineth in darkness and the darkness comprehended it not." Now the "darkness" is the foolish minds of men, made blind by vicious desires and unbelief' (*ibid*. IV 2).

God in Christ sets about the task of enlightening us: 'Our enlightening is the partaking of the Word, namely of that life which is the light of men. But for this partaking we were utterly unfit, and fell short of it on account of the uncleanness of sins. Therefore we were to be cleansed. And further, the one clean-

---

[1] In *De Trinitate*, trans. A. W. Haddan, T. and T. Clark, 1873; and *Homilies on the N.T.*, translations published by Parker, Oxford, 1854, 1875.

sing of the unrighteous and of the proud is the blood of the Righteous One, and the Humbling of God Himself' (*ibid.*).

In this life, even in the 'state of faith', it will be possible to 'see God' only, as Paul says, 'in a glass darkly' (*Sermon* III [Ben. MS 53] 11). At the end, 'our justification shall itself be perfected unutterably. For then "we shall be like Him, for we shall see Him as He is".' But now, 'the corruptible body presseth down the soul, and human life upon earth is all temptation . . .' (*de Trin.* IV 3). Even when you see God, you will not be able to describe him. Now, you have to say, 'It is not this' (*Serm.* III 9). Now, God is 'incomprehensible', and can only be sought; he can be found only to the extent of finding how incomprehensible he is (*de Trin.* XV 2).

Augustine stresses much more than do the eastern fathers the moral incapacity, even of man who is being redeemed, to 'see God', to have any clear knowledge of him. Man still subject to temptation is in no state to receive 'revelation' of God.

To be sure, he has some information about God, as much as God has seen fit to give him: '(the Word) speaks to us by enlightening us, what ought to be spoken to men, both of itself and of the Father. And therefore He says, "No man knoweth the Son but the Father; neither knoweth any man the Father, but the Son, and he to whomsoever the Son will reveal Him" '; and Augustine goes on to quote some passages of the New Testament which, he believes, tell us what we ought to say of God. This was not to 'reveal God' (Augustine insists again on the 'uncleanness of sins and punishment of mortality' that disables), but to provide a true pattern of humanity, in order that we may be in the end 'refashioned after the image of God' (*de Trin.* VII 3). And so, when he preaches on the 'Great Thanksgiving', Augustine has little to say about 'revelation' of God at all; he concentrates on the example of humility and the teaching of humility. He just mentions in passing that what is 'revealed' is ' "All things are delivered unto Me of My Father" ' (*Sermons* XVII-XIX).

If we achieve purity of heart, here and now, we shall, in a manner suited to our infirmity 'see' God (*Sermon* III); but 'when . . . this image shall have been renewed to perfection by this transformation, then shall we be like God, because we shall see Him, not through a glass, but "as He is"; which the Apostle

Paul expresses by "face to face". But now, who can explain how great is the unlikeness also, in this glass, in this enigma, in this likeness such as it is?' (*de Trin.* XV 11).

This presents an even sharper contrast with the strictly qualified hope of the eastern fathers that we glanced at a moment ago. Augustine seems to be both more pessimistic about man now, and at the same time more ('biblically', perhaps) optimistic for him in the end. His mind *will be* capable of comprehending God.

The fact is that with two major qualifications (we have mentioned one, his strong sense of sin; we leave the other for the moment) Augustine is more explicitly and elaborately 'intellectualist' than any of the authors we have so far considered. His main concern is with the rational activity of the individual human mind; its knowledge of things, but much more its knowledge of itself. It is here that he expects to find God 'mirrored' (*de Trin.* IXff.); not for instance in any inter-personal relationships of men. Bertrand Russell, commenting on Augustine's theory of time, writes: 'The theory that time is only an aspect of our thoughts is one of the most extreme forms of that subjectivism which . . . gradually increased in antiquity from the time of Protagoras and Socrates onwards. Its emotional aspect is obsession with sin, which came later than its intellectual aspects. St Augustine exhibits both kinds of subjectivism. Subjectivism led him to anticipate not only Kant's theory of time, but Descartes' *cogito*. In his *Soliloquia* he says: "You, who wish to know, do you know you are? I know it. Whence you are? I know not. Do you feel yourself single or multiple? I know not. Do you feel yourself moved? I know not. Do you know that you think? I do." This contains not only Descartes' *cogito*, but his reply to Gassendi's *ambulo ergo sum*'.[1] (The same subjective intellectualism occurs in his *de Trinitate* (XV 12): 'I know that I know that I am alive'.)

This 'intellectualism' is demonstrated further by Augustine's constant tendency to see sin in terms of unreason.[2] It comes out most clearly when he discusses 'original righteousness', and the manner of the transmission of 'original sin'. 'If Adam had remained in Paradise he would indeed have begotten children,

---

[1] Bertrand Russell, *Western Philosophy*, p. 374.
[2] See T. A. Lacey, *Nature, Miracle and Sin*, Longmans, 1916, pp. 115f., 130.

but in accordance with the dictates of reason, and without any excess of concomitant emotion.'[1] It is because of this lustfulness that sin is transmitted. It is precisely because Jesus was not born this way that he was sinless.[2] Augustine's rationalism was so extreme that he seems to have been unable to conceive of the possibility that God might have intended man 'from the first' to have large elements of irrational spontaneity in his make-up.[3] Even in a child there 'is' (somehow) a full human intelligence.[4]

Man in heaven is man defined in terms of perfect mind, capable of complete and immediate comprehension: 'There we shall see the truth without any difficulty, and shall enjoy it to the full, most clear and most certain. Nor shall we be inquiring into anything by a mind that reasons but shall discern by a mind that contemplates . . . ' (*de Trin.* XV 25).

However, as we suggested, this intellectualism is qualified by two factors. On its own, it might well have led Augustine to suppose that God could here and now be 'revealed' to the rational (Christian) mind. He does not seem to approach the 'vision of God' itself, wonderful though it is, with the same 'religious awe' that leads the eastern fathers to suppose that the Mystery will always be unfathomable, and not just unspeakable. Nor does he accept the philosophical agnosticism that is part of the eastern position (see his defence of the powers of mind in *de Trinitate* XV 12ff.). But he does here and now find man, even when Christian, too sinfully irrational for any clarity of vision. (The stress on sinfulness as separating God and man is 'biblical'; the understanding of sin basically in terms of unreason is not.) Man is too wicked for God to be revealed to him.

The other qualification to Augustine's intellectualism is his acceptance of the Pauline and Johannine and ultimately, Christ-like, exaltation of love, *caritas*, *agape* (cf. *de Trin.* XV 17ff.). Of course, it is possible t use the word in very different ways; but at least the *Confessions* suggest as Augustine's aim and experience much more than a cold, intellectual love of God. This of course links with Augustine's certainty that it is sin that separates man and God; sin and love are mutually exclusive

---

[1] N. P. Williams, *The Ideas of the Fall and Original Sin*, Longmans, 1927, p. 362; quoting *de nupt. et concup.* I 1, 6, 7, 8.
[2] Lacey, *op. cit.*, pp. 139-40; cf. *Enchiridion* 10.
[3] Williams, *op. cit.*, p. 343.
[4] Lacey, *op. cit.*, p. 119, quoting *de civit.* XXII 24.

possibilities for the will. It may be that Augustine is being in-
consistent, and more Christian in his inconsistency. Man is not,
in the end, just 'rational will'; he is love that can be real apart
from reason (Augustine seems to allow for this, *de Trinitate, ibid.*).
Love is the greatest gift of God. Through the Holy Spirit, 'the
love of God is shed abroad in our hearts, by which love the
whole Trinity dwells in us' (*de Trin.* XV 18). So perhaps it is
fair to suggest that for Augustine not only does sin disallow a
clear understanding, a 'revealing' of God; but the love of God,
enabling our love of our neighbour and (so?) of him, provides
an entirely adequate *present* relationship with him, for which
'revelation' is not necessary, save in the more limited sense of
'information about'.

Augustine is not of course the only ancient Christian writer
to accept 'love' as the primary term for our relation with God;
Chrysostom does so too, with notable passion, when talking of
the imperfection of our 'knowledge of God', both in his sermons
and in his treatise περὶ ἀκαταλήπτου (*L'incompréhensibilité*).
And this must be so for many whom we have not examined. It
is this, rather than a strong sense of sin, that provides a safeguard against the aridity of an intellectualism that would see
God's activity towards men predominantly in terms of the
providing of 'knowledge'.

Thomas Aquinas[1]

Aquinas agrees with Augustine, against Chrysostom (whom
he mentions explicitly), both in his confidence in man's ultimate
ability to 'see God' with his mind and in his accompanying
stress on 'intellect' as the highest and best of man. 'Therefore
the opinion of some (e.g., Chrysostom) who consider this (the
excess of the intelligible object above the intellect) inclines them
to the idea that no created intellect can see the essence of God.
This opinion, however, is not tenable. For as the ultimate
beatitude of man consists in the use of his highest function,
which is that of the intellect; if we suppose that the created
intellect could never see God, it would either never attain to
beatitude, or its beatitude would consist in something else beside God . . . ' (*ST* I 12.1). And he supports this with an overt

---

[1] In *Summa Theologica*, Dominican translation, R. and T. Washbourne, 1914ff.

reference to man's intellectual curiosity, which he believes must be satisfied (*ibid.*).

However, even angels cannot know God without his express aid; and we, embodied for the present and *in via*, cannot manage even that so directly; we have to abstract from things seen individually, if we are to 'see' universals which are beyond the power of sense. Some further 'illumination' is necessary (*ST* I 12.4-5). And probably his disagreement with Chrysostom is not complete since he admits a sense in which God can never be comprehended by any but God.

Moreover, in addition to man's 'physical' inability to 'see the Essence' of God, there is the fact that the less a man's love toward God, the less he can comprehend: 'The intellect which has more of the light of glory will see God the more perfectly; and he will have a fuller participation of the light of glory also who has the more of charity; because where there is more of charity, there is the more of desire; and desire in a certain degree makes the one desiring apt and prepared to receive the object desired ... the diversity of seeing will not arise on the part of the object seen (but) ... on the part of the diverse faculty of the intellect' (*ST* I 12.6). There is then an ethical disability, too.

Although we have 'nature' from which we can abstract the knowledge that God exists, and is first cause; and although we have various extra information 'revealed'; we cannot, in this life, really claim to 'know God': '... by the revelation of grace in this life we cannot know what God is, and thus are joined to Him as to one unknown; still, we know Him more fully according as many and more excellent of His effects are demonstrated to us, and according as we attribute to Him some things known by Divine revelation, to which natural reason cannot reach, as for instance, that God is Three and One' (*ST* I 12.13). And this is how he interprets the 'Great Thanksgiving', as information about the Trinity (*ST* I 31.4).

However, more definitely than I was able to find in Augustine (whom, however, he quotes to this effect), Aquinas is willing to allow a real sense in which 'perfect love' is a possibility now, and is the manner of relationship to God and men demanded of us and possible for us. 'Now it is charity that unites us to God, who is the last end of the human mind (*sic*), since *he that abideth in charity abideth in God, and God in him*' (*ST* II/2 184.1).

And this is perfectly possible, quite apart from a perfect knowledge, in so far as there is a total tendency to love of God and neighbour (*ibid.* 2).

Earlier he has said: 'We must assert that love which is an act of the appetitive power, even in this state of life, tends to God first, and flows on from him to other things, and in this sense charity loves God immediately, and other things through God. On the other hand, with regard to knowledge, it is the reverse, since we know God through other things . . . to love God is something greater than to know Him, especially in this state of life . . . aversion from God, which is brought about by sin, is removed by charity, but not by knowledge alone; hence charity, by loving God, unites the soul immediately to Him with a chain of spiritual union' (*ST* II/2 27.4).

Practically speaking, the position seems to be very similar to that of Augustine.

Protestant Theology: John Calvin[1]

Calvin, as T. H. L. Parker points out, was educated in the humanist tradition, and for him again man is primarily intellect. Man consists of body and 'soul', 'which is his nobler part', imprisoned in it. Man mirrored God, was 'made in his image', in the sense that 'his intellect was clear, his affections subordinated to reason, all his senses duly regulated, and he truly ascribed all his excellence to the admirable gifts of his Maker'; this was 'Adam before the fall'. And in Adam's case the glory of this shone in every part of his body. In the restoration of man, 'knowledge', according to Calvin's understanding of Paul, takes priority; 'true righteousness and holiness' come second (*Inst.* I 15). And so, from the first lines of the book, he concerns himself with 'the knowledge of God and of ourselves'.

In line with normal Christian tradition, Calvin is sure that even sinless man could not know God without God's 'revealing himself' (*Inst.* II 12). Man still has some idea (*notitia*) of God, innate, and not as Aquinas and schoolmen suggested, deductive; and 'the symmetrical arrangement of the world is like a mirror, in which we may contemplate the otherwise

[1] In *The Institutes of the Christian Religion*, the Calvin Translation Society, Edinburgh, 1845. See also T. H. L. Parker, *The Doctrine of the Knowledge of God*, Oliver and Boyd, 1952.

invisible God' (*Inst.* I 5). But the corruption of the human mind is so great that the only knowledge that unredeemed man can in fact have is little more than Aquinas allowed he could have by deduction: 'that there is a God.' 'With respect to the Kingdom of God, and all 'that relates to the spiritual life, the light of human reason differs little from darkness; for, before it has pointed out the road, it is extinguished; and its power of perception is little else than blindness' (*In Eph.* 4.17).[1]

The divine answer to this situation is 'revelation', 'the knowledge that quickens dead souls' (*Inst.* I 6). To nature, God has to add his Word (in Scripture) 'to make himself known unto salvation' (*ibid.*; the same phrase is repeated, *Inst.* II 6). The 'revealing' Word comes, in a preparatory way, in the Old Testament, but pre-eminently in the man, Jesus of Nazareth. He mediates the full 'knowledge of God' in a form we can appreciate: 'Accordingly, at the beginning, when the first promise of salvation was given to Adam, only a few slender sparks beamed forth: additions being afterward made, a greater degree of light began to be displayed, and continued gradually to increase and shine with greater brightness, until at length all the clouds being dispersed, Christ the Sun of Righteousness arose and, with full refulgence, illumined all the earth' (*Inst.* II 10).[2]

And so the whole of salvation is understood in terms of 'revelation'. It is not 'just' an exhibition of God, or of the grace of God. It is the *grace* of God that is 'revealed', and the forgiveness of God. It includes an opening of men's eyes to see. It is a most powerful act, because it is the 'revealing' of *God*. But it is primarily 'a revealing'. And so the whole service of the Church becomes a sort of 'preaching', which, by God adding to it his Holy Spirit, may be 'revelation'.[3] Everything, sacraments included, is aimed at man's conscious intellect: 'The office of the sacrament is to aid the infirmity of the human mind' (*Inst.* IV 17).

The 'knowledge of God' is a 'propositional knowledge', but one which demands a response (*Inst.* I and II). It is perceiving 'that' God is a Father, author of salvation, propitious; yet, 'properly speaking, we cannot say that God is known, where

---

[1] Parker, *op. cit.*, chs 1 and 2; the quotation, p. 29.
[2] Parker, *op. cit.*, p. 66ff.   [3] Parker, pp. 81-99.

there is no religion or piety' (I 2). 'Faith . . . consists in knowledge. . . .' 'Faith includes not merely the knowledge that God is, but also, nay chiefly, a perception of His will towards us. It concerns us to know not only what He is in Himself, but also in what character He is pleased to manifest Himself to us' (*Inst.* III 2).

The main point of God's activity in Christ being seen as the providing of 'knowledge of himself' here and now, there is a great stress, obviously, on the clarity of the knowledge now available. Otherwise, the traditional Christian belief from the New Testament onwards in the finality of Christ would be destroyed: 'But when at length the Wisdom of God was manifested in the flesh, he fully unfolded to us all that the human mind can comprehend, or ought to think, of the Heavenly Father. Now, therefore, since Christ, the Sun of Righteousness, has arisen, we have the perfect refulgence of divine truth, like the brightness of noon-day. . . . (God) will not add revelation to revelation, but has so completed all the parts of teaching in the Son, that it is to be regarded as his last and eternal testimony' (*Inst.* IV 8). And so 'As soon as the minutest particle of faith is instilled into our minds, we begin to behold the face of God placid, serene, and propitious; far off, indeed, but still so distinctly as to assure us that there is no delusion in it' (*Inst.* III 2). (The contrast with Augustine's exposition of Paul's 'in a glass, darkly' is remarkable. Augustine says it can *not* mean that we see from a great distance, clearly.)

Calvin admits, with Aquinas, that the 'essence' of God cannot be known; but he can hardly mean the same thing by 'essence' as Aquinas at least thought he meant, for Calvin says: 'Cold and frivolous, then, are the speculations of those who busy themselves with the question, *quid sit Deus*; when it is more important for us to know *qualis sit*, and what accords with his nature' (*Inst.* I 2, as quoted, Parker, *op. cit.*). According to Calvin, so far as we could want to know, it is 'himself' that God has 'revealed', and for Aquinas that would mean the 'essence' of God; no cold or frivolous thing. Though formally in agreement with others, Calvin believes we have a very much clearer knowledge of God than Aquinas or the earlier fathers would have allowed.

Calvin, of course, does qualify even this. We have already

noticed that he suggests our knowledge of God is distant; it is somehow clear without being as clear as we shall have it in heaven. And although he sees man, and God's activity to man, primarily in intellectual terms, we have also shown in passing that the will and devotion of man are involved. And he has, even if they are secondary, other terms than 'enlightening' for the work of Christ.

Calvin is not wholly determined by his humanist tradition in his understanding of man, and the way God must deal with him. But we have found in the *Institutes* the greatest confidence in the (non-biblical) definition of man here and now in terms of conscious reason; and the strongest emphasis on 'revelation' as the manner of God's being gracious towards him. This is at least sufficient to support if not to prove our earlier suggestion, that it is the rationalist rather than the 'biblical theologian' who demands 'revelation' of God in the present.[1]

It may also not be coincidental that we find this stress on 'revelation' at a time of controversy, from a representative of a Christian group in the process of putting up defences to exclude many other Christians. In the time of Irenaeus, and in the time of Calvin, to cry 'revelation' is to divide Christians from each other (*Inst.* IV 18 *et passim*). Some just will not believe that God is 'revealed' in the way you wish.

And it is probably also significant that Calvin in the *Institutes* seems not a little embarrassed by Paul's eulogy of 'love' in I Corinthians chapter 13; for instance, he quotes verses 2 and 13, only to explain them away, in favour of (a very intellectual) 'faith' (*Inst.* IV 5 and 17). And in this again Calvin contrasts with the theologians we have so far studied.

This is not to suggest that Calvin was wrong to make his protest; but it may be worth pondering the result that might have come, had he based his protest more on the 'biblical' and less on the rationalist traditions of the Church.

It may be fair to contrast Calvin with Luther at this point. At any rate, Gustaf Wingren can suggest that Luther differs markedly from Barth just here where Barth loyally reproduces Calvin's emphasis on 'knowledge', at the expense of other

---

[1] For a critical questioning, in a different but related context, of Calvin's rationalism and philosophical presuppositions and their effect on his attempt to be bound by the Bible, see P. van Buren, *Christ in our Place*, Oliver and Boyd, 1957, pp. 13, 22, 38 (and n. 3), 39, and the 'Conclusion', p. 140ff.

aspects of Christian life. 'The main question with Luther is the question of righteousness. But with Barth the main question is whether we have knowledge of God, or whether in ourselves we lack such knowledge and must receive it from the outside.'[1] However, although Luther may have preserved a more balanced understanding of God's activity, it has to be admitted that Barth is able to quote appositely from Luther to support his revelation theology.[2]

A brief glance at Schaff's *A History of the Creeds of Christendom*[3] offers some further illustration of the position argued here.

The Lutheran Confessions (Augsburg, Luther's Catechism, the Formula of Concord) have no articles expressly devoted to 'revelation', and only mention incidentally that, for instance, God 'revealed' the Law. They are much more concerned with sin, guilt and righteousness, the subject, for example, of the first article of the Formula of Concord.

The Reformed Confessions tend to give a much greater priority to 'revelation', and the question of how God is to be known. The Gallican, Belgic and Waldensian formulae have their second article devoted to this issue; the Westminster Confession begins with it; and there is the same tendency as in Calvin to see the corruption of Adam's reason as the most serious consequence of his disobedience. The intellectualist tendency in Reformed Protestantism in particular had its most marked effect in the Society of Friends. Here the logic of this element in Protestantism was fully worked out; for instance, the traditional concern of Christians in their worship with more than just their own minds disappeared. The sacraments that had already become sermons vanished altogether, which was only reasonable. The *Confession* of the Society of Friends, published in 1675, began: 'Seeing the height of all happiness is placed in the true knowledge of God . . . the true and right understanding of this foundation and ground of knowledge is that which is most necessary to be known and believed in the first place.'[4] The whole activity of God is seen in terms of an immediate enlightenment.

It is interesting for an Anglican to find that the Articles

---

[1] *Theology in Conflict*, p. 26. Though Wingren is probably mistaken when he traces this emphasis only as far back as the nineteenth century. See above, ch. 1.
[2] E.g. in *CD* I/1, p. 134.
[3] Hodder and Stoughton, 1877.　　　[4] Schaff, vol. III, p. 789f.

of Religion do not use the word 'revelation', or the phrase 'knowledge of God', or anything of that sort. The purpose of Christ's coming and death was to be a sacrifice for sin, and to effect our justification; no intellectual effects of fall or restoration of man are thought worth mentioning. This is particularly noteworthy, as the Calvinistic tenor of the Articles is elsewhere very noticeable. However, the Articles are very short, compared with the Confessions, and it would not be proper to try to base any argument on this absence.

Modern Times

There is no need to attempt even as brief a selective survey, as has been offered above, for later theologians, to the present century. This is adequately done by H. D. MacDonald, in *Ideas of Revelation*,[1] though from a rather different, less critical, standpoint.

MacDonald is surely right that the predominant interest in 'revelation' during the recent past sprang from its denial by the Deists (p. 2ff.). He then traces the vicissitudes of the word through the next centuries. He also notes the intellectualism that often accompanies its use, and suggests (what is fairly commonly held) that this stems from Descartes. Or rather, not so much from Descartes as from a selection of one element in Descartes' own rather wider understanding of the 'thinking self' (p. 19ff.). We have found reason to suggest that this stress on 'mind' may be found among Christians long before Descartes hardened the distinction between *res cogitans* and *res extensa*. 'Revelation' too had become important, for a while, centuries earlier, for Irenaeus, in the face of gnosticism (which also, perhaps coincidentally, tried to separate 'God' from the physical world).

The real oddity, on which I shall comment more in the sixth chapter, is that after considering the variety that he notes and explains, MacDonald is even more sure that 'revelation' is an important category for Christian talk of God. It does seem very strange that the confusion of Christian belief about 'God has made clear' could allow any other conclusion than that 'God has not made clear'.

[1] Macmillan 1959. Cf. also the same author's *Theories of Revelation*, Allen and Unwin, 1963.

The documents Schaff collects from the Orthodox and Roman Catholic Churches would suggest that they only began to have much to say about 'revelation' in the nineteenth century, and this again, largely in face of contemporary denials.[1]

I am not concerned for the moment to do more than point out the possible origins of a predominant concern with 'revelation'; to show that it represents only a minor and really quite recent way of understanding God's dealing with men. I would not myself accept the evidence so far offered as proof of the uselessness of this word and the ideas it can convey. Like 'Trinity', 'transubstantiation', 'existential', it could be a necessary addition to the basic vocabulary of Christian theology. After all, it has always been used, even if in differing ways and only on the periphery of Christian talk. In an age of mass education, when more and more people are encouraged to exercise their minds, and have more and more time for conscious relationships with others, it could be entirely proper to emphasise the cognitive aspects of Christian faith and life.

It is the question of the usefulness of talk of 'revelation', irrespective of its origin, that occupies the next three chapters.

But the fact remains that if my reading of the material discussed so far is correct, a very heavy question mark is placed against a good deal of contemporary theology, which attempts to find 'revelation of God' in Bible, or Bible and tradition.[2]

---

[1] *Op. cit.*, vol. II, pp. 214, 241, 252, 446.

[2] R. Latourelle, S.J., in *Théologie de la Révélation*, Desclée de Brouwer, 1963, discusses the theme of 'revelation' in the fathers at rather greater length. His exegesis of actual texts presents a picture not significantly different from that offered here—e.g., on Thomas Aquinas '. . . la révélation (that we have so far received) est une connaissance imparfaite, un moment de notre initiation à la vision' (p. 185). He is, however, very much more ready than I to weld such very cautious statements as there are to be found in the Bible and the fathers into a 'concept of (present) revelation'; although in the last pages of the book he seems quite sure that 'cette connaissance de foi . . . saisit imparfaitement et obscurément son objet'; and, 'La révélation par excellence appartient à l'eschatologie' . . . 'la vision en image (quoting I Cor. 13.12) ne donne qu'une image confuse.'

5

linguistic analyses [handwritten marginalia at top]

✓ *for its validity re : reveals* [handwritten annotation]

HOW TO TEST RELIGIOUS LANGUAGE

I T is necessary to look briefly at the ways in which religious language in general may properly be used, before we go on to examine the ways in which 'reveal' in particular is rightly or wrongly employed. That is the first of the two problems outlined in the first chapter: In what sense if any may 'God' be said to be 'revealed', when Christians are so confused and unsure of him and his supposed 'revelation'?

The question of the meaningfulness of 'theological' language, language used (by anyone) to talk directly of 'God', or of 'the things of God', has been increasingly discussed over the past thirty or forty years.[1] It is quite easy for most Englishmen to know what is meant when they are told 'there is a table in the room next to us'. To check that they have understood (and that the information they think they have been given is correct), they can go and see. It is as easy to tell what is meant by 'there is a kangaroo in the garden', or 'there is a pink albatross on the bird table', again, because it is easy to check, however hard it may be at first to believe. But when you are told 'there is a very reticent ghost haunting this pub', or 'there is an invisible God in our midst; and not only is he hidden from sight, but he cannot be touched or measured, and is really ineffable', it is much harder to tell what is meant. Even those who, for instance, accept the title 'Christian' will very often disagree about what is intended.

[handwritten marginalia in left margin: *he* ✗ *yes, the problem ? religious certainty*]

[1] See F. Ferré, *Language, Logic and God*, Eyre and Spottiswoode, 1962; also I. T. Ramsey, *Religious Language*, SCM Press, 1957; A. MacIntyre in *Metaphysical Beliefs*, SCM Press, 1957; *New Essays in Philosophical Theology*, ed. Flew and MacIntyre, SCM Press, 1955; E. L. Mascall, *Words and Images*, Longmans, 1957; R. Hepburn, *Christianity and Paradox*, Watts, 1958; *Faith and Logic*, ed. B. Mitchell, Allen and Unwin, 1957; T. R. Miles, *Religion and the Scientific Outlook*, Allen and Unwin, 1959; ed. S. Hook, *Religious Experience and Truth*, Oliver and Boyd, 1962; G. MacGregor, *Introduction to Religious Philosophy*, Macmillan, 1960; and for a history of the philosophical method that gave rise, *inter alia*, to this discussion, J. O. Urmson, *Philosophical Analysis*, O.U.P. (1956), 1958.

It is *so* difficult to tell what is meant, that many have concluded that it is impossible. It is not that they believe Christian
assertions about 'God' to be untrue. It is that Christians cannot
give them a clear enough account of what they are trying to say,
for it to be possible to agree *or* disagree. It is so unclear that it
makes no sense whatsoever. It does need a lot of clear thinking
to find, for instance, what may be meant when we 'speak' of
God whom we call 'ineffable'—'unspeakable'.

In face of this real dilemma, I find it hard to have to argue
the need for clarity in theology: the need to know as precisely
as possible what words can and cannot do, the need to keep
your eyes open for any gap between their capabilities and the
job you may be asking of them. 'Christianity' so obviously (to
me) deserves the clearest possible forms of verbal expression
(when it calls for words at all) and is strong enough (I believe)
to stand them, that any form of lazy or defensive verbal smoke-
screen seems self-evidently blasphemous or faithless or both.
The aims of clarity in affirmation where affirmation is war-
ranted, and steadfast agnosticism where agnosticism is demanded by the facts, may be difficult to achieve. But I find it so
difficult to imagine a Christian needing to be persuaded that
these are proper aims, that it is only as an *argumentum ad
hominem* that I would offer a 'text'. Paul in correspondence with
the church in Corinth demands clarity as a part of Christian
love for others; to speak meaningless gibberish may be exciting,
but its excitement is purely selfish: 'So also you, unless you
utter by the tongue speech easy to be understood, how shall
it be known what is spoken?' (I Cor. 14.9). And when there are
things that he may not speak, he does not try (II Cor. 12.4).

Current 'analytical' methods of determining the intentions of
utterances by scientists, moralists, metaphysicians, theologians,
and many more, are at least one set of tools for achieving clarity
and honesty. There may or may not be disturbing implications.
But these are tools which the Christian theologian is bound by
love for Christians, non-Christians, and God himself, to try to
use.

However, 'philosophical analysis' does not seem yet to be
widely known in theological circles, or, if known, accepted.
So it is necessary to give a brief account of some of the main
ways (relevant to our enquiry) in which 'religious' language

may be used, and to sketch a defence of the positions taken. I do not hope in these few pages to persuade the sceptical more than that there is a case to be made, and can only refer him to the books already mentioned. There will, as a slight aid to clarity, be no more than a few footnotes to point the relevance of any conclusions for our investigation of 'revelation'. Such relevance should become clear in the chapter that follows this one.

I. FORMAL LANGUAGE

Some language the theologian uses is purely 'formal'. That is, it has to do with explaining his technical terms by other better-known words, and showing how his terms interrelate. He may talk about 'three Persons in one Substance'. He may say that when he uses the term 'Person' it is to mean what Tertullian may have meant by 'person', a 'party' with certain legal rights and duties; and not, for instance, what a modern writer, perhaps influenced by existentialism, might mean by 'person'. He may define 'substance', again in legal terms, and say that in his use it does not mean a 'stuff' as such but anything on which a party at law (a 'person') could make a legal claim. He will then have shown something of how he means his terms to work. He has not yet said anything about 'reality', about man or about 'God'. He has only defined his terms.

It is fairly obvious that this is necessary, if we are to understand what he means when he goes on to use these terms to discuss some actual problem. If part of the time he were to use 'person' to mean a 'legal fiction', and part of the time to mean a 'self-conscious being that can demand a response from other such beings', we would clearly be in the devil of a mess; as puzzled as Alice confronted with Humpty Dumpty and words that meant whatever he wished at any moment. We may fairly demand that whatever else the theologian does, he should be consistent in his use of words.

If he uses a word without explicitly re-defining it, we ought to be able to assume that he is using it as it is used in other contemporary contexts. Unless he tells us he means by 'person' 'party with legal rights and duties', we may fairly expect it *not* to mean that. If he does use an ambiguous term (such as 'person') and gives no explicit definition, we may expect that such defini-

tion will be implicit in the first few contexts in which the term
is used. This will tell us which meaning (or even which complex
range of meanings) he intends. We then expect this meaning or
range of meanings to be maintained throughout, unless he
actually tells us that he intends to alter it. Even if he does tell
us that he intends to use a word in various senses, we may be a
little annoyed, and wish either that he had found other distinct
terms, or that at least he would mark his redefined terms in
some way so as to distinguish them. It would be less deceiving
if he were, for instance, to talk of 'Word (a)', 'Word (b)', (c),
(d), (e), for the various senses in which he may use 'word'.
Suppose then, as a further example, that he defines 'deity', and
does so in terms of 'that which cannot in any way be limited',
and defines 'incarnation' in terms of 'being limited by time,
space and physical-ness'—and means the same thing by
'limited' in each case. He cannot then talk of 'deity' becoming
'incarnate'. He has explicitly said he cannot.

This has, of course, no immediate bearing on any problem
of the possibility or impossibility of a being Christians believe
in and call 'God' being in some way identified with a man
called 'Jesus'. It just tells us that if this theologian tries to
describe such a belief, in terms of 'incarnation of deity' as he
understands those words, we can tell before he starts that he is
going to contradict himself, make nonsense. He has told us that
he will. He may be godly and a holy man, but until he redefines
his terms, he is just being silly. He has warned us that he is not
going to make sense of something we may actually believe; and
we must draw the obvious conclusion.

He may well be loath to accept this. He may call this silliness
a 'paradox', and may insist that it is a good and holy way of
talking. F. Ferré offers a defence of paradox, up to a point.[1]
To the question, 'Is it raining?' we might answer: 'It is and it
isn't!' Of a particular girl, we might say, 'She's pretty and she's
not.' These are necessary paradoxes, because current English
(or American) has no one word to describe an intermittent
drizzle, or a girl who has, say, a pleasant profile but is dull
full-face. We do not mean, 'It really is raining hard, and yet at
the same time, in this same place, it is not raining at all';

[1] Ferré, *Language, Logic and God*, p. 153ff. Cf. also, interestingly, Daya Krishna in *Religious Experience and Truth*, ed. S. Hook, p. 231ff.

'Everyone finds her ravishingly beautiful and is disgusted at
her ugliness.' These instances Ferré offers are slightly lazy
conventional phrases. We understand them to mean, 'It is raining (a little) and (yet) it's not (raining very hard).' 'She's
pretty (when you look at her in profile) and (yet) she's not
(when you look at her from other angles).' These 'paradoxes'
are perhaps useful, as Ferré suggests, as a sign that language
needs clarifying, as a *demand* in fact for further explanation. They
may not be used as 'Halt' signs saying: 'Please do not look any
closer, it might spoil my argument.'

It may take some while to clarify what is meant, the sense in
which the girl is pretty, the sense in which she is not. It may be
an instinctive judgment, that the speaker may need time to
justify. But until greater clarification has been achieved, all
further discussion must stop. We cannot proceed to argue
from this point, until we know what this point is. We cannot
decide how to photograph her, whether to let her play Cin-
derella, let her enter the beauty contest, until we know what
we mean by these hasty and imprecise terms. If we do see these
words as a sign that we should think out more clearly what we
mean, they are useful. We may perhaps call such a useful contradiction in terms a 'paradox', as a sign of its virtue. But if
we just enjoy mystifying, if we enjoy a contradiction for its own
sake, if we are too lazy or mischievous to clarify it, then it is a
vicious contradiction, and has no good use whatever. If we can
only produce such vicious contradictions, we should admit
openly that we have not yet thought enough (or been told
enough) to say anything noteworthy. And we should hold our
peace.

The theologian may very properly say, 'God's imminence
and transcendence look like a paradox, the way language is
normally used; but I mean that God is involved in the world,
imminent, in *this* way, and is independent of it, transcends it,
in *that* way.' But if he just says, 'God is imminent and transcen-
dent and that is a very striking contradiction, and it shows that
I am talking about God', we may safely ignore him. The word
'God' does not make nonsense somehow meaningful.[1]

To reiterate, the fact that a theologian produces nonsense

[1] Some instances of the recognition of this, in another context, are given by Flew,
essay VIII in *New Essays*.

about 'God' does not of course prove conclusively that 'God' may not be talked about—still less, that there is no 'God' about whom to talk. It only shows that this particular theologian cannot; or at best, that he is lackadaisical, and not sufficiently concerned for his readers. Yet, if no theologian ever produced language about 'God' that did not contradict itself into meaninglessness, then it would be obvious that 'God', in empirical fact, could not be spoken of. He would be literally 'ineffable'. So Christians, for instance, would have to admit that they had nothing to say.

This is the importance of 'formal' logic, in theological talk. Even if such talk *is* consistent, it does not prove the theologian right.[1] But if it is self-contradictory, he is just mouthing words, he is producing (a rather tedious) nonsense. He is proved not worth listening to, before he even starts to discuss supposed 'facts', or 'Christian truth'.

This could mean that a great deal of traditional language about 'God' needs to be discarded. In theology, words such as 'infinite', 'unknowable', 'ineffable', and so on, are put into what otherwise seem to be quite simple assertions. Strictly, these words (and the word 'God' is of course, often chief of them) seem to make any assertion containing them meaningless.[2] 'The divine providence is ineffable.' If that is the case, you cannot know about it at all, at least not so as to write books about it. You cannot speak about it. You have said so.

But I. T. Ramsey proposes a way in which the demand for further clarification that we have seen this sort of self-contradictory language makes may be met.[3] The 'paradox' is not to

---

[1] Most theists seem to have given up supposing that the formal logic of actual words can *prove* their case, that the 'existence' of God is a logical necessity. ' "God" is a being so complete that his non-existence is inconceivable'; 'causality is such, that there must be a first cause, which is to be called "God".' Hume and Kant, two centuries ago, showed the flaw in arguments of this sort, which are purely circular, the conclusion being only lightly concealed in the first term. 'The unicorn is such a perfect animal that it is not conceivable that there should not be one.' See Ferré, *op. cit.*, and MacGregor, *op. cit.* (For a sense in which it might be proper to talk of 'God's' 'necessary being'—but not 'logically necessary'—see J. H. Hick, *SJT* 14.4. See also Ferré, again, pp. 32ff. and 48ff., on J. N. Findlay's essay in *New Essays*; also, in *Religious Experience and Truth*, W. N. Clark, p. 224ff., and W. E. Kennick, p. 261ff.)

[2] There are other words that produce a similarly destructive effect, but less obviously: 'perfect', 'first', etc. See McIntyre, *Metaphysical Beliefs*, p. 187.

[3] I. T. Ramsey, *Religious Language*. The following is not a guaranteed 'interpretation'; rather an understanding (or misunderstanding) based on that book. Ferré, *Language, Logic and God*, similarly suggests that no theologian in fact, even the most

be left as a 'marvel' (of obscurity). These purely negative qualifying words (they often translate Greek words with an alpha-privative, ἀ-παθής, ἀ-κατάληπτος, etc.) should be used, Ramsey suggests, not to proclaim from the start, 'This sentence is nonsense'; but to produce a 'truncated cone' of meaning. An ordinary activity (e.g. planning to supply need, and supplying it—providence) is refined by one or more of these 'theological' words, so that the less relevant aspects of the metaphor are discarded, and a dwindling number of appropriate aspects are left, to tell about 'God': a 'cone' of meaning. Strictly, as has been said, these words produce un-meaning; the cone comes swiftly to a point, and nothing communicable is left. But the intention is that as the cone of meaning narrows down the listener (or the speaker himself) will say, 'Yes, I see what is being got at.' And he will make the desired moral and emotional and self-committing and worshipful response. It is a sort of 'Dutch auction': you keep reducing the value till someone makes a bid. And then the language will have served its purpose, it will have produced some quite specific effect, which another ordinary, 'sensible' sentence could not have produced. Whether or not you wish to use this sort of language, produce this sort of effect, is a matter of choice. But it is language doing a job which its users think is a valid one. To take Professor Ramsey's term, it is producing a 'disclosure situation'; it is eliciting (or expressing, or both) a 'personal' response.

To take as an illustration again the sentence, 'The divine providence is unsearchable.' I take it that this would be a shorthand way of saying what follows: God plans for and meets need. But he does not do this selfishly and foolishly as a squirrel stores up odd hoards of nuts for the spring—that is easily understood by observation. Nor is God like a railway company, whose set mechanical pattern of operation (with a few odd variants!) you could quite soon deduce by careful observation. And so we continue the qualifications, until I say, perhaps the

---

possessed by paradox, really intends just to contradict himself, and produce 'holy nonsense'. It matters to him, which words he starts with, and precisely which words he uses, apparently, to negate them (but, in fact, Ferré suggests, to qualify them). He also suggests that the Thomist 'doctrine of analogy' is useful at this level, as an insistence that the way ordinary language is used of 'God' should be carefully examined, and an attempt in part to effect such a scrutiny (p. 76ff.). See also J. Wren-Lewis, *Return to the Roots*, Modern Churchman's Union (after 1955), p. 21.

best analogy is to be drawn from the very complex and difficult plans and provisions that a good parent makes for a child, with all the 'ifs' and 'buts' and constant revisions of those plans that fresh circumstances make necessary. This is a much more difficult providence. But even this sort of planning and providing I may understand; I know the sort of person the average 'good' parent wants his or her child to be. I can even perhaps imagine the sort of parent who has a total concern for the child, so that the parent's whole mental and physical powers are given over to ensuring that in every circumstance which may occur there shall be a way through that will bring the child to the rich, free and loving adulthood that is the parent's plan for him. But by now my mind is boggling; not only at the complexity but at such a willingness to spend oneself in selfless care (for this is not a domineering attempt to live the child's life for him). This is as far as I can go; all I can say is that this truncated cone of mean-ing points to what I want to say about God. This expresses my own (heavily qualified) optimism, and seeks to elicit a similar response to life in 'God's world' from others.[1] The language is, to my mind, doing a legitimate job. There is no 'verifiable' language that can as such express or elicit any sort of optimism. Genuinely 'scientific' language may be used to express some form of optimism or humility or other moral attitude; but that only means that it has been put to another, non-verifiable, use.[2] And the sort of language instanced above expresses, and seeks to elicit, a particular form of optimism, humble, trusting, loving —which no other sorts of language can do in this way.

The language is still meaningful, I have not yet qualified away my paradigm. *It is still possible to understand the sort of response I expect*; I am not asking for just any response. But I know that what I want to say about God is beyond even the refined level of the paradigm which I have reached: it is both more com-plex, and more loving. And that is why I say, 'God's provi-dence is unknowable.' I can only point, and hope my listener will say 'I see', 'The light dawns.' My listener may, if he will,

---

[1] See below, *Commitment: Demand and Response*, p. 179.

[2] As when A. Isaacs in *Introducing Science*, Penguin, 1963, suggests that there is a 'sense of humility' 'appropriate' to the vastness of the observable universe (p. 17). For the illegitimacy of this sort of attempt to argue an ethical position from a factual statement, see R. M. Hare, in *The Language of Morals*, Oxford (1952), 1961; and later in *Freedom and Reason*, Oxford, 1963.

say, 'No, you should have let your cone of meaning continue to the tip, to meaninglessness; you should have continued to an outright contradiction. I refuse to respond as you suggest.' But it is a valid linguistic method. It is not now just obscurantism. Similar methods of shaping language for persuasion and teaching purposes are employed by others besides theologians. The Freudian psychologist takes the word 'sex' and (in this case) inflates it quite beyond its normal meaning(s). But it is the best way to make his point. The philosopher takes a word like 'mind', and refines-out popular 'mis-use' of it, and produces a more tenable set of words to describe such 'truth' as 'mind' previously described. But 'mind' no longer means the same things.

The theologian, then, can use such a method to refine the language at his disposal, and then use it to produce his effect, to express or elicit commitment to God. But he means his language to be 'true'. He intends it to express or elicit a particular sort of commitment, not just any commitment. It is fair then to ask him to check very carefully the language he is using. He is taking a human situation and pointing it in a particular direction, sometimes with elaborate qualifications, often more briefly just with the help of words like 'infinite', 'ineffable'. The addition of such a strictly nonsense word does of course make any statement incontrovertible precisely by making it meaningless, as we saw above. But if the nonsense word is being employed 'usefully', in the way we outlined, and not just as a blind defence, it cannot by itself justify any assertion or exempt it from criticism. As Professor Ramsey insists, the 'model', the analogy, must be analysed carefully to make sure that the user is evoking or expressing what he intends. The original 'paradigm situation' must be examined, to find the sort of response it evokes in normal conversation; the qualifications must be scrutinised to make sure that they leave the intended aspects of meaning at the top of the truncated cone. Does 'passionless' (ἀπαθής) have any of the overtones of 'apathetic'? If you use it to qualify the divine charity, in what sense do you really want the qualification to be understood? It might well be thought that you meant it in the sense of the popular saying, 'as cold as charity'. Ἀπαθής strictly has no meaning; something that cannot be affected is inconceivable. The job that the alpha-privative is

doing , when this word is used of God, is to point away from the
human situation, to say something that some ordinary human
paradigms cannot. But that does not tell precisely what aspects
of the human situation are less and less appropriate as analogies
for talk about God. The alpha-privative, without further qualification, is too blunt an instrument. It could be aspects of
human care, or hate, or wrath, or the intensity of human
emotions, any or all, that are to be knocked away to make
human metaphors appropriate for talk of 'God'. But we need
to know precisely which aspects are discarded at the base of our
cone of meaning, and which still remain just below the apex.
We need to be sure that for the purpose in hand this is a proper
qualification of a proper human metaphor. This is a further care
that the theologian must exercise in his 'formal' logic.[1]

II. FACTUAL LANGUAGE

Some language that the theologian uses is straightforwardly
'factual', in a scientific sense. It 'describes', in terms that may
be shown by public physical tests to be accurate or less than
accurate. It makes a claim that can be checked by sight or
touch or smell, by measuring, by counting, and so on. The
meanings of statements of this sort are quite clear. 'A molecule
of water is made up of four atoms of hydrogen and two of oxy-
gen' ($2H_2O$); 'a Christian congregation is made up of people
who have an unusual ability to love.' 'Fossils of organisms x
first appear in geological strata dating from n million years ago';
'the pattern of living to which we have given the title "Christian" first appears in Mediterranean society nineteen centuries
ago.' 'This idea of original sin is in the book of Genesis'; 'the
table of which you speak is in the front room.' Although some
assertions of this sort are harder to check than others, they are
all 'verifiable', or 'falsifiable' in appropriate ways. These are
the technical terms.[2] The assertions may be true or false, but

[1] This demand for 'formal' clarification applies for instance when God is said
to be 'revealed' without ceasing to be hidden; cf. *inter alios* K. Barth, *CD*, I/1,
pp. 192, 344; I/2, p. 106; IV/2, p. 297. But see below, next chapter.
[2] When 'philosophical analysis' was first moving from the position of 'logical
atomism', it was suggested that 'the meaning of a statement is the method of its
verification'. This criterion was found to be not completely satisfactory (even for
'scientific' language), and was modified to that of 'falsifiability' (Urmson, *op. cit.*,
p. 107ff.). A great many quite proper 'scientific' propositions, it was realised, could
not be finally and conclusively verified; it is never, for instance, possible to perform
all the experiments necessary to 'prove' a general 'law'. It is much less question-

you can tell what they mean clearly enough to know how you would set about trying to see if they were right or wrong. There are basically simple tests, or at least (for instance, with 'historical' propositions) more complex but agreed processes based on such tests. You expect other people to reach the same conclusions as you do yourself. If you always get different results from those that many others obtain, you go to your doctor, and then to your optician, your psychiatrist, or someone else who tries to cure abnormalities in the reception of physical sensations.

If a theologian makes a statement of this sort, about things that can be seen, felt, smelt, heard, counted, etc., his language must obey the rules for talk that purports to convey factual, verifiable, or at least falsifiable information. He must not pretend that his language is of this sort, when it is not; nor must he panic, and say, 'This is a fact, but a holy fact, about the observable world; and you must not try either to verify or falsify it; I will not let it be proved true or untrue.'[1]

begging to ask, 'What are the circumstances in which a supposedly factual assertion might prove false?' If there were none, this would show that there were no 'facts' at stake. The words might be serving some other quite useful purpose, but the sentence would not be 'factual'. It was suggested then that only such assertions as may be verified or at least could be falsified are meaningful at all (e.g., for the former view alone, A. J. Ayer, *Language, Truth and Logic,* Gollancz, 1936), but this has seemed to most an unnecessary and quite artificial restriction of normal usage. It makes more sense to say that only such propositions are *factually* meaningful. See below; and especially F. Ferré, *op. cit.,* pp. 1-5.

M. Polanyi, *Personal Knowledge,* Routledge and Kegan Paul, 1958, protests against a too ready assumption of 'pure objectivity' even in our appreciation of 'scientific facts'. Polanyi would seem to prefer an objectivity that was seen to consist in a consensus based on trust of others. However, it is not legitimate to argue (and Polanyi strictly avoids this) that 'religious faith' is straightforwardly analogous to the scientist's trust in assertions that cannot be finally and conclusively proved. 'Religious faith' is not just the same thing in another field. There is a discussion in A. C. Danto, 'Religious Faith and Scientific Faith', *Religious Experience and Truth,* p. 130ff., in which 'B' tries to make this case which I have argued is not valid. I think that 'A's strongest points (but he does not mention them) are scientists' frequent unanimity (which contrasts with the confusion of religious assertions, as I shall emphasise later); and, related to this, the *practical* difference between religious and scientific 'faith'. A research scientist can carry out experiments, and a technologist can apply the results, if necessary, without believing them: both quite effectively. If they are effective, no one minds. But this is very definitely not the case at least with Christian religion, where going through the specified activities without any 'faith' is never allowed ultimately to be satisfactory; and where even near-identical 'faiths' do not produce identical practice or 'results'.

See further T. R. Miles, *Religion and the Scientific Outlook,* esp. ch. 4. There is no need to commandeer the words 'fact', 'factual', etc., by an arbitary definition that excludes religious assertions. If another wishes to talk of 'non-empirical facts', he may. But when such 'facts' will not accept the responsibilities other, empirical facts have to bear, then neither may they claim the privileges—e.g. 'objectivity'.

However, it should be easy to see that language that is just about 'God' does not work at all in the same way as 'scientific' language.[1] The scientist promises that his assertions can be proved true, at least ultimately, by sense-data; he positively (if he is a good scientist) demands that they be checked. The Christian or Jewish theist, on the other hand, openly claims that it is wrong to try to test statements about 'God', and anyway, impossible. 'Plankton is rich in protein' is a claim that any impartial laboratory can examine. Has it a protein value? How much has it? Enough for it to be fair to say it is 'rich in protein'? 'God is rich in mercy' is a sequence of words that looks similar. But those who say these words say it is wicked to try to 'test' their truth. We may not sin more, to see just how rich in mercy God is. We will probably be told that to approach God in this frame of mind is to ensure that we find out nothing at all. And yet we will be told, perhaps quite vehemently, that it is 'true' that God is 'rich in mercy', but it is true in some non-scientific way, in some way that cannot be tested.

The theist can of course ignore that element in his tradition which tells him not to try to test 'God', and not to make test-demanding, scientific-type 'descriptive' statements about him. He may forget this and, for instance, pray for one of two otherwise identically treated seed-beds, and not the other, to see if prayer to 'God' works. Suppose the bed that is prayed for does considerably better than the other. What would be proved? Only that thinking about seed-beds (and perhaps 'God'; and perhaps, devoutly) makes a good fertiliser. This would still not prove 'God'. It might of course persuade; but tricksters as well as honest salesmen can persuade. It might even persuade a believer that the one supposedly addressed was not worth the name 'God', if he could be swayed by such petty conjuring. But all it could *prove* would be the power of some thinking (and perhaps speaking) of some people, to produce hitherto unexpected effects.[2] Statements like 'God is rich in mercy' cannot

[1] Cf. D. Cairns, *A Gospel without Myth?* SCM Press, 1960, p. 152: 'It would, indeed, be no wise defence of the Christian faith to try to assimilate its knowledge to the knowledge of empirical fact, or to claim that it could submit to verificatory procedures like those suited to the exact sciences.'
[2] Cf. C. A. Coulson, in *Science and Christian Belief* (O.U.P., 1955), Fontana, 1961, p. 38ff., where he insists that 'psi' phenomena (such as these might be) do not transcend time and space, but only our present understanding of them. See also T. R. Miles, *Religion and the Scientific Outlook*, p. 102ff.

be proved scientifically; and though they may be meaningful in some other way, *scientifically*, *factually*, they are (and are intended to be) meaningless.

It is, of course, possible to 'describe' an imaginary character. But it is not a factual description; it cannot be true or false. I can make my 'Mr Pickwick' a thin vegetarian lover of hymn-singing, and no one can properly dispute my description. Only if I claim to be portraying Charles Dickens' 'Mr Pickwick,' can I be shown to be right or wrong. But that is only because I am now really talking about an actual book that anyone may read. Even if I quote exactly and extensively Dickens' own words about 'Mr Pickwick', I will still not be making true or false statements about him. Dickens himself may not have succeeded in describing Mr Pickwick as he imagined him. But the description is not true or false for that; it does not claim to be about the author's imagination. As a picture (even with its noted inconsistencies) it stands in its own right. Nothing that anyone can do or could have done can make it 'true' or show it 'false'. So, it is possible to describe 'God' in the way I might a fictional character; but it will not be a case of truth or false-hood. That only enters in if I talk about ' "God" for St Paul', 'the "God" of the Old Testament', 'the "God" my mind (or Sigmund Freud's mind) projects'. But then, I am not describing 'God', but things said by Paul, assertions in the Old Testament, the workings of my brain, or that of Dr Freud. We shall look again at this way in which God may be in a sense 'described' later in this chapter, and more extensively still in the next. For the moment it is only necessary to repeat that it is impossible to make scientifically true or false statements about 'God himself'.

The theologian may, of course, use a mixed sentence, only part of which purports to be of 'God', while the rest is a purely verifiable assertion. 'God in his rich mercy enables John, Cyrus and Jeanne to love Ivan, Fritz and Ahmud.' It is possible to check if John, Cyrus and Jeanne do love; if they do not, the statement as it stands is untrue. But whether they do or do not, there can be no check whether the possibility is granted (or withheld) by 'the rich mercy of God'.

It may be claimed that there is some common Christian 'experience' of 'God', say in 'person to person encounter'. It

cannot be checked whether it be of 'God' (though it can be
checked to see if it is consistent with other ideas, Christian
ideas, of God). But it can be checked, even if with difficulty,
whether or not there be some 'common experience', and even
whether all who have it, say it is of 'God'. If there is no evidence
for such common experience, obviously the claim as a whole is
false. The theologian should accept this. He may, however,
openly say, 'Ah, but this is an experience of *God*, and so even
qua experience, cannot be checked'—and he might well argue
for this as we argued above. It has however now ceased to be an
'experience', because an 'experience-that-cannot-be-checked'
is very different from 'an experience'. The theologian should
either use another word or write out in full, 'There is a common
experience-that-cannot-be-checked of God.' But an experience-
that-cannot-be-verified (or a claim to an experience that cannot
be verified) is an experience (or an experience claimed) that
cannot be experienced, like a 'visible object that cannot be seen'.
The assertion is nonsense in the full form; in the short form,
deceitful nonsense. 'God' may insist on being mysterious, but it
is not for the theologian to substitute the mystification of word
spinning for such real mystery of God.[1]

III. POETIC LANGUAGE

To return to theists' talk that is mainly or solely about 'God'.
It is claimed that it is 'true' in some way that cannot be checked,
in some non-scientific way. It is 'true', although it does not offer
a falsifiable description. This claim is, of course, dismissed by
some philosophers (and by many who rely on 'common sense').[2]
Assertions that cannot be verified are said to be 'meaningless'.
Neither true nor false, but meaningless.

'All the world is produced by God.' We are told we cannot,
indeed we may not, try to test this sort of statement. 'All heat is
produced by essination.' Since we do not know what 'essination' means we cannot check this sentence, either. So, as it

---

[1] This affects, for instance, any claim that 'God is revealed *to us here and now*'. If
the theologian's claim includes *us*, or other actual people and events, then it is
open to empirical falsification. But see further, the next chapter. Contrast, e.g.
P. Tillich, *ST* I, p. 143f., for a 'knowledge' of 'revelation' that can be had but
cannot be subjected to any scientific scrutiny.
[2] See Ferré, *Language, Logic and God*; Hepburn, *Christianity and Paradox*; some of
the writers in *New Essays* and in *Metaphysical Beliefs*; many writers in *Religious
Experience and Truth*.

stands, it is useless. It does not help us light fires, install air-conditioning, melt aluminium (or even endure hell). It is use-less, because it is uncheckable. And so the first sentence, too, must seem useless. It does not tell us how to put men into orbit in the earth's atmosphere, how to stop them from putting each other in small pieces into the earth's atmosphere, how to mine minerals, or *how* to live at peace. It tells us nothing about the world at all, its use or control. How can so technically pointless an assertion be useful? It is too meaningless to be true or false. It is as helpful as 'gued flamsiel tybe euval sef karn'.

And yet, very little of our speaking has to do with giving technologically useful information about the characteristics or control of our environment.[1] We use words to ask questions, to express concern, to give commands, to make petitions, to elicit affection, to announce commitment to a course of action, to give vent to our emotions. We find many uninformative uses of language very worth while. . . . Theology, talk about 'God', is perhaps one of these: a worthwhile way of talking that does not give information about anything, or at least, only very indirectly. No more than 'Ouch!' or 'Damn!' What sort of use has it? Can it be 'true' or 'false'?[2]

It is, for instance, tempting to think that the Bible especially has the 'truth' of a poem, or some other work of art, a truth that can only be put in one way, and that cannot be analysed or investigated, but only 'received'. There are drawbacks in this position.[3] It is quite possible, for instance, to say that Mr William Golding's myths present a 'true', a helpful, picture of the human situation, without accepting either that the narra-tive is of events that happened, or more important, without accepting the author's Christian intention. It is possible to say that a poem such as 'Paradise Lost' is 'true', whether or not you believe in a devil or a hell or a god. Neither you nor the poet may believe that this is more than an effective, even the most effective, way of saying—something else. An unfalsifiable picture of 'God' as a fictional character (see above) might be

[1] Ferré, *Language, Logic and God*, chs 4, 5 *et seq.*; Miles, *Religion and the Scientific Outlook*, ch. 3.

[2] Ferré, *Language, Logic and God*, p. 104, *et passim*; Hepburn, *Christianity and Paradox, passim*, and in *Metaphysical Beliefs*, p. 85ff.

[3] Hepburn, again, in *Metaphysical Beliefs*, p. 85f., deals with some of these difficulties. See also MacGregor, *Introduction*, p. 312ff.; Miles, *Religion and the Scientific Outlook*, p. 152 ff.

'true' in this way. 'True' here seems to be a psychological term, meaning 'persuasive' and 'illuminating'. It helps you understand the world and your self, and even deal with both, in a way not hitherto possible. But most Christian theologians would want to say their talk of 'God' was exclusively true. Not 'a helpful view of life', but 'the only true view of life (and more)'.

The 'most' in 'most Christian theologians' is however important. Not everyone who claims to be Christian would claim exclusive truth for his views. It is fair to say that to allow only 'poetic' truth to Christian assertions is to stand outside the main stream of historic Christianity. It is the view, broadly speaking, of gnosticism, theosophy, Jungian psychology[1] and Hindu apologetic. It is, of course, often admitted by Christians that some or much of the Christian scriptures are 'myths', in the sense of powerful stories that express vividly a view of life that works. Patristic writers used much of the Bible as though it were myth in this way. But that all Christian talk of 'God', 'creation', 'redemption', and 'heaven' is myth *of this sort* has been consistently repudiated by the Church Catholic. I, too, regard the 'poetic' view of Christian truth as inadequate. Christian statements about 'God' ought not to be in the end reducible to picture statements about man and his world, tales just used for their psychological effect, and exchangeable for quite different stories if they lose their attractiveness and evocative power.[2] There is, however, another sense, to be out-

[1] See, for example, J. A. C. Brown, *Freud and the post-Freudians*, Penguin, 1961, p. 43ff.; and others.

[2] F. Ferré, in an article in *SJT*, Dec. 1959, and in the last chapter of *Language, Logic and God*, where he refers to this article, suggests that Christian faith provides the most satisfactory 'organising image' by which a man might live in the world. These 'organising images' have 'responsive' meaning, as opposed to 'reactive' meaning; they may not be dismissed as 'merely emotive', just because they cannot be tested in the same ways as cognitive statements (statements that purport to give factual, verifiable or at least falsifiable information). They are useful; they are tested by living them. This does go some way beyond the poetry-art-myth analogy; but it is very questionable whether many of his fellow Christians do accept their faith with this understanding alone (though obviously it is possible, and Professor Ferré may do); and it is also unlikely that they would commend it for its 'fulfilment, breadth of vision, and sense of truth within this world'. The Cross stands too firmly against the world to let the world finally determine our 'organising image'. The following pages attempt to show that the predominant purpose of Christian language is to be found elsewhere. But Ferré's insistence on a total reference for Christian theology is surely acceptable. See also A. D. Kelly, 'Can we Talk About God?', *CQR* CLXIII No. 348: 'Talk about God can be described as a way of understanding our world' (p. 317). See also J. A. T. Robinson, *Honest to God*, SCM Press, 1963; and, of course, P. Tillich, *Systematic Theology*, and other works, *passim*. Miles, in *Religion and the Scientific Outlook*, p. 152ff., suggests that this

lined below, in which Christian language about 'God', it will
be suggested, has to be accepted as 'myth'. Then an explanation for this seemingly narrow insistence on 'exclusive truth'
for the Christian 'myths' will be offered.

It is worth noting in passing that a theology that delights
in paradox may well be as effective for those who cultivate it, as
myth-and-poetry is for others—and in the same way. There is a
numinous quality about sentences with holy words that are not
allowed to make sense. They may have a powerful, even psychotherapeutic result. Words used in this way may stir the hearer,
irrespective of their truth, falsehood or meaninglessness. However, it seems fair to insist that those whose talk about 'God'
can only be judged by its emotive effects should openly admit
this to be the way they use language, admit that it is the speaking that matters, and not any particular meaning in what is
said. Most Christian theologians would want to say that irrespective of their psychological power, only one (complex)
'myth' is true. 'God so loved the world . . .' is more than a
strong, even the strongest, way of saying, 'The world of men is
a place where you matter, and is worth all the concern you
can yourself muster.' This 'myth' is accepted in a way that the
stories of Hercules or Prometheus or Dostoievsky's Christ
and the Inquisitor are not. 'God is love' is not the same as 'love
is God', which could be expressed in innumerable different
'myths' or 'parables'.

This use of language is nonetheless important. It is important
for the theologian to realise the overtones of the words and
images he uses. He may mean one thing, when he says, 'God is
our Father' ('God' cares); but what will be the effect? 'God' is
a cross old man who either ignores or beats you? He does need
to choose his words carefully and qualify them vividly, so that
their meanings and overtones (for him and for his listeners)
may coincide, powerfully. His words do need, whenever possible,
to be 'poetically' true. But I suggest they need to be more.

sort of approach is an attempt to retain 'theism without tears'; 'not because it
demands no moral effort . . . ,' but because no tears need be shed over the failure
to achieve any factual meaning for theistic statements. I am not sure that Miles'
own position—'the way of silence qualified by parables': esp. chs 15 and 16—itself
escapes this criticism (see below). 'Parable' certainly suggests to me a quite incidental illustration, and does not convey the very intense attachment of most mono-
theists (Christian, Jew, Moslem) to their complex of myths, which is most like an
attachment to a 'real' person.

To summarise so far: Christian talk of 'God' must be self-consistent. Because it refers to an unusual 'being', it has some special ways of fining down the words it does use; but it must do this carefully. It has no excuse for exempting from observation any assertions that connect this 'God' with observable states of affairs; yet when it just talks of 'God', its talk is not of that sort. Neither is Christian talk of 'God' just a powerful myth, a psychotherapeutic pattern of imagery. All these factors are important; but finally, Christian language about 'God' is neither a dead logical system, a series of scientific facts, nor an imaginative poem. The main use and meaning of Christian language, and the ways of deciding its truth and falsehood, lie elsewhere.

iv. COMMITMENT: DEMAND AND RESPONSE

Christian language about 'God' is intended to express and elicit (and so, but very incidentally, to describe), commitment to him.[1]

'Wilt thou have this woman to thy wedded wife . . . so long as you both shall live? The man shall answer, "I will".'

This is commitment. The primary function of the words, where words are used, is not to say something informative, something that might prove true or false.[2] The first purpose of the words is to be a self-committal. They are 'performative'.[3] The father (or friend), in answer to the request, 'Who giveth this woman to be married to this man?' has nothing to say, but usually just gives his daughter's hand to the priest to give to the man—'commits' her to the church to be 'committed' to the groom. It does not make sense to ask if a committal is self-consistent, or gives us true information about the world, or is pretty. A committal is an act, it just happens or does not. If it is a private act, there may be no need for words or overt gestures at all; no need even for conscious thought: 'He realised later

---

[1] See A. MacIntyre in *Metaphysical Beliefs*; also Miles, *Religion and the Scientific Outlook*, ch. 16; P. van Buren, *The Secular Meaning of the Gospel*, SCM Press, 1963, esp. ch. 4; R. Abelson, 'The Logic of Faith and Belief', in *Religious Experience and Truth*, p. 116ff.

[2] Ferré, *Language, Logic and God*, p. 56. The 'I will' is not a brief way of saying 'I shall do it' (no man is commanded to prophesy); nor even, 'Yes, see, I am doing it.' The 'I *will*' ('I do will it') is of course intentional.

[3] Cf. T. R. Miles, *Religion and the Scientific Outlook*, p. 185, where he refers to J. L. Austin. See further, below, p. 192, n. 4.

that from this moment he had committed himself to the strange brick-layer'.

However, if the committal is to be public, words may well be used. If it is very important or complex, words may be essential for the committal to be to one course of action rather than many others. Some element of description may need to be part of the act.

Committal may be to a person. It may be casual, it may be intense. You may commit yourself to a young man for five-minutes' dancing and desultory conversation, or for fifty years of marriage. Often the circumstances make plain the area of commitment, the general type of relationship being entered on, so that again words are not needed. The setting may even suggest the intensity and intended duration of the commitment. A silent nod could be the act of commitment in the dance-hall, the moonlit orchard, or the bedroom.

But words are useful. They help the person to whom you are committing yourself to know what relationship you intend; they let other people know; they help you clarify the position for yourself. 'He had not meant to go so far. He should have spoken. But now he realised that he had committed himself at least to housebreaking.' A question, 'Wilt thou . . . ?' or an answer, 'I, N take thee M . . .' makes clear *what* commitment you intend.

Commitment to a person is of course commitment to a line of action, trivial or momentous: to the 'Twist', or a business partnership, or a round of golf. Or commitment to a course of action may have no reference to any particular person or group; it may be to generosity, or laissez-faire, or atheism. Professor R. B. Braithwaite has suggested[1] that a statement like 'Love is Good' is mostly used as a commitment to loving acts and attitudes; and that 'God is love' is a picturesque way of saying much the same sort of thing: 'Just as the meaning of a moral assertion is given by its use in expressing the asserter's intention to act, so far as in him lies, in accordance with the moral principle involved, so the meaning of a religious assertion is given by its use in expressing the asserter's intention to follow a specified policy of behaviour' (p. 15f.). Statements of Christian belief

---

[1] *An Empiricist's View of the Nature of Religious Belief*, C.U.P., 1955, p. 10ff.; cited by Mascall, *Words and Images*; also by Ferré, MacIntyre, Miles and van Buren.

are used for 'claiming intentions to follow an agapeistic way of life' (p. 19).

E. L. Mascall criticises this understanding. His first objection (and it is the only one that concerns us here) is that it cannot be true that 'to declare that a course of action is right is to express one's intention to follow it if possible'; it cannot be true for it would mean that 'the man who says he believes a certain act to be wrong but that he intends to do it all the same, is not merely an honest moral weakling, or a hard-headed cynic; he is a muddle-headed thinker . . . '. But Mascall does not offer a fair estimate of the 'normal use' of moral assertions. Quite apart from these indirect ways of expressing your intentions, it is obviously possible to express what is quite explicitly an 'intention' and not intend to carry it through. You may say to the policeman, 'I do not intend to drive my car, I have left the keys with my friend in there', when all the while you intend to drive as soon as the policeman has got out of the way. You are still sober enough to know how to use language quite correctly. You have used it clearly, and meaningfully enough, to deceive.[1]

So you can declare 'Drink is a curse' loudly, as your abstaining boss enters the office; when really you treat alcohol as the one thing that makes life bearable. You can bark, 'Road hogs who exceed the speed-limit should go to gaol', when you are passed at forty by another car doing fifty, in the centre of the town. And your wife may be taken in. If you assert a moral

---

[1] Mascall (in *Words and Images*) earlier clouds the issue by changing Braithwaite's 'moral assertion' into '*thinking* I ought to do the action' (my italics). There is obviously more chance of a man *thinking* a course of action right, and not intending to follow it, than there is of his asserting that it is right, and not intending to do it. However, a man might even do this without consciously deceiving, without knowing that he was 'misusing' language. He would then be deceiving himself. He might for instance be adding an unconscious rider to 'honesty is right' ('but not for me, just now'), 'I do intend to be trustworthy' ('but not in this one instance, these few instances'). This way he might try to persuade himself he is really an honest man, a moral person; basically trustworthy. George Orwell's pigs (in *Animal Farm*) realise that the slogan 'All animals are equal' is strictly a programme to which all are committed. It is not a programme they intend. So they have to modify it; they cannot leave it as it is, a moral assertion that is not their intention. And in fact they deceive the other animals with just such a subtle qualification ('but some are more equal than others') as many a man uses to persuade himself that some virtue is really his intention. Mascall makes his point by ignoring the deceit (not just muddle-headedness) in common practice. For a defence of a 'preceptivist' or 'imperativist' view of the language of morals, see R. M. Hare, in *The Language of Morals*, and in *Freedom and Reason*, especially ch. 5, where he deals with the problem of 'backsliding' and *akrasia*. See also R. Abelson, in *Religious Experience and Truth*, p. 125; and Miles, *Religion and Scientific Outlook*, chs. 5 and 6.

principle, and you seem to be sincere, and not joking or obviously trying to deceive, you may fairly expect your hearers to understand that you intend to act on this principle; and this is probably what they will conclude. If you fail to act this way in many circumstances, they will think you a liar. You may, of course, quite honestly modify your principle in a complex situation, and add a rider. This qualified assertion then becomes your commitment to action in this particular case. 'Drink is a curse; but here it is necessary to save life, and only alcohol can do it.' You may, even more likely, have very mixed intentions, and be not really very sure what they are, nor able to declare them. You may declare an intention rather wistfully. You wish this were your sole intention. This is what you wish you could commit yourself to. All this may be more or less clearly understood by your hearers. But the assertion of a moral principle, aphoristically or casuistically, is normally taken as a commitment to the appropriate course of action.

Commitment as such cannot be true or false, logically. It cannot be meaningless, or self-contradictory. It just happens. Judgments of 'true' or 'false' are only relevant where words or significant acts suggest a particular pattern or intensity of commitment. They make it possible to decide whether the words or acts are appropriate or not, 'true' to the commitment (itself neither true nor false). Do they convey more—or less—than the commitment intended? Do they really fit the commitment being made? 'Do I really mean to stick with this girl for life?' The words can make the commitment being offered or elicited precise.

Necessary though this judgment often is, it may however be difficult to form. If a man acts clean contrary to his directly or indirectly expressed intention, it is fair to suspect that he was deceiving. But it is not proof. Only a machine of a complexity as yet unattainable might be able to tell, by sorting electric currents in the brain, exactly to what, and how far, a man really committed himself, at one moment. And it might have been a total commitment at that moment, and completely real; and yet withdrawn the next. Committal is not, as we have already seen, an assertion that something observable is going to happen, 'I shall in fact be faithful.' It is just the act of announcing decision publicly or privately; the act of accepting a new friend, a new pattern of behaviour. It may be a course of action which may be maintained for life, constantly renewed, or at any moment repudiated (however good or bad the repudiation may be), without the reality of the act of commitment itself being *necessarily* proved or disproved. *Which why a marriage document — licen. why are changers*

On the optimistic supposition that most people do not intend to deceive (the analyst of the 'use' of language is not usually so pessimistic as to think it necessary to discuss the infinite variety of deceit), it is possible then to decide how we may use the language of commitment best, to clarify our commitment, to make it public, and to elicit the committal of others to precise undertakings.

It seems that, more or less, Christian talk about 'God' is directly or indirectly the language of commitment[1]. The 'more or less' is necessary because on the one hand, while few Christians use such language without any commitment at all, many may suppose it to be primarily descriptive;[2] and because on the other hand it seems to be the only way in which language about 'God' may be defended logically, and more important still, perhaps, theologically.

Committal of yourself to a course of action cannot be either logical or illogical. Commitment to two mutually contradictory courses of action at one and the same time is illogical. But commitment to one self-consistent (though perhaps very complex) course of action is just a matter for individual choice and cannot be logically proper or improper; so neither can the words in which it is (accurately) expressed.

A widower may announce, 'I intend to live as though Elsie were still my wife. I will still do the things she persuaded me to share with her. I will still meet new people, make new friends, just as we used to do.' Without sentimentality, or pretence, he may commit himself once and for all, or time and again, to a relationship with the memory of one who is quite obviously no longer with him, as though she was still there. (The wisdom

[1] There is also Christian talk *to* God, vocative and imperative (or jussive, perhaps better). But it seems to depend, logically and actually, on language that appears to be 'about' God, 'O God, *who declarest thy almighty power most chiefly in shewing mercy and pity*: Mercifully grant....' It always suggests either a prior commitment, however tentative, or is in fact such a commitment: 'O God, make me thine.' But talk *to* God will be widely accepted as the most *important* Christian use of words, in practice.

[2] Or primarily myth; both of which we suggest are a misunderstanding.

or rightness of his decision is not at issue.) The words of his committal cease to be appropriate, when he decides to marry again. Though he once may have said them quite properly, now they no longer fit the new line of action he intends.

A girl marries in wartime, just before her husband goes to the front line, where his company is wiped out. There is no news of him, though someone from a nearby unit who escaped thought the husband had lived and had been taken prisoner. The girl insists on living as his wife, and not his widow. Their relationship was such that she can do no other. To her, this sort of commitment comes as a demand. It is not strange or untoward; it is little stranger than the constancy of friends of hers who know their husbands are alive in prisoner-of-war camps. 'I am still in love with John, and he is alive, and my husband.' Even after seven years she maintains this commitment. She does not pretend he is there with her (that would be pathological). She is just committed to him, to a particular course of action, even though now she may legally presume him dead, and herself free to remarry if she wishes.

What she says does not factually 'describe' her husband. She is in no position to make descriptive statements about his present condition. What she says will not be shown to be true or false by a later reading of prison-camp records. Her language only ceases to be appropriate, when time weakens the hold John has on her (she is no longer 'in love'), or when she is finally and reliably told he *is* dead. She can then do as the widower, and live *as though* John were alive. But not as the 'grass-widow' of a living man.[1]

It is also possible to take the course of letting your thinking and living be guided by some 'character' in past history or in fiction. 'I will live *as though* Beau Brummel (or Boadicea or Buonaparte) were my guide and tutor.' And you might elaborate, for your own sake, or someone else's, what you meant by that. You might of course be told, 'That's not Beau Brummel you're patterning yourself on; that's your own romanticising of him.' And if you wish to be honest, you will then either commit yourself to the historical Brummel, by changing your way of life accordingly; or you will amend your promise to, 'I will

---

[1] The relevance of this sort of situation as a paradigm of Christian talk about God is further explored and defended and qualified in the next chapter.

live as though my impression (or Miss Georgette Heyer's impression) of Brummel were my guide and tutor.' 'I believe in him.' Either way commitment and the words which express it are still logically impugnable. Either way you are (probably) committed to living in sartorial elegance, even in Georgian luxurious squalor. Only if you do not live this way is the language of your commitment again misleading.

'I believe in God . . . and in Jesus Christ . . . and in the Holy Ghost . . .', should, as Braithwaite suggests, be taken as a declaration of an intention to live in a particular way; it is well summarised by his coined 'agapeistically'. If it does not express this intention, it misleads. Where Braithwaite misunderstands, as has been pointed out,[1] is in supposing that this is all that the Christian commits himself to. 'The Christian' intends (I think) a fuller, and more complex self-committal. 'I intend to live in love, in as complete as I may *humble*, loving *dependence* on God-who-acted-first-in-love-towards-us-in-Christ; in love to him and all he loves; in a love which my understanding of some events 1900-odd years ago, and of other events since that I believe are related, elicits from me, *demands* of me.'

There are many varieties of this Christian commitment, even within seemingly monochrome Christian communities, traditions, institutions. (There are even forms of commitment which fall outside this definition, but to which I would not wish to deny the epithet 'Christian'; for instance, when Christ is the most illuminating myth, or one such myth among many.)

But by and large, the Christian form of *agape*, of love in dependence, in humility, is integrally bound up with commitment to 'God', who, it is believed, must be said really to 'act' now, and really to have 'acted' 'in Christ'. It is a love (to men and so to 'God' himself) which is both seen as elicited by 'God' before being offered, and as necessarily empowered by him, because otherwise impossible. It is essentially love in response to a love which is believed to be prior.[2]

[1] Ferré, *Language, Logic and God*; Mascall, *Words and Images*; Cairns, *A Gospel without Myth?*, p. 152.

[2] It might seem at this point as though we were smuggling in pseudo-descriptions of 'God', in talking of him as 'acting'. But the ensuing discussion should make it plain that this language is 'descriptive' only of the commitment intended (and that incidentally); we have already seen this in the paradigm of the war-widow above. It does mean that all language about God is in a sense 'mythic', as we noted above, and as is allowed by, e.g. R. Bultmann, *Jesus Christ and Mythology*, SCM Press, 1960,

There may be other forms of *agape*, even humble *agape*, with no mention of 'God', or with the understanding 'as though "God" were real (but he is not)'. But the central Christian commitment is to a life of humble *agape* in total dependence on 'God' who *is* believed to be 'real' and 'living' and 'active'.[1]

The Christian's commitment is essentially love in response to 'perfect love'; and though the Christian may see men who love as the manner of 'God's' actual loving and enabling of love, he has usually been unable to wait for men to elicit it, and has never been able to wait for perfect human love to arouse and empower it, but has found 'God' drawing the response from him. The 'myth' of the prior love of 'real God in Christ' is essential to the Christian commitment.[2] This belief in 'God' who is 'real' creates, then, a possibility of commitment to forms of *agape* not open to those who do not or cannot accept it. The statement of faith in the 'living God' is an integral part of the course of action.[3]

The way of living and loving itself may, of course, be possible

---

pp. 60-2. But Christianity, *pace* Bultmann, etc., I think usually offers its 'myth' at least primarily, not as an 'understanding of the world', but as the best way in which its commitment to love may be verbally expressed.

For the sense in which 'God acts' is used at this point, see below, and chapter 7.

[1] This is not to say, 'We Christians beat everyone at humility in love'; such a boast is obviously self-contradictory. It is only to say that Christian assertions offer a form of commitment that in fact escapes the danger of being a concealed boast: 'Where then is the glorying? It is excluded. By what manner of law (or, religion)? of works? No, but by a law of faith' (Rom. 3.27; cf. I Cor. 1.29ff.).

[2] This is of course not unlike the Kantian 'Moral Argument' for the 'existence of God'. (See G. MacGregor, *Introduction to Religious Philosophy*, p. 120ff.) But it differs in two ways. It does not try to 'prove' anything, except the intelligibility of the language used. And it does not see God as the guarantor of 'the moral order', but as the enchanting Lord of love.

[3] I do not think that P. van Buren, *The Secular Meaning of the Gospel*, has fully realised how different the ethic of Christianity (and, less importantly, its 'understanding' of life) must become, if there is no 'gospel'. (This is logical 'must', not a prophetic-descriptive one.) Just the attractiveness of Jesus in the Gospels, or in the whole New Testament and tradition, does not seem to me an adequate substitute for belief in the gracious activity of God—not as a ground of love, an eliciting of love. The same sort of criticism applies to W. and L. Pelz' *God Is No More*, Gollancz, 1963; and perhaps also to T. R. Miles' *Religion and the Scientific Outlook*, unless he means more by his 'way of silence qualified by parable' than was obvious to me on reading.

These all seem to be attempts to salvage more of Christianity than is really possible, if mythic language *as myth* is disallowed. If for instance the case I have argued here is thought to be not radical enough, then it does seem to me that though recognisably 'Christian' ethics may still very well be possible, they will be different from any of the traditional Christian patterns of commitment from the New Testament (including James!) onwards. I do not think this difference should be disguised.

without every individual Christian offering an explicit verbal commitment; or at least, with very few words. The community as a whole probably needs to be more explicit on some occasions, and so has its creeds and sermons. In Baptism, and especially the Eucharist, individuals and the community can commit themselves primarily by symbolic acts to God who in the sacraments is believed to act first; and the words are only incidental. They may even not be well understood. But the self-committal may be real, in much the same way as the accepting of salt or the grasping of the tent pole in a Bedouin home is a real commitment: committal in this case to 'God' in the belief that he has loved first.

This cannot be shown to be a better or worse way of living agapeistically. It is just other. It is a way to which, or in which, some people do commit themselves. As committal, if it does indeed ever happen, the accepting of this way of living is just a fact. Neither 'true' nor 'false' but a fact. And the words used are valid, if they express accurately the committal intended.

However, at the risk of being tedious, it would be best to qualify this analysis a little further.

This is the way in which some people would wish to commit themselves. The difference between a just-believer and a just-non-believer on this definition would be the difference between the man who wishes he really desired to be fully committed to this way of life (the man who sees his present commitment as inadequate), and the man who sees no need of commitment or growth in commitment. The first (in Johannine terms) sees himself as standing under judgment, and as insufficient; the latter thinks he is managing well enough (cf. John, ch. 9).

The first sees at least that he cannot be satisfied with less than total commitment, if he is to continue as a believer. This is how he uses the name 'God'. He uses the name 'God' at least to express his understanding that a *total* commitment is demanded of him. For him it is entirely proper, and only proper, to be wholly committed. To put it perhaps more accurately still, he finds elicited from him a response such that he realises he can never draw a line and say, 'This far and no further.' If another man can say he is committed to a 'God' who does not elicit, demand, this total commitment, then it is to a different 'god'. For the man who is committed to *agape* in the central Christian way, nothing deserves the name 'God' that is seen as demanding less than this, less than total, dependent, humble, loving, free obedience. No believing that does not at least hope for total commitment can properly be called 'believing'.

It is misleading to say, 'I commit myself to offering to him the love the living God elicits (demands, makes possible), the response from me of loving obedience; or at least offering the desire to want to love and obey', if you never even think of your present lovelessness as unsatisfactory. And if you are willing to regret your lack of *agape*, but never in fact intend to love, you still need to change your claim: 'I believe in God who makes me dissatisfied with myself.' The formula 'God is love' is deceitful, just as a 'moral assertion' (in Braithwaite's sense), if you are not committed (just as the widower ceased to be committed) to the appropriate course of action. You should change from 'God is love' to 'God is Judge and may be love', or to 'God is apathy', as your formula of commitment. If you have not the slightest intention to let your love increase, it would be perhaps more honest to drop the 'God', and say instead, 'my god (or daemon) is love, judge, apathy'.[1]

A large part then of the commitment I have suggested the Christian makes is to 'God' who elicits and empowers his love (the Christian commitment is to a love elicited from him and empowered for him). Language about 'the Holy Spirit' is often used to make this part of the commitment. Language about the Trinity, the three persons united in love, makes best sense when seen as expressing the goal of Christian commitment, the perfect love of persons in community.[2] It is this understanding of Christian love as elicited, empowered, moulded, by the gracious love

---

[1] It means, as we shall see, that there is no justification for saying *this* 'God' is 'revealed', if the appropriate commitment is not forthcoming. This really restates in part what was said above. Just as the Christian has no licence to make untrue statements about the world, so he has no licence to suggest he has committed himself to a course of action which he does not intend. For impassioned statements of this call to complete commitment, see D. Bonhoeffer, *The Cost of Discipleship*, SCM Press, 1959 (though I find a lot of the detail of his exegesis forced), and W. and L. Pelz, *God Is No More*. (Though again I would suggest that much of the exegesis is extremely arbitrary. The reader is offered words of Werner and Lotte Pelz rather than words of Jesus. But they are very powerful words. And see above, p. 186, n. 3.)

[2] See L. Hodgson, *The Doctrine of the Trinity*, Nisbet, 1943; and J. McIntyre, *On the Love of God*, Collins, 1962, p. 181ff.; though such a 'family' understanding of 'God' is often refused because an originally other than Christian definition of his unity is widely accepted. It is odd that often those who most stress Jesus' and the Spirit's 'revelatory function' are least willing to let Jesus and the Spirit 'reveal' a fresh, other, non-rationalistic understanding of God.

of another, that makes Christian language more than Braith-waite's picturesque moral assertions.

But it is obviously false to claim that your assertion is more than an imaginative moral one if, in fact, you do *not* find that, living committed in this way, you or others are enabled to live agapeistically. If Christian commitment does not meet with success, then Christians have not committed themselves to 'God' who enables love. If it *is* successful, it does not 'prove' God. We have not found a new basis for 'scientific' descriptions of him. It only 'proves' the psychological oddity, that people who really believe odd things, odd 'myths', can produce odd, even useful results. If it fails, it shows the terms of commitment inappropriate; just as the war-widow's may become in-appropriate.

I have suggested that most Christian commitment is centred on Jesus of Nazareth, as *the* act of God, and most often as God himself.[1] This commitment depends on historical research and may be shown still appropriate or now inappropriate by it. It cannot be 'proved' by historical research; but it can be more or less drastically modified by such enquiry.[2] This is the centre of commitment to God who acts in history. It is a commitment to allowing events which actually happened to affect your life.[3] Either these events, or similar ones (and, of course, others which now happen), or very different ones, happened. If you are committed to the historic figure, Jesus of Nazareth, as the central historic event for your life, the event you call '*the* act of God in history', then to be consistent, and to be honest, you must let the form of your commitment depend on the uncertainties of historical research that tries to find what Christ himself did, said, was like. In the same way, the romantic needed, to be honest, to alter the terms of his commitment to his hero.

There are other forms of Christian commitment in which historical research is not so important. It is possible to be com-mitted to 'the Christ of Faith', of my faith, my church's faith, Luther's faith, Paul's faith, what I think Paul's faith was, or

[1] 'God was in Christ, reconciling the world to himself' (St Paul); 'My Lord and my God' (The Fourth Gospel); 'Jesus Christ my God' (Ignatius of Antioch); 'Very God of very God' (the 'Faith of Nicea').
[2] Cf. D. Cairns, *A Gospel Without Myth?*, ch. 8; H. Zahrnt, *The Historical Jesus*, Collins, 1963, p. 104.
[3] For a further statement of what is intended by a phrase of this sort see the next chapter.

what my favourite theologian thinks Paul's faith was; or a com-
bination of these and more. These are not 'better' or 'worse',
'truer' or 'less true' than the ones described as 'central'. They
are just other, and should be admitted to be other—to be, for
instance, faith as in a fictional character. But they may of
course still fall into the same category of commitment to 'God',
who is seen as eliciting a response that cannot stop short of total
agape.

The task of theological language is to make the terms of self-
committal clear, to the committed and the uncommitted. If you
claim to be committed to a historical person, with all the ambiguities that involves, then you cannot at the same time be un-
affected by the work of the archaeologist and textual critic.
Are you committed to a general 'New Testament' understanding of Christ? Then literary research into these documents
must affect you. If in the New Testament solely to Paul's
Christ, then admit it. Only if you are driven back beyond any
connection with the New Testament, with its particular understandings of humble, dependent *agape*, then perhaps it would be
more honest to surrender the name Christian. This is to make
clear the 'area' of the commitment.[1]

A lot of theological language, that of the Trinitarian and
Christological definitions, was first used to make clear the aim,
extent, degree of commitment; to make clear that it must aim
to be total. This was what was meant by 'there was not when
he was not'/(οὐκ ἦν ποτε ὅτε οὐκ ἦν). Commitment to Christ must
be total, as to 'God', not to 'a god'. And it must be to Christ
that this commitment is made, to the man Jesus of Nazareth,
as God; not to a largely *a priori* idea of God, in which 'Jesus'
is finally irrelevant, either in Nestorianism or monophysitism
(both of which are attempts to avoid letting Jesus affect the basic
understanding of, commitment to, 'God'). Even in its com-
promise, the Church has often failed to allow the scandal of

[1] For the most part, as MacIntyre, *Metaphysical Beliefs*, suggests, commitment is
to Christ as understood in the way some simple or complex 'authority' represents
him. He is accepted as 'seen' through a Baptist type of reading of the Bible, through
one or more of the many Anglican readings of the Bible, early Fathers, perhaps,
and recent Fathers, maybe; through a Roman Catholic reading of the Bible,
Fathers, developing tradition of the Church, ratified by Papal pronouncements, to
the present day. The individual commits himself to Christ as he is presented in
some smaller or larger, cohesive or nebulous, ancient or infant Christian community.
Theological language is a community attempt to express and elicit such commitment.

this precise particularity really to dominate its commitment. But it seems, if only formally, that it has seen this to be the real if unattainable centre of its life.[1]

In the last analysis (historically speaking), the very centre of commitment that can be called 'Christian' is commitment to the real past events of a person who did some things, and not others—either did them, or did not do them—Jesus of Nazareth: commitment to these events, this person, so that they, or he, is called 'God'; and what is meant by 'God' and what is intended in commitment depends on what can be known of him.[2]

The Christian commitment to a life of humble, dependent *agape* (or desire for it) is neither true nor false, if it happens at all. Traditional Christian assertions (though not necessarily in archaic speech) seem to be the only vehicle by which it may be expressed or elicited. There are none other suitable for precisely these lines of action. It is 'true' or 'false' in so far as it accurately expresses the commitment that the Christian intends, its aims, intensity (and, in the end, its success). It does not 'describe' *God* in any meaningful way, in any way that can be shown more or less apt or inapt. It 'describes' God no more than the war bride's language[3] 'describes' the actual condition of her husband. She hopes it may, even believes it does: that is part of her commitment. Theological language does however often seek to describe Jesus of Nazareth; as we have noted.[4] Only incidentally does it *describe* anything, and that is just the commitment, without reservations, to dependence on God as (and not 'as though') alive—to God whose chief 'act' that elicits this response was the birth, life, death, resurrection-ascension of Jesus of Nazareth. It describes incidentally a commitment to respond in love which its chief job is not to 'describe' but 'express'. It describes, more or less accurately and just in passing, faith, believing, which cannot be proved, only accepted, modified, rejected.

---

[1] Cf. P. van Buren, *The Secular Meaning of the Gospel*, ch. 2, the whole of Part II, and esp. ch. 7; see below, ch. 7.

[2] Further difficulties in talk of 'knowing' Jesus are examined below.

[3] Above, p. 184.

[4] In fact, even if it can validly be maintained, against the conclusions reached here, that there is a true element of description of God in theological language, that will not greatly affect what follows; the question still remains, 'Can God be said to "be revealed" when Christians are so variously and ineffectively committed to him?'

V. CONCLUSION

The non-believer, the uncommitted, may still insist, Christian faith is only a complex of myths, a world-view, with odd psychological effects on those who accept it, 'good' or 'bad' effects depending on the critic's standpoint.[1] But for the believer, however much of myth he may allow clothes the language of his commitment, even irradicably forms it, it is still primarily a language of ethical commitment, not an evocative or psycho-thereapeutic picture of the world. Rather than offering to describe the world,[2] he is promising to act in the world.[3]

Theologians' talk then, must be consistent; must be verifiable where it talks of facts; should be persuasive; and must express accurately the self-committal Christians wish, and find it possible, to make.[4]

We have so far only hinted at the light this brief survey of uses of 'theological' language may throw on problems of 'revelation'. However, it was necessary for clarity's sake to state the presuppositions that lie behind the ensuing discussion, and it is now possible to continue with the major theme of the essay, without too many pauses and parentheses; the need for this chapter should then become plain.

[1] Cf. G. Nakhnikian, in *Religious Experience and Truth*, p. 164.

[2] It is odd how the feeling that Christian language must be *describing* 'something' that others do not 'know' persists. J. A. T. Robinson in *Honest to God* objects strongly to using the word (or name) 'God' to mean 'a person' who can be shown to be or not to be a part of 'reality'. 'God' is not 'a being', 'a person' (p. 29ff.). But Robinson then (following Tillich) goes on to redefine what should be meant by 'God' in what seem to be intended as equally 'descriptive' terms. 'God', 'the transcendant', 'is a feature of all our experience—in depth'. Statements about 'God' acknowledge this element in our experience (pp. 52, 55). There is some chance that Robinson does sometimes intend statements with 'God' in them in the way we have here suggested ('God is personal' is said to mean 'personality is of ultimate significance', p. 48, and this is a commitment). But by and large, 'God' as 'an element in all experience' becomes just what Robinson began by rejecting, a part of 'reality' that may or may not be.

[3] Contra S. Hook, in *Religious Experience and Truth*, p. 63: 'The language of religion carries with it a mood of acceptance and resignation to the world as we find it, which tends to dissipate the mood of social change and reform.' See also below, ch. 7.

[4] The distinctions that I make above between 'first' and 'other' (understood) 'purposes', 'primary' and 'other' functions, 'direct' and 'indirect' language, might have been made more clearly with the help of the terms suggested by J. L. Austin, in *How to do things with Words*, Oxford, 1962, and also in *Philosophical Papers*, Oxford, 1961: but I hope that I have, if a little clumsily, avoided the over-nice abstract distinctions that he objects to. See also D. Evans, *The Logic of Self-Involvement*, SCM Press, 1963, for a theologian's appreciation and use of Austin's tools.

6

KNOWLEDGE AND REVELATION, MISUNDERSTANDING AND DISOBEDIENCE

I T would be possible so to redefine the word 'revelation' that
the proposition 'God has revealed himself' would be compatible with just *any* other proposition. It could be done by
giving 'reveal' a new meaning for each argument; so that, for
instance, it might on some occasions actually mean 'make more
obscure than before'. But we have suggested that such equivocation does not really suit Christian theology. We assume that
there are 'normal' ways in which 'reveal' (and 'know') are used,
and that the theologian intends one of these, unless he specifically says not, and never something totally different.

It is possible to make what look like assertions about 'the
Christian experience of "revelation" ' and all the while (even
intentionally) ignore the empirical facts of Christian intention
and achievement. In this case, we have seen, the assertions are
probably false.

It may be suggested that talk of 'the Christian revelation'
has a powerful effect on men's minds; it may even be true. But
unless the effect is to elicit a positive commitment to *agape*, it
is not talk about a Christian 'God', it is not 'revelation of God
in Christ'.

It may be supposed that the Christian failure or refusal to
offer a total commitment, or, when offered, act on it, is irrelevant
to a consideration of whether 'God is revealed'. But in this case,
again, it is not a Christian 'God' who is being spoken of at all.

Bearing these conclusions from chapter 5 in mind, we examine statements about 'God' being 'known', or 'revealed'.

We need to be sure of the human situations from which we
are starting, how the language is normally used, the direction in

which we are qualifying this language for 'true' talk about God, whether such 'verifiable content' as these assertions may have proves true or false, and whether it is appropriate to Christian commitment.

I. TO KNOW   *How do friers "know"*

'Knowledge' of Facts

The simplest uses of 'know' are in such sentences as, 'I know $x = 2y$'; 'I know the right (or best) way to London'; 'I know how to write.' It becomes more complicated in 'I know London'; 'Yes, I know the man you mean'; 'I *know* Jack, and I know he couldn't have done a thing like that.'

In normal, unambiguous usage, 'I know $x = 2y$' and other similar assertions are all falsifiable. It is quite proper for someone to say, 'No, you do not, for I can prove that x does not equal $2y$.' You cannot 'know' that $x = 2y$ if it does not. 'I believe $x = 2y$' is not refutable, at least not in the same way. By electro-encephalography it might be shown that you were making an untrue statement about your own mind.[2] But you may very truly believe an untrue statement that $x = 2y$; and your statement about your (mistaken) belief cannot be falsified. You may of course still insist on saying, 'I *know* $x = 2y$' when in fact it does not, but then you are using 'know' in rather a different way, to say forcefully, 'I really do believe $x = 2y$.' It is not the place of the analyst of linguistic usage to say that a word should not be used in a way in which it is commonly used; his task is only to point out the differences between usages, and to insist that no illegitimate deductions should be made by confusing them. The 'normal' usage 'I know (= "I know-and-can-prove") $x = 2y$' is primarily a statement about some external fact[3] and as such can be checked. If you say, 'I know the way to London', but in fact get yourself lost, I may, gently or

---

[1] Again, it is not being claimed that only that which may be verified (better, falsified) is worth saying; but that where an assertion does have this logic, the need to examine the possibilities of verification cannot be evaded.

[2] Or you might be said to be making 'an untrue declaration': so R. Abelson, 'The Logic of Faith and Belief', *Religious Experience and Truth*, p. 118ff. Much of this analysis is however supported in Abelson's article. I think that the stress he places (and cf. I. T. Ramsey's *Freedom and Immortality*, SCM Press, 1960) on the different logic of first as opposed to second and third person statements will probably prove wrong. At least, I would not wish to base any further argument on such differences as appear to some to hold.

[3] 'I know and can prove $x = 2y$' is also a statement about your own mind, but this is not its primary purpose. Cf. Austin, *Philosophical Papers*, p. 44ff.

forcefully, call you a liar. This is normal usage. 'I know (=
"I know-and-no-one-may-disprove; I believe") $x = 2y$' is
only a statement about (or, perhaps, assertion of) your own
mind, and though external checks may persuade you to change
your mind, they do not disprove your statement. This is not the
normal way to use 'I know'; this is the sort of statement you
make when you are losing your temper, and is, for instance,
akin to swearing. Unless we have very strong reason not to, we
assume that the man who says 'I know $x = 2y$' is saying something that can be checked, and that he, probably, has checked
(by whatever tests are appropriate).

In 'I know London', the amount of knowledge expected will
depend on the speaker. The provincial motorist can validly
make the claim, if he can navigate his car across the City, and
find the main shopping centres and places of interest; but the
London-based commercial traveller can say, 'Ah, but you don't
know London like I know London'; and the London taxi-driver
will mean even more by 'I know London.' The man who says,
'I know London' probably implies some qualification, and will
accuse you of pedantry if you take him up on some aspect of the
City that he is not likely to know. He most likely means, 'I know
London sufficiently for some specific purpose.' But if within
these implicit or explicit limits he proves mistaken, then he
does not 'know London'.

'Yes, I know the man you mean' may be as simple as 'I know
the way from here to London.' 'I recognise the man from your
description; he is the one who catches the 7.53 a.m. from the
stop opposite.' 'I know sufficient about him to distinguish him
from other men; I know him.' This is still obviously falsifiable
—you can properly say, 'No, you don't know the one I mean;
he goes by the 7.38 a.m. train into the City.'

'Knowledge' of Persons

However, 'I know that person' is often a much more complex
claim, and requires a more detailed analysis; especially as this
is often taken as a model for talk of 'knowing God', and because
the importance, delight and the very complexity of this type of
'knowing' can be used as excuses for refusing to think clearly
about it.

(i) *'I and Thou'*   It seems fair enough for the purposes of discussion to divide the personal uses of 'know' into three classes. Obviously, however, any one instance of 'knowing a person' may be compounded of elements from more than one 'class'.[1] Out of these we may be able to find a proper way of talking of 'knowing God'. The first we look at and the richest is the 'knowing' that comes with close and frequent contact. A man newly wed may have a very inaccurate image of his wife, perhaps flattering, but quite probably unreal; even of her physical appearance, and particularly of her character. The image he has of her will probably be compounded of his conscious ideal of womanhood, a projection of himself, his mother, sisters, previous girl-friends, film stars, and a whole multitude—and be qualified only by those factors in her character that have already penetrated through to him. . . . The closer contact of living together for months and years modifies the image (as well, of course, as the reality), and he learns, for instance, her real likes and dislikes, strengths and weaknesses. You can tell objectively[2] if he has come to know her more truly—or better, 'has come closer to knowing *her*'—by the success or failure of his conscious and unconscious predictions of her behaviour, even of her unpredictability. This you can check. And you may find that the ideal remains powerful enough to swamp his response to the real person, especially if the fanciful is more pleasant than the real. This is then the refuge of a sickly mind. The saner response will be to accept the real person his wife is, and allow the 'image' to be reshaped progressively by the changing reality. But it is important to note that the reshaping depends very much on close and frequent physical contact, the continuous noting of facial expression, tone of voice, durability of enthusiasm; and an ideal image (or even an anti-ideal) can reassert itself, if husband and wife are separated.

[1] The examples below are of 'knowing' a person in an active, positive relationship. It is of course possible to have a full and true knowledge with little if any sympathetic or antipathetic relationship. Such might be the knowledge gained by a psychiatrist of the strictest Freudian school. The tests for such a claim to 'knowledge' are much the same. But see below for a proviso.

[2] A 'complete objectivity' (as noted above, p. 172, n. 2) is not being claimed (and is probably, anyway, nonsense). It is here assumed that it is meaningful to talk of some impressions of the world around as more, others as less objectively formed. The test is by comparison with others' (and one's own previous and later) reactions. The assumption cannot be 'proved' but has to be 'accepted' if discussion of the world by two or more people is to take place at all. I am not prepared to attempt the futility of debate with anyone who disputes this.

In the sense in which, for instance, Martin Buber uses the
'knowledge' of the 'I' for the 'Thou',[1] any image can be the
gracious 'Thou' that is presented to the 'I', and does not have
to have an 'objective reality'. It is just the irrelevance of objectivity that 'makes' the relationship. It is self-authenticating.
But I cannot be said to have such a 'personal relationship'
with my wife, one that may be called 'knowing *her*', if my relationship is with an image of her formed purely or predominantly
subjectively, i.e. with scant reference to the person she really is.
Making sure that my very authentic relationship is authenti-
cally with my wife is a matter of setting my understanding of
her gained 'relationally' over against her observable behaviour,
and seeing if they match. The 'knowing' of which Martin
Buber writes is valid, however small the connection between
the Thou encountered, and any 'I', any self, itself capable of
entering such a relationship; so I can even 'encounter' a tree as
my 'Thou',[2] though of course it cannot 'encounter' me. My
relationship with the tree, or with any other imaginary self,
may be entirely 'authentic', in Buber's analysis. It authenti-
cates itself. But once I claim to have, or to have had, a relationship with a particular person, a person who is not only my
'Thou', but is himself capable of being 'encountered', initiating
or receiving a relationship, description has come in; the claim is
open to falsification. So, it will easily be seen that it is not my
wife that I 'know', if she never or rarely behaves as I expect;
I do not 'know' my wife if I am constantly surprised by her,
constantly misjudge her temper. It is only some person my mind
presents to itself: the claim to relationship is on its own an
assertion solely about my state of mind. On the other hand, the
claim to 'relationship with', 'knowledge of', *a person* is a statement about externally verifiable or at least falsifiable fact, and
can usually be quite easily checked. The relationship that
exists only in my mind may be called 'I-Thou' relationship,

[1] M. Buber, *I and Thou*, T. and T. Clark, 1937. I cannot find a difference 'in
kind' between this type of 'knowing' and the 'impersonal' ones described above.
This is just more complex, more emotional. However, it does seem different enough
in degree, important enough for human living, to warrant a distinct vocabulary.
Even in non-technical discourse we reserve special ways for talking about persons.
It is the logic of this sort of language's use of 'know' that we now examine. For a
theologian's appreciation of this language, cf. J. Baillie, *The Idea of Revelation*, p. 28:
'an important new advance'. For further illustration see p. 238.
[2] M. Buber, *op. cit.*, p. 7.

and raises no questions of objectivity. The other may be called an 'I-Thou-Thou-I' relationship: it supposes that the 'Thou' that encounters my 'I' is also a real 'I' that can or does encounter, let itself be encountered by, me as 'Thou'. The only circumstances in which an 'I-Thou-Thou-I' relation is likely to happen are the day-to-day contacts of, say, a marriage. The only situation where a claim to such a relationship can be justified is one where objective checks can be made. The only justified claim to such a relationship is one that is at least not falsified by my own or others' experience.

I think that a Christian using this language would want to claim an 'I-Thou-Thou-I' 'knowledge of God'. He would not, I think, just be claiming that the relationship was satisfactory, 'authentic'; he would be saying ' "real God", "God who is known to others", is my Thou.' At the time of encounter it would (I gather from Buber) be impossible to say 'who' my 'Thou' is. But afterwards the Christian would very likely wish to say, 'My "Thou" is God, the Father, "revealed" in Christ'.[1] And then he has admitted that the relationship is more than self-authenticating. He has qualified the claim with a verifiable or at least falsifiable description; falsifiable at any rate by reference to what is normally meant by 'God, God the Father, God revealed in Christ'. He will not be claiming that his mind has spun a mental 'Thou' into relationship with itself. It is a 'Thou-I, I-Thou' relationship, initiated by the 'Thou' who is God. This I think the Christian would have to insist, if he were using this type of language.

But the paradigm we have suggested for language of this kind *does not seem to allow us to claim this sort of relationship with God*, the sort of relationship that is objectively shaped by physical contact with the Other, and empirically verifiable from moment to moment by the accuracy of conscious and unconscious forecasts of moods and wishes. He does not, at present, offer himself to us in this way, the richest form of 'knowing' a person. *We do not yet have an 'I-Thou, Thou-I' relation with God*.

(ii) *Indirect 'Knowledge' of Contemporaries* There remain the other two classes of the use of 'know' in personal relationship language, dependent on this first for their meaning. By assiduous

---

[1] Admitted, for instance, by D. Cairns, *A Gospel without Myth?*, p. 213ff.

reading of gossip columns, newspaper reports, film magazines, you could reach the point where you could validly say, 'I feel I know Bing Crosby like I know the man next door.' 'I *know* Gina Lollobrigida.' This would be a little artificial, a trifle precious; but the 'I-Thou' relationship could be authentic enough and the 'image' fairly objective (as accurate as the press reports). It is not an 'I-Thou, Thou-I' relationship; it is not specifically shaped by the other person. But it is still objective; it can be tested. If you expect your star to fall for a film director, and instead she falls for a camera-man, you do not know her very well. And there is always the (faint) possibility that you might both meet—that the relationship would become two-way, 'I-Thou, Thou-I'—the chance that your relationship with her would prove directly continuous with your relationship with the imaginary her. However, till this happens, you have to keep the 'I *feel*' before the 'I know', or the italics. If you are pressed on this point, you have to say, 'Well, no, not really; we've never met face to face, I don't really know her like that.'

Even this does not provide us with a paradigm for talk of 'knowing' God. The closer, the more 'real' a relationship of this sort is to become, the more it has to rely on people who *are* in the first sort of relationship with the other person; people who are in day-to-day objective physical contact. And we have noted the obvious fact that God does not grant this first type of relationship to any in our world for it to be the basis for us of the second kind of relationship with him.

(iii) *'Knowledge' of Characters in Fiction and Biography*   With varying degrees of objectivity, you can 'know' fictional and other literary characters, and enter into 'relationship' with them. There are the people of your daydreams, the slightly more independent population of your sleeping dreams; the men and women in novels, who are created by someone else, in ways you cannot control; and the historical personages that you meet in biographies, who are already created in large measure for their biographers—and here this third group merges with the second, which is living biography. Even in these cases, you have large scope for forming images of these people to your own liking, witness our frequent annoyance at the way film-

makers, playwrights, actors, have 'misinterpreted' a character
from a favourite book. The only objective check is to read more
biographies, more interpretations of the character, to discuss
him or her with others who have read the book, seen the play.
It is much more difficult, but it is possible to make some
objective checks, and so make sure that the character you
'know' is the one intended by the author and not just the
product of your own imagination. And any of these figures,
imaginary, biographic, can become your 'Thou'. But if one
man says, 'This is what Gladstone would have done' and
another says, 'Don't be daft'; if one little boy says, 'Robin
Hood wants us to practise shooting arrows' and the other says,
'No, he wants us to stalk cat-deer'—then obviously they do not
both 'know' 'Gladstone', or 'Robin Hood'; at least, not the
same Gladstone or Robin Hood. They do not both 'know' the
same person, however real may be to each of them the image
they call by the same name, 'Robin Hood', or 'Gladstone'—
real as 'Thou', and authentic as different imaginary characters.

For the non-Christian, or non-theist, this must seem the most
likely paradigm for talk of 'knowing God'—a relationship with
a diffuse imaginary person whom a number of contemporaries
claim to know, and about whom they disagree largely, showing
how much he is a product of individual imagination, an adapta-
tion to taste of a stock of rather vague common traditions.
'God' seems to be not just one imaginary character, but many.

A Paradigm for 'Knowledge of God'

There is, however, the possibility of extracting from these
three classes of ways of 'knowing a person' a paradigm for talk
of 'knowing God', which may be a little more acceptable to the
Christian, though not as bold as he would perhaps like. It is
certainly one whose validity he should be able to maintain in
talk with fellow Christians; he might even be able to defend it
in conversation with a sympathetic non-Christian. It is really
a sub-group of the second or perhaps the third class, but with a
significant element of the first. It is the sort of relationship
that can accompany the long correspondence of pen-friends.
The uncontrolled imagination can play a large part in it (the

Cf. A. Farrer, 'Revelation', *Faith and Logic*, ed. B. Mitchell, p. 93: 'As many
persons of Godhead as there are human destinies' (though Farrer thinks the problem soluble).

third type of knowing), witness the surprise of pen-friends at
meeting, even when they have exchanged photographs. It is
a relationship whose other term has some connection with an
actual living person (here it is analogous with the second type
of knowing). And the 'other' can correct mistakes about himself, mistakes that become obvious in the letters he receives;
this personal control of the relationship by the 'other' gives the
analogy with type-one knowing. It is still even with the best of
correspondents far from the 'I-Thou, Thou-I' relationship of
day-to-day contact where full advantage is taken of the possibility for objectivity. But it can provide the Christian with a
model for some of the things he would wish to say about
'knowing' God.

A fair illustration would be as follows. There is a refugee,
X, in a mid-European camp. He corresponds with a sick man,
A, in an American sanatorium. The American is a fairly well-
known author, who often used to be in the papers for odd
exploits; even now, magazine articles are written about him.
There is no real chance of their meeting, the American cannot
travel, the refugee has T.B. and will never get a clearance.
Still, the refugee has a fairly lively impression of his friend-at-a-
distance, from the stories and reactions of others who claim to
have known him, from the biography produced by friends with
the help of the man's son, now dead; and from the letters he
receives at frequent intervals.

Something like this the Christian may claim for his 'knowledge of God'. To a large extent it depends on the impression
of others: the Bible and a greater or lesser area of the very varied
Christian tradition, and the 'experience' of his contemporaries.
But he will claim, it is 'knowledge' of a living person. More or
less often he will claim to have received, quite consciously,
messages from the 'God' he claims to 'know'. And he will probably claim, if not in quite the same words, that this 'God', or
'the Holy Spirit', shapes his response to him by other means
besides these messages consciously received—that 'God' does
this perhaps predominantly without his being aware himself
of 'God's' activity. This latter assertion obviously has no
immediate parallel in the paradigm under discussion, but
broadly the situation is similar enough; the claim to 'know a
person', through others' impressions of him qualified by the

living person himself, but in a way less immediate and less sure than actual physical nearness would allow.

However, there is already a very real logical difference, which cannot be argued away, even if its importance can be called in question. If the refugee has doubts (Is this author real, and not just a publicity stunt by a publishing firm? Are my letters from him authentic, and not just a trick someone is playing on me?), he can write to someone else at the American hospital, or to fellow countrymen living near who might be able to make sure for him. If he had the money, he might be healed, or bribe his way to America to check for himself. The objective reality of the person with whom he corresponds is 'verifiable', at least theoretically. The Christian plainly cannot, by definition of the term 'God', make this sort of check by sense-data (see above), either at second or first hand. He cannot check in this way that Christian origins and history are not a huge fraud, that his own experience of God is not self-deception aided by others.

But the real importance of this theoretical possibility of *first-hand* verification is definitely questionable. In the living situation of the refugee, verification is to all intents and purposes as impossible as it is impossible for the Christian to obtain first-hand evidence to verify his 'knowledge of God': the refugee, like the Christian, has to decide for or against continuing the relationship, for or against deciding it is with a real person, without reference to data that are not in fact available.[1]

In actual fact, the refugee will probably not question the authenticity of the other person, *A*, unless a third person calls it in question. Suppose then that he meets refugee *Y*, and finds that he too has been corresponding with *A*. He may swop impressions. 'He minds a lot about the United Nations.' 'Yes, funny the way he detests the whole show.' 'Detests it? I've never met a man keener on it. Look, this magazine quotes him as saying he's leaving all his money to it; and he's praised its work no end in letters.' 'Rubbish. You should see what he told me about it, interfering in national sovereignty; he always

[1] It might be objected, see above, that it is not for any man to test his relationship with another, but to trust; and *a fortiori*, not to test 'God'. But it is not 'God' that we are suggesting the Christian should test, but his own supposed 'knowledge' of him; testing how far it is 'God' that he 'knows', and how far just a projection of, for instance, his own far from perfect self. This is not just permissible it is imperative.

was one to protect individuals, people or nations.' 'Are we talking about the same man?'

Either they are not talking about the same man, or one at least is victim of a hoax, or one at least has a very mistaken impression of him. If the letters to both are genuine, then they both have a very insufficient impression of the real person, and have not realised the possible complexities of his character. Though to give such impressions, he would have to be schizophrenic. . . .

Suppose that refugee Z now appears on the scene and shows Y that he has mistranslated the American's letter, and himself backs up X's impressions of A, from his own correspondence with him, then although Y may not be persuaded, X will have good reason to trust his own beliefs about A and to continue the relationship. He could still validly say, 'I know a real person, A.' The more people he could find who agreed with him about A, the more right he would have to say, 'I know A.' The more he found like Y, who disagreed with him, and even with each other, about A, the less right would he have to say 'I know A.'

If he were the only one who claimed to know A, there would be little problem because little possibility of falsification. If he is one of many claiming a knowledge of A, the problem becomes acute. If by and large they agree among themselves, their claim to a common knowledge of A is good enough. If they disagree, then some, many, all, do not 'know' A in any significant sense of the word. One or two may in fact know him, but will find it hard to persuade anyone else that they do.

The relevance of this for the Christian should be clear. If, as has been argued, this paradigm, or one very like it, for his talk of 'knowing God', is the best he can hope to defend, then there are two corollaries. The greater the diversity of the groups to which he allows the name Christian, the less his justification for saying they 'know God', in any meaningful sense of that word; the less his justification for saying 'God has made himself known.' Then, the only way to justify a claim to 'know God', a claim that 'God has made himself known', is to restrict the list of the enlightened to a group that agrees about 'God' on as many major and minor issues as possible.

Obviously, it will not seriously damage the claim if Group One says, 'The number of candles on the altar does not matter much to God, but if anything he prefers two'; and Group Two says, 'The number does not matter to him, but he prefers six.' But if both say this does matter to him, and disagree, the claim is badly shaken. If they agree that love between Christians is important to God, but cannot agree on how he wishes church unity to happen, the claim is badly shaken. Two people can validly claim to 'know' a third if they disagree about him only on matters which they do agree are unimportant. If they do not know his mind on some matter which *is* important to him, they do not 'know him', or they do not 'know him' at all well.

The second way to justify the claim, by reducing the number of claimants, is superficially more promising. But it is not open even for one present major Christian body to make the claim just for its members; there is too much diversity within even Roman Catholicism or Orthodoxy and certainly in any large 'reformed' body for the claim to be valid. The claim could only be made at the expense of becoming entirely sectarian. It is, of course, possible for a group to persuade itself that its 'knowledge of God' is continuous with such 'knowledge of God' as may be evidenced in the New Testament. It is doubtful whether such a group could sufficiently *prove* either claim to make their use of the word 'know' meaningful.[1] It would be difficult enough to make good a claim that the New Testament writers themselves had a common 'knowledge of God'.

The 'pen-friend' paradigm (or something like it) provides the Christian with his closest analogy for his talk of 'knowing God'; it allows for a large element of imagination, a place for the experience of others, and room for control by the one 'known'. The Christian has to admit that his talk of 'knowledge of God' lacks one of the paradigm's possibilities of verification, the theoretical possibility of immediate contact. The more important check by presence or absence of general unanimity *is* possible, but in the present state of Christian obedience the application of this criterion of general agreement in belief and practice is little short of disastrous.[2] Christians have a number of vague and contradictory beliefs and even these seem to have very little

---

[1] This is not to say that the group could not persuade others of the 'truth' of their case; only that it could not *prove the point*.

[2] This has little bearing on the question, 'Does God exist?' It is only concerned with the problem, 'Is there knowledge of him?' To be sure, if there is none at all, the question of his 'existence' ceases to be very pressing.

effect on their practice. To call this 'knowledge of God' is absurd if it is not blasphemous.

'Knowledge of God' and the Hebrew yd'

So much for 'to know a person' in current usage. It does not offer any possibility of conveying the wide range of meanings that we found could be communicated with the Hebrew *yd*'.[1] In the latter, we noticed, there is usually if not always a change of meaning for a different relationship, a change that is quite real and can be seen from the context. In English, to 'know' your brother, your wife, your father, your son, are all similar. In the Old Testament (and in the New), to 'know' a superior, especially God, means to obey him; to 'know' your wife means primarily coition; and so forth.[2] Admittedly, in English, if you say you know a particularly holy person well, yet are yourself amoral or wicked, it sounds strange; but it is not the contradiction it would appear in the Old Testament or the New. The English word usually means 'to have information about', or 'to be acquainted with'; even, 'to have and keep a very deep and rich acquaintanceship with'. But it is always describing the cognitive and mental element in a relationship. It is much narrower and more precise than *yd*'. This does mean that translation of the biblical terms, from the Old Testament and from the New, is difficult. Because our English word does not alter its sense for the different persons known, it is far too easily assumed that 'knowing God' in the Bible, for instance, means 'knowing him as a friend'. So far is this from the case that when a writer does want to say that Moses had this sort of 'knowledge of God' he has to add 'as a friend' to make it explicit (Ex. 33.11). Just 'Moses knew God' would have meant something rather different; it would mean Moses was obedient. This 'obedience-knowing' is the only sort of 'knowing' that is expected of most men, in the Bible.

From this it follows that in the logic of 'the biblical use' (it is fairly constant) not only do differences of opinion about 'God' invalidate the claim to 'know' him, the claim to any posi-

[1] See chs 2 and 3.
[2] 'To know' is used of sexual intercourse, in the legal phrase, 'to have carnal knowledge of', and in some Christian books about marriage, but probably only with conscious reference to the Bible. It is not normal contemporary English usage (cf. *O.E.D.*).

tive relationship with him; but *failure to act* on 'knowledge' claimed invalidates the claim 'to know'. In this idiom, the failure of Christians to maintain or restore unity is an even stronger proof that there is no 'knowledge of God', than their failure to agree on the terms God would will for unity; this along with all the many other failures of Christians, to understand and obey.

This note of 'obedience' cannot be made artificially a part of the logic of the English 'to know'. However, it is part of the logic of a significant use of the name 'God' as we have seen in the last chapter.

When a Christian says 'God is love', and beats his children unmercifully, we feel he has not understood his own words. God is he who makes an absolute demand upon us, there is no limit to the obedience he may expect of us. To claim to 'know' God, in any full sense of the word, without offering to him the response he demands, is meaningless. You may 'know' a weak personality without being noticeably affected; you cannot in any full sense of the word 'know' a person very much more forceful and attractive than yourself, without being affected by him. You cannot claim to 'know God', unless your whole life is God-like.

Christians cannot claim *any* sort of 'knowledge of God' unless they agree about him; they cannot really claim 'knowledge of God' unless they act without conflict on what they say they know of him. Nor, of course, till this has happened, can it be said that 'God has made himself known'.

Bearing this in mind, we now turn to see what possibilities there may be for talking intelligibly and truly of 'revelation' as an act or activity of 'God': 'revelation' of 'himself', 'truths about himself', 'his will', 'his demands', or anything else.

II. TO REVEAL

Etymology

The word 'reveal' has a much more restricted current use than 'know'. The use in present English is very much the same as that of *glh* in Hebrew, and ἀποκαλύπτειν in Greek. The

⁶See above, p. 185ff. This is another way of stating what was said above, that language about 'God' is the language of commitment.

stem-word 'veil' is not as obvious to the English user as it would be in the Latin word from which it derives, or in the Greek,[1] but the word is used largely in contexts where 'unveil' would still be quite appropriate, if a little artificial. So there is no difficulty in translation. And we noted in the first chapter that this common meaning of 'reveal' is generally accepted by theologians.

Literal and Metaphorical

It might be possible to use 'reveal', very literally to mean just 'take away one physical object that was covering another physical object': 'uncover'. But the word would probably not be understood in this way. 'To reveal a hidden trap door in pitch darkness' would sound silly. 'Reveal' usually means 'to uncover for sight', literally or metaphorically. It implies that someone will be able to say, 'I see', or 'I have seen;' 'I see with my eyes' or 'I "see" intellectually' ('I understand').

It might be used for 'make *available* for sight'; it can just possibly be used in this way, even if no one does 'see'. 'The statue lay revealed all morning, without one viewer entering the room.' Certain physical objects (or conditions, such as 'darkness') that would hinder a potential viewer have been removed. But this use is not frequent. Normally, to 'reveal' means actually to 'make seen',[2] for the 'veil' that is to be taken away includes metaphorically any optical or mental factor that prevents sight: the 'unveiling' is the removing of all hindrance to 'seeing', including any in the intended viewer's eyes or mind or both, and so cannot be said to have happened until the 'seeing' itself has happened. 'To reveal' then mostly implies 'to reveal *to someone*'. It prompts the question, 'Who did see?' Even when the 'veil' is a physical one, its removal will not usually be called a 'revelation' unless someone does see the hitherto hidden object. 'The mayor pulled the silken cord, the curtain fell hesitantly, and the Abomination was revealed to the horrified gathering.' And in the novelettish situation, 'He stripped off his shirt, there, alone in the room, to reveal the strong muscles of his arms and

[1] Latin, *revelare, velum,* curtain, veil; Greek, ἀποκαλύπτειν, κάλυμμα, veil.
[2] See G. F. Woods, in *Theological Explanation*, Nisbet, 1958, p. 87ff. But the analysis offered there of this word does not take into account some of the critical considerations dealt with below. See also G. MacGregor, *Introduction to Religious Philosophy*, p. 30f.; and the references in ch. 1, p. 10f.

chest and back', 'reveal' is used because the hero's body is being 'shown' to the reader, who has not 'seen' this before.

Normally, then, if 'reveal' is used, the question may fairly be asked 'Who saw?' If no one 'saw', then the word is being used a little oddly only of the physical uncovering of a physical object. If the word is *not* being used solely in this way, if it is being used of an optical (or *a fortiori*, of an intellectual) 'unveiling' to 'make *seen*', then the 'revealing' is as incomplete as the perceiving (visual or mental, or both) of the person or persons it is intended shall 'see'. It should be clear to the user, and to the hearer or reader, which sense is meant.

We noted in the first chapter that theologians seemed to accept that 'revelation' implies the effecting of an extreme clarity of perception. And this is, to be sure, its normal sense.

We have glanced in passing at the rather remote possibility of 'reveal' being used to talk of the purely physical 'unveiling' of a purely physical (solid) object. It is not usually now thought that 'God' is such a physical object that may be uncovered by the removal of another physical obstruction, and so 'revealed' just as simply as that. Even if the ancient Hebrews and others have thought of 'God' veiled only by the 'firmament of heaven' or by cloud if he descended below it, modern Western theologians do not so much as think it worth registering their disagreement (except occasionally by pretending that the ancient Hebrews did not really believe that either). But it was noted earlier that many New Testament writers place some stress on the fact that people *saw* Jesus' physical body: he was, in this sense, 'revealed', physically—both available for seeing, and actually seen. When it is believed that Jesus 'is God', it can be said, 'God was made visible', 'God was actually seen.' But to say that the 'physical-body-of-Jesus-who-is-God' 'was seen', is not the same as to say the 'self' of 'Jesus-who-is-God', or the 'self' of God, 'was seen'.[1]

[1] See ch. 3, esp. p. 106ff., where it is noted that the Fourth Evangelist makes this contrast explicitly. It is also the theme of more than one Epiphany hymn; for instance, 'Within the Father's House', *A. & M.* 488. Verse 2:

'The doctors of the law
   Gaze on the wondrous child,
And marvel at his gracious words
   Of Wisdom undefiled.

Yet not to them is given
   The mighty truth to know,
To lift the fleshly veil which hides
Incarnate God below.

To say that Jesus was (at least) an ordinary physical human being, seen by his contemporaries, is theologically very important; he was not just a figment of mid-first-century imagination. It is a meaningful assertion, it can be 'verified' in the same rather indefinite way as other statements about past events; and, at the present stage of historical research, it seems quite justified. To use 'reveal' or 'revelation' for this 'making seen' is a little grandiose, but quite intelligible. He whom Christians call 'God incarnate' was 'revealed', even 'will be revealed' (which the New Testament also says and intends in much the same way). But in this sense it cannot, of course, be said that he is still 'revealed'.[1] He is not now 'on view'. He has not, by becoming physically visible, necessarily 'revealed' himself to me, literally or metaphorically. And save for a few possible exceptions (noted in chapter 3) this is the only even implicit 'revelation of God' of which the New Testament writers speak—the past and future making seen of the physical being, Jesus.

This sort of physical 'revealing' could happen to a book, as a thing of parchment (papyrus, or paper) and ink. It could be hidden and then disclosed to view. But 'the Bible is God's revelation' does not even among the superstitious mean that a first copy of the book was dropped from heaven. It is not as a physical object brought into sight that it is called 'divine revelation'. It might be said of the Tables of the Law, by some; or of the golden book of a later sect. But this is obviously not the usual level at which talk of 'biblical revelation' moves.

Finality

Such a literal, physical 'revealing' of an enduring object could (theoretically—it would depend on its durability) be for all time and for all people. It could be a 'final' 'complete' event. But a 'revealing' that includes a 'making seen', if it is to be 'for all times and for all people', must happen for each individual. The statue may have been 'revealed' to many, but not to me, until I have been brought into the room that houses it,

> 'The secret of the Lord
>   Escapes each human eye,
>   And faithful pondering hearts await
>   The full Epiphany.'

[1] See H. R. Niebuhr, *The Meaning of Revelation*, Macmillan, N.Y., 1941; Macmillan Paper-back, 1960, p. 148.

and there do see it. It is not possible to transfer the 'objectivity' or 'finality' of the literal 'revealing', 'uncovering', of a solid body, to the normal use of 'reveal'. If 'reveal' is being used to mean 'make seen' (still more, if it is being used as a metaphor for 'make known'), it has only happened as the 'seeing' (or 'coming to know') has happened.

Whatever else the theologians may mean by the 'finality' or 'objectivity' of revelation[1] they explicitly do not mean that there is no more 'seeing' or 'making seen' to be done. John Baillie writes, 'The divine act of revelation cannot be said to be completed unless it be apprehended as such, just as I cannot be said to have revealed anything to you if you do not at all understand what I have desired to convey. . . . It follows that God reveals Himself to me only in so far as I apprehend Him. Such apprehension, however, must be a fact of my own present experience or nothing at all, and that is why more than one of the writers whom we have been quoting insist that "all revelation is in the present moment".[2] The 'revealing' as such, the actual 'making seen', is not understood as objective and final (only a literal uncovering could be that and still relevant). The 'revealing' that interests the theologian is one that continues, and makes us 'see' now.

In the strictly literal sense again, it might be possible to call Jesus' walking quite visibly around the Galilean and Judaean countryside a 'final and objective revelation' of him. But if the 'revealing' of him was truly 'final' in this or any sense, that would at the same time mean there was no more seeing for us now: he is for us no longer a 'visible object'. The written Book, the engraved stones, could on the other hand have been 'finally and objectively revealed', and could still (as things that last) be wonders for the pilgrim to gaze at. But even those to whom Bible or Decalogue are most precious cannot now point to any relic that has that sort of finality or objectivity.

This may seem trivial; but it really is important to explore some of the odder blind alleys and fence them off. It drives us to

[1] For the terms see e.g. P. Tillich, *ST* I, pp. 123-4, 147ff.; J. I. Packer, *Fundamentalism and the Word of God*, p. 118; K. Barth, *Against the Stream*, p. 207, etc.
[2] In *The Idea of Revelation*, p. 104f. He cites specifically E. Brunner; see also G. Aulén in *Revelation*, p. 300; J. I. Packer, *op. cit.*, *ibid.*; P. Tillich, *ST* I, *ibid.*; and cf. p. 40: 'Since there is no revelation unless there is someone who receives it as revelation, the act of reception is a part of the event itself'; S. Bulgakoff in *Revelation*, p. 171ff.; K. Barth, *CD* I/2, p. 238.

think, What other roads are there to securing some 'objectivity' and 'finality' for 'God's saving revelation', if the simplest ones prove so useless? Still, we have seen that it is generally admitted that if there is objectivity or finality, it lies elsewhere.

However, the 'finality' can be made to refer to the completeness of what is 'revealed'; it is 'final' because nothing more is needed. It is 'the last word', and nothing may be added, subtracted, modified. Other people may well still need to be allowed to 'see', but there is nothing to show that has not already been shown. It is the criterion by which to judge whether later viewers have seen truly or not. This sense is made possible by an ambiguity in the word 'revelation' that we shall look at more closely in a moment. A 'final revelation' in this sense is not talking about a completed 'making seen' but a 'definitive *revelatum*'. It does not suggest that everyone has seen who will see; but it does suggest that there is somewhere a clarity that can 'define' what shall be seen by later viewers. If this clarity is lacking, it is not 'definitive'.[1] The university authorities can place the prototype of the new B.A. hood on show in the museum, for the local tailors to copy. It is the criterion for all future hoods, but it is actually definitive only while it is readily available for imitation or comparison. This is important.

Some New Testament writers say that Jesus is the 'image' of God, or use some equivalent expression to describe him (John 1.14; II Cor. 4.4; Phil. 2.6; Heb. 1.3); and so he is in that sense 'definitive' of God. He is the point at which to start if you are talking about, or better, obeying, God; he is, too, the criterion for other sources, for instance, the Old Testament. But, as we have seen, these writers recognise quite readily that we do not and cannot yet fully appreciate him. So, though he is in this sense potentially 'definitive' of God for those who believe in him in this way, he is not yet the definitive '*revelation*' of God. For a later theology, Jesus the Christ 'is' God, and of course 'God' is the final and complete criterion of 'God'. But we have seen that neither for this later theology does the 'incarnate Son co-equal with the Father and the Spirit' yet allow us to know the 'self' of God. The physical 'revealing' of Jesus the

---

[1] This re-definition is made explicitly by P. Tillich, *ST* I, p. 147ff.; it is implicit in many of the other passages cited in the last note.

212 *Has Christianity a Revelation?*

Christ, the Word of the Father, is not the 'final' 'definitive' 'revealing of God'. We shall look further in the last chapter at belief in Christ as the still indefinite 'definition' of God.

The content of a book could more easily be 'definitive' than could a man who lived a normal or shorter than normal span. For him to be 'definitive' beyond his own age, he would need a 'definitive' record. Many would make this sort of claim for the Bible.[1] But that it does not in fact (whatever might be the case) 'definitively reveal' anything is shown beyond dispute by the vast number and variety of sects that do appeal to it in this way.

However, many writers, including all those so far referred to, make some allowance for our lack of comprehension, while still persisting in talking of Christ as the 'final' (in this or some other sense) 'revelation' of God. We do not pretend yet to have answered all the implicit defences of this usage, and we will offer further criticisms as our discussion continues.

'Final Revelation' and ἐφάπαξ *in the New Testament*

There is one further important fact to grasp while we are still trying to find some 'finality' in 'revelation'. This assertion of the 'completeness in principle'[2] of 'revelation' seems to be an attempt to reproduce the insistence of some New Testament writers on the 'once-for-all-ness' (ἐφάπαξ)[3] of God's act in Christ. On this point, Emil Brunner explicitly quotes a number of the references noted here, and they seem to be echoed in other writers.[4] But this perhaps more than anything else demonstrates the odd gap between the quite intelligible ways of thought about God and Christ of the New Testament writers, and the much less readily intelligible ways of thought of modern exegetes and systematic theologians.

It makes quite good sense (and again, we shall look more at this in the last chapter) to say of parents who have brought about the conception of a foetus: 'They have founded a family.' A couple who adopt a child have 'saved it' (from, for instance, the anonymity of an institution). The rescuer who has brought

---

[1] J. I. Packer, *Fundamentalism*, for instance; esp. p. 91ff.
[2] G. S. Hendry, art. 'Revelation' in *ThWB*.
[3] Rom. 6.10; Heb. 7.27; 9.12; 10.10; cf. Rom. 5; Heb. 9.26, 27, 28; 10.2; I Tim. 2.5; Acts 4.12; John 19.30, etc.
[4] E. Brunner, *Reason and Revelation*, p. 31; P. Tillich, *ST* I, p. 152; G. Aulén, in *Revelation*, p. 300; W. Nicholls, *Revelation in Christ*, p. 37f.; K. Barth, *CD* I/1, p. 133ff.

the girl successfully to the bank, and then been drowned himself, has 'sacrificed his life for hers'. The girl who says 'I will' has 'accepted' the man as husband. All these, and many more, are 'once-for-all'. Something completely objective is achieved. A decisive start has been made to a new series of events. It is their beginning, and gives them their character. If all goes well, no fresh start is needed. And yet the event itself is pointless, if the series does *not* happen. If the foetus dies before or very soon after birth; if the adopting parents die, and the child is returned to the orphanage; if the girl is killed by the shock, or by pneumonia; then the family was not founded, the child was not saved, the life was not sacrificed for another life, but for nothing. There are many happenings like this, decisive for a pattern of events, complete as beginnings—yet essentially that, essentially starting-points, essentially open-ended. They are complete—but pointless if their series is not continued and probably if it is not concluded. The New Testament writers describe the life-death-resurrection-and-glory of Jesus in terms drawn from situations like this: 'salvation', 'redemption', 'adoption', 'acceptance'.[1] And Paul admits their logic: 'If acceptance by God is through the law, then Christ died for nought' (Gal. 2.21).[2] If the free justification, redemption, propitiation, forgiveness that were the purpose of Christ's 'one act of righteousness' (Rom. 3.24-25; 5.18) are not freely accepted by men, but can be earned by them, then the once for all 'Christ event' is in vain. It is a completed beginning and decisive, but it is essentially open-ended. It is pointless if its series is not completed. It has been done, but it awaits men's acceptance. It is 'once for all', but it awaits my response. All the terms the New Testament writers use to interpret the purpose of God in Christ can be used in this way. They can, of course, be used also of the finally completed process itself, when the 'salvation' made possible by the saving event has been fully received; an instance is σώζειν itself in Paul, most often used of the completion of the series. But when these words describe what God *has already* once for all done in Christ, it is as the completed start of an open-ended series.

---

[1] Ch. 3, at the end. This the 'inauguration of the end time', Heb. 6.5; Rom. 8.23, etc.
[2] Cf. Heb. 6.6: if the series is not continued, there is an implied—and blasphemous—demand for a fresh start.

And the point of this excursus is that 'revelation', as it is normally used, *just cannot denote such an event.*[1]

'Revelation' (as we have seen it actually in use) describes not just the start alone of a series, but its start and its completion all in one. It is not the finished first stage of a larger process which waits to be completed by our response. 'Revelation' describes both the offer *and the acceptance.* As John Baillie said in our quotation above, 'revelation' includes apprehension. It describes the completion of the circle, and so cannot be open-ended. It cannot at all describe the purpose of God in Christ in the ways the New Testament writers saw it.[2]

In case the reader feels he is having a fast one pulled on him, it is worth repeating that this is the very insistence of the writers we have cited. Having explained that they do not mean that God only once 'revealed himself', they have themselves rejected one possible (and the only natural) meaning of 'once-for-all' or 'final' 'revelation'. The sole alternative we were able to find preserves the phrase 'final revelation', but only by a form of equivocation. In fact, it transfers the 'finality' to the content. We have already criticised this, and suggested that it is wishful thinking (and not 'biblical'). But even if our criticism is rejected, it is important to realise that this verbal shift which the theologians we have noted have themselves found necessary has itself lost us all sense of a historic 'once-for-all-ness'.

The 'revelation of God in Jesus Christ is final by being definitive for all time, the criterion of every claim to have received the revealing of God'—this can only mean that the *content* of the 'revealing' is final. If it were the provision of this criterion that was supposed to be final, we would be landed straight back in the dilemma our theologians were trying to escape; because we might as well call the provision of the criterion its 'revelation', and ('provision' or 'revelation') it is still as incomplete as our receiving of it. Anyway, it is the 'content' that the theologians say they intend. And the content of a mental 'making seen', now separated from the act of 'making seen' itself, is an abstract 'timeless fact'. It can be 'definitive', but only if there is some way of preserving it, making it available.

[1] As was seen by O. C. Quick, *Doctrines of the Creed*, Nisbet, 1938, p. 132.
[2] 'Completed final revelation' would, in NT terms, imply a completely 'realised eschatology'—which is, if taken literally, nonsense; and a nonsense the NT writers avoid.

But if we are really talking of a 'definitive content of an act', we have completely abstracted it from time, space, history and 'once for all' events (including the single and unique complex of events that was Jesus of Nazareth). The only defence for 'final revelation' that the theologian aware of the difficulties of the phrase can offer, shows that to talk of God's purpose in Christ as 'revelation' cannot, even by the most devious means, fail to lose an undisputedly important element in some major New Testament writers' interpretation of that purpose.

To see God's intention for the life, death, resurrection-and-glory of Christ predominantly or solely as 'self-revelation' is to lose sight of either the 'once-for-all-ness' or the present relevance of those events.

('Definitive revelation' is also, as we hinted much earlier, banal. If Jesus 'revealed God', then *of course* what he 'revealed' is definitive of anything that later claims to be 'revelation of God'. The phrase is barely concealed tautology, as well as poor exegesis.)

To return, then, to the uses of the word 'reveal' itself.

The Initiative of the Agent

'Reveal' is used of something hitherto unseen, for instance the hero's body beautiful. It may be 'revealed' again, later in the story, of course; but this is then in contrast to the intervening period of hiddenness. It has been 'revealed' (in what we have suggested is the normal sense of the word) only to those who have seen it; it may still need to be 'revealed' to any who have not shared the experience.

Because 'revealing' talks of things otherwise hidden, there is often quite a heavy stress on the part played by the 'revealer' (or the thing or event that 'reveals'). Whether or not the object shall ever be seen often depends on his decision (on this event happening); on the 'revealer's' initiative. So, having something 'revealed' to you contrasts with 'finding it out for yourself'.[1] The word is often used with an overtone of surprise; at what is 'revealed', or that it is 'revealed' at all. It is a dramatic word, often part of startling headlines: 'Butler Reveals All'.[2]

This makes 'reveal' an attractive word to many theologians

---

[1] Barth, *Against the Stream*, p. 207.
[2] Cf. G. F. Woods, *op. cit.*, p. 89.

for talking about God. It is especially so in a theology that
stresses Man's dependence on God, his inability to achieve a
proper relationship with God by his own efforts.[1] For such a
theology, if a man knows anything of God, if he has any conscious relationship with God, this must be God's work, by
'revelation'; 'revelation of truth about God' or even 'revelation
of God himself'. If God had not 'revealed', all this must have
remained hidden. And this dependence on the other person
holds in our own coming to know our friends.[2] The word may
be useful, perhaps especially for post-Augustinian theologies;
but this seeming usefulness does not of itself justify its employment. It may well be true to say that Man needs God's 'self-
revealing' if he is to 'see God'. That does not itself necessarily
mean that God has yet met, or at least at all fully met, that need.

It has been said that God 'stands revealed', as it were, in the
whole of Nature; if only for those who already have, or who are
given, eyes to see:[3] in other words, the stress on the initiative
of God that 'reveal' can convey may not always be intended.
This latter use does seem self-contradictory,[4] and a word like
'discoverable', (easily) 'discernible', would seem more appropriate. But this would still be very hard to defend. The variety
of gods that those willing to look for one in 'nature' have found
is even greater than the variety of Christian understandings of
'God'. 'One God' really is not 'discernible', still less in any
meaningful sense 'revealed', even to enlightened Christians (!)
in the world as it is.

But before we proceed further we must examine the ambiguity of this noun 'revelation', that we keep using; we have
already noticed in passing an aspect of this vagueness of meaning.

The Ambiguity of 'Revelation'

The noun 'revelation' can mean the same as the verbal noun
'revealing': the activity of one who 'reveals' ('A complete self-
revelation is not easy'). It can also mean 'the thing revealed',
(just as 'construction' can mean the 'act of constructing' or the

[1] Ch. I, p. 9. The present writer shares this belief in Man's dependence on God,
but not in the 'revelation' which he thinks is illegitimately deduced from it.
[2] See below, p. 235.
[3] Calvin, *Institutes* I 5, though with the latter emphasis.
[4] Cf. P. Tillich, *ST* I, p. 133ff.

'thing constructed'). It will normally only mean this when it is used wholly metaphorically; a physical thing that has 'been revealed' is not itself called a 'revelation' ('He looked at the uncovered marble. "Take that revelation away", he roared'). But in 'The visitor announced that he was an escaped convict; this revelation left us all aghast', 'revelation' does probably mean, 'this fact which he revealed'; though it could still be intended to mean 'his revealing this', 'his actual telling us this'. In the sentence, 'The statue revealed was a revelation of the sculptor's advanced technique', the statue is not being called a 'revelation' because it has been 'revealed', but because it 'reveals' something further itself. Here 'revelation' has a third sense, 'a thing which reveals' (just as the statue might be a surprise, a thing that surprises). The word is likely to be ambiguous. The important point to note is that it cannot logically mean, nor ought it to be used to try to mean, two or three things at once. In the sentence, 'This paper has kept you informed of every move in this significant, squalid affair; and we are proud of this revelation', it is not entirely clear whether the paper is proud of 'the squalid affair revealed', or 'having revealed' it, or the 'revealing light' it may throw on some wider situation.

The ambiguities of the noun 'revelation' do not of course disqualify it altogether from theological use; they only make a certain degree of care necessary. For instance, it might be possible to persuade a reader that God can (or does) 'reveal himself in the Bible', and to summarise this with 'The Bible is God's revelation.' On the basis of the slogan 'The Bible is God's revelation' you could then argue that this means 'God has revealed the Bible' (we have said it is 'his revelation'). You could even add, 'All that we need to know of anything is revealed by God to us in the Bible: we have said, it is his revelation.'[1] None of these need in fact follow from the other, but the jump is made with little effort because of the 'blind-word' 'revelation'. It is particularly easy to make the leap from 'revelation' as act to 'revelation' as content; we saw this when

---

[1] The argument in J. I. Packer, *Fundamentalism*, though not precisely in these terms, seems to run along these lines. God has revealed himself, the communication of this is in Scripture, therefore Scripture itself must *be* revelation—pp. 42f., 91ff. Then on p. 96 he admits that this can easily further become an encouragement to 'Enquire Within Upon Everything', though he himself rejects the practice.

we were examining 'final revelation' above. And there is the further ambiguity which we have also already noticed, in any use of 'reveal', between 'make seen', and 'make available for sight'. The fact that the same word can denote the continuity of 'making seen' and the finality of a (physical) 'unveiling to view' has probably helped to persuade more than one writer that he could hold these contradictory ideas together.

'Reveal' and 'revelation' are good words for woolly thinking, but not so good if the aim is precision.

However, the example 'The Bible is God's revelation' has brought us to the next section, 'propositional theology'.

The 'Revealing' of Facts

'Reveal' can be used of disclosing facts. This is now entirely metaphorical; both the 'veil' and the 'removing' of it are figures of speech. It means 'to make known', 'to make seen', in the also metaphorical use of 'see'. It would not be used of the learned professor finding some scientific 'law', hitherto unknown. It is not possible just to 'uncover' a fact, in the way you might (just possibly) 'reveal' a statue in the dark. He would only be said to have 'revealed' the discovery if he made his results (and probably method, too) available for others. He might publish and nobody read his work; he would then have 'revealed' his findings only in the sense of 'made them knowable'. The question this would prompt would be the one, 'Who can now "see", "get to know"?' But again, 'reveal' would probably not be used of this making available; it is more likely that it would be reserved for the actual 'making known'. When at last other scientists had read or heard or seen the findings, and when the popularisers had told us in our morning papers, then it might be said that he had 'revealed' what he had found. And now it would be proper, and necessary, to ask the question, 'Who has seen, who has learned the results, and understood them?' Again, it should be clear which sense is intended.

If you have some documents in code, or in a foreign language, you can display them. The documents, things of paper and ink, are 'revealed'. They are 'revealed to people' when

1 *Daily Express*, Thursday, 7th February, 1961. An inner-page headline: 'B.E.A. WILL REVEAL ALL . . . British European Airways is to take the unusual step of telling its 750 pilots *exactly* why it has sacked Captain X' (my italics). A *complete* telling of the relevant facts is a 'revelation'.

people come and see them. You have not 'revealed' the *contents* until, for instance, you have published a translated or decoded version. The contents themselves are not 'revealing' (of, say, the situation in Russia) unless their implications are under-stood. You may mean that these various 'revealings' have happened for diplomatic circles, for the newspaper world, for the British public as a whole, or a wider circle still. But in each instance it is proper to ask, 'For whom is this visible, or knowable?', or, 'Who has seen this? Who has got to know and understand this? And what precisely may be seen or known, or has been seen or known?' If you receive no one clear answer, or alternatively many clear but conflicting answers, you are probably justified in deciding that nothing has been 'made clear'; there has been no 'revealing'.

In other words (as should be fairly obvious) it ought to be possible to test the claim, 'We have had *X* revealed to us', in the same ways as the claim, 'We know *X*' may be tested (see above). The main difference is that, if anything, 'revelation' used without qualification is normally taken to imply a quite complete making known of whatever it is claimed has been 'revealed'. The word may of course be used seemingly loosely (see above), because there are generally accepted limits to the amount of 'knowing', 'seeing', 'understanding', that can normally be expected of this subject in question, in the circumstances that obtain; but if 'revealing' is said to have happened, then within these implicit or explicit limits a complete knowledge or, at least, a complete availability of knowledge is being asserted;[1] and the claim holds good, only if it can pass the normal tests of consistency and successful application among those who claim to 'know', those who claim to have received the 'revelation'.

'Propositional Revelation' and the Bible

Such 'propositional revelation' is unpopular with many theologians, and has been for some while. 'Personal revelation', the 'revealing of God in Person-to-person encounter', is pre-ferred.[2] There are good arguments in favour of the preference; however it is much harder to find circumstances that will justify

---

[1] To avoid unnecessary repetition, only the meaning 'made known' rather than 'made available for knowing' will be discussed below, except where the latter is relevant to the enquiry.

[2] See ch. 1.

a claim that a 'person' is revealed, than that certain propositions are 'revealed'; and the latter is hard enough. We shall
start at this point both because difficulties here are *a fortiori*
difficulties in talk of 'personal revealing', and also because there
can hardly be 'revealing' of or through or in Jesus of Nazareth,
unless we have clear and authoritative (even 'revealed')
statements about him.[1]

(*a*) *The Literal Content*   It might be said, 'The contents of the
various books of the Bible were revealed by God to their authors;
and so the total content of the Bible is revealed by God to us.' If
by 'the content' is meant only the actual words in a particular
order as conventional signs on paper, this is fairly simple. There
are already some qualifications: Does this imply the 'Received
Text', or some scholarly modification? The text in the original
languages (where recoverable), or in an 'authorised' translation into one language? But these are not very important;
it is easy to find Christian groups who accept one basic text
(or one authoritative translation). The same words and sentences are known by, or can easily be known by, all the members
of such a group. This genuinely contrasts with the fact that these
words and sentences are not known by other people, and are not
available for them to know (they may be very distinctly
'available' for all living now; but there have been many for
whom this was never so). The words and sentences of the
Bible are or have been 'hidden'; but it may fairly be said that
to certain people they are 'revealed'. As was noted above, the
assertion that 'God' did it cannot be checked in the same way.
But the assertion that 'These words and sentences are revealed
to us' can be checked, and at this level may well be justifiable.

(*b*) *The Meaning*   If however, in 'content' is included the
actual *meaning* of the words or sentences, the claim becomes
much harder to validate. Every member of the group would
have to have accepted the same 'meaning' for each word and
sentence of the accepted text; or, at least, would have to offer

---

[1] J. I. Packer, *Fundamentalism*, p. 91ff.; and, in a slightly different sense, admitted
by W. Nicholls, *op. cit.*, p. 62. Cf. H. D. MacDonald, *The Idea of Revelation*, Macmillan,
1959, p. 192: 'If there were no adequate record, then would each new age need
again the revelation. Bethlehem and Calvary would need to be repeated to bring
God to man.' For attempts to avoid both 'propositions' and 'fundamentalism',
while retaining 'revelation', by or through or in Jesus of Nazareth, see below.

the same meaning, if called upon, to show that the one meaning was in fact available to him. It is very unlikely that any but the very smallest group could make good such a claim,[1] particularly if records of the beliefs of past members of the group have been preserved. It seems unlikely that any group has seriously and for any length of time made a boast like this. Many may have been tempted to make the boast, while really using the word 'reveal' loosely, with vague but large tacit qualifications.

Surely God has 'revealed' in Christ that he is love? This was (perhaps) not known before, now it is known. All Christians will say it!

If only the sentence 'God is love' (and its equivalents in other languages) is meant, as we saw above, this is probably fair enough. Most if not all Christians would agree. Then ask them the *meaning*, what the love of God is like, what he does as love, what he demands as love, what response he actually enables as love: and you will find again there is little 'revealed' beyond the words.[2] Moreover, they may be so qualified by such words as 'impassible', 'righteous', 'holy', 'eternal', as to have widely different meanings or very little meaning at all.

A number of further qualifications may be made. It may be insisted, in particular, that it was only claimed that the meaning of the Bible was 'revealed', in the sense of 'made available for knowing'; and that only for those who had eyes to see, minds to understand. This in effect narrows the group, which is the easiest way of making good such a claim (see above). Still, the smaller group must make good the reduced claim. A group, however small, must be able to offer a single meaning when called upon. If they could do this, they could fairly claim that the meaning was revealed to them. But by now we have excluded any 'revealing' of the total meaningful content of the Bible to Christian people as a whole. It would be possible still to insist that the meaning was there, available, 'revealed', if only Christendom would open its eyes. But when something

---

[1] J. I. Packer, *Fundamentalism*, does not attempt to do this.

[2] I offer no documentation, assuming that the sad facts of the Christian situation are obvious enough. (Perhaps D. L. Edwards, *God's Cross in our World*, SCM Press, 1963, *Prologue*, would do for a start.) If anyone can prove me wrong at this easily 'falsifiable' point, show me that a large number (not even necessarily the majority) of professing Christians are unanimously obedient to a single vision of love, then I shall recant—recant the negative conclusions of this analysis; though not the analysis itself. And I shall shout (I do not sing well) a thousand Te Deums.

mystery; · maybe the better word for the Chn
belief; Its own existence. than knowledge ?
revelation?
222   *Has Christianity a Revelation?*

so-say 'revealed' is still so obscure that no one or very few can
actually *see* it, there is small point in saying it is 'revealed'.
Such an assertion could even look like deliberate deception.
It is never 'seen', it is not in any real sense 'available for sight'.
It is much truer to say that it is *not* 'revealed', than that it *is*
'revealed' (if 'reveal' is still being used in anything like its normal sense). If the meaning of the Bible is 'revealed' (even truly
'revealed') to a very few alone, or one man alone, it may be
nice for them; it is hardly relevant to others, especially as there
is no way for them to judge between conflicting claims. There
is small point in saying a thing is 'revealed' if it is not and cannot be 'seen'.

(*c*) '*Revelation*' '*in*' *the Bible*   It then becomes necessary to make
some (Idealist?) contrast between 'content' and 'form'.[1] Usually
this is expanded as: The Bible is not a set of 'revealed propositions', each in turn 'revealing' some 'truth' about God. The
'revelation of God' comes 'in' or 'through' the words of Scripture. God has not allowed himself to be tied down and codified.
The temporary embarrassment can even be made a defence:
the very relative and problematic nature of the 'form' of the
'revelation' can be offered as a sign that the 'revelation' itself
cannot be 'talked about' or criticised.[2] But a tactical withdrawal is often really a retreat, and does not in itself make the
citadel less vulnerable. The metaphysical distinction of 'form'
and undefinable 'content' may seem to put a magic invisible
barrier around the 'revelation' claimed, that no philosopher,
Bible critic, historian or psychologist can pierce; but if the
'revelation' is supposed to happen *to anyone*, it is still liable to the
test by consistency. And this is always the part of the wall that
verbal magic cannot make untouchable. If various Christians
do not receive the same 'revelation' 'in' or 'through' the Bible,
then there is still nothing 'revealed' to them. And this defensive
retreat does mean that it is impossible for a particular claim to a
'revelation' to be checked against the Bible itself, because words

---

[1] K. Barth, *Against the Stream*, 'The Bible contains this revelation . . .', 'the form
in which it (the revelation) confronts us is relative and problematical'; pp. 218,
223; W. Nicholls, *Revelation in Christ*, pp. 45, 109; S. Bulgakoff, in *Revelation*, p. 156;
J. I. Packer, too, *Fundamentalism*, p. 97, though he suggests in the following pages
that the distinction is easy to make, and rarely important, and insists mostly on
'verbal revelation'.
[2] K. Barth, *Against the Stream*, pp. 215, 223ff.

and sentences in it have no longer a clear 'revealed' meaning by which to judge. Really this position is as untenable as J. I. Packer points out in his book to which we have been referring. If you start (as he rightly supposes many varied theologians do) by assuming that a Christian is necessarily committed to belief in a 'revelation', then you are equally bound (even closer than he, with his few very cautious qualifications, allows himself to be) to a belief in 'verbal revelation'. This we have already seen.

What this book would suggest is that a Christian does not have to be tied to the assumption that Dr Packer makes for him, common though the assumption be among many contemporary theologians.

It is perhaps worth noting in passing that this 'form-content' defence of 'biblical revelation' seems very hard to maintain in its purity. It easily breaks down into a biblicism indistinguishable in practice from that labelled by opponents as 'fundamentalism'—rather as 'transubstantiation' was intended to curb 'gross' superstition, but soon became the basis for accepting 'bleeding host' legends.

(d) 'Revelation' to 'Me'   This further possibility we consider is largely a hypothetical one; but common practice[1] could produce this sort of formulated apologetic and a Christian Existentialism does in fact approximate quite closely to it.

The defence might run like this: 'Through the Bible, God speaks to me, in my situation. He reveals the truth of himself to me as I am, so that I may understand about him, and about myself in this world.[2] And this, since I am (or my group is) unique may well mean that I quite properly get something quite different out of the Bible, out of any one short passage, from anything any one else may find there.'

And this, whether it be the *sortes biblicae* of superstitious Protestant individualism, or a more sophisticated technically

[1] See e.g. E. H. Robertson, *Take and Read*, SCM Press, 1961, p. 55ff.: 'The group should realise that their own questions are being answered in their Bible study.' The author himself, however, insists on trying to find the meaning the original writer intended.

[2] Cf. R. Bultmann, 'Everything has been revealed, in so far as man's eyes are opened concerning his existence and he is once again able to understand himself', quoted above, p. 13; though existentialist language really belongs a little later in the discussion.

'existentialist' approach, may seem promising. We still have 'revelation' (of a sort) connected with the Bible; and we have again turned what seemed to be an embarrassment into what appears to be a defence:[1] 'No one can dissuade me from believing that God is revealed to me in or through the Bible, if in fact I do believe that. I believe it because I do.' Still less than for the approach we called ' "revelation" "in" the Bible' can what others find in the Bible, be they critics or fellow-worshippers, affect the 'revelation' I believe in.

And of course, consistent solipsism is impregnable. This is the final narrowing of the group. No one can dispute 'my voices'. At least they cannot till my voices direct me in my relations with other people, or till I try to let them see something of what was 'revealed' to me. And when they too claim their conflicting voices, the problem returns: Have we 'revelations' of many gods; or does the One God choose to remain hidden and ill-known? — *each diff voice, a diff. opinion*

(*e*) *A 'Self-Authenticating' 'Revelation'*   'Truth of God is revealed to us' looks like a statement about the experience (actual or, less probably, potential) of a number of human beings. As such, it may be tested, verified or falsified.[2] The contemporary Christian situation does not seem likely to do anything but falsify the claim. But perhaps 'revelation' is 'self-authenticating'. Its very nature means that it cannot be tested, it is 'revelation of God', and refuses all controls. You may not look for the largest cohesive Christian sect and choose their 'God'. 'God' presents the truth of himself to you, and you accept (or, some would allow, reject). Other people's different experiences and even more divergent accounts of them leave untouched 'God's self-authenticating revelation to you'.[3] This could be so. It would

[marginal notes: ha; yes; X =; a claim theologian make, but it he got to be a ruse.]

---

[1] Versions of this defence, based on the nature of the certainty of the individual's faith, which makes what it believes unassailable can be found in J. MacQuarrie, *An Existentialist Theology*, SCM Press, 1955, p. 169; G. Bornkamm, *Jesus of Nazareth*, Hodder and Stoughton, 1960, Introduction; P. Tillich, *ST* I, p. 144; J. Knox, *Criticism and Faith*, Hodder and Stoughton, 1953: 'The distinctive, central item of Christian faith (the faith that is "immune from any peril from criticism") is that God supremely revealed himself in Jesus Christ.' This defence is criticised in D. Cairns, *A Gospel without Myth?*, ch. VIII; also H. Zahrnt, *The Historical Jesus*. See below, ch. 7, *'Revelation' in Apologetics*.

[2] See above, ch. 5.

[3] See K. Barth, *Against the Stream*, pp. 208, 214ff.; G. Aulén in *Revelation*, p. 308; G. S. Hendry, art. 'Reveal' in *ThWB*: 'There is no criterion of revelation apart from revelation itself. At most it can be examined in regard to its own internal

If the same one God says contradictory "truths" to different people, we prove the lie of their religious theory. — *Yes*

still not give you the right to say that 'God has given a self-authenticating revelation of himself' to you and to others who think very differently of him. Diverse 'self-authenticating revelations of God' do not justify 'The truth of the one God is revealed to us'.[1]

Unanimity would not prove that there was a 'Christian revelation of God'; but the fact of disunity proves there is none. *(= X)*

'Revealing' 'Partially', 'Gradually', or of 'a Mystery'

Much of what follows is stating the obvious, but it is necessary as a foundation for the ensuing discussion. If I claim to have 'revealed' $2xy$ to A, my claim is only true, if A has 'seen' $2xy$. If he has 'seen' only $2x$ or $2y$; or only xy—then that is all that I have 'revealed', whatever my intention or my efforts. This could be called a 'partial revelation' of $2xy$. But the point is: if 'reveal' is used at all, something very precise must be meant by 'partial'. The 'part' must be clearly definable in itself, and preferably in its relation to the whole, for it to be said to be 'revealed'. Does this mean that all $2xy$ was 'partly revealed' (e.g. if $2xy$ were 'half-revealed', that would mean $1xy$). Or is it $2x$ or $2y$ that is 'revealed'; or x or y; or less than that? Is it the whole, seen still dimly; or a part, seen completely; or even a part seen, but still not with complete clarity? Unless these questions can be answered, it is not legitimate to talk of a 'partial revealing'. 'The clouds parted and the town was revealed, lying in its little valley.' This means something very precise. As much of the town as could be seen normally from this position in good visibility was seen. If the cloud only thinned, showing the town up as an otherwise undifferentiated darker patch against the surrounding country, then it was the outline of the town that was 'revealed'. If from this position a hill hid part of the town, then only a particular fraction of the town was revealed. If 'the town was revealed' to a number of viewers, then they all saw something quite precise. The context may show

---

self-consistency . . . but there is no external test by which it can be authenticated; for revelation by its nature is unique and incomparable; it cannot be explained or proved, it can only be received in faith and humility.' If Hendry only meant that there can (by the unprovability of statements about 'God', see above) be no proof of claims to 'revelation' apart from how it is 'received' by us, that would be unexceptionable. But this would be an 'external' test, and so is probably not his intention ('internal self-consistency' above).

[1] This we have really already shown above, p. 198, 'I and Thou'.

that it was only a fraction of the whole, but sufficient for their purpose; what they needed to see was in fact shown them. But if, explicitly or implicitly, it is admitted that they did not see all there was to see, all that needed to be seen; if some thought they saw the town, others a battleship and others a bare field, then, though they may have seen something, it cannot be said that 'the town was revealed to them'. Only something quite limited may be meant to be 'revealed', perhaps to a limited number of people; but unless they have all seen all that was intended, that intended 'revealing' has not happened. 'I tried to reveal the lay-out of the room to them by the light of a match, but they only saw the first couple of yards.' The first six feet were 're-vealed'; but not the lay-out of the room.

Similar limitations apply to talk of 'gradual revelation'. Again it may mean successive steps (*gradūs*) or stages in the achieving of clarity of vision; or the uncovering of successive areas of the object; or both together. In every case what is seen must be clearly seen for it to be 'revelation'; even if it is itself still vague at this stage, at least the vagueness must be fully perceived.

It may even be 'mysterious': a dark shapeless thing, or a mobile, shifting, colour-changing, waxing and waning thing. But if some see only one, some another facet of its mysterious character, then to that extent even its 'mysteriousness' is not 'revealed' to them. However limited, there must be some clarity before 'It is revealed' becomes meaningful.

It may be accepted that neither the contemporary state of Christianity, nor its past history, allows an unqualified claim to have received a 'revealing' of the will of God to be sustained; and yet a last attempt may be made to salvage some form of 'biblical revelation'. God is not *fully* revealed, in any of the ways analysed above (or in any other way). God's will is not *fully* 'revealed' to anyone. But many have received a '*partial* revealing' of God which comes nearest to fulness in the New Testament and its witness to Christ. This is all for which we may hope, while we are still imperfect. It is only our imperfection that keeps us from a full understanding of what God is always 'revealing' in the Bible.

The 'partiality' of the 'revealing of God' in the OT, and of our acceptance of it now, are noted more or less explicitly by, e.g. W. Nicholls, *Revelation in Christ,*

God's ways for men are partially 'revealed'—in or through
the Bible (and perhaps elsewhere). It may mean that some parts
of the truth of God are clearly seen and known, 'revealed'. For
it to be generally true, there would need to be a large measure
of agreement on at least some topics of importance, by most
of those who accepted the Bible as being in any way a 'revealing' of God's will. Again, some small group might claim to have
seen the truth of God's will clearly on some point; but while
others cannot or will not 'see' this as God's will, it is truer to
say that it is not 'revealed' than that it is. It is also difficult to
maintain that 'parts' are clearly seen, unless the limits of the
'parts' are clear. Obviously, if the limits are indistinct, the
parts are *not* clearly seen. If some group claims that God's will
for the unity of Christians is 'revealed' to them completely,
both why and how it should be, it is fair to ask them whether
God's will on this point goes as far as affecting the shape of the
Church's Ministry, or the relation of Church and State; and if
it does, how far does it affect these questions. If the group does
not know if God's will for unity affects these issues, they do not
know the truth of his will for unity clearly. If they do claim
that they do know the way God's will on this point affects other
issues, they are implicitly claiming much more than a knowledge of 'part' of God's will. For different people really to 'know'
different 'parts' of God's will, the 'parts' must interlock without
conflict, which is even more difficult.

The next possibility is that the claim means that many people
can see the whole of the truth of God's will partially, hazily,
dimly. If the 'mist' obscured only minor matters of detail (how
many candles on the altar; shall a cleric be called 'priest' or
'presbyter'?), then the claim would seem good enough. But if
the mist seems to cover matters that are accepted as vital (shall
the Church accept historical criticism of its sacred canon of

---

pp. 53ff., 75-80; J. I. Packer, *Fundamentalism*, pp. 52, 129; P. Tillich, *ST* I, p. 162,
'always fragmentary'; K. Barth does not seem so happy with this sort of distinction
(he prefers to talk of the OT asking the 'right question' which the NT answers),
but it may be implicit in what he has to say of 'fulfilled time'—*CD* I/2, pp. 119
and 53ff. *Against the Stream* (pp. 225-40) seems to admit that 'divine revelation' is
not very good at getting through to Church or individual. That 'God' is only
'partially revealed' to us, as he was only partially to old Israel, is of course rather
oddly maintained alongside a belief that his 'revelation of himself' is complete,
final, absolute, etc.; it is our intransigence and then our finiteness that are blamed
for the no more than partial success. The possibility that God might not be intending to 'reveal' does not seem to have come to mind.

scriptures; how far shall it experiment to combat secularism and what shall it do to stem the de-Christianisation of Western Europe?), then the point seems to have been reached when it must be admitted that there is much more mist remaining than has been removed; there is at least so much remaining that it is not legitimate to cry 'a break in the mist!', 'a revelation'. The 'revealing' is too partial to merit the term 'revealing'. To the third possibility, that the claim means 'a "partial" revealing of "parts" of God's will', all the above objections again apply (but doubly); and the claim is already so heavily qualified as to be pointless. A doubly veiled 'revealing' is not usefully a 'revealing' at all.

This also means that talk about a 'gradual' or 'progressive' 'revelation of the truth of God' is not very helpful either.[1] It includes the difficulty we have just noticed, for it must suggest that God is already 'partially revealed' (if the 'progress' is thought to have begun). But there are further objections still.

A rectangular jig-saw puzzle may be started by four people, one at each corner. To begin with their sections may seem totally different, even though parts of what will be the picture are genuinely being 'gradually revealed' to them. Four diverse people who meet a fifth at home, on the train, at work, or in the club, respectively, may have widely differing aspects of his character quite truly 'revealed' gradually to them. But a jig-saw with widely contrasting sections, a man so disintegrated as to show four different 'selves' to different people, do not offer very promising analogies for the 'self-revealing' of God who is One. The supposed recipients of the 'gradual revelation' do not seem to be on the same gradient.

There remains the defence afforded by the traditional belief in the 'mystery' of God. He cannot (perhaps 'by definition') be comprehended by the human mind. Or it may be said that in his 'revelation' he remains 'hidden'; the very fact of 'having to reveal himself' makes abundantly clear that he is 'hidden'; and he never loses this initiative of having to step out of hiding to present himself to us.[2] We talked about 'the mystery of God'

---

[1] The term is defended for instance by G. F. Woods, *Theological Explanation*, p. 91.
[2] K. Barth, *Church Dogmatics* I/2, p. 84ff., *et passim*. For Barth the cross 'reveals the hiddenness of God'; but the 'resurrection and ascension are the event of his self-declaration'; *CD* IV/2, p. 133, *et passim*.

in our first chapter and offered some other instances of discussions of this idea.

God's love may well be too profound for us ever to understand. But it is not traditional teaching to suggest that it is self-contradictory. If any 'mystery' is 'revealed' to present-day Christians with their kaleidoscopic beliefs, it is a mystery of diversity, and that by definition is not 'God'. The traditional image of the 'mystery of God' is an ocean too deep to plumb; but the total course of Christian theology makes it look like a maze so complex that everyone gets lost in his own way. If there is a 'revealed mystery', it is this that is 'revealed'. Of course, the diversity may be in our 'seeing' of what 'God' really would like to 'reveal'. But that still means that it is not, so far as we are concerned, 'revealed'.

'Partially', 'gradually', 'mysteriously' rapidly become words for giving a semblance of meaning, when none really remains. When 'reveal' is so heavily qualified, it is not being refined down towards an apex of meaning, to fit it to talk of 'God'. It is having its meaning completely destroyed.[1] The theologian is using a word that normally describes 'making clear' to mean 'leave unclear'. It is not very helpful.

Can Talk about 'God' be barely Propositional?

So far, propositions about 'the truth of God', 'the will of God', and so forth, have been discussed as though they were like any other proposition; as though they were asking only for an intellectual assent and no more. This was only for simplicity's sake, and did not beg the question as to whether there are better ways of talking of God. We mentioned the further possibilities, and gave warning that they would be even more difficult to defend.

It was suggested in the last chapter, however, that there is always a strong implicit element of demand or commitment or both in any sentence in which the word 'God' appears (at any rate if the word is being used at all normally); even if there is also an element of simple proposition in the sentence.[2] If this is

[1] See above, ch. 5.
[2] Surely if this logic of sentences about 'God' were recognised, the rather barren conventional antithesis between 'propositional' and 'personal' 'revelation' would be resolved. The notion that Christianity is a matter of the 'mere' intellectual acceptance of a set of ideas, culled from the Bible, or the Bible and other sources, is shown to be unsatisfactory by the Bible and many of the other traditional

perhaps our hunches, n faith, in a rev. can only be substantiated, or proven false, as we obey it by life practice. If it works then, we have confirmation. If not, we're deceived so, then it becomes even more difficult to justify a claim that the 'truth of God' or the 'will of God' has been 'revealed'. It cannot then be said that God's will concerning, for instance, the use of property has been 'revealed' until the full force of his demand on our property (whatever the demand may be) has been felt. And the full force of God's demand cannot be said to have been felt until it has been felt irresistibly. It has not been felt irresistibly until obedience is offered. Sets of words containing the name 'God' may be 'revealed'; even some commonly acceptable meaning for them may be 'revealed'; but they do not 'reveal' the will of God on any matter until it is so fully 'seen' that it elicits obedience. It is not enough for Christians to agree on terms for unity, or terms for missionary activity; until they actually obey what they think is the will or the love of God, they cannot meaningfully claim that his will or his love is 'revealed' to them. The man in the train may say, 'Yes, I know God is love, it has been revealed; and it means I should look after my family and myself and let the rest of the world go hang; and I act on this.' It would probably mean that all that was known, 'revealed', was the sequence of words, 'God is love'. That *God* is love, appears to be still unknown.

It might be possible, as was noted, for some Christian group, which was closely organised, and which held strictly a common definition of belief, to claim that its beliefs, the words and sentences, were 'revealed'; it might even claim that a single meaning for them was 'revealed', though there is less likelihood of it making good that claim. Nowhere does there seem to be a level of obedience, consistent throughout a Christian group, high enough to allow the group to make good a claim that the will of God in its irresistible force has been 'revealed' to it. Again it might be admitted that only a qualified claim was intended: 'I only mean *something* of the demand and attraction of God is revealed. Obviously it is not all revealed.' But the same difficulties as were noted above attend this attempt to qualify the

---

sources themselves; they say that the Christian is the one who is, or wishes to be, totally committed. But the attempt to conjure some sort of 'personal confrontation' out of the pages of a book, and so elicit a 'personal commitment', is no satisfactory alternative, as we have seen. The proper solution is to realise that propositions 'about God' in Bible, Creeds or Confessions are sets of words expressing, inviting or demanding commitment; they are not 'understood' unless the demand implicit in them is felt, and strongly felt.

word 'reveal', and it will as soon be so qualified, made so 'partial', as to cease to be 'revelation' at all. Judged even by the most general and platitudinous statements of what is 'proper Christian behaviour', Christian disobedience is living disproof of any claim that the will of the holy God is 'revealed'.

The 'Revelation' of 'God' as 'Person'

'Reveal' is often used by critics of novels, biographies, plays and films, particularly of insight given into the depths of a person's character; a scene may be 'very revealing', of the characters displayed, or more generally, of 'human nature' at large.[1] 'Revelation' has happened, when a particular trait, or group of traits, or the total person, respectively, is 'fully known' (as fully known as convention or the individual speaker allows is possible).

The 'revealing' in this sense may still be a 'making known' of facts. In this way a patient might be 'revealed' to his Freudian psychiatrist; all the important or relevant facts about him, even (though this is unlikely) all the facts about him that could be known, are known. These facts may be known by a detached observer; there is no need for him to become emotionally involved with his patient, in order that the latter may be 'revealed' to him; nor need the 'revelation' lead to any such involvement; there need be no involvement, or so little as to be negligible, and yet it may be said that the person in question has been 'revealed' to the psychiatrist.

However, it is also possible to discuss human beings in terms other than those of cold detached observation, to discuss the possibility of commitment to them, the possibility of becoming myself involved. In such terms a person is likeable, attractive, hateful, forceful, compelling. The detached observer may, of course, see all this and see, too, why it should be. But unless he has been 'attracted', 'repelled', or whatever is appropriate, it cannot be said that the 'attractiveness', 'repulsiveness', of the man in question has been 'revealed', for he has not found for himself any attraction or repulsiveness. It can only be said

---

[1] Miss Dilys Powell, in *The Sunday Times*, 22nd January, 1961: 'There is, or should be, revelation of character. . . . One knows how these men will react to circumstances inside the prison walls. But not outside. One doesn't know them except superficially' (review of *The Hole*).

that the psychiatrist has noted the effect of his patient on others: his attractiveness, repulsiveness for them.

This only emphasises that a test for a 'revealing' having happened, depends on a precise definition of what is said to be 'revealed'. If, for instance, 'person' is used differently from its use in the paragraph but one above; if it is used to mean something like 'a-being-to-whom-no-human-can-refuse-some-emotional-response', then obviously such a 'person' cannot be said to have been 'revealed', where no response is offered. It has not been realised that this is (in this sense) a 'person'. It may even be debated whether 'person' *can* mean the human as detachedly observable; or whether it must mean the human as incapable of being observed detachedly. Obviously, both senses are used, both reactions are possible. The debate as to which is the 'right' way to use the word is not relevant here and is anyway only an illogical method of discussing the rival merits of different ways of regarding human beings. Both uses are legitimate in their respective contexts. But it is important to know how 'person' is being used, if a claim that 'a person has been revealed' is to be tested. A claim that a person as detachedly observable has been 'revealed' can be tested in the same ways as any other claim to have received a 'revelation' of facts.

A claim that a 'person' as 'one-to-whom-some (emotive?-emotional?)-response-must-be-given' has been 'revealed', has to be tested by the emotional response offered. Suppose there is such a response. Many people say that X has been 'revealed' to them as a 'person' (in this sense) and attracts them. Y says that X has been 'revealed' to him as a 'person' (in this same sense) and X repels him. Both statements could be untrue, and neither the many nor Y 'know' X as a 'person'. But in this particular case, both may be quite true. X may be the sort of person who does attract many, and will repel a man like Y. Y may need to be 'converted', to become a different person (more pleasant, or less pleasant) if X is to be 'revealed' to him as attractive. If a number of people of *similar* character claim that another 'person' has been 'revealed' to them, but respond very differently, some are attracted, some repelled, then probably there has been no such 'revealing'. More important still, if a number of people of very *diverse* character claim that another 'person' has been 'revealed' to them, and all respond *in the same way*, all are attracted or all are repelled, then again there has probably been no 'revealing'; for the other person, if really 'revealed', would have attracted some but repelled others. Of course, in any normal situation, seemingly different people may be attracted to a common friend, either because, though different, they have in fact some subordinate trait in common; or because they find very different points of attraction in the common friend; or both. But in neither of these cases are they responding to a 'revealing' of the entirety of the other 'person'. If Y hates to be dominated and insists on being in control in any relationship, while X wishes to be mastered and cannot bear taking the lead, they will not respond in the same way to the 'revealing' to them of Z, who is strong enough to dominate anyone he meets, or to the 'revealing' to them of A, who prefers to be on equal terms with all his friends.

There are then further tests that may be made of a claim that a 'revealing' has happened, when what is said to be 'revealed' includes factors to which some emotional (or moral) response is expected. (Of course, this does not apply only to 'persons' but to such things as works of art.) These are 'further tests', because the ordinary tests for such a claim still hold good. X and Y must not only offer the appropriate emotional response but also be able to give an accurate 'observer's' account of Z or A, to make good their claim that the latter are really 'revealed' to them as persons.

We have examined ways in which 'reveal' may properly be used, and particularly with regard to 'personal disclosure'. It seems unlikely that an unqualified claim that a person (in either of the senses of the word discussed above) is 'revealed' will often be justified. A human being is so complex, and his fellow is so slow to comprehend him, that the most that is likely is the 'revealing' of a few facts, a few aspects of personality. A claim that a person is 'revealed' may include this as an implicit qualification; he is 'revealed' as far as circumstances normally allow. Such a claim without even implicit qualification might perhaps be made by one life-long friend of the other, by one of a long-married couple of the other, and be made with justice; but it is not very likely.

If 'cold facts about a man' are 'revealed', there is still no *logical* necessity for any involvement on the part of the one who

has come to 'know'; before, or after. If a 'person' (in the second
sense) is 'revealed', that means by definition, that there has been
some response; but it may range from falling in love to a violent
antipathy. However, if there *is* to be a positive response, a
commitment, a friendly involvement, it will probably have to
wait for some sort of 'revealing'—whether or not it is a true
'revelation', and however 'partial' it may in fact be (see above).
It may be amplified or even radically corrected later; but this
will have been the starting-point of a friendship. A 'revealing'
remark, act, series of events, may be very important for the
coming into being of a friendship.[1]

There is perhaps more likelihood of a personal reaction, in
conscious commitment or its deliberate refusal, if 'John' sets
out deliberately to 'reveal' himself to 'Joan', sets out to produce
an open confrontation; more than if Joan simply notices John
in 'revealing' situations that just occur. John's intention to show
the sort of person he is gives notice of an already-existing liking,
'reveals' at least a provisional commitment on his part already.
The fact that he has taken the initiative may make it easier for
Joan to respond.[2]

He will send flowers, try to kiss, talk, to 'show his affections'.
He sets out to 'reveal' himself. But it cannot be said that he has
succeeded in 'revealing' himself, unless Joan is able to reach a
true assessment of John now, and his likely future behaviour;
an assessment which friends now, and her own future experience
will not belie. If less than John's whole self is 'revealed',
obviously it can only be said that this or that intention, aspect
of character, was 'revealed'; and this may even be very decep-
tive, concealing John's true character, distorting Joan's appreciation of him by concentrating her attention on certain traits
(good or bad) that are in fact unimportant in his total make-up.
In this case, 'John was revealed', or 'John revealed *himself*',
are inappropriate, and if 'revealing' language is used at all, it
has to be carefully qualified. 'He revealed the superficial attractiveness that was naturally his; but carefully concealed his true

---

[1] See G. F. Woods, *Theological Explanation*, p. 87ff.
[2] It is interesting to note, however, that the man who tries hard to 'reveal'
himself, to make his actions tell, is often accused of insincerity for his ostentation.
'Are you doing this because you love me; or because you want to deceive me into
supposing you love me?' are both meaningful questions. For sure, 'Both because I
love, and I want you to know, for my own sake, and for yours if you wish to respond'
may be a quite proper answer.

intentions.' The episode was far from 'revealing', except of the one aspect, which is, of course, very clearly seen. Another girl (or the reader of a book in which John and Joan appear) may have found the events 'completely revealing'; but however much John intended to 'reveal' himself to Joan, if she was too stupid, shallow, psychotic, to understand, he did not 'reveal himself' as he had intended.

In the end, only if John is willing to be 'revealed', or if necessary to 'reveal' himself, is it likely that he will be at all fully 'revealed' to Joan. He could if he wished conceal himself, even if they were wed. The 'revealing' depends, to a large extent, on his initiative.[1]

The conditions for asserting meaningfully that 'God' as 'Person' is 'revealed' can now be discussed quite briefly.[2] In the first chapter we gave some references to places where the arguments for this way of talking may be found. In the first part of this chapter we talked about 'knowing a person', and the ways a claim to such 'knowledge' must be tested. We suggested that they could (and in the case of claims about God, should) be verified, even if, on occasions, the sense just of 'knowing' the other is tremendous, and drives all critical thoughts away. It is really no defence against this to claim that you can never really 'know' another person as precisely as a scientist 'knows' the result of a laboratory experiment; or that you have to intuit your 'knowledge' of another person and so it cannot be verified in the way sense-experience may.[3] It does not matter how the 'knowledge' came; the real question is, 'Have you got it?' and most often this may be easily verified or falsified.

The word 'mystery' may recur in this sort of discussion, but we have already noticed its shortcomings.

We have examined the sort of 'knowledge of a person' that may be gained from a book. The Christian usually claims that such 'knowledge of God' as he believes he has depends on the

---

[1] Above, p. 215; G. F. Woods, *Theological Explanation*, p. 87ff.

[2] 'Revelation in Events' (e.g. art. 'Revelation', *Handbook of Christian Theology*, Collins, 1960, p. 330) is a phrase that often describes such 'personal revealing', but needs no separate treatment.

[3] J. Baillie, *Our Knowledge of God*, O.U.P., 1939, p. 201ff.; *The Idea of Revelation in Recent Thought*, p. 25ff.: 'I cannot analyse for you in any exhaustive way how my friend revealed himself to me as what he is.' One is occasionally made to suspect that the reason for using 'personal' language of 'God' lies just in the apparent difficulty of criticising it. But it is more probably a proper reverence for him.

Bible (as record of the primary 'events' of Christian history), to a greater or lesser extent on Christian tradition, preferably up to the present day; and on constant control by the Holy Spirit. It was seen that the only plausible paradigm for this sort of 'knowing of God as person' was already of a very distant and uncertain 'knowing'; and that even a claim to this sort of 'knowing' was very difficult to make good. The same applies, whether it is said that 'God' as 'person' is 'known' or 'revealed'; or whether it is said that it is 'in Christ' that we 'see' or 'know' God as 'person'. The latter adds the further difficulty of deciding how Christ himself is 'known'. It might, according to traditional Christian belief, have been possible in Christ's lifetime to have 'known' God, quite 'objectively'. But it has already been seen that the early writer who most insists on this possibility, the Fourth Evangelist, does not seem to think that such 'knowing' happened; and even if he had thought so, the diversity of New Testament witness to Christ would have shown him to have been wrong.[1] However, so far as *we* are concerned, 'knowing' Christ and 'knowing' the Father are on much the same level of difficulty.

The first sense of the 'revealing of a person' that we noted amounts to the 'revealing' of lots of facts about him. We have already discussed the difficulties of claiming that we have lots of true facts about the One God 'revealed' to us. It has also been suggested that to talk of 'cold facts' about 'God' is a contradiction in terms.

But it has also, indirectly, been shown that to talk of the 'revealing' of 'God-as-person-who-demands-response' (in fact, submissive, obedient, loving, response) is not justified either. To say that the 'will of God' is *not* 'revealed in its irresistibility' is much the same as to say that God is not 'revealed as a "person" (in this sense)'. There is not sufficient obedient response on the part of Christians to warrant saying that 'God-as-irresistible-person' is 'revealed' to them. And to say that God could be 'revealed' as other than irresistible—as one to whom just any or no response at all could be offered—is completely to redefine 'God'.

If God is to be 'revealed' to us, we probably all still need a radical conversion, whether it be sudden or gradual. It does

[1] See ch. 3.

not seem to happen in a lifetime or, if it does, it is to so few that it has little effect on the rest of us.

That we should depend on God for any 'revelation' of him seems from our experience of human friendship quite intelligible. But we still await it. He certainly does not seem to 'stand revealed' (in any meaningful sense of 'revealed) in 'Nature', or anywhere else.[1]

What is there left to say of Communication between God and Man?

It may be that the theologian, admitting all the difficulties, only wants to say that he believes that 'God' does allow men to understand and respond to something of his own character and demands. Though it may be (rather, *is*) impossible to check objectively that some idea is 'from God', and though many fellow Christians may dispute any 'given' idea, yet he may well want to believe that 'God' somehow communicates with men. Among the many ideas that men have of 'God', and of how to respond to him, are some that 'God' himself has given. This he finds he must believe, that some come from 'God' as a gracious gift. And he might want to use 'reveal' for this 'providing information'; not necessarily to suggest against the evidence that all is clear, but to insist that it is 'provided'.[2] We have noted that one of the reasons for the use of 'reveal' is to stress the initiative of the actor, and the dependence of the recipient. However, it is not really honest to use a word that means 'provide clear information' to describe the providing of notoriously unclear information.

A modern examination technique is to pose a question, offer

---

[1] This is not the same thing as to say, with much traditional theism, that God *must be* 'invisible', 'incomprehensible', *by definition*. The present writer does not find *a priori* definitions about what 'God' 'must be' very persuasive. But the chances are that the supposed deductions to God's 'incomprehensibility' really just explain the commitment the believer makes. Just as 'proofs' of the 'existence' of God now seem to be elaborations of the believer's understanding of his faith, so it is actual experience that leads to the formulation: 'God has not made himself comprehensible', 'has not revealed himself'. Both ways of arguing seem to be found in the Fathers; see ch. 4.

[2] E.g. J. Baillie, *The Sense of the Presence of God*, O.U.P., 1962, p. 187f.: 'What is true in any religious system is from God; what is false is of our own imagining. Man can know nothing of God except as God himself reveals himself to him. No man can by searching find out God, except as God himself takes the initiative both in prompting the searching and in directing the finding ... though how far each people responded to what God was thus minded to teach them, and how far they mingled such response as they made with corrupt practices and notions of their own is, of course, another question.'

one correct among a dozen false solutions, and ask for the right
answer to be chosen. The information has in some sense been
'given'. It can hardly be said to have been 'revealed'. To depend on God for information, but still to be left in uncertainty,
seems to be the lot of the Christian. It is not that there is no
possibility of giving positive content to the word 'God'; it is that
even within 'the Christian tradition' there are too many possibilities. When one bundle of possibilities is chosen and called
'the revelation of God', this is only a disguised way of saying
'This has my allegiance; I commit myself here.'[1] However we
choose as Christians, we cannot claim that God has made the
right choice at all generally plain. However plain we might like
to say it must be, it is still not plain enough for most of us to
'see'. In this uncertainty there is no 'revelation'.

Conclusions

If God intended to 'reveal himself' in Christ, in the events
of his life and death and resurrection and in his teaching, he
failed. It seems more faithful to assume that this was not his
intention. That he intends finally to 'reveal himself' to us we
may well hope; and we may believe that the events of the life
and death and resurrection of Christ, and the continuing life of
the Church, have made possible our 'conversion', so that we
may become the sort of people who really will be able to 'see
God'. But to suggest that this has already happened, does
happen, is to deceive both ourselves and others. There is little
more point in saying that though it is never realised, yet a
'revealing of God' is now possible. A possibility that cannot at
present be realised is not at present relevant. A 'revelation' of
what cannot now be seen is not a 'revelation'. We may believe,
trust, that Christ has made the 'revealing of God' a possibility
in some sort of future. It is surely nonsense, even pernicious
nonsense, to pretend that it is a present fact.

---

[1] T. R. Miles, *Religion and the Scientific Outlook*, pp. 195-7.

Additional Note to p. 197: '*Knowledge of Persons*' A striking illustration of the point
being made is provided by N. W. Clerk (C. S. Lewis), *A Grief Observed*, Faber and
Faber, 1961, especially p. 17ff. But the whole book seems to me to illustrate the
difficulty of talk of 'knowing people', 'knowing God'; and at the same time to
express what I wish to convey, a willingness to trust without any certainty,
'meaning', or 'revelation'.

7

CHRISTIANITY WITHOUT REVELATION

IT is infuriating to be told that you may not say, 'almost perfect', 'almost complete', because 'something is either perfect or not, complete or not'. Everyone knows what is meant by 'almost perfect', 'almost complete', 'almost full' (even 'the larger half'). This essay is not attempting to impose such a piece of purposeless pedantry. Many terms that are strictly absolute are so qualified; and it is much tidier than a circumlocution such as 'has come close to the point of completion'. I have insisted, time and again, that 'reveal' *may be qualified*, and *meaningfully*. All that is demanded is that if the word is intended to express 'theological' (or other) truth, the qualifications should be carefully examined, so that both writer and reader, speaker and listener, may know as precisely as possible what is being said. But I then suggested that the theologian who is at all aware of the actualities of the Christian situation will admit that any talk of 'revelation of God' must be so heavily qualified that it would be less confusing to use another word. After all, if a young couple are told that their home is 'almost complete', and find that it still lacks wiring, pipes, plaster, floors and roof, they will be justifiably grieved; not because the builder has no right, with notice, to use ordinary words specially qualified, but because in this case he has deceived them.

We have tried, then, to show that the qualifications with which a realistic theologian finds he has to use the words 'reveal' and 'revelation' suggest that he would do better, in company with the New Testament writers, to keep these words for the 'future consummation' (however that is understood) and just possibly for the physical seeing of Jesus of Nazareth, long ago. It is not that the present writer is more pessimistic about the

Christian situation than is anyone else. Many older and wiser
Christians are less sanguine still. But if John Baillie was right
when he wrote:

> 'There is much that we do not know. Now we know in part, as
> St Paul says, and it may sometimes seem to us to be only a very
> small part. Now we see only, he says again, as in a mirror dimly.
> The clouds and thick darkness remain, and the light piercing
> them sometimes seems scant enough',[1]

then does it not follow that 'revelation' is too grand a word to
use yet? It really does seem to claim so much more than is
justified. Even if we qualify it with words like 'partial', 'veiled'(!),
'mystery', are we not as likely to deceive others as is the
builder who says 'almost complete' for 'just started'? May we
not even delude ourselves?

This final chapter is concerned with showing where 'revelation' may be causing confusion; and with ways in which, once
'revelation' is restricted to the meanings and contexts I have
suggested, the confusions may be avoided. Once the predominant stress on this one word has been removed, a full and largely
traditional theology may be stated and even defended, and
perhaps lived.

We start by unravelling some of the muddles involved in
much talk of 'natural' and 'revealed' religion; particularly to
see if the antithesis is essential to the preservation of Paul's
distinction between 'grace' and 'works'. The next question we
ask is whether it is possible to talk of 'revelation', even 'revelation as encounter', without becoming narrowly and esoterically
'intellectualistic'. And the last of these specimen problems is
that of the value of talk of 'revelation' in apologetics and
evangelism.

The second part of this chapter is devoted to a summary
statement of the sorts of implications that an acceptance of the
position argued here might have for a much wider field, really
for theology as a whole. It is intended primarily as a statement,
and not as a further attempt to persuade the hitherto uncon-

---

[1] *The Idea of Revelation*, p. 148. These words are from the penultimate paragraph
of the book. It is only fair—but by no means destructive of the point being made—
to give their continuation: 'But it is the Light of the World. It is more light than
we are ever likely to use. It is enough to see to do our work by, and until we have
done our work we have no cause to repine. When our work is done, it is promised
that we shall know even as we are known, and that we shall see face to face.'

vinced. But, by the same token, a reasoned rejection of the theological position there outlined has very little bearing on the validity of the arguments of the preceding chapters. It is not to be supposed that the rejection of the contemporary use of 'reveal', etc., *proves* the Christian necessity of the doctrinal tenets sketched in these pages; but it does lessen the necessity, even the persuasiveness, of some of the alternatives.

The third section attempts a defence of 'salvation' as a more useful term than 'revelation' to summarise for Christians the purpose of God in Christ. Again, I do not hope to prove that the word *should* be used; only to show that it stands much better the tests that I have applied in greater detail, but with negative results, to 'reveal'.

This is preliminary to a final rounding off of the discussion as a whole.

The arguments that follow may perhaps help at least to persuade that the case against 'revelation' is not just a piece of hypersensitive finicking, but has far-reaching implications for theology and life. And these implications are by no means necessarily negative or hurtful; some may even find them positively liberating.

I. THREE MUDDLES CAUSED BY 'REVELATION'

'Natural' and 'Revealed' 'Knowledge' and the 'Grace' of God

Is 'knowledge of God' 'revealed' or 'natural'? Is it 'innate', or 'of grace'? Of the many discussions of these problems, we take that of William Nicholls' *Revelation in Christ* as near enough typical; at least it provides sufficient illustrations of the arguments that occur.[1]

Nicholls begins by looking at the variety of 'the religions of the world, great and small, high and low' (p. 15ff.). In their variety, they do not tell us 'how we are to choose which to embrace'; there is not even some objective universal core. 'Most ordinary people . . . are right to reach the conclusions they do. The multiplicity of man's religious ideas make it seem *a priori* unlikely that they are well founded . . .' (p. 17). Other argu-

---

[1] See also E. Brunner, *Revelation and Reason*; K. Barth, *CD* I/2 §17, *et passim*, *Against the Stream*, p. 205ff.; P. Tillich, *ST* I, p. 133ff.; J. Baillie, *Our Knowledge of God*, chs 1 and 2, p. 75ff., *The Idea of Revelation*, chs 3 and 4, *The Sense of the Presence of God*, p. 168ff.

ments dispose of 'metaphysical deductions' and 'pure atheism' as alternative positions. Out of this vagueness, variety and straight denial no 'knowledge of God' could come. 'If God exists, he is the unknown God, and will remain so unless he makes himself known' (p. 25).

The only 'live' alternative, then, must be 'revelation'. 'Ordinary people are right to reach the conclusions they do' only 'if they leave out revelation'. 'Revelation' allows us to claim 'the true knowledge of God' (p. 15). By contrast with any general 'knowledge of God', 'revelation' (apparently) is convincing, and persuasive (pp. 16, 20), and allows us to give good reason for our ideas (p. 24). And only Christianity has this 'revelation'.

As a statement of preference this is fair enough: *I* say that *I* will call only Christianity 'revealed religion' (p. 30).[1] But it seems to be intended as an argument in favour of Christianity, showing (somehow) that Christianity lies outside the uncertainty created by the general diversity of 'religions'. And, as such, it is blatantly circular. The fact that Christians may claim to have 'inside knowledge' does nothing to prove their beliefs, does nothing even to distinguish them from the crowd. 'Revelation . . . is a universal religious conception.'[2] Seen from outside, however much it says it has 'received' its faith, Christianity looks like just another attempt to construct a god from a selection of this-worldly data. The purely formal category 'revealed religion' does nothing (if it is formally and objectively applied) to mark Christianity off from the perplexing variety of what generally goes by the name 'religion'.

In fact, a man has to choose, without some handy *a priori* clue of this sort. (It is odd that Nicholls, who rejects *a priori* arguments for the Christian 'God' (p. 31ff., cf. p. 21f.), nonetheless finds them worth while in arguments against competitors.)

And it has to be admitted that it is a very insecure argument for Christianity against (allowing the term, now) 'other religions', to point to 'their' diversity. If their variety means 'revelation' is still needed, it is quite as urgently required to answer the enervating dilemma of the kaleidoscopic possibilities of Christendom.

---

[1] Above, p. 238 and n. 1.
[2] H. Kraemer, *The Christian Message in a non-Christian World*, Harper Bros, 1938, p. 69; though the statement is rather sweeping.

Nicholls next makes the fairly common point that only 'revelation' in 'events that might not otherwise have happened') could have allowed God to preserve his initiative (pp. 28, 33). If 'God' were to 'reveal himself' in events that are 'repeatable' (we seem expected to infer), he would necessarily become pas-) sive before men's gaze, and so really not be 'God' at all.[1]

But, even allowing for the moment the distinction between 'repeatable happenings' and 'unique event' (*ibid.*), the objectionable 'passivity', 'loss of initiative', or 'bonds' are inserted for him in the argument of the man who is speaking for 'natural' or 'general' 'knowledge of God', before he can say (maybe) yes, (maybe) no. It is no essential part of the case. If a man thinks he has seen a glimpse of God in the slow sure growth from seed to full plant, and becomes patient and persevering, he may say, 'How clever of me to find God who was lying captive for me to find'; but he may as well say, 'How good of God in his freedom to show me this truth about himself.' The New Testament scholar may say, 'How gracious of God to show me so much of himself through the writings of Paul'; but even he may say, 'How clever of Paul to produce such a rich theology, and of me to understand so much of the truth of God that lies passive there for me to find.' A distinction cannot be forced between a 'natural' and a 'revealed' knowledge of God; or between a 'general' and a 'biblical' 'revealing of God', by the blind assertion that the former in each case could never be a gracious act of personal initiative (such as befits God), while the latter must; that the former must 'bind' God, while only the latter could leave him free. If either has happened (which we find very difficult to believe), it is for us God's gracious act. But another man might see both Bible and nature as ways to spy on a passive god. Nicholls himself talks of God standing 'revealed

[1] Cf. also G. S. Hendry, *art. cit.*, *ThWB*: 'Is there not a natural revelation, i.e. a knowledge of God which is always and everywhere *available to* men?' And further, K. Barth, *CD* I/2, §13.2, 'Jesus Christ the Objective Possibility of Revelation', where Barth seems to be supposing all along that if God is in any sense truly known apart from Christ, he will (again, *per impossibile*) have lost his 'freedom'. 'But if we conclude from this ("revelation in Christ") that God was able to and had to reveal Himself to us in this familiar form, that it was the very thing we needed—we must not forget that we can only say so in thankful retrospect upon what God has really done—not on the ground of an *analogia entis* already visible to us beforehand, of an affinity and aptitude for God's revelation, belonging to the world since creation, familiar to us and recognisable in it despite the Fall, *as if God were now utterly bound to it*' (*ibid.*, p. 37, my italics).

through Christ' (p. 39), though perhaps he did not intend the inconsistency.[1]

Already implicit in the preceding argument is the also very common distinction between 'nature' and 'history'. Nicholls uses it further for I think a unique argument: the fact that Christianity bases its talk about 'God' on 'events' makes it philosophically meaningful in a way which all other religions, and metaphysics in general, based as they are 'on permanent features and characteristics of the world' (p. 28), can never be; because a historian could prove the Christian records untrue ('falsification'), and repentance, faith, and the resultant personal contact with God through Christ are Christian talk's 'verification' (p. 31). Admitted, the historian might[2] falsify Christian historical assertions; but the *interpretation* put on them (which is the point at issue) simply is not 'meaningful' in this way at all. As we have tried to show in an earlier chapter, it is neither 'true' nor 'false', in the way that scientific (including 'historical') assertions are.

But the distinction itself between 'history' and 'nature' is purely arbitrary. 'History', as it is used in statements like this, means only 'human history' and as such is part of 'natural history'. Human history just happens to be more interesting to us. This is well said by H. R. Niebuhr:

> 'The events of history to which Christian revelation refers may be regarded from the scientific, objective, non-committed point of view as well as nature can be. . . . At best . . . historic description will make use of the category of individuality, pointing out the uniqueness of each event and the particular way in which general principles are made concrete in it. But such uniqueness is a characteristic of all events in time.'[3]

A harvest (and every harvest is 'unrepeatable') might as well be the particular gracious (even 'revealing') act of a personal God as might a particular journey or a particular death; and so might the growth of a particular acorn. The fact that many Christians claim to see God clearly in a very limited number of events does not *in itself* make their claim any different from

---

[1] Cf. quotation from Barth in previous note.

[2] *Contra* many theologians, see above, p. 189.

[3] H. R. Niebuhr, *The Meaning of Revelation*, p. 55ff. This is probably the best treatment of 'revelation' without actually questioning the word itself, that I have met: the most aware of the difficulties that are part of the traditional claims.

those who claim to see God in a more extended series of events. Some qualities of these events may make a difference, but just 'uniqueness' cannot; that is a 'quality' of all events in time as events. There is nothing implicit in the notion of the 'self-revealing' of a 'personal God' that can make Nicholls' view somehow more logical, Christian or 'biblical' than the belief of, for instance, Leonard Hodgson: that 'revelation' is God's enlightening of the minds of men when they see the implications of any events, in the history of nature or the history of men.[1]

A child finds it hard to see the love and care of parents in the normal routine of being fed and clothed and trained for adulthood; if there are no treats, no special attention, no at least apparent preferential concern, he or she begins to feel neglected. 'Mummy and Daddy do not love me any more.' The insistence on seeing God 'personally' at work over a limited area, and 'in particular events', is very similar. It is understandable, at any rate in a child. But it is not logical. The many similar but in fact unique events of routine care are the stuff of family 'personal' relationships. It is for the Christian to pray that he may respond to God acting in person in every particular event; which means in everything that happens, because it will always be 'particular'. God may seem to use some events more than others to shape us to be the people who will ultimately 'know' him; we may believe he lets us know more of his purposes and his self in some happenings than in others. But all events are his. 'Not a sparrow can fall to the ground apart from God.' To restrict God's 'personal' activity to a few particular events is, *per impossibile*, to keep God from being God.

Obviously this raises problems about cruel and evil events in 'nature' (and so in 'history'!); but so does any doctrine of God as 'Creator', and the semi-deistic attempts to relegate God's personal activity to nice events, or 'revelatory' events, leaving a machine or a devil (or an indefinable 'x' that we would rather forget about) made by him to do the routine or nasty things, only multiply hypotheses without answering the primary question.[2] It is no part of the plan of this book to attempt a theodicy. It is a fact that Christians think they most clearly see

---

[1] This sentence was intended as a direct quotation, but I lost the reference. I think it fairly represents opinions expressed in L. Hodgson, *For Faith and Freedom*, Blackwell, 1957, vol. II, e.g. pp. 3 and 20ff.

[2] Hodgson, *For Faith and Freedom*, vol. II, ch. III, 'God and Evil'.

God at work in one of the nastier events of human (and natural) history.[1]

The distinction between 'nature' on the one hand, and 'history-and-grace' on the other, is unreal. So far as logic is concerned, God is as free to act 'graciously' in one part of natural history as in another, and cannot (by logic) be restricted to those areas of it which obviously affect men, or particularly concern them. Conversely, that we believe he was 'incarnate'[2] in a very restricted number of events—a human life—does not logically force us to believe that this was a more 'personal' action than any other we believe him to have done.

But there is an overriding unreality in this argument about 'revealed' or 'natural' knowledge of God. Circumstances do not seem to justify a claim either that God is 'revealed' in all (natural) history; or that he is 'revealed' in some smaller (say, human) area of (natural) history.[3] Neither side has won, and neither has (yet) taken the prizes.

It is still possible to decide (as, for instance, does Karl Barth) that there *is* only one area where God acts graciously, only one area of 'revelation': 'Here—but only here—(Christianity) sees revelation . . . and it sees God. . . . Revelation in the Christian sense takes place and God in the Christian sense is, in accordance with the news of Jesus Christ.'[4] There is no logical necessity (Barth would not allow it), and it is not proved more intensely 'personal'. It is just a decision to find 'revelation' here, and nowhere else. This is something completely 'new' and 'other'. And so long as the talk remains abstract, this can sound quite well. As a commitment, it is logically unassailable. But when those who claim to find here 'revelation' of God disagree among themselves as to what, or perhaps better, 'who', is found, it does not look very like 'revelation'.

---

[1] We discussed in ch. 5 what it means to talk of 'God acting': it is primarily a commitment to respond in love in events as they happen; but it is more than that. It is the essential 'myth' that allows us to intend an *agape* that is not 'self-sufficient', but believes it finds its power in this 'God' who acts.

To say that 'all events are acts of God' could be 'pantheistic' (and so a commitment just to accept, and otherwise do nothing, in response to events). But it is of course intended to mean 'all events are acts of the God of love', and so is a commitment to finding ways to love in all events, and to expecting to find love possible.

[2] See again ch. 5.

[3] See ch. 6 above.

[4] Barth, *Against the Stream*, p. 211ff.; cf. *CD* I/2, *ibid.*, 'Jesus Christ the Objective Possibility of Revelation.'

And once 'revelation' is translated into terms of 'reconcilia-tion' or 'obedience' as it most often is[1] (and as we saw it had to be if it were to be 'God' 'revealed'), the difficulties increase further. If this 'revelation' *does* create a man anew, make a completely new obedience possible; and if anything meaningful is being said by that, then it should be possible to tell who has and who has not received the 'revelation'. They will be totally 'other'.

They will, for instance, now love in a way that has only now, and only for them, become possible. That this distinctive-ness is not apparent is the major brake on the Church's mission and ministry. Once 'revelation' is said to achieve an empirical response, the fact that *it has not happened to people* becomes at once apparent. It is possible, with Karl Barth and others, just to decide that 'here' there is 'revelation'. But it is not possible just to 'decide' that these men have been made different by receiving 'revelation', if they have not.

If still it is insisted that 'revelation' *has come* to men who *have not fully received it, are not fully reconciled, still do not perfectly obey,* then an important concession has been made. There is *not* a 'complete newness', a 'total otherness'. The people in the 'area of revelation' look very like those who are outside. If the people in the 'area of revelation' achieve their obedience through 'revelation'; and if the 'revelation' is the sole possibility of their obedience; then it begins to look as though those seemingly outside who behave in much the same way have received 'revelation' too. Or else they have performed without the grace of 'revelation' what others have had to await this grace to achieve. . . . Nichols at least is caught in this inconsistency. On page 92 of *Revelation in Christ* he judges, 'One cannot know the living God without being drawn into a way of living' that is appropriate; but earlier, he has refused to allow the world at large the benefit of the obverse of this judgment (p. 18), even quoting but apparently dismissing as of no consequence a 'word of the Lord' on this very point: 'By their fruits ye shall know them.' Once 'revelation' is supposed to have some empirical effect, the edges of the area of the 'revealing' are irreparably

---

[1] Barth, *Against the Stream*, p. 215; *CD* I/2, p. 792; P. Tillich, *ST* I, p. 161ff.; W. Nicholls, *Revelation in Christ*, p. 92; cf. J. Baillie, *The Sense of the Presence of God*, p. 90ff., and the quotations there.

blurred by Christians themselves, and the *a priori* distinction between 'nature' and 'grace' is again destroyed.

(The only conceivable further defence of the position, which luckily no one seems to have offered, is to assert that there is a 'newness', but it cannot be seen except by those who are made new; this would be *battalogia*. Some of the distinctions drawn in the discussion of 'grace' and 'nature' do tread almost as close as this to calling good evil and evil good. The wisdom of God may be foolishness with men; but the profane babbling of men is not the wisdom of God.)

The position of John Baillie and Leonard Hodgson[1] among many others, is surely more intelligible. If a particular Christian response to a situation is thought to be due to the grace of God, and only possible through his action, then it seems necessary to allow that a similar response to a similar situation by a non-Christian is the action of God. This is not sentimental. It may be very hard to find obviously God-inspired actions outside of historic Christianity. It is also quite hard to find them within.

If it is allowed that 'revelation' is unreal apart from its acceptance, and if its acceptance is a moral thing and so is unreal apart from its moral result, then similar moral acts must betoken a similar 'revelation'.

The only fault in the argument is the one pointed out in the previous chapter, and emphasised again since, that there is not a sufficiently uniform or intense moral response to 'God' to warrant the claim that he is 'revealed', has 'made himself known', has elicited a full response to himself. A claim that 'God' is 'generally revealed' (in the sense that includes an ethical response within 'revelation') is even more difficult to sustain than one that he is 'particularly revealed' (in the same sense)—and that is hard enough. The only possibility of retaining the word is so to qualify it that it loses its meaning indirectly instead of explicitly.

This does, however, emphasise the positive point that John Baillie and Leonard Hodgson and others have made, that it really is impossible to draw a tight line around 'the Church' or 'a church' or any other 'locus of grace' and say God is only at work, only savingly at work, inside. To make the 'arrogant

---

[1] *Our Knowledge of God; The Idea of Revelation; The Sense of the Presence of God;* and *For Faith and Freedom* I, respectively.

assumption'[1] that God only saves where the 'revealed' 'name of Jesus Christ' is explicitly confessed, is to tell God what he ought to be about. Instead, as John Baillie says:

'We have to take history as we find it. Above all, we have to accept the action of God as we actually discover it to be. We cannot pretend to know in advance how God *ought* to act for the enlightenment and salvation of the human race. We are not in a position to lay down rules or conditions. The only question which—shall I say as a good empiricist?—I have a right to ask is: Do I in fact find God coming to meet me in Jesus Christ as nowhere else, or do I not?' (*ibid.*, p. 207).

Not even if we believe that Jesus Christ is the salvation of the human race, may we tell God that he may only let that salvation avail, where there is a consciously enlightened commitment to the incarnate Lord. We must look and see.

We have not found that 'revelation' (nor any more precise form such as 'particular' or 'historical' 'revelation') is at all necessary to safeguard any real distinctiveness of the Christian faith, or to express a belief in the gracious personal initiative of God. In fact we have found the antithesis of the 'natural' or 'revealed' 'knowledge of God' (based in part on the logic of the word 'reveal' itself) to be quite false; and worse than that, to be the mainstay of an exclusiveness arbitrarily imposed on God and man. In our relations with other men, we are servants with the power (we may believe) to love; not masters with a knowledge to proclaim.

'Revelation', Intellect, and Human Personality

We have already suggested in our fourth chapter that 'revelation' became important only when Christians began unduly to emphasise the role of the intellect in the service of God. Now there is a sense in which this is admitted on many (though not all) sides, as we saw in the introductory chapter. For instance, Gustaf Aulén has written: 'The word "revelation" is heavily burdened with intellectualism';[2] and we referred to other writers who make a similar charge—against some uses of the word. But they do seem to suppose that this 'intellectualism' can be avoided, while the word is still used. 'What is offered to

---

[1] J. Baillie, *The Sense of the Presence of God*, p. 191.
[2] In *Revelation*, p. 275. Cf. J. McIntyre, *On the Love of God*, Collins, 1962, p. 255ff.

man's apprehension in any specific revelation is not truth concerning God, but the living God himself.'[1] And the question we ask here is simply, Is this really so? Does this idea of 'personal self-revelation' avoid a de-personalising 'intellectualism'; or is it not rather itself a very highly sophisticated intellectual notion indeed?

The best defence of the use we are here doubting is in the form of an attack. Austin Farrer in his essay 'Revelation'[2] says that to have God 'disposing of us', 'dealing in us', is insufficient for the Christian; we must have a more 'personal' term, such as 'dealing with'; and that must include 'awareness', and so 'revealing': 'God is believed to dispose of us and our destinies at all times, but that is not to say that he deals *with us* but rather (if the phrase be allowed) that he deals in us; it certainly does not mean that he is revealed to us' (*ibid.*, p. 100). This would, then, run clean counter to our suspicion that 'revelation' implies a de-personalising intellectual activity by God.

Farrer argues that we *must* include the notion of 'revealing', if our talk of God is not to de-personalise us. Yet there is really very much less justification than he suggests for an insistence on the word 'reveal' as being an essential part of 'personal dealing' (which is actually the real subject of his essay).[3] Farrer

---

[1] W. Temple, *Nature Man and God*, p. 322; cited by J. Baillie, *The Idea of Revelation*, p. 33; also by W. M. Horton, 'Revelation' in *A Handbook of Christian Theology*.

[2] In *Faith and Logic*, ed. B. Mitchell.

[3] The basic term that is used to prove the appropriateness of 'reveal' is 'deal with (personally)'; and it is to this that Farrer devotes most of his discussion. This at least would suggest that 'reveal' is for him a subsidiary term of secondary importance: it cannot be defended in terms of its own meanings. G. S. Hendry, *art. cit.*, *ThWB*, has much the same difficulty. 'Revelation is essentially a dialogue, in which God speaks his word, addresses it to man's understanding, and seeks to elicit an understanding response.' If 'revelation' is essentially a dialogue, why call it 'revelation' at all; why not call it what it essentially is? The discussion so far should have shown in fact that, though 'conscious dialogue' may be part of God's purpose, even his final purpose, neither is it a very appropriate term for God's activity towards men now. To see God's present activity as directed predominantly towards dialogue with the conscious mind is to run counter to biblical faith and the present observable Christian position.

H. H. Farmer, in *Revelation and Religion*, Nisbet, 1954, also finds embarrassment with the word 'revelation', and explains in his Preface that though it is in his title, he really means to talk of something else. And see also H. R. Niebuhr, *op. cit.*, p. 152ff., where there is a long string of sentences starting 'Revelation is . . .'; 'revelation' is mostly anything but 'revelation'. For instance, it is 'that moment when we are given a new faith, to cleave to and betray, and a new standard, to follow and deny'. This is finely said. But why, save intoxication with the word, call it 'revelation' at all? Compare the argument of A. R. George (*Communion with God*, p. 103ff.) against K. Kirk's use of the related term 'vision': if the latter has to substitute 'close communion' for his theme word, it would be less misleading to

explains: 'Now "dealing with" involves two parties who must be aware of each other's actions.' But as an analysis of the term as it is normally used this is just not true. A teacher 'deals with' rowdy pupils without trying to increase their 'awareness' of himself, personally. Perhaps Farrer understands a more refined sense of 'deal with personally'. But a parent can 'deal with' a child tactfully, and with every respect for the emergent personality, long before the child can be aware of many of the actions of the parent, or most of the intentions behind them, long before the child is aware of the parent as a person at all, or at all able to respond on a personal level. Compared with God as 'a person' (if that be a proper phrase), the most fully 'personal' of us, I think a Christian would want to say, is very much a child, to be 'dealt with' as a child, and not be expected to see the full 'personality' of him with whom we have to deal. In fact, the parent who tries to 'reveal himself' too soon, who tries to elicit a precocious personal response, is not acting 'personally' at all; he is not looking for a 'personal relationship', but just for a foil for his own personality. That is not God's way with us.[1] And even among adults, among people at a roughly similar level of 'personal development', 'dealing with personally' does not have to include such a degree of awareness as would justify using the term 'revelation' (unless, obviously, it was so heavily qualified that it was not 'revelation' at all).

Perhaps I may be allowed to adapt an illustration of Farrer's. He does not find it necessary to offer an explicit defence as such of the use of the word 'revelation' at the outset; nor does he seem to see that the difficulties the use of such a concept entails are not an essential part of the *scandalon* of the Christian faith. However, he does at one point say,

> 'If the Godhead had been incarnate under a complete incognito, what would have been the result? Those who had to do with him would have had to do with their Creator, but only as children who take it for quartz may handle diamonds; it is no handling of diamonds to them. His companions would have felt the impact

---

surrender 'vision' altogether. (But even a claim to 'close communion' with God, on any conscious and responsive level, would be hard to defend against the criteria outlined in chs 5 and 6 above.)

[1] There is a sense in which D. Bonhoeffer (*Letters and Papers from Prison*, SCM Press, 1953) rightly argues that God has brought Western man at least to a form of 'adulthood'. But that is very much an adulthood without 'awareness of God'.

of a divinely good life, and perhaps passed on the influence. It would have dwindled as it spread and left at length not a ripple on the surface of history' (*ibid.*, p. 100).

In fact, the picture of children handling diamonds is remarkably appropriate; just add that not all thought them attractive at all, and of those who did, some found them quartz, some glass, some plastic, and that a few did think them to be of an unimaginable value; and you have a vivid parable of the actual divergent reactions to Jesus of his first followers and acquaintances:[1] and even so, the impact *is* still felt.

We have suggested that so far from 'revelation' safeguarding the personal integrity of those with whom God 'deals', a 'revealing' too early might well have been actually destructive, and anyway, does not seem to have been the way God chose. Yet even if these parts of Farrer's positive defence of 'revelation' do not stand, is our counter-charge, that 'revelation' is distortingly 'intellectualistic', really true?

I must confess that I 'feel' this more powerfully than I think I can argue it logically. It is only possible to offer some pointers which may or may not be persuasive.

If the action of God is seen predominantly as the providing of true information about himself (and if 'faith' for instance is seen as 'assent' to these propositions, and little or no more), then only the 'mind' seems to be engaged, and this will leave most people 'cold'. This is the critical position William Temple and many others have adopted, as we mentioned again at the beginning of this section. And yet J. I. Packer, for instance, reminded us that even if we were to have a more than 'propositional' 'revelation' (for instance, one that engaged us more, demanded more commitment, some 'personal' response), through Christ, we would still need 'revealed propositions'.[2] This did seem to us inescapable. (That it is very hard to show that we have them is not immediately at issue.) So even if it is believed that the words and sentences of the Bible 'mediate' a more 'personal

---

[1] Farrer's argument as it stands is purely deductive, and is in marked contrast with his explicit rejection of *a prioris* on the preceding page (compare Nicholls above): 'What we can show in general is not the possibility of revelation, but the impossibility of forecasting the nature or bearing of God's personal action until he reveals it.' In this case, however, Farrer assumes that he can 'forecast' the conditions for the incarnation of Godhead having a continuing effect. There must, he assumes, have been a 'revealing'.

[2] Ch. 6, p. 219f.; cf. ch. 1, p. 12ff.

revealing', the latter still depends on a previous quite heavy work of intellectual appreciation. The analogy we offered in the previous chapter for the 'knowledge of God' (where 'know' is used in its current English sense) suggests the same conclusion. God seems to be offered for our 'knowing' in a complex of activities most nearly akin to the reading and interpreting of letters.

Moreover, even supposing a fairly high degree of literary ability on the part of those to whom God is supposed to be addressing himself, the requirement that they should 'read out' of the material offered them a sense of being 'encountered by a person' makes a still further demand on intelligence. Admitted, an active imagination (for this is what is really being asked for) does not depend on literary ability; but it is one form of intelligence, and not universal, even among highly educated people.

A 'mystical' 'revealing of God' would of course not be subject to these immediate criticisms, for it does not seem to depend on intellectual ability at all. But it would even further restrict the area of God's working if he were thought predominantly or only to act towards us in 'revelation' of this very rare kind.[1]

The modification of the intellectualism that Christianity inherited from classical philosophy, and for which 'revelation' is such a congenial term, to a concern for 'personal relationships' is certainly an improvement (though we have suggested that just to see the imperative and 'invitatory' logic of statements that seem to 'describe' God would be a simpler and more readily defensible alternative). But in 'personal relationships' it is still conscious mental appreciation of the other person that matters. This is obvious from the methods used by its protagonists to argue this way of talking.

H. D. MacDonald, as we have already seen, traces the over-intellectual understanding of 'revelation' to Descartes, and himself argues that 'it is an error to take the thought element in

---

[1] I have not thought it necessary to mention mysticism before this point, as no one seems to have suggested this sort of 'revealing' as a key concept for the understanding of the ways of God to men. Most books on the subject of mysticism take pains to stress that this is not for all. Even so, I would doubt whether this either may properly be called 'revelation', in face of the diversity of the 'knowledge' that results. And this is not a criticism on the superficial level of just noting the variety of semi-technical terms used to describe such experiences. It is simply that no sure working knowledge of the active, purposive God of the Christian hope of salvation seems to result. See R. C. Zaehner, *Mysticism*, O.U.P., 1957, who accepts the criterion of the presence or absence of 'love' that we have used here (e.g. p. 203ff.).

consciousness as the whole',[1] yet does not question at all the stress on 'consciousness' as such. It is to the 'conscious self' that God addresses 'revelation' (this is, of course, implicit in the words themselves). But 'revelation' is so uniquely the purpose of God, and 'consciousness' the only aspect of man worth God's consideration, that MacDonald can write: 'If there were no adequate record . . . Bethlehem and Calvary would need to be repeated to bring God to man'.[2]

Of course it is possible just to deny the insights of modern scientific and empirical psychology; and it would be silly to attempt a defence in a few lines. But by no means all Christians find this denial necessary; MacDonald himself allows a qualified approval. And modern discoveries, supporting the interpretative guesses of Freud and others, would suggest that not just conscious *thinking*, but *consciousness itself* is only a small part of what goes to make up the individual. Even if he is not 'thinking', it is only the intelligent man who is for much of the time awake to his surroundings and other people; and even he is being very largely shaped by influences of which he is not aware at all. If God's predominant or sole activity is 'revelation' aimed to 'conscious selves', then it is to an elect intelligentsia, with very little regard for the mass of mankind.

Both the former writer and John Baillie insist that 'there is a "self" that becomes aware',[3] affected by, but not produced by social conditioning—and closed to the probing of the psycho-analyst. MacDonald merely asserts this, with the support of further assertions by other writers; Baillie offers a deductive 'proof' of it: 'It is impossible to think' any other conclusion justified. Almost inevitably, if you argue *a priori* from the content of your own thoughts, rather than inductively from controlled experiment and observation, the end product will be 'intellectualistic'. If the 'material' you start out with is what you 'think' of man, your conclusions about him will be in terms of thinking, or some form of consciousness that is near enough akin.

[1] *Ideas of Revelation*, p. 60; see above, ch. 4, p. 160ff.
[2] *Ibid.*, p. 192; quoted in full above, p. 220, n. 1.
[3] MacDonald, *ibid.*, p. 52; cf. J. Baillie, *Our Knowledge of God*, p. 201ff.; *The Idea of Revelation*, p. 25ff. The view of man implicit in a choice of 'revelation' for the predominant term by which to describe God's action to man runs counter to a view of man that may be culled from the Old or New Testaments; see for instance, W. D. Stacey, *The Pauline View of Man*, Macmillan, 1956; especially ch. XV, dealing with 'mind' (νοῦς).

Certainly this is the case that Gustaf Wingren, whom we quoted in the first chapter, makes against Karl Barth. It is probably worth quoting the latter on this point; for as we have suggested, the defence he finds it necessary to make really admits the case we have been arguing. Barth, as we have pointed out, believes that the 'Word of God' is powerful, not just 'words about God'(1) But in the prolegomena to his *Church Dogmatics* he writes:

> 'Revelation itself and as such is language. . . . We are not absolutising the human possibilities of the intellect. We might well be of the private opinion that it would be better and nicer if God had not spoken and did not speak with such deliberate "intellectualism" and that it would be more appropriate to God if "God's Word" meant all sorts of different things' (*CD* I/1, p. 150).

I would follow Wingren in suggesting that 'revelation is the choice of Barth and the philosophers of the nineteenth century (and perhaps that of those of the two preceding ones), rather than (as Barth would prefer) God's. But 'revelation', however it is understood, is, I would suggest, incurably 'intellectualistic'.

'Revelation' in Apologetics and Evangelism

There is a similar stress on consciousness, on 'hearing', on 'proclamation', as making real the 'saving event', in many contemporary theologians. An interesting example is Rudolph Bultmann. We have already noted his insistence on the centrality of 'revelation' and we have seen something of his interpretation of it in terms of 'self-understanding' (ch. 1 above). Here there is a strong apologetic and outward-looking motive. The Christian message must be 'demythologised' to be intelligible to those who hold a modern world view.

Bultmann says, 'In faith, I deny the closed connection of the worldly events, the chain of cause and effect as it presents itself to the neutral observer . . . (but) . . . not as mythology does; I deny the worldly connection of events when I speak of myself, for in this connection of worldly events, my self, my personal

---

(1) E.g. *Against the Stream*, p. 214ff.; cf. *CD* I/1, p. 162ff. Barth is quite confident. Is not the 'Word of God' powerful in the Bible? But Barth talks of its power when heard; in the Bible (largely OT, but cp. John 1.1ff., Heb. 4.12-13) it is powerful quite irrespective of hearing, and so of intellect.

existence, my own personal life, is no more visible and capable of proof than is God as acting.' To speak of God acting in any way observably is to 'deliver up the faith in wonders (God acting somehow "within" events) to the criticism of science and in so doing validate such criticism'.[1] On the other hand, to insist on 'personal encounter', or some such phrase, as the manner of God's acting may be thought to render 'faith' impervious to assaults by 'science'. It may safeguard the Christian from making the sort of assertion that will prevent the 'modern man' from taking him seriously. It may also allow faith really to be faith, to be total trust, independent of all support: 'There cannot be any trust or love without (this) risk'.[2] The Christian will be able to talk truly and effectively to people around him.

But is this the best, the truest and most effective way to proclaim Christian faith in an age of science? C. A. Coulson maintains a strong case against the practice of putting God 'in the gaps', as an apologetic method.[3] It is short-sighted. It is also blasphemous. For an earlier age, it seems, anything unusual was specifically God, God acting personally, in lightning, earthquakes and the like. And then 'science' pushed him out. And Coulson warns against seizing on some halt in the progress of scientific discovery (for instance, the uncertainty about the plotting of the course of the 'particles' in an atom) as the point where 'God' may be believed to take over direct and personal as opposed to indirect, impersonal, control. The religious have done this too often in the past, and by identifying 'God' with the inexplicable, have allowed him to be destroyed when the explanation turned up. The proper Christian way is to believe that God is in control 'personally' of all. Then, as the unholy alliance of sceptic and credulous usher their 'God' willingly or unwillingly out through the back door, the Christian can serve the real God still occupying the whole house, which has always been his, and fully his. The unnatural alliance is only exorcising an imaginary djinn from chimeric sanctuaries. The credulous

---

[1] R. Bultmann, *Jesus Christ and Mythology*, SCM Press, 1960, p. 64ff. Cf. the same author's essay 'The Concept of Revelation in the New Testament', in *Existence and Faith*, quoted above, ch. 1.

[2] *Jesus Christ and Mythology*, p. 73.

[3] C. A. Coulson, *Science and Christian Belief*, O.U.P., 1955; Fontana, 1958. See also D. Bonhoeffer, *op. cit.*, pp. 124ff., 131ff., 143ff., etc.; 'I should like to speak of God, not on the borders of life, but at its centre . . . in man's life and prosperity. . . .'

lodged him there, the incredulous dislodged him; but this was never the Lord God Almighty. It is surely impolitic to make your 'God' a djinn in a jar; it is even more certainly impious.[5]

The Christian apologist who tries to lodge God in the fast-nesses of 'consciousness', 'dialogue', 'encounter', 'the self', seems to be falling into this very trap. The way persons come to be, what really happens when two people become conscious of each other, are as yet very poorly explored realms.[2] And so it is very tempting to see God here, where science is still imprecise. But as a common criticism of Bultmann goes, after all the demytho-logising, the core he still clings to of 'revelation' of the 'Personal God' confronting the 'personal creature' is as much myth as any of the Christian tradition that has been discarded or re-interpreted.[3] And it is vain to hope that here science will leave for good a quiet place for a harried 'God' to rest.

Bultmann does of course defend himself against something like this charge; but it seems to be only by playing with words. As was quoted in parentheses above, he talks of God acting (somehow) *'within'* events: 'Faith insists not on the direct identity of God's action with wordly events, but, *if I may be permitted to put it so*, on the paradoxical identity which can be believed only here and now against the appearance of non-identity.'[4] He assumes that the reader will permit him to put it so; but this conundrum—When is an action not an event? When it is paradoxically non-identical with an action—begs the whole question. If God is said to be acting 'within' or 'through' a set of events, then either some further events will happen that would not otherwise have happened, and that is 'miracle'; or the original assertion is false; or it is meaningless. It is meaningless, if the action of 'God' is so defined that it means an action in which nothing happens. If something does happen, it is observable; if it is not observable, it has not happened, and was not an action.

However, let us suppose that Bultmann is talking meaning-

---

[1] 'Miracle is simply the religious name for event'—Schleiermacher, *On Religion* (Harper Torchbooks, 1958, p. 88). R. Bultmann regards this view as 'weak'—cited by D. Cairns, *A Gospel without Myth?*, p. 117.

[2] See for instance G. Walter, *The Living Brain*, Duckworth, 1953; Penguin, 1961.

[3] See especially P. van Buren, *The Secular Meaning of the Gospel*, chs 1 and 3, commenting on the even more 'extreme' position of S. M. Ogden, *Christ Without Myth*, Collins, 1962.

[4] *Op. cit.*, p. 62; my italics.

fully of the 'action of God'. He then defines the sort of 'action' he believes God performs. 'When we speak of God as acting, we mean that we are confronted with God, addressed, asked, judged, or blessed by God. . . . When we speak in this manner of God as acting, we conceive God's action as an analogue to the actions taking place between men' (p. 68). The world is a machine, into which the 'God' intrudes from time to time to confront men; only such events as consciously (or perhaps implicitly)[1] confront men with God are 'acts of God'. 'Only such statements about God are legitimate as express the existential relation between God and man' (p. 69). The result is a sort of deism, with as yet no apparent apologetic or evangelistic advantage. The area of 'myth', of miraculous invasion, has been reduced, but the scandal of the break in the 'chain of causality' remains.

The weakness of Bultmann's position appears again when he defends himself against the charge that he means by 'faith'— 'a purely subjective psychological experience' (p. 70, see above). (That too would, we know, be an empirical event, and we could tell by ordinary observation, or even by electronic machines, whether it were happening or no.) Faith, Bultmann answers, is not subjective (or not merely subjective); it grows out of real events that happen. It is analogous to 'the love of my friend, my wife, my children, (which) meets me genuinely only here and now as an event. Such love cannot be observed by objective methods but only by personal experience and response. From the outside, for example, by psychological observation, it cannot be perceived as love, but only as an interesting detail of psychological processes which are open to different interpretations.' And this is pure assertion, without any evidence. That my wife is offering me 'love' (even in the broadest sense) is psychologically and usually quite patently observable; that I accept this as love, that I 'understand myself as loved', is equally observable. It does not take much patience or ingenuity or even ill-manners to watch such events taking place. The observer does not see the love as 'love-towards-himself'; but he can see well enough if love between my wife and me happens or not. Whether faith in

[1] *Ibid.*, p. 75. That it is encounter with God may not be consciously appreciated; but for it to be 'encounter with God', it must result in a new 'self-understanding'. The latter, *selbsverständnis*, is not just an intellectual appreciation; it is practical. But the word chosen shows where the emphasis still lies.

God is to be called 'purely subjective'; or whether it grows out
of objective events, in a way analogous to the love between my
wife and my self, it is observable. With patient observation, it
would be possible to find what subjective states of the individual
were conducive to faith in God, if faith is just subjective (which,
as Bultmann says, is unlikely), or what social and architectural
surroundings produce faith in God (or, allowing Bultmann's
phrase, Christian 'self-understanding') 'objectively'. In fact,
this is already known in some detail. 'Christian sociology' has
made considerable progress in France and America.¹ And if this
is the only area of God's action, it should soon be possible to see
him at work; to watch clinically, and decide if there is an active
God or not. Christian talk about 'God' is reduced without
becoming any more defensible.

Bultmann is sure that 'the event of God's revelation' is a
'wonder' (p. 73ff.). It changes things, 'it occurs in our actual
lives and transforms them'. If this is what the 'revealing' act of
God does, then it alters the physical structure of the brain, in
a way it would not otherwise be altered. This is as much miracle
as an alteration to the physical structure of a limb. This is no
adequate apologetic.

It may not be entirely fair to judge Bultmann's approach to
'the modern man', and the latter's quite proper questions, from
this book which is addressed to fellow Christians in the main.
But the book is a defence of the former approach; and it just
does not seem to answer the questions.

Bultmann is surely not guilty on the charge sometimes brought
against him, of watering Christianity down just to suit a modern
palate. He does not choose the ground of 'self-understanding'
just because it is apologetically useful; he is sure that this is the
proper ground of Christian theology, whether there is a problem
of communication or not. Nonetheless, he does suppose that the
proclamation of what is then, to him, the full faith, solely in
these terms, will disarm the scientific objector, so that he is faced
only with the true *scandalon*, the demand for faith in God's
'revealing' action towards him in Christ. And in this supposition, I suggest, he is deceived.² To state Christian faith in
terms of 'revelation', and that in terms of God addressing the

¹ And see e.g. M. Argyle, *Religious Behaviour*, Routledge and Kegan Paul, 1958.
² Note also, Bonhoeffer, *Letters and Papers, passim* and esp. pp. 121ff., 125ff.

individual as person, has no real apologetic value, and does not ensure an unimpeded impact for Christian preaching. It is not likely to help the Christian talk to the man who thinks 'scientifically'. In Bultmann's case it only seems to succeed because he is juggling with words.[1] Each time he makes a statement that looks like the sort of empirical assertion that would pin him down to an observable, causality-breaking act of God, he throws the key-word high in the air, and says triumphantly, 'See, it doesn't touch the ground at any point.' As soon as you ask about the next word in the argument, up that one goes, too, until they seem all to be spinning excitingly on their own. Actions of God are only paradoxically identical with observable events. What are they like, so we can understand at all? Like events between persons. But are these not observable? No, they are not mere *feelings* (just psychological events). And so on. It is only if you look very carefully that you catch him with a ball very firmly in his hand; for instance, when you ask, 'Why should it be assumed that "mere feelings" alone are "psychological" and "observable"?'

It is hard to say how far the general concentration on 'revelation' is motivated by the hope that it may focus the activity of God on to an area of man's life where that activity may not easily be disproved. John Baillie's 'the revelation of mind to mind . . . defies precise analysis'[2] is in effect defensive; and Paul Tillich says 'the knowledge of revelation' cannot 'be subjected to the experimental tests through which truth is established'.[3] We have noticed other examples of this same defence in the previous chapter (*Revelation to Me*, p. 223). Its apologetic value would be enormous, if the argument were valid; but it is not. 'Revelation' offers no true advantages in talking to the non-Christian.

[1] It is interesting that D. Cairns, *A Gospel without Myth?*, finds it necessary to use a not dissimilar 'circus' metaphor to describe Bultmann's efforts to secure a safe position. Much of his criticism of Bultmann's defence by subjectivity I would agree with, as far as it goes; but I have found it necessary to go further, and criticise the common understanding of Christianity in terms of 'revelation' which I think lies behind the superficial plausibility of Bultmann's case (an understanding Cairns also shares with Bultmann). Cairns, *op. cit.*, p. 127, notes that R. Gregor Smith in *Kerugma und Mythos* IV has argued, as I have, against putting 'God in the gaps' in this sort of apologetic; but for all his protestation, Cairns (*ibid.* and p. 213ff.) does seem himself to risk just this.

[2] *The Idea of Revelation*, p. 25.

[3] *Systematic Theology* I, p. 143. We ourselves have noted that seeming statements about 'God' cannot be verified; but the 'knowing' of them may.

This is not to deny that the attempt of a Bultmann or a Tillich, or more conservatively of a Baillie, to find effective ways of talking to people today is good and brave. It is just to deny that a concentration on 'revelation' and related terms is the best way to do it.

II. IMPLICATIONS FOR DOGMATICS

I have suggested that the word 'revelation' has tended to lead its users into at least three false positions. Although most theological writers would qualify the term in some of a variety of ways, yet the clarity the unqualified word suggests has led them to forget their more careful reservations, and use it to argue a sharper distinction between Christian and non-Christian than the facts that lie behind their own expressed reserve would warrant. 'Revelation' has also led to an intellectualistic position, which often their broader sympathies have made them hope to escape. And a concentration on 'revelation' and ways of thought stemming from its use has offered an apologetic position that seems secure, but that really surrenders a belief in an all-active God without producing any effective defence for the reduced faith that remains.

Now, supposing that even after careful scrutiny the greater part of the case offered so far were accepted, the vast question still remains: What effect would this have on theology as a whole? In particular, what effect would this have on the work of various (and often very different) systematic theologians who have based a great dogmatic structure seemingly on the very shaky foundations that I have here tried to expose? Obviously, to discuss this adequately could mean a book for each writer, hardly worth while before the hypothesis itself has been tested; it could then be better done by experts in the works of the various dogmaticians (or even by the latter themselves . . .). Having found most of the theologians I have attempted to criticise of considerable positive value on many occasions, I would hope that often it would only be superstructure and padding that would disappear, and that many 'free-standing' insights would remain.

The simplest way available to offer an outline of the effects an acceptance of the position argued here might have, is to look at the way the interpretation of some clauses of the 'Nicene'

Creed is affected by a predominant use of the term 'revelation', and to suggest how the clauses might be understood without this dominating word.[1]

'*According to the Scriptures*'   In this case, it must be confessed that the clause is taken out of context and used as a peg. (Though in part defence it may be remarked that the Church did commit itself more or less to a set canon of Scripture as part of the same process as that which produced in the end this Creed,[2] and this clause makes clear the Church's intention to understand its salvation primarily if not solely from this source.)

I have shown, I hope conclusively, that it is not 'scriptural' to understand the life, death, resurrection-and-glory of Christ in terms of 'the revelation of God'. Many theologians whom we quoted in the first chapter, and more besides, have thought it was. How significant their mistake is depends on how vital they suppose submission to scripture to be.

Karl Barth writes: 'The intention of the authors of the Bible was not to express opinions which we are open to contradict with our own opinions. They speak from a Word that does not allow us to enter into discussion with them.'[3] Emil Brunner is as firm: 'The Christian Church stands and falls with the written New Testament, and the written Apostolic testimony to Christ is not only the foundation of all the later witness of the Church to Christ; it is also its norm.'[4] Both these writers insist that they do not mean 'verbal inspiration'; but we have shown not just that the phrase 'revelation of God' is no 'biblical' phrase, but that it is not a 'biblical' idea (or, so commonly, 'concept').

[1] I have suggested (ch. 5 above) that the main purpose of Christian talk of 'God', etc., is to express commitment to a way of *agape*. It is not possible to do more than hint in the following pages at how the various credal statements may serve this end. P. van Buren's *The Secular Meaning of the Gospel* contains a discussion in detail of this main purpose of Christian theological talk, and suggests interpretations with which I would largely agree. I have noted above that I differ from van Buren in finding it still necessary to accept the 'myth' as part of my (expressed) commitment. This allows me to intend love-in-dependence in a way that just the evocative power of New Testament and other Christian writings does not (cf. van Buren, ch. 6). I also, obviously, find it much less easy than he to use talk of 'revelation' as part of this commitment (and so, related terms: the 'discernment', 'significance', 'understanding' supposed to be available to Christians). See also T. R. Miles, *Religion and the Scientific Outlook*, the final chapters. These are, however, rather less satisfactory than van Buren's work, in that they are *theologically* less perceptive.

[2] See especially J. N. D. Kelly, *Early Christian Creeds*, Longmans, 1950; *Early Christian Doctrines*, A. and C. Black, 1958.

[3] *Against the Stream*, p. 217f.

[4] *Revelation and Reason*, p. 127.

Paul Tillich allows explicitly for 'additional sources beyond the Bible'; so how far finding that 'the Bible' does not talk of 'revelation' in his sense would worry him, it is hard to tell. But he does say: 'The Bible, however, is the basic source of systematic theology.'[1] Rudolph Bultmann insists: 'The church's preaching, founded on the Scriptures, passes on the word of the Scriptures. It says: God speaks to you *here*.'[2]

If it is really thought that an unscriptural theology has failed, then these theologies which give a large or even overwhelming place to 'revelation' have failed. But I would still hope that it is only the framework that is ill-constructed, and that much of value remains that might be pieced together some other way.

The Creed prefers Scripture. It does not itself talk of 'revelation' (though it is very short, and we must not argue much from its silence)[3]

'*Maker of heaven and earth*'; '*by whom all things were made*'; '*for us men*' The assertion that 'God' 'by the Son' *made all things*; and that the Son *came down from heaven for us men* should mean that the whole of man's life in the world is seen as the sphere of God's creative, sustaining, and redemptive activity.

But as we have already seen in the preceding section of this chapter, a stress on 'revelation' concentrates at least the effects of the coming of Christ onto a small section of mankind—and within that small group sees the whole redeeming activity of God directed towards the even smaller area of life that may be labelled 'consciousness'. This is true at least in the ways we have already mentioned, for (as instances again) Rudolph Bultmann and Karl Barth.[4] Paul Tillich has much wider sympathies with the whole of human culture; but his attempt to channel this into talk of 'ultimate concern' is essentially an effort to make all life 'religious'; and this, as Dietrich Bonhoeffer suggested, is

---

[1] *ST* I, p. 40.
[2] 'How Does God Speak through the Bible?', *Existence and Faith*, p. 168.
[3] '*Light of Light*' refers to the manner of the Son's 'eternal' origin, and not his 'incarnate' function.
[4] Cf. C. West, *Communism and the Theologians*, SCM Press, 1958, p. 288; although the author thinks highly of Barth's more speculative theology, he has this to say: 'Barth's field of greater knowledge and interest, as a Christian in the world, is culture and philosophy, where ideas and attitudes are the fundamental moral factors. This leads him in a number of instances to misjudge social and political problems . . . where the final moral fact is the deed itself, the way the neighbour is in fact treated, or the state in fact organised.'

probably to misunderstand the world;[1] it is certainly to narrow it.

The fact has to be faced that 'revelation' *is* 'a universal religious conception'.[2] To make God seem only or mainly interested in 'revealing himself' is to make him seem concerned with a 'religious' area (or, favoured word, 'dimension') of man's life. And as Bonhoeffer saw, this is a shrinking area, a vanishing dimension; and the attempt to retain a 'religious God' in it is essentially faithless, and necessarily forlorn, because neither God nor man will stand for it. I have argued elsewhere[3] that this is a proper understanding of Bonhoeffer, that he was right to see the world this way, and equally right (on the basis of the Old and New Testaments) to see God's purpose this way; and I do not wish to spend too much time elaborating the point here. But accept a belief that Christ is Lord of the World, Lord of its history, so that events that really happen are in some sense at least his; a belief that God is Creator of the real world, and that it is redeemed by Christ; and a belief that God justifies, accepts a man by grace, as he is, irreligious and sinner, and not for any ability of the man to understand sophisticated theology, nor for any willingness to shrink and cringe to an ecclesiastical size and temper: accept this belief, and it must make mere 'revelation' a woefully inadequate term by which to interpret the full-blooded faith of Christendom.

The same inadequacy in the face of the Creed can be seen from the point made earlier: not only is 'revelation' 'religious', it is intellectualistic. It narrows the purpose of the coming of Christ from 'us men' to 'us thinking men'. That this is not guess-work is shown in practice. The current intellectual presentation of 'the Gospel' makes an impact in Universities, at least in this country; undergraduate surveys at Oxford and Cambridge (admittedly the numbers are not so striking in a non-residential one such as London) suggest a quarter are fully, and as many again partly, committed as Christians of some allegiance. This is far higher than the figures for the country as a whole, and especially for the 'working class' areas, where just cogitating plays a smaller part in what is nonetheless often a full

---

[1] *Letters and Papers from Prison*, p. 147f. I think this criticism of the Tillich of the 'religious socialism' days still holds; at least much of the terminology is constant.

[2] H. Kraemer, quoted above, p. 224.

[3] 'Man's Coming of Age', *Prism*, December 1962, No. 68.

and 'authentic' life. And yet the intelligent can hardly be
thought to find it easier to love.

It would be foolish, of course, and self-defeating, to run to
the other extreme, and pretend that Christians can afford to
neglect or despise intellect. 'Consciousness' and 'cognition' are
parts of the wholeness of man, and if God has in any way set
about redeeming man, then that must affect man's conscious
thinking. As education spreads, and manual work becomes very
gradually less deadening, and as society becomes (as it seems to
be doing) more bourgeois, then thinking good and holy (and
perhaps even true) thoughts about God, and how to respond
to him, and how to tie this into cohesive patterns of ideas, may
become more widely important. But this is not yet so. For the
present (which is where we obey), 'thinking Christians' must
learn to recognise and accept and co-operate with 'unconscious
Christianity' (Bonhoeffer, p. 172).

So, till men and women more generally make in their often
already quite full and 'authentic' lives a larger place for reflection and philosophising, 'revelation' will produce a theology
that largely ignores and perhaps even helps to alienate them.[1]
Again, 'revelational theology' fails our test by the Creed.[2]

'For our Salvation'; 'for the remission of sins' The latter phrase
describes the effect of the *one Baptism*, but it was always of course
firmly believed that this forgiveness stemmed ultimately from
the life, death and resurrection of Christ. Gustaf Wingren
chooses this theme as the criterion for judging a theology (in
this instance, Karl Barth's) based on 'revelation'. Had I felt the
need to choose one crucial theme, I would probably not have
chosen this particular one; but it is certainly valid; and Wingren
himself mentions that he could have used a whole host of others.[3]

'Salvation' is a wider term than 'forgiveness'. I hope to defend

[1] It would be futile to suppose that a 'religionless' approach, a 'living for others'
would present evangelism with a panacea. It would be equally futile to suppose that
just 'thinking other thoughts' (such as the ones reproduced here) allows an escape
from an over-heavy intellectualism. There are no easy escapes from Christian
ineffectiveness.

[2] It also fails against the standard of the sorts of understanding of man that may
be culled from Scripture, as we have already suggested. Cf. W. D. Stacey, *The
Pauline View of Man*, p. 202: 'Any contention that localises the divine energy in one
element in man must be fundamentally wrong.'

[3] *Theology in Conflict*, p. 82; further references and quotations are at the end of
our first chapter.

an understanding of this fuller term 'salvation' in the third section of the chapter. For the present, a quotation from Hodgson may make my immediate point for me: 'The concentration of attention on Christ as the revelation of God's lordship in judgment and mercy minimises the significance of his work on earth as an objectively achieved act of atonement. It belongs with the unsatisfactory kind of atonement theology that Rashdall derived from Abelard.'[1] 'Revelation' is unsatisfactory as the main or only term whereby to understand salvation in Christ.

I would only point out, in contrast, that Paul Tillich argues at some length for the 'identification of revelation and salvation'.[2] Karl Barth seems to make a similar equation, at least in earlier volumes of his *Church Dogmatics*. If you follow up references to 'Atonement' in the index of I/2, you read pages that talk of 'revelation', occasionally and significantly paraphrased by 'reconciliation' (esp. p. 152). In the final discussion of dogmatic method we are told: 'With the doctrine of the atonement, we come to the real centre—not the systematic, but the actual centre—of dogmatics and Church proclamation. God the Mediator is the present, the absolute present, *in which we find ourselves as hearers of God's Word*' (p. 882; my italics). When Emil Brunner writes: 'The miracle of the revelation of Jesus Christ is in its uniqueness. . . . The Atonement takes place either once for all or it never really takes place at all';[3] again the two terms seem to be in apposition. And for Rudolph Bultmann, it is 'revelation' that 'gives life'.[4] In no way are these redefinitions adequate as interpretations of the theology that lies behind these clauses in the Creed;[5] I have already suggested their inadequacy as interpretations of the New Testament.

'Came down from heaven, and was incarnate by the Holy Ghost of the Virgin Mary, and was made man, and was crucified also for us under

---

[1] *For Faith and Freedom* II, p. 227; referring to H. Rashdall, *The Idea of Atonement in Christian Theology* (London, 1919), cf. Hodgson, p. 55. Hodgson himself sees 'revelation' as part of the redeeming activity of God, 'stripping off successive layers of misconception' (p. 54), and with this I would not quarrel, save to suggest that God is choosing to do it too unevenly for us as yet to say that we have even a 'partial revealing' of the fulness of God. Cf. O. C. Quick, *Doctrines of the Creed*, p. 223f.

[2] *ST* I, p. 160ff.
[3] *Revelation and Reason*, p. 306.
[4] *Existence and Faith*, p. 71.
[5] See J. N. D. Kelly, *Early Christian Doctrines*, ch. 7.

*Pontius Pilate*① Paul Tillich rightly says, 'The early church was well aware that Christology is an existentially necessary, though not a theoretically interesting, work of the Church. Its ultimate criterion, therefore, is existential itself. It is "soteriological", i.e. determined by the question of salvation. The greater the things we say about the Christ, the greater the salvation we can expect from him'.[2] Tillich goes on to make the point that, nevertheless, any form of docetism or monophysitism is self-defeating, because Christ becomes great but irrelevant.

Tillich himself, as we have noted, sees 'salvation' in terms of 'revelation'. He prefers to talk of Jesus as the 'Logos'; and this leads him to say, 'In the terminology of the Nicaean controversy, the power of the Christ is the power of the divine Logos, the principle of divine self-manifestation' (p. 164). And this is just untrue, terminologically. 'Logos' is not mentioned even in the original creed that the Nicene Fathers used, and certainly not in our Constantinopolitan version.[3] The fact is that 'the Word' alone has never been an entirely satisfactory term (though Kelly rejects the idea that the Nicene Fathers explicitly refused it just because it was favoured by Arius).[4] That is not our immediate point—which is, that a 'Logos-Revealer' Christology seems to produce an 'adoptionist' Christology. Tillich himself insists on combining 'adoption' with 'incarnation' (p. 171ff.). In his understanding of the 'saving revelation' of the 'New Being', the latter must fully participate in existence to conquer it (p. 173); and he is able to say, for instance, '. . . men also participate in the manifestation of the atoning act of God. They participate in the suffering of God who takes the consequences of existential estrangement upon himself, or, to say it succinctly, they participate in the suffering of the Christ' (p. 203), which implies much more than 'adoptionism'.

For a reason that is similar enough within his own particular theology, Karl Barth writes: 'This man would not be God's

---

[1] We do not intend to discuss the virginity of Mary's conception or parturition of the Lord. This is well discussed in W. N. Pittenger, *The Word Incarnate*, Nisbet, 1959, p. 66ff. Note especially his quotation of two Roman Catholic authors to the effect that it is impossible to argue *a priori* the necessity for God of the virgin conception; God either procured it or he did not (p. 69f.): it is not integral to Christology.

[2] *ST* II, p. 168.
[3] J. N. D. Kelly, *Creeds*, p. 227.
[4] *Ibid.*; cf. G. Pawson, *Mirfield Essays*, Faith Press, 1962, p. 44.

revelation to us, God's reconciliation with us, if He were not, as true Man, the true, unchangeable, perfect God Himself.'[1]

But where, for instance, there is no desire such as that in Barth to assert the absolute uniqueness of the 'revelation of God in Christ' (and we have suggested that this is a bad starting-point, even if here the stress on 'unique revealing' does help preserve a fuller Christian confession), then a theology based on 'revelation' produces some (often quite sophisticated) form of adoptionism. Donald Baillie quotes A. S. Pringle-Pattison: 'In order to give us authentic tidings of the character of God, Jesus did not require actually to *be* God.' Baillie himself is sure that more must be said than this; but this is the way the argument tends to run.[2] If the message is not absolutely unique, as in Barth, then the bearer does not have to be so very different from the rest of us. Once the (unjustified) attempt to find uniqueness in the 'revealing' is (rightly) discarded, 'revelation' alone cannot preserve the truly Christian emphasis on the uniqueness of the saving act of God in Christ.

This happens very noticeably in the position argued by Norman Pittenger. The second chapter of his work on Christology (*The Word Incarnate*) is devoted entirely to 'revelation'; in it he makes the distinction between 'general' and 'special' 'revealing'. He prefers 'Logos' ('the expressive principle in Godhead') to 'Son' as that of God who (which?) was incarnate (pp. 79, 186f.), and the purpose of Christ is primarily 'to reveal' (cf. pp. 252ff., 161f.). So the 'indwelling of the Logos' in Jesus for this special concentration of a 'general' revealing is unique 'only in degree' (p. 188ff.); in fact the 'degree-kind' antithesis is false (p. 236ff.). Jesus was 'the unique focus for a universal presence and operation' (p. 192). Pittenger approves the 'Antiochene' Christological approach, thinks highly of Theodore of Mopsuestia, and by no means poorly of Nestorius, and is content with the former's phraseology (e.g. ὄργανον) (pp. 89ff., 178ff.). Among modern attempts to talk of the 'very God and very Man', he praises Donald Baillie's book, already quoted, but thinks that other aspects of God's working than just the 'paradox of (prevenient) grace' should be seen at their highest

---

[1] *CD* I/2, p. 155.
[2] D. M. Baillie, *God was in Christ*, Faber and Faber, 1948, pp. 61-4; quoting *Studies in the Philosophy of Religion*.

in Christ (p. 196ff.). This is not to belittle Christ, because it is the most that could possibly be said (p. 188). And when the most that may be has been said, Jesus should not be called 'God' (pp. 111, 125).

The starting-point of 'revelation' seems to produce a very similar result in the essay by Hugh Montefiore in *Soundings*, and of course in Donald Baillie's work, though with some reservations in each case. Jesus as 'revealer' is no more than the supreme example of God's working in all men.

And just in terms of 'revelation', this is not satisfactory. How can the crucifixion of a human being who was not God show that God is love? It might show the devotion he could inspire, but if it showed anything of 'God' himself, it would be his cruelty, so to reject a man who loved as Jesus did. It is logically impossible to have someone else show your own care and concern for you.[2]

So too if 'salvation' is to be seen in terms other than 'the self-revelation of God', then it is essential to feel free to call Jesus 'God'. Another than God might even persuade me of God's love; but the love and suffering of another than God could obviously not be the suffering love of God himself. God does not love at second-hand. David Edwards writes: 'We must admit . . . that almost all the classic theologians of Christendom, Catholic or Protestant, have denied that God can suffer. Behind their theology may be detected the philosophy of the Greeks. The God of Aristotle is the unmoved mover, the passionless spectator. Although they teach the full divinity of Jesus, they suggest that it was the human, not the divine, "nature" in the Son which suffered, and that the Father was not involved.

'The liturgies and hymns of orthodox Christendom have often been braver than its theology in speaking of the Passion of God, the Blood of God, etc., and now in our time the weight of theological opinion seems to be shifting.'[3]

If the death of Christ is in any way sacrificial, expiatory,

---

[1] *Soundings*, ed. A. Vidler, C.U.P., 1962, pp. 164ff., 171ff.; but contrast p. 166, 'God was active in Christ not primarily to show himself to man but to do something for man'; and *God was in Christ*, p. 119, in the setting of the whole chapter; but again contrast e.g. p. 198.

[2] Cf. D. M. Baillie himself, *op. cit.*, p. 64.

[3] In *God's Cross in our World*, p. 113f.; and the rest of the chapter, with a number of apposite quotations, from a variety of writers. Cf. also J. McIntyre, *On the Love of God*, chs 6 and 7.

redemptive—if it is 'saving' in anything like the senses that have been understood from the earliest days—, then it must be the Passion of God, the Blood of God, the Death of God. Anything else is morally intolerable.

'*God of God, Light of Light, Very God of very God . . . was crucified also for us under Pontius Pilate*' Very God died. A concentration on 'revelation' tends to produce a Christology that is inadequate, even in its own terms,[1] and certainly inadequate to express the credal faith.

'*The Holy Ghost, the Lord, the giver of Life*' A 'Logos-revealer' Christology tends to leave the Holy Ghost neglected. Many of the activities that might be appropriate to the Spirit of God are ascribed to the Word of God. An instance we have just seen is Norman Pittenger's understanding of Christ simply in terms of the full expression of the universal Logos, with no reference to the place of the Spirit in the Incarnation despite the large part

[1] There is not room here to defend further the position taken, except to make two brief points. First, it is odd that many who see Jesus as 'revealing God' have allowed God neither to 'reveal' that accepting the limitations of space and time and ignorance was never impossible for him; nor to 'reveal' that ability to suffer is an *essential attribute* of his. Yet if Jesus 'manifests' anything of God, then the latter should be obvious and the former at least possible. (Cf. the quotation from W. Temple, D. M. Baillie, *op. cit.*, p. 66.) That none of this *is* widely seen is just part of the evidence that gives the lie to talk of 'revelation'. And secondly, to reject the Antiochene Christology is not to be committed to any form of docetism (Apollinarian, Eutychian, anhypostasia, or any other; the slogan-calling between writers on Christology goes both ways—cf. W. N. Pittenger, *op. cit.*, p. 105ff., on Hodgson) in one's estimate of the man Jesus. He was a man of his time, who prayed and worshipped and loved, and said he was not 'good' as God was. In his relationship to God and man, he was one with us, a human organism with a conscious and unconscious mind, powered by the same Spirit as we are. (This is where Baillie and Pittenger are absolutely right; Jesus *did*, we may believe, respond to God as the fullest—the complete—instance of the gracious working of *the Spirit of God*—not *the Logos*—in men.) But more than this, the Son (or the Word)—a 'person' of God was accepting as his own every experience of the man Jesus, in a way that is unique, in a way in which God has refused with any other man. Of course Jesus was not conscious of this; at least, the Synoptic tradition would not suggest he was. (For the difficulties of saying this, and yet the need, see the quite incidental discussion in A. Farrer, essay 'Revelation' in *Faith and Logic*. It is odd that it does not seem to be taken into account by D. M. Baillie (*op. cit.*), who gives much more weight than we should allow to the Johannine material as *verba domini*.) Jesus hardly could have been conscious of God's unique relation to him, and still remained man. But in faith we may believe Jesus was God, suffering for his world. In his relation to God, and to man and to the rest of the world through the Spirit, Jesus was 'continuous' with us; in the self-identification of the Son with the foetus, babe, child and man, Jesus is unique; he *is* God. Something like this at least orthodoxy has always tried to preserve, however poor its formal language, and mine.
   'God allows himself to be edged out of the world and on to the cross. God is weak and powerless in the world, and that is exactly the way, the only way, in which he can be with us and help us' (D. Bonhoeffer, *Letters and Papers*, p. 164).

given him in the Gospels throughout Jesus' life, and despite the
fact that making a place for both Spirit and Word in the
Incarnation allows the traditional Christian insistence both on
the continuity and discontinuity of the activity of God in the
man Jesus with his activity in all men. There is mention of the
Spirit in the prolegomena to Pittenger's discussion of the Incarnation; and then only passing references (at least in my memory
and the index) till he is allowed formally to reappear in a short
discussion of 'the Trinity' at the end.[1]

Even if a theology based on 'revelation' is less arbitrarily
'binitarian' in practice, it can (particularly with the help of the
unilaterally inserted *filioque*) restrict the activity of the Spirit
to an enabling of the reception of 'revelation'.[2] This is already
to ignore his activity below the levels of consciousness (Rom.
8.26f.).

The restriction must then follow of the activity of the Spirit
to the Church, the area where 'revealing' happens (and
probably to the listening fringe just beyond the Church who
need his enabling if they are to respond by grace). This limitation does certainly have better precedent in the ways of thinking
about him of those who produced the Creed.[3] I would only
revert to the argument in the first section of this chapter: where
the fruits of the Spirit are found, there the Spirit must be. He is
Lord and *Life-Giver* as well as he *who spake by the prophets*.

'*I believe in one God-the-Father*[4] *Almighty . . . and in one Lord Jesus Christ
. . . God of God, Light of Light, Very God of Very God . . . and I believe in
the Holy Ghost, the Lord, the giver of life . . . who with the Father and
the Son together is worshipped and glorified*' Trinitarian theology is
a function of Christology and Pneumatology, as they are of
Soteriology. If a predilection for talking of 'revelation' affects
the last three, it must also shape an understanding of the
Trinity. Leonard Hodgson defends his thinking about the
Trinity against Claude Welch's repudiation of it with these
words: 'Dr Welch, following Barth, holds that the doctrine is
more securely grounded if it is regarded as an implication of the

---

[1] Cf. N. W. Pittenger, *op. cit.*, p. 229: 'A full discussion of this point (the Spirit)
is inappropriate (*sic*) in a treatment of the Incarnation.'
[2] K. Barth, *CD* I/2, pp. 203-79, esp. p. 250ff.
[3] J. N. D. Kelly, *Creeds*, p. 155ff.
[4] J. N. D. Kelly, *Creeds*, p. 131ff., 195.

fact of revelation. Revelation implies Revealer, Revelation, Revealedness. God as Revealer is Father, as Revelation is Son, as Revealedness is Spirit, and the Bible is the revelation of the lordship of God in all three modes of existence.

'I find three difficulties in Dr Welch's presentation of the Barthian position.

'1. The doctrine is not an attempt to expound the significance of the content of the revelation which God has seen fit to give us: it is a deduction from an analysis of the theologian's idea of revelation. Dr Welch confirms my estimate of Barth's theology (see p. 229 of my book) as being on this subject rationalistic rather than biblical.'[1]

In, for instance, Karl Barth's teaching, 'personality' can only be ascribed to the unity of God.[2] The supposed internal logic of the word 'revelation' is more important than anything that might conceivably have been said to have been 'revealed'. (A predilection for 'Logos'—*expressive principle*—rather than 'Son' also assists in this neutralising of the 'persons' of God.)

If (and this is something which the whole of this discussion gives us even further cause to doubt) Jesus is in any sense 'God revealing God', he should at least show that 'God' is able to talk 'to himself': 'Abba, Dad.' None of the attempts to find language for this from descriptions of the individual are adequate: neither the 'psychological' terms of Augustine, nor the 'modes of existence' of the Cappadocians. The individual talking to himself is mentally unbalanced, not more but less than 'personal'. The individual who has three parallel 'modes of existence' (God's 'modes of existence' are supposed by Barth to be 'eternal'; he is not formally Sabellian) is a sort of super Jekyll-and-Hyde, not more but less than personal.

It is interesting that Augustine looks for his terms in descriptions of the activity of the mind of the isolated self-sufficient intellectual, who 'loves what he knows', etc., instead of in descriptions of the unit of God's concern of which the New Testament ('revelation'!) speaks, 'the Body of Christ', 'the people of God's possession', the community. If God is really making us to be like himself, and he is self-sufficient unity, then

---

[1] *For Faith and Freedom* II, p. 226f.; citing C. Welch, *In This Name*, Scribners, 1952, p. 168ff.; L. Hodgson, *The Doctrine of the Trinity*, Nisbet, 1943; cf. K. Barth, *Church Dogmatics* I/1.

[2] *CD* I/1, p. 403.

by helping us become a plural agapeistic community, he is going about this assimilation in a remarkably odd way. But the 'flight of the alone to the Alone' is not the aim of the Christian.

If we want to believe that Jesus was God suffering to bring us to God and that the Spirit is God praying us to God (and, of course, we have to *choose* to believe these), then we are committed to saying things about God that are at least formally compatible with this belief, however little positive content we can yet give to the words. It is as Three that our God has acted towards us.

An insistence, as in the Old Testament, on the oneness of 'God' was not motivated by a philosophical delight in mathematical unity. 'The Lord your God is one Lord; and you shall love the Lord your God with all your heart and with all your mind and with all your soul.' It is an ethical unity, demanding a complete singleness of response. It is opposed to the moral anarchy of a polytheism in which one god may be played off against another. The unity in love of the 'family' which is our God allows no such licence.

It is not a unity patterned on, determined by, human relations; it is a unity which God reproduces, still dimly, in us in love in community; a unity of which we can still speak only formally. The unity of God is such that each 'person' is more fully personal than any human individual; but it is a unity in love that is more intensely 'one' than the most integrated human being. In real love, *agape*, the unity is most real, and yet the lovers are not absorbed by one another, but most truly individuals. It is, we may believe, to share in such a unity that God is shaping us. When at last we love like that, we shall be 'seeing God'; the 'persons' of God will have at last succeeded in 'revealing themselves' to us.

There *is* polytheism in much atonement theory, playing Son off against Father, Love against Justice; and again in the over-clear distinctions between 'nature' and 'grace', where man tries to curtail the *perichoresis*, God's freedom to act as one Creator, Redeemer, Sanctifier, in the whole world. What I have outlined is the only 'orthodoxy' (right worship) that seems to me to allow God to be God independently of the world he creates and redeems and hallows. Only so may I speak of 'selfless' love, *agape*, in God, 'apart from' the loved beings he has made.[1] This is the only fully Christian monotheism.

The credal form stresses the 'threeness' of the Lords who are our God. A theology based on 'revelation' again tends to confuse the credal statement.

Then, briefly, where there is a predominant stress on the 'revealing of God', the *One Holy Catholic and Apostolic Church* becomes something that only happens when 'revelation' is received, and 'appears and disappears after the manner of the Cheshire cat'[2] (a sort of docetism in ecclesiology). The Church's disunity is concealed in a specious talk of a 'definitive revelation'; and its unity is made to depend on intellectual niceties. The *one baptism* becomes a preaching and proclamation for us to hear,[3] rather than our objective adoption by God. That one element in its eschatological hope that we have seen the early Church did not suppose it was already enjoying, the 'revealing' of the Christ and perhaps the Father, is supposed already in some sense to have happened, before *the resurrection of the dead and the life of the world to come.*

The word 'revelation' is a source of great confusion. A theology based on it is inadequate for the exposition of the traditional faith of Christians, even in the traditional terminology.

III. 'SALVATION' AS AN ALTERNATIVE

I have suggested that theologies based on 'revelation' are not able to convey to us the full richness of Christian life and faith, and have given instances (many of which are by no means 'news') of the sort of impoverishment that seems to result when this is the dominant word (or, of course, 'concept'). My plea that the New Testament, and the facts of the Christian position, and the strictly limited possibilities of talking sense about 'God', should be taken seriously is not an irrelevant pedantry. For better or for worse, it is doctrinally and 'existentially' of vital importance.

By and large, examples have been taken from a few prominent

---

[1] L. Hodgson, *The Doctrine of the Trinity*, p. 225; J. McIntyre, *On the Love of God*, ch. 5, and p. 181.
[2] L. Hodgson, *For Faith and Freedom* II, p. 119; cf. K. Barth, *Against the Stream*, p. 225ff.
[3] K. Barth, *ibid.*, p. 74.

contemporary Protestant writers. Even if the examples have the effect I wish, the intention is not malicious. It is done in the hope that these writers' (and others') more positive insights may have freer and fuller play, if the bonds of this misused category can be struck off. But the questions still recur—Are the ways of speaking I have preferred (or any other ways for that matter) for talking about 'God' really better than those based on 'revelation' which I have dismissed? Are there ways that may be defended, theologically, empirically, linguistically?

Again, as this is the conclusion of a fairly specific study, I cannot do more than outline an argument.

From the evidence we have examined it seems fair to deduce that there are three major reasons for the choice of the word 'revelation' and for its retention even by theological innovators.

(i) The first reason seems to me a positive one. 'Revelation', as we have noted more than once, stresses the initiative of the agent; it speaks of 'grace', at least in the sense of 'prevenience'. And 'grace', the 'gracious activity of God' (focussed, of course, in and through Jesus of Nazareth), must, I have suggested, be accepted in some form if there is any desire at all to remain in the historic Christian tradition, committed to *Christian* 'agape' (see ch. 5, above). 'Revelation' talks of the grace of God; but 'salvation', I suggest, does so more effectively. It is better 'theology'. This I have already argued, in the preceding section, and will not add much here.

(ii) The second reason for the choice of the term 'revelation' is almost as old, but not, I have suggested, as good. 'Revelation' answers the demand of the intellectual man, 'Give me knowledge.' He may be first-century Gnostic, fourth-century neo-Platonist, sixteenth-century Humanist, eighteenth-century Cartesian, nineteenth-century Idealist, twentieth-century Existentialist; but in one form or another talk about 'revelation' meets or tries to meet the need that he feels. I have suggested many reasons for denying either that 'revelation' (of his 'self') in any meaningful sense can be taken as God's purpose in Christ, or that it was so taken by the earliest Christians. I do not wish to repeat any of these arguments. But one further point is perhaps necessary. If my reading of Christian history to the present day be correct, there is *no clear 'knowledge of God'*. And if there is no clear 'knowledge of God' a further point follows:

Supposing a girl answers a ring at the door, and finds a large bunch of red roses and white carnations. There are at least three possibilities. If there were a note attached, the flowers would be a pleasing way of sending a message. In fact there is no note; but even so, someone may be trying to 'say it with flowers'. This is one possibility: the flowers are a message. But to say what? The girl looks at a magazine that has an article on what flowers mean, but does not like the result. She looks in an encyclopaedia, and the variety of possibilities sets her in a whirl. She even counts the petals to find whether they are supposed to tell her that someone loves her, or has ceased to love her; the odd number of petals in each bunch on its own says 'someone loves you', but taken together they say 'someone no longer loves you' (and she still does not know who, does not even know if she has met the sender, or if the flowers were intended for her in the first place). Supposing that everything has gone to plan from the sender's end, and the flowers really have arrived just as he meant them to, there is small likelihood that he intended to *say* anything at all, give any information, any insight into his own intentions or character. Just a gift lacking clear explanation does not immediately suggest that a message is intended.[1]

The second possibility (but this a very faint one) is that the conveying of a *sort of* message is the flower-sender's intention. He may be a crank who enjoys mystifying. 'If you had understood', he is going to say later, 'you'd have got no end of a treat', and he will tell the girl, and enjoy her disconsolation at failing her impossible test. It is a message, but a very loveless and cruel one.

But the most likely possibility is that the gift without clear information is intended as a gift. The flowers are meant to be enjoyed: arranged, smelled, gazed at. The donor may wish to remain anonymous for the time being, or for good. For the present, to understand the flowers as a message is completely to misunderstand them. They may even be a preparation for a later disclosure; but for the moment they are meant as a gift of flowers.

So, if there is no *clear* 'knowledge of God' resulting from the events of the life, death, resurrection of Christ, not only is there

---

[1] A similar metaphor is used for an argument of this sort in G. Wingren, *Theology in Conflict.*

(as we have seen, by definition) no 'revelation', but their
purpose can hardly be seen as instructional *in any sense*. Not even
heavily qualified 'revelation', not even the first stage of instruction or enlightenment, can be the purpose of these events. It is
still possible to see them as a gift, a gift that different people
may treat in a variety of ways. But supposing that these events
have 'reached us' (by their causal effects, including such records
of them as they engendered) as the agent intended (and if we
believe him love omnipotent, it would be odd to deny it)—then
it is impossible to see them as a message, information, the giving
of insight. We may believe them to be a preparation for a future
disclosure; but for the moment, if they have any purpose, they
are meant just as the gift of a man's life for his friends. The
friends could find that sufficient.[1]

'Salvation', like 'revelation', talks of the gracious initiative of
God; but 'salvation' is not, I shall suggest, such an inadequate
term for the interpretation of the purpose of the historically
primary Christian events in which that 'gracious initiative' may
be seen. After all, 'salvation' (or terms like it) is the interpretation of the first people reached by these events.

(iii) The third reason for preferring 'revelation' we have
already looked at. It is a more recent factor. 'Revelation' has
seemed a readily defensible term. It is very hard to prove from
where someone has obtained a piece of knowledge; so it is hard
to disprove his claim that he has it by 'revelation'. We have
seen at some length that this may defend an individual claim,
but cannot defend one by any existing 'church'; and I would
argue that whatever initial apologetic drawbacks 'salvation' as
an alternative may seem to have, there is rather more chance
of defending it, linguistically.

The word 'save' has been chosen as our example, not because
it is thought to be particularly 'typical' for the thought of the
New Testament; but because, of many kindred words (see ch. 3
and above, p. 265ff.), it is the one chosen by the Niceno-
Constantinopolitan Creed. In the New Testament it is used by
Paul primarily for God's completion of his purpose (but com-

---

[1] If God has given us no clear message, we must realise we have much less to talk
about, much less verbal proclamation to make, than we sometimes suppose. Cf.
T. R. Miles, *Religion and the Scientific Outlook*, ch. 15, 'The Way of Silence'; 'You
say "I do not know" and try to talk; I say "I do not know" and remain silent'
(p. 163). Cf. J. Downing, 'Jesus and Martyrdom', *JTS* XIV. 2.

pare Rom. 8.24; and note that δικαιοῦν, δικαιοσύνη, etc., used mostly of God's first act of acceptance in Christ, may also be used of the consummation: Gal. 5.5). It is used by the writer to the Ephesians in the sort of context in which Paul might have used δικαιοῦν (Eph. 2.8). Compare Titus 3.5; and the overtones of the synoptic ἡ πίστις σου σέσωκέν σε (e.g. Luke 7.50).

I now attempt to show shortly that 'save' does not have the drawbacks that make 'reveal' so awkward for a logical theology.

It has already been pointed out (above, p. 212ff.) that words like 'save' are logically capable of expressing the 'now but not yet', the 'complete but open-ended' 'act of God' which so many of the New Testament writers see in the life, death, resurrection-and-glory of Jesus of Nazareth. The aim in rescuing a man drifting half-drowned out to sea is to restore him to the degree of security enjoyed by 'the average man' on dry land. Then he will be said to be 'safe'. But already when the rescuer dangling from the helicopter has secured a line round the man in the water, the latter has been 'saved'. This is quite genuine and meaningful. However far he may still be from the final 'safety' intended for him, without this preliminary act there would seem to have been no chance of the final safety at all. The man on the end of the rope *has* 'saved' him.

He has saved him *from* the water, and *for* the doctor, for the hospital treatment, for a return to his family, perhaps for life to a normal old age. The rescuer has created a situation in which the final 'safety' in view has again become a possibility. His act is in itself complete, final, irreversible—but open-ended. If the man slips irretrievably back out of the life-line, then he has been 'saved' in vain; but even that cannot destroy the fact that he was 'saved'.

By the same logic, it is possible for 'save' to be heavily qualified, and still remain meaningful in many contexts. 'He only managed to save the library in part; much of great value was lost.' 'The surgeon's prompt action saved his eyesight, and he was able to walk without help, though he had to learn Braille for reading.' A very 'partial saving' is still a 'saving'; it is even more importantly so, if it is part of a 'saving process'.[1]

An event may take place which makes a common final 'safety'

---

[1] Contrast 'revelation', above, p. 225ff.

a real possibility in a way in which it was not before, for a variety of people. Ultimately, for it to be a 'common salvation', they will, of course, have to come to offer the same response to their situation. But for a long while they may react in differing, even completely opposed ways. They can be 'saved' without knowing it, or even while consciously rejecting the 'safety' they have been granted. An example would be the co-operation, lethargy or continuing panic (even in a few deranged cases, refusal) that might be the response of various people trapped in a mine when rescuers were actually moving freely among them.[1]

Our instances so far have been a little impersonal. It is necessary to offer a typical example in which people are more involved as people.

The citizens of some Swiss canton might in the sixteenth century have claimed that the 'reformer' (or, alternatively, 'preserver') of the area's religion had 'saved them' from heresy, for the 'True Faith' (one of the varieties of possible complex forms of Christian commitment). This would be true; and, obviously, only time would tell for how long they were 'safe', and what level of 'safety' in this sense they were going ultimately to reach and maintain.

The hero had 'saved them', even while the opposing armies menaced. He had 'saved them' even while children and many others did not realise what was going on; and even while many in their hearts rebelled against the new ways imposed or the old ways preserved. He had been instrumental in creating a situation in which a particular form of Christian commitment was a real possibility; whereas without him it *might* not have been so. Presumably the level of 'salvation' intended was one in which every man, woman and child as they were able would respond to and accept the chosen 'Faith', and in which this response would be so full that the situation would be indefinitely maintained. So long as this remains a possibility, in each generation, the original saving act is still saving, the canton is still saved for this 'Faith'.

I have said that the 'hero of the Faith' created a possibility which without him 'might not have been'. This of course, by the nature of the case, cannot be proved. Meaningfully to call the events in which he was prominent 'saving' does not make it

---

[1] Contrast 'revelation', above, p. 226ff.

necessary to *prove* that without him the 'saving' could not have happened; it is not necessary, because it would be fruitless speculation. That is the nature of historic events: there is no way of comparing them with what 'might have been', for events that did and 'events' that did not happen are totally unalike. For them to be 'saving events' only two things are necessary. They must still, in some way, have some of their original effect, be it through buildings, institutions, folk-prejudice, deliberate teaching, or any other means: this should be quite 'objective'. And there should be some people still sufficiently interested to judge them 'saving', rather than quite irrelevant or positively pernicious. For in a situation of this sort, 'save' will be most often used with heavy overtones of approval (or possibly, sarcasm). It could be used neutrally, by an 'impartial' historian (were such a dullard to be found), to mean just 'have some effect'. But most often it will be used by those who commit themselves, to some degree, to the continuing possibilities that stem from these events. (The unrepentant rescued suicide will not talk of being 'saved'; the communist student of sociology might talk of the children left in the institution being 'saved' from the decadence of a bourgeois home.)

Sincerely to call particular events 'saving' is to commit yourself in some manner or other to possibilities that they still genuinely enable. It is not to make unverifiable claims about the origins of the events in question; nor is it, at least not necessarily, to claim that the possibilities they seem to enable are immediately available; nor even, necessarily, that only these events make this sort of possibility real.

And it is surely meaningful to call the primary, historic Christian events (or those of them traditionally accepted as having happened and whose records still convince) 'saving' in this sense. By (one way or another) creating a 'church' and later 'churches', in which the tradition of commitment to humble *agape* of which I have spoken has been preserved, these events have made such commitment a present possibility. By creating communities in which this commitment is, more or less, offered, they have provided a variety of environments in which those who wish to may share in this sort of commitment, and even be encouraged to carry it through. These people can then say that the original events have 'saved them' from a life lacking to a life containing the possibility of commitment to this sort of *agape*; even to its acting-out.

This is not to offer to prove that without these events their life would have lacked this note. If they say things that suggest as much, it is only a strong way of insisting that the form of their commitment is to these events and no others as 'saving'. It is not to assert that other sorts of *agape*, even very similar or just possibly quite indistinguishable forms of *agape*, are impossible without this commitment; that is a matter for empirical investigation. Nor is it to deny that the manner of even quite intense commitment to Christian *agape* can differ a great deal from believer to believer. We still have no 'revelation'. It is, however, to assert that the end product is an *agape* that will be expressed in common action; rather than by 'war' *or* 'peace with honour' *or* 'appeasement' *or* 'non-resistance'; rather than by 'preaching the good news' *or* 'healing' *or* 'educating' *or* 'irrigating' *or* 'leaving alone'; but it allows that, for the time being, the only point in common will be that each individual committed in this way will hope that each next day will be less selfish than the last. The events are still 'saving' in the way we have described here while the commitment is of the sort we outlined in the fifth chapter, a commitment always dissatisfied with the level of achievement, a commitment to a love that is 'empowered by God' in the life, death and resurrection of Christ.

These events in 'history' cannot be *proved* to be '*God's* 'salvation'. But within the limits we have made here, it can, if desired, make good sense, to say 'here *is* salvation' (even 'salvation for the world'); it makes good sense, so long as a man does wish to commit himself in this way to a Christian possibility of love.

I have suggested some of the effects on theology as a whole of seeing the primary Christian events in terms of a 'myth' of 'salvation'; these seem to me to be good effects. But they depend largely on the prior theological value of talk of 'salvation' itself. It just does seem that a much greater stress is placed on the 'grace of God' (which stress I have hoped to preserve) if he is believed to have done something that can really be said to have happened, rather than something that patently has not. In the sense I have analysed, 'saving events' *may* be said to have happened in the life, death, resurrection and glory of Jesus;

'revealing events' have not. The choice between 'salvation' and 'revelation' is between on the one hand a mythic understanding of and a committal to, a sequence of events that has happened and still happens, and on the other hand an equally mythic understanding of events that have yet to be found occurring anywhere, as the 'gracious activity of God'.[1]

Many Christians believe that the 'salvation' already available will be completed in a much fuller and more striking form than has yet appeared. This will be in an unspecified 'future'. And this is an important part of the total complex formula of Christian commitment. It allows the Christian to be both realist and optimist at one and the same time. It allows him to express his *intention* to let neither others' nor his own failures to love, nor the failures of love to effect its aims, deter him from his commitment. It allows him to commit himself confidently to a 'salvation' that is already available, without *having* to give unqualified approval to any aspect of life as it may now be lived: none of this is yet without reservation that for which he has been 'saved'. At the same time, he is able to criticise radically the failures of the present without having to surrender his concern for what does happen here and now; he believes that all that happens is material out of which God 'does' or 'will' construct what will be wholly good. He is committed neither to cynical despair nor rosy optimism. Instead, he is characterised by hope.

This does mean of course, as is widely recognised, that the Christian eschatological hope is misunderstood if it is taken as a pseudo-scientific prediction; and equally, if it is taken as an excuse for speculation about 'time' and 'timelessness' (enjoyable though these fancies may be). The form in which God answers this hope is up to him.

[1] I do not think that this is a 'purely' (or at least, arbitrarily) subjective view of 'salvation'. It could be more 'objective' if it included the (albeit biblical idea of the) defeat of demons and devil; but that would be so objective as not, on its own, to 'save' *me*. The Church (difficult though it is—and I as part of it) and its traditions (including the Bible), and its sacraments as factors in 'salvation', are as 'objective' as seem possible, without becoming irrelevant. And 'salvation' in terms of commitment to, and the acting out of love in community seems to be the real concern of the New Testament writers. It is 'salvation' *from* fear, sin, hate, slavery; salvation *to* 'agape' empowered by God in Christ through the Spirit. The end is perfect love. Salvation as rescue from the anger, wrath, justice of God, from hell, or from corruptibility, is too future to be relevant and too loveless to be Christian (even if Paul talks of it). 'Salvation for resurrection' is an important part of commitment in trust till the end of life.

This is (as is often noted) in many ways like the hope of the Communist. The latter believes that the dialectical 'saving' process is well under way; out of feudalism, bourgeois capitalism or socialism, it is active to produce the final bliss of 'Communism'. In fact this is put forward as a 'scientific' prediction; but that is only a strong way of expressing his commitment to the 'salvation' which is seen as already possible, and which makes the present a time to criticise, and also a time for decisive action. The logic is very similar, and marks as vividly the life of the man who makes either 'leap of faith'.

The assertion of certain success in neither case excludes present efforts ('sit down ye men of God . . .') as it might; and for this very reason—that the assertion is tacitly understood predominantly as a commitment.

For the Marxist, 'the end' is the Communism where man finds his self so freely that society will run without compulsion. It is a powerful hope for those who accept it. For the Christian, 'the end' (but only the end) is when all share in the Divine Society, and awareness of the Persons of God is such that they may be said to be 'revealed'.

IV. CONCLUSIONS

The logic of words like 'save' means that it and they are well suited for the theological interpretation of the historical events of the life, death, resurrection and glory of Jesus of Nazareth. They are much better suited than words like 'reveal'.

Happily enough for the Christian, the New Testament comes out of the total examination rather well. Even though the later makers of theology seem to live in verbal Spanish castles, the earliest Christian writers keep their feet firmly on the ground, they live here and now. They do not pretend to an awareness of 'God' which their lives and experience cannot substantiate. But they believe that 'God' has made them his people, at the cost of the death of his 'Son', and through the coming of the 'Spirit'; and to this 'God', in the pattern of behaviour his actions suggest and which the 'Son' has taught, they commit themselves. And even this summary might not include the beliefs of some whom they would have been loath to exclude. For within this very broad pattern of self-committal-in-dependence, the New Testament canon itself records no 'revelation', no clarity that would make exclusiveness easy; only a great variety of response and belief. The central core, as it appears in retrospect, was a committal that in deed, and later in word, treated the 'Son' as 'God'; and that treated the new possibility of life in love in the freedom of the community as 'God', too. This was 'the Spirit'. And it is to such a pattern of free self-committal-in-dependence within community that today's Christian may surrender himself. The pattern of obedience can be continuous with the first pattern; there is a community that has always preserved something of this pattern and its possibility. There is no 'reason' for this action, no 'reason' why others still uncommitted should take it. Some do choose to.

But within this pattern of obedience, 'God' cannot be said to be 'known', without very heavy qualifications. He cannot be said to have 'revealed' himself, unless the word 'reveal' is evacuated of most if not all meaning. Moreover, examination of some of the contexts in which 'revelation' is used suggests that, even if it could be modified successfully, meaningfully, it would still not be a very useful word for a truly Christian theology. It tends to be part of a way of thinking that so emphasises one aspect of man that the rest is lost; neither 'rational' nor 'personal' consciousness can stand for the whole man. This sort of theology is useful neither in apologetic nor in preaching. It will not, save by accident, convince the sceptic of the meaningfulness of Christian talk, nor the believer of God's grace.

The conclusions we have reached are not the result of deductive reasoning about the 'nature' of God. They are the logical conclusion of the understanding that if 'God has acted', 'does act', in human and general affairs, then only in what actually has happened, does happen, may his actions be found. If someone suggests that somewhere within general or human history 'God' is 'revealed', the suggestion has to be checked, not by wishful thinking, nor by its attractiveness, but by looking to the area of events to which this believer points. And there, allowing for all the qualifications the speaker wishes to make, either someone, something, 'God', is 'revealed', or not. We have decided it is truest to say he is not 'revealed'. This is not to tell 'God' how he ought to act (to tell him he ought somehow to have 'revealed' himself, or at least now to 'reveal himself', is

to do that). The way I have suggested is to allow God to act
as he wills, and to elicit the response that he wishes. It is altogether more polite.

We Christians do not commit ourselves very deeply. The
'fruit of the Spirit' is not very evident in us. We are sure 'God'
has 'done something for us'. But we are frightened of the bold
language of the first believers, who seem to have been willing
to let their faith (or at least the chance of talking about it
meaningfully) stand or fall by 'God's' success in making them
love. It is much less risky to talk of 'God's action' in terms that
cannot be belied. It is much easier to make 'I am justified by
God' mean 'He has forgiven me', than to let it mean 'He has
set me in such a relationship with himself, that from now on I
can obey him and love him.' Thus we concentrate on supposed
'events' (such as 'God's forgiveness') that cannot be given the
lie; or on our own 'personal' experience, emotional or intellectual, that no one can easily examine; and so on 'revelation'.
To save God's grace from unflattering comparisons with other
supposed currencies, we inflate it to a level where no exchange-
rate need be quoted.

And this is faithlessness. This is a failure of nerve, a failure
to trust God to do anything at all. We build vast complex
theological schemes, in which a speculative 'Fall' is mended by
an abstract 'satisfaction', or an imaginary 'revelation' provides
a 'knowledge' that no one knows, without anything having to
happen to real people. It is because we are afraid that if we say
that 'God acts' in the real world, and does noticeable things to
observable people—if we say, this is really what he is about—
he may fail us, and shame us. And we are not willing to risk
this insecurity.

Not that traditional Christian commitment allows a condi-
tional trust: 'I will believe, so long as he gives me a successful
family life'; or, 'if he makes my parish come alive within the
next five years'; or, 'so long as I do not sin much more, but
learn to love a great deal'. The believer wishes to commit himself absolutely: that is, at any rate, the trust that is demanded
of him. But he expects 'God' to act; and he does not need to
fill in the silence, when nothing that he thinks is typical of 'God'
happens, with a lot of talk about all the wonderful invisible and
unprovable things 'God' 'has done' and 'is doing'. If he looks

for real acts of 'God', he may even find actual events that are happening to which he can commit himself, as to 'acts of God'.

Dietrich Bonhoeffer, in his letters from prison, quoted above in the notes, pleaded for Christians to allow 'God' to come in, from the edges of life, to the centre, to concern the whole man and the whole society. This is a difficult demand, but the only understanding of 'God's' demand that allows 'God' to be 'God'. Then all events, in all their ambiguity, are 'acts of God', places where men and women may respond to him, depend on him, obey him, in any of a finite but often vast number of different ways. In this uncertainty stands the Christian, not very faithful, not very different from other people; often, he himself knows, less obedient. Where he stands, with the insights he has, he prays to obey, he tries to obey, he tries to relax into a dependence on God that he believes will be far more demanding than any attempt to obey on his own.[1] And still he finds a greater obedience, sometimes, perhaps often, in those who do not believe. In the end, he trusts that the way he has chosen, and it alone, will make final and complete obedience to 'God in Christ' possible. For this he prays. For this, he is never satisfied with his own beliefs, with his own customary moral judgments. Any event may be 'God' demanding a new, perhaps dangerous, decision and action of him. At no point can he rest and say, 'This is revelation: now I know for sure.'

There may be momentary certainties for the Christian; but never an assurance into which he may relax. All attempts to build these false certainties are idolatrous. Bible, Pope, Church, Tradition, Experience, Encounter, Sex, Prosperity, Society, Learning, Arts; the list of gods is very long. For the man who wishes to commit himself in the pattern that is at the centre of Christian life, none of these gods can receive the unconditional allegiance he must offer to the One who still insists on hiding himself, and leaving us unsure.[2]

But even in this uncertainty does not the Christian seem to assume that he has some insight into the character of 'God'? Although he may allow the name 'Christian' to a variety of patterns

---

[1] Following D. Bonhoeffer at least some of the way, I would suggest that this is dependence in strength, not in weakness, a voluntary humility not forced by any failure or by guilt. Cf. C. Green, *Union Seminary Quarterly Review* XIX. 1, p. 21.

[2] Cf. W. and L. Pelz, *God Is No More*, p. 20ff., and ch. 7; also D. M. MacKinnon, in *Objections to Christian Belief*, ed. A. R. Vidler, Constable, 1963, p. 31ff.

of obedience, there are some patterns he will doubt, and some he
will exclude altogether. Does this not suggest that to be Christian
at all he must implicitly be claiming that at least *he* 'knows
God'; is he not, in fact, claiming that *he* 'knows God' fairly
well, if he claims to be able to decide between actions more or
less pleasing to him? He patterns his action as far as he can on
the action of Christ in living and dying, and says this is the
central 'act of God', central to his purpose, and our redemption
for 'God'. Is not this to suggest that he believes this act to be in
some sense 'characteristic' at least; and if characteristic then to
that extent, by definition, 'revelatory of character'? In what
sense could an act be 'characteristic' if it 'showed' nothing of the
actor's personality?

We have seen that it is very hard to believe that God *intended*
to 'reveal himself' (because there is such poor and diverse
'knowledge' of him) or at all *meant* even some lesser 'insight' into
his character, when he gave us his gift-without-authoritative-
explanation in Jesus Christ. But even if nothing of this sort were
his intention, could we not watch him at work, and draw some
valid conclusion? Leonard Hodgson in his Gifford Lectures
again and again insists that God has acted, it is for us to work
out the doctrine. But really we are so bad at understanding this
'act of God' to which we would commit ourselves, that it is just
not possible yet to claim any sure success. Though we are sure
this is the right place, the God-given place, to quarry under the
Spirit's direction for 'knowledge of God', we seem as yet to be
only chipping at a few outcrops which we have yet to prove
belong to the main seam that we believe is there, but still
remains well hidden beneath the soil.

It is in fact quite meaningful to talk of someone 'expressing
themselves', even 'expressing their love', without anyone having
understood. The theory of some school teaching is that if you
give a child some fairly plastic, adaptable materials, and just
leave him, he will 'express himself' with them. There may be
little to express; he may express himself badly so that his teacher
fails to understand; he may express himself fully, but from his
mess only another teacher would be able to understand much
of the tensions and delights and hopes and fears of the child's
life. It is perhaps possible for him fully to express himself, for this
teacher to believe he has, and yet for no one to understand at all.

Taking this further, a mother may show love to her children
and yet may express this love in many ways, which the children
may not comprehend. The children may even respond with
hostility. The parent may die before the children grow to
understand, before the children ever 'see' the love, before the
actions in which the love is expressed ever 'reveal' the love, or
better, 'reveal the lover'. But the love has been 'expressed'. And
if the children grow, and themselves love, the love has been
well expressed; even if the parent's character still remains a
mystery. The children may in later years understand the cost
of the love that has been lavished on them, and if the parent
lives long enough, may then see the care and realise the effect
it has had, which so 'reveal' the parent that in the end a full
adult relationship is possible. But still the 'expression' of love
is real even if it 'reveals' nothing. It was a fully 'characteristic'
activity, but it may never, or only after a long time, be 'revealing'.

It will have been possible for the children to commit themselves to the mother, possible for them to understand that some
ways of behaving are more fitting than others, long before there
has been anything that might be called a 'revelation' of the
parent. The children have probably learned very slowly, and
some better than others, which ways are best. They may always
respond in very various, even contradictory ways. The parent
has expressed her love, has acted fully 'characteristically',
without at any point even dreaming of 'revealing' herself,
without even unintentionally 'revealing' herself. And the children have been part of the broad pattern of the behaviour of the
family, a pattern they may or may not learn to adopt as their
own. Love has been 'expressed', character has been 'expressed',
and effectively; and even 'revelation' has been prepared for,
with as yet no 'revelation' happening.

When the Christian wants to say that 'God has acted most
characteristically in Christ', has 'expressed himself most fully in
Jesus' life, death and resurrection', he may meaningfully say
this and no more. He may say that he commits himself to a
pattern of obedience dependent on 'God', modelled he hopes
more and more closely on this act—within a community that is
committed in ways like this. He may say that if 'God' *is* ever
'revealed' to him, he will expect to find that this is the act that

most fully 'expresses God', of all the events that have happened
in the world's history. He might even say, as another way of
announcing the same commitment, that if he ever fully understood this central 'act of God', he would 'fully understand God'
(which would then be, of course, strictly tautologous). But he
is not committed by this to a claim, even implicit, that *now*
God is 'revealed' in this act, still less that this is the present
purpose of this act. In committing himself to this 'act of God
in Christ' he is not claiming to understand it very well at all;
he is not claiming it 'reveals' God to him. To claim that *his*
understanding allowed him to 'see God' clearly would be to
condemn his fellow Christians who differed from him, and,
really, to make himself the judge of God. We may believe that
looking back imaginatively at the life, death and resurrection
of Christ we are 'seeing' the work of God; but we are seeing
without comprehending. We just may not pretend that we as
yet understand or love enough to be 'seeing' God himself.

To claim that the life, death, resurrection of Christ is *the*
characteristic 'act of God', the one 'act of God' among men that
is not distorted by human sin (set though it is in the context of
that sin) is a 'leap of faith', a commitment. It does not imply—
if well understood it does not allow—a claim that so 'God is
revealed' to me, to you, to his Church, to his world.[1]

A Christian may say that he is 'called by God' to a particular
course of action, to some total way of life. He 'knows' this is
'God's will' for him. He is at least saying that he is sure he must
do this; he is expressing his intention to behave this way. But
he would not be justified, it has been suggested, in claiming that
so he 'knows the mind of God'. At least, God has not placed
him in a position where that can be more than a windy boast,
which many of his fellow Christians will deny. He may still use
a form of words like this to express his commitment-in-depend-
ence. He hopes that what he is going to do is God's will; he is
going to do it as an act of obedience to God, as thoroughly and
whole-heartedly as he can; if it is obedience to *God*, he can do
no less. He is going to act as though he knew in all certainty
that this was precisely 'what God wanted'; even though he

---

[1] If this be true, and if our relativising of the 'nature-grace' distinction is valid,
then it must follow that the Christian is committed to service *rather than* evangelism;
to loving, *rather than* talking about, God and Man.

realises that he has not this precise knowledge. If the Christian looks at his total situation, he will realise that he must offer this total commitment; but still in uncertainty, without the comfort yet of 'revelation' and 'knowledge of God'.

Talking to the man who is not committed in this way, the Christian will probably only be able to explain his language as a poetic, pictorial way of expressing moral decisions, the intention to perform certain acts. And he may have to accept that the other man will find this an unnecessarily confusing way of talking. He may explain that his particular obedience-in-dependence can only be expressed (and so, by extension, discussed, thought about) in these terms. And the other man may see that the Christian has a myth that enables him to make certain decisions, express certain attitudes; yet may still reject the myth as mere myth, and the attitudes as 'unrealistic' or even pernicious. But the Christian who uses his language to express commitment to the love of the Holy Trinity cannot expect what he says to be very useful for the man who refuses such commitment. He cannot even be sure that his commitment as a Christian will be its own argument. The Crucifixion, the fullest act of commitment to love in uncertainty of which the Christian knows, is also the world's completest rejection of its God. Jesus on the cross in fact 'reveals' nothing; he just demands our still confused and inarticulate faith and obedience. 'Revelation' is not till the consummation. Even so, Come Lord Jesus.

APPENDIX

Table to Illustrate New Testament Theological Priorities

This table is not expected to persuade the unwilling of anything more than that there is a serious case to be made for the position suggested on p. 124 above. The reader who does not believe that the New Testament writers greatly prefer 'saving' and 'redeeming' words to 'communication-revelation' words, for God's purpose (past, present and future) in Christ, may be encouraged to read through his New Testament again. *Proof* of this suggestion can only come from a careful study of all the contexts from which these figures are drawn, and that is beyond the scope of this book.

All the 'communication' words ('see-reveal', and 'know') discussed above are included in the first table. These are, as that discussion has, I hope, shown, predominantly used of communication of information, or of the making seen of the Christ in the past or in the future. A table of these words used to present God's purpose in Christ, past or present, as 'self-revelation' would of course have instances only in one passage in Matthew, one in Luke, and perhaps a few (but I have argued none) in John; *and that is all*.

The second table is of as many words (and cognates), chosen at random, from contexts where the 'saving' purpose of God in Christ is referred to explicitly or implicitly. *And obviously, for this table, instances could be multiplied manifold*, whereas for the first one, the tally is complete.

TABLE I—*'Communication' words: 'revealing', 'seeing', and 'making known' etc.*

The words as used in	Paul	Synoptics (inc. Acts)	John	the Rest	Totals
ἀποκαλύπτειν, -ψις	23	10	1	7	41
βλέπειν	1	4	1	17	23
(ἐν-) δεικνύναι	5	3	6	10	24
δηλοῦν, -ος	—	—	—	3	3
ἐμφανίζειν ἐπιφανής, -εια	—	—	2	1	3
ἐπιφαίνειν,	1	1	—	6	8

The words as used in	Paul	Synoptics (inc. Acts)	John	the Rest	Totals
θεᾶσθαι	—	2(+2?)	5	—	7(9)
θεωρεῖν	—	4	11	—	15
ὁρᾶν φαίνειν	5	16	23	5	49
φανεροῦν, -ός, -ωσις	13	4(+2)	16	6	39(41)
ἐπιγινώσκειν, -γνωσις	10	4	—	10	24
γινώσκειν, γνῶσις	18	5	31	2	56
εἰδέναι	5	6	18	1	30
γνωρίζειν	7	—	1	1	9
					331(335)

The figures in both tables (which I have insisted, are only a guide to the seriousness of a position suggested) should be taken plus or minus 10 per cent, to allow for differences as to the relevance of some contexts.

TABLE 2—*'Saving activity' words: a random selection from a wide field of choice*

The words as used in	Paul	Synoptics (inc. Acts)	John	the Rest	Totals
ἀγάπη, ἀγαπᾶν ἅγιος (e.g. οἱ ἅγιοι)	77	21	89	27	214
ἁγιάζειν, -σμός ἄφεσις	60	18	4	39	121
ἀφίημι (sc. ἁμαρτίας) δικαιοῦν	3	46	3	2	54
δικαίωσις, δικαιοσύνη (θεοῦ)	75	4	1	4	84
εἰρήνη	32	3	8	13	56
ἐκκλησία	60	27	3	26	116
καλεῖν, κλῆσις	32	7	—	16	55

The words as used in	Paul	Synop- tics (inc. Acts)	John	the Rest	Totals
(ἀπο) καταλλάσσειν	13	—	—	—	13
κληρονόμος (-ία)	16	6	—	13	35
κύριος	417	340	70	176	1003
(ἀπο) λυτροῦσθαι, λύτρον, -ωσις	7	6	—	5	18
σωτήρ, -ηρία -ήριον σωζεῖν	43	71	8	55	177
χαρίζεσθαι	14	3	—	—	17
χάρις	83	4	5	34	126
					2,089

Even if e.g., *φιλεῖν, φίλος* were substituted for *κύριος*, which rather swamps the rest, the total, 1,118, would still be about 350 per cent greater than that for the first table, for only as many words.

ABBREVIATIONS

AV   Authorised Version (of the Bible)
BJRL   *Bulletin of the John Rylands Library*
CD   Karl Barth, *Church Dogmatics*
CQR   *Church Quarterly Review*
DSS   Dead Sea Scrolls
EVV   English Versions (of the Bible)
HDB   *Hasting's Dictionary of the Bible*
NEB   New English Bible
NTS   *New Testament Studies*
OED   *Oxford English Dictionary*
RSV   (American) Revised Standard Version
RV   Revised Version (of the Bible)
SJT   *Scottish Journal of Theology*
ST   Paul Tillich, *Systematic Theology*
ThWB   *A Theological Word Book of the Bible*, ed. A. Richardson,
            1950
TNT   Rudolph Bultmann, *Theology of the New Testament*
TWNT   *Theologisches Wörterbuch zum Neuen Testament* (Kittel)
VB   *Vocabulary of the Bible*, ed. J.-J. von Allmen, 1958

SELECT BIBLIOGRAPHY

This is a list of books referred to in the text or notes, which deal fairly explicitly with the major themes of this work. Other writings referred to can be found by using the Index of Authors.

ALLMEN, J.-J. VON (ed.)   *Vocabulary of the Bible*, Lutterworth Press, 1957

ARNDT AND GINGRICH   *A Greek-English Lexicon of the New Testament*, C.U.P., 1957

AUSTIN, J. L.   *Philosophical Papers*, Oxford, 1961
  How to do things with Words, Oxford, 1962

BAILLIE, J.   *Our Knowledge of God*, O.U.P., 1939
  The Idea of Revelation in Recent Thought, O.U.P., 1956
  The Sense of the Presence of God, O.U.P., 1962

BAILLIE, J. AND
MARTIN, H. (eds.)   '*Revelation*', Faber and Faber, 1937

BARTH, K.   *Church Dogmatics*, I/1, I/2, IV/2, T. and T. Clark, 1936ff.
  Against the Stream, SCM Press, 1954

BARR, J.   *The Semantics of Biblical Language*, O.U.P., 1961.

BARRETT, C. K.   *The New Testament Background*, S.P.C.K., 1956

BONHOEFFER, D.   *Letters and Papers from Prison*, SCM Press, 1954

BRAITHWAITE, R. B.   *An Empiricist's View of the Nature of Religious Belief*, C.U.P., 1955

BRUNNER, E.   *Revelation and Reason*, SCM Press, 1947

BULTMANN, R.   *Gnosis*, A. and C. Black, 1952
  Jesus Christ and Mythology, SCM Press, 1960
  Existence and Faith, Hodder and Stoughton, 1961

BUREN, P. M. VAN   *The Secular Meaning of the Gospel*, SCM Press, 1963

BURROWS, M.   *The Dead Sea Scrolls*, Secker and Warburg, 1956

CAIRNS, D.   *A Gospel without Myth?* SCM Press, 1960

CHARLES, R. H.   *Apocrypha and Pseudepigrapha*, Oxford, 1913

DAVIES, W. D.   *Christian Origins and Judaism*, Darton, Longman and Todd, 1962

EVANS, D.   *The Logic of Self-Involvement*, SCM Press, 1963

FERRÉ, F.   *Language, Logic and God*, Eyre and Spottis-
                    woode, 1962
FLEW, A. AND   *New Essays in Philosophical Theology*, SCM
  MACINTYRE, A.   Press, 1955
  (eds.)
GASTER, T. H.   *The Scriptures of the Dead Sea Sect*, Secker
                    and Warburg, 1957
GEORGE, A. R.   *Communion with God in the New Testament*,
                    Epworth Press, 1953
HARE, R. M.   *The Language of Morals*, Oxford, (1952), 1961
                    Freedom and Reason, Oxford, 1963
'HASTINGS'   *Dictionary of the Bible*, T. and T. Clark, 1963
HEPBURN, R.   *Christianity and Paradox*, Watts, 1958
HODGSON, L.   *For Faith and Freedom*, vol. II, Blackwell,
                    1957
HOOK, S. (ed.)   *Religious Experience and Truth*, Oliver and
                    Boyd, 1962
KELLY, J. N. D.   *Early Christian Creeds*, Longmans, 1950
                    Early Christian Doctrines, A. and C. Black,
                    1958
KITTEL, G.   *Theologisches Wörterbuch zum Neuen Testa-
                    ment*, III, Stuttgart, 1949
KNIGHT, G. A. F.   *A Christian Theology of the Old Testament*,
                    SCM Press, 1959
KNOX, J.   *The Death of Christ*, Collins, 1959
KOEHLER, L.   *Old Testament Theology*, Lutterworth Press,
                    1957
LATOURELLE, R.   *Théologie de la Révélation*, Desclée de Brouwer,
                    1963
LIDDELL AND SCOTT   *A Greek-English Lexicon*, Oxford, 1940
MACDONALD, H. D.   *Ideas of Revelation*, Macmillan, 1959
                    Theories of Revelation, Allen and Unwin,
                    1963
MACGREGOR, G.   *Introduction to Religious Philosophy*, Mac-
                    millan, 1960
MACINTYRE, A. (ed.) *Metaphysical Beliefs*, SCM Press, 1951
McINTYRE, J.   *The Christian Doctrine of History*, Oliver and
                    Boyd, 1957
                    On the Love of God, Collins, 1962
MASCALL, E. L.   *Words and Images*, Longmans, 1957
MILES, T. R.   *Religion and the Scientific Outlook*, Allen and
                    Unwin, 1957
MITCHELL, B. (ed.) *Faith and Logic*, Allen and Unwin, 1957
MOULTON AND   *The Vocabulary of the Greek New Testament*,
  MILLIGAN   Hodder and Stoughton, 1930
NIEBUHR, H. R.   *The Meaning of Revelation*, Macmillan (N.Y.),
                    (1941), 1960
NICHOLLS, W.   *Revelation in Christ*, SCM Press, 1958

PACKER, J. I.   *Fundamentalism and the Word of God*, I.V.F., 1958
PARKER, T. H. L.   *The Doctrine of the Knowledge of God*, Oliver and Boyd, 1952
PEDERSEN, J.   *Israel*, O.U.P., 2 vols, 1926-47
PELZ, W. AND L.   *God Is No More*, Gollancz, 1963
PITTENGER, W. N.   *The Word Incarnate*, Nisbet, 1959
POLANYI, M.   *Personal Knowledge*, Routledge and Kegan Paul, 1958
QUICK, O. C.   *Doctrines of the Creed*, Nisbet, 1938
RAMSEY, I. T.   *Religious Language*, SCM Press, 1960
RICHARDSON, A. (ed.)   *A Theological Word Book of the Bible*, SCM Press, 1950
SCHAFF, P.   *A History of the Creeds of Christendom*, vols. II and III, Hodder and Stoughton, 1877
THORNTON, L. S.   *Revelation and the Modern World*, Dacre Press, 1950
TILLICH, P.   *Systematic Theology*, vols. I and II, Nisbet, 1953ff.
URMSON, J. O.   *Philosophical Analysis*, O.U.P., 1958
VERMÈS, G.   *The Dead Sea Scrolls in English*, Penguin Books, 1962
VRIEZEN, T. C.   *An Outline of Old Testament Theology*, Blackwell, 1958
WINGREN, G.   *Theology in Conflict*, Oliver and Boyd, 1958
WOODS, G. F.   *Theological Explanation*, Nisbet, 1958

SELECT INDEX OF GREEK AND HEBREW WORDS

INDEX OF REFERENCES

THE OLD TESTAMENT (GREEK: LXX)

APOCRYPHA AND PSEUDEPIGRAPHA (R. H. Charles)

THE FATHERS

SCHOLASTIC AND REFORMATION

INDEX OF AUTHORS

SUBJECT INDEX

verifiable - falsifiable   167 "opposite = appropriate

q u a logion q the Lord   42 'yada' - to obey
130   Jesus "the renewing mouth q God" Ⅳ Gospel   not to have sex
190 "then was not when he was not" - Ⅳ Gosp. prevenience   intercourse, and
                                            9 × 8 said at Gen.

W: write same letter to Scottish friend q own
q Theology. (get a access f.   x   49 ErιεβΔναη - doubt
                Sem. library,   margil
                                            59 on qt v8t5

The question is: Is there actual realization   163 argumentum ad homine
        in each hope?
                                        34 Gen 32:24 - a revis
182 Ⅱ Sec 2. on using language intended to deceive.
                                        35 Ex 3
74 Ⅱ Ref vocab = Jewish. priesthood etc.   y 39-40 Jer. 31:31
        a promise q the eschaton?
118-119 Ⅱ Perodoxy ? ... - says knowledge "is Ⅱ Sec 1:2 etc. is ethical behavior.
30 Ⅱ Sec 2 X because rev. is rarely q God living, men are las
                    mistakes. Hence, 'false prophet'
            quote Augustin 150 "..." and 152 "counsel "corruption "t Gen surely.
40 Ⅱ Sec 1:3-4 proper cult - conduct 40SE
  also 39   is Sec 4.5 "sub-apostolic age"
47 Peter's OT was LXX, would that have taught Peter 1:3
        69 "known, God = to obey him "   a
  68 known, God - to obey him "   a
is the "knowledge" esoteric   thru Philo .
        68 known, God - to obey him " mystical absorption - thru Philo.
55   * "absorption mysticism" 61 - deification, mystical absorption - thru Philo.
        "knowledge i ethical actions enabled by God." doing i knowing, q q obey
                                                        "AATh 507
X 56 on God reveals his will, power to do it . about f. Ⅱ Sec except ....
57 on the writers x Jewish
5-7 Ⅱ Sec 1:3 "perfection" q life 'worship - perfect way q q = revealed in law -
                                                            Jus
61 Hermetic - knowl. q God as an end in itself - 2t. end. 62
... u Paul we have th. merit q God u Spirit.

131 creo series, "imitator q the   104 unity "on"   63 + 1 Cor 1:18f
        passion q my God"   103 Jn 17:11   64 Ⅱ Cor 12:1
                                        +kham"
135 Ⅱ Sec 3 √   + prayer   66 on wrath q Ⅳ nl X
                                    106 Jn 14:9   Rom 9:18f
240 14 Ⅱ Sec 1: "as a cause,   115 I Jn 1:5 "on walk   Ⅳ Gospel 3 etc
        q a real light "inherent   in lite
26 21 14 Brown quote Ⅱ Sec 1:10 f   122 Heb 9:24, 26, 28   66 f Rom 1:18 f
                Peter apologetic   x   143 the light "in th   68 Col 1:9-10
278 Ⅱ Deb 1:7-8 14/ not saved from,   gospel q John   68 f Col 3:13
  -229   but only to -   149 Augustin on Jn -   also on "de
                                    "light shin i dark, but .."   mirrors
                                    163 J Cor 14:9   69 Phil 3:8-10
                                    206 # Jn - drunkat   84 t Col 1:26
                                        love, tan not be   Gal 2:14
                                        abt Ⅱ Rev 11:7-8 ?
                                    211 quote - on Ⅳ Gosp   95 Mt 5:8
                                        Jesus i how to know   98 Jn 1:48
                                        God   2:24-5.
                                    206 Heb. "once q all"
                                        14 quote